A COMPANION TO
MEDIEVAL SCOTTISH POETRY

A COMPANION TO MEDIEVAL SCOTTISH POETRY

Edited by

PRISCILLA BAWCUTT
JANET HADLEY WILLIAMS

D. S. BREWER

© Contributors 2006

All Rights Reserved. Except as permitted under current legislation no part of this work may be photocopied, stored in a retrieval system, published, performed in public, adapted, broadcast, transmitted, recorded or reproduced in any form or by any means, without the prior permission of the copyright owner

First published 2006
D. S. Brewer, Cambridge
Paperback edition 2010

Transferred to digital printing

ISBN 978-1-84384-096-1 hardback
ISBN 978-1-84384-247-7 paperback

D. S. Brewer is an imprint of Boydell & Brewer Ltd
PO Box 9, Woodbridge, Suffolk IP12 3DF, UK
and of Boydell & Brewer Inc.
668 Mt Hope Avenue, Rochester, NY 14620, USA
website: www.boydellandbrewer.com

A CIP catalogue record for this book is available
from the British Library

This publication is printed on acid-free paper

Contents

Preface		vii
Abbreviations and Short Titles		viii
Contributors		xi
Introduction: Poets 'of this Natioun' *Priscilla Bawcutt and Janet Hadley Williams*		1
1.	Late Medieval Scotland: a Study in Contrasts *Elizabeth Ewan*	19
2.	'I will my proces hald': Making Sense of Scottish Lives and the Desire for History in Barbour, Wyntoun and Blind Hary *R. James Goldstein*	35
3.	'Mark your Meroure be Me': Richard Holland's *Buke of the Howlat* *Nicola Royan*	49
4.	*The Kingis Quair* and the other poems of Bodleian Library MS Arch. Selden. B. 24 *Julia Boffey*	63
5.	'Of Wisdome and of Guide Governance': Sir Gilbert Hay and *The Buik of King Alexander the Conquerour* *Joanna Martin*	75
6.	Henryson's *Morall Fabillis*: Structure and Meaning *Roderick J. Lyall*	89
7.	*Orpheus and Eurydice* and *The Testament of Cresseid*: Robert Henryson's 'fine poeticall way' *Anne M. McKim*	105
8.	Religious Verse in Medieval Scotland *Priscilla Bawcutt*	119

9.	William Dunbar *John Burrow*	133
10.	Gavin Douglas *Douglas Gray*	149
11.	Medieval Romance in Scotland *Rhiannon Purdie*	165
12.	Sir David Lyndsay *Janet Hadley Williams*	179
13.	Guide to Further Reading *Priscilla Bawcutt and Janet Hadley Williams*	193
Index of Manuscripts		211
General Index		213

Preface

A Companion to Medieval Scottish Poetry provides an up-to-date guide to an exceptionally rich body of late-medieval writing. The opening chapters introduce the highly distinctive literary culture and history of Scotland in the fifteenth and early sixteenth centuries. Several of the subsequent chapters give detailed coverage of individuals, including comparatively neglected figures, such as Richard Holland and Walter Kennedy, as well as the most famous early Scottish poets – James I, Robert Henryson, William Dunbar, Gavin Douglas and David Lyndsay. Attention is also paid to topics, themes and genres that were important in Scotland at this time, notably the historiographical tradition, alliterative poetry, religious verse, romances, and the legendary history of Alexander the Great. In the last quarter of a century, there have been major advances in the study of medieval Scottish poetry and in related scholarly disciplines, such as palaeography, manuscript studies, and lexicography (the completion of the great *Dictionary of the Older Scottish Tongue*). These are documented in the concluding chapter, a Guide to Further Reading.

To assist readers unfamiliar with Middle Scots, the letter forms yogh (*ȝ*) and thorn (*þ*) in quotations have been modernized respectively to *y* and *th*, and scribal abbreviations have been expanded.

The compilation of this book has been a stimulating joint effort. We warmly thank our contributors for their willingness to devote their expertise to the *Companion*, and Caroline Palmer of Boydell and Brewer for her assistance at each stage. Finally, we should like to thank our dear husbands, Nigel and Ian, for their good-humoured and learned support. They have been true companions to us and to early Scottish literary studies.

Priscilla Bawcutt
Janet Hadley Williams

Abbreviations and Short Titles

In bibliographical references here and in the text, place of publication is Edinburgh unless otherwise indicated.

Asloan MS, ed. Craigie
    The Asloan Manuscript. A Miscellany in Prose and Verse written by John Asloan, ed. W. A. Craigie, 2 vols, STS (1923–25)
B   poem numbers in Dunbar, *The Poems*, ed. Bawcutt
Bannatyne MS, ed. Ritchie
    The Bannatyne Manuscript Writtin in Tyme of Pest 1568 by George Bannatyne, ed. W. Tod Ritchie, 4 vols, STS (1928–34)
Barbour, *Bruce*, ed. McDiarmid and Stevenson
    Barbour's Bruce, ed. Matthew P. McDiarmid and James A. C. Stevenson, 3 vols, STS (1980–85)
Bawcutt, *Dunbar the Makar*
    Priscilla Bawcutt, *Dunbar the Makar* (Oxford, 1992)
Bawcutt, *Gavin Douglas*
    Priscilla Bawcutt, *Gavin Douglas: A Critical Study* (1976)
DOST   *A Dictionary of the Older Scottish Tongue*, ed. W. A. Craigie, A. J. Aitken et al. (Chicago, Aberdeen and Oxford, 1937–2002)
Douglas, *Shorter Poems*, ed. Bawcutt
    The Shorter Poems of Gavin Douglas, ed. Priscilla Bawcutt, STS, 2nd edn (2003)
Douglas, *Virgil's Aeneid*, ed. Coldwell
    [*Eneados.*] *Virgil's 'Aeneid' Translated into Scottish Verse by Gavin Douglas*, ed. David F. C. Coldwell, 4 vols, STS (1957–64)
Dunbar: Essays, ed. Mapstone
    William Dunbar, 'The Nobill Poyet': Essays in Honour of Priscilla Bawcutt, ed. Sally Mapstone (East Linton, 2001)
Dunbar, *The Poems*, ed. Bawcutt
    The Poems of William Dunbar, ed. Priscilla Bawcutt, 2 vols (Glasgow, 1998)
EBST   *Edinburgh Bibliographical Society Transactions*
EETS   Early English Text Society
    ES Extra Series; OS Original Series
ER   *The Exchequer Rolls of Scotland*, ed. J. Stuart et al., 23 vols (1878–1908)

FMLS   *Forum for Modern Language Studies*
Hary, *Wallace*, ed. McDiarmid
        Hary's Wallace, ed. Matthew P. McDiarmid, 2 vols, STS (1968–69)
Hay, *Buik*, ed. Cartwright
        The Buik of King Alexander the Conquerour by Sir Gilbert Hay, ed. John Cartwright, 2 vols, STS (Edinburgh and Aberdeen, 1986–90)
Henryson, *The Poems*, ed. Fox
        The Poems of Robert Henryson, ed. Denton Fox (Oxford, 1981)
History, ed. Jack
        The History of Scottish Literature. Volume 1: Origins to 1660 (Mediæval and Renaissance), ed. R. D. S. Jack (Aberdeen, 1988)
IMEV   *An Index of Middle English Verse*, ed. C. Brown and R. H. Robbins (New York, 1943); *Supplement*, ed. R. H. Robbins and J. L. Cutler (Lexington, Ky, 1965)
IR   *Innes Review*
Ireland, *Meroure*, ed. Macpherson, Quinn and McDonald
        The Meroure of Wyssdome composed for the use of James IV ... by Johannes de Irlandia, ed. Charles Macpherson (vol. 1), F. Quinn (vol. 2) and Craig McDonald (vol. 3), 3 vols, STS (Edinburgh and Aberdeen, 1926, 1965, 1990)
JEGP   *Journal of English and Germanic Philology*
Longer Scottish Poems, Vol. 1, ed. Bawcutt and Riddy
        Longer Scottish Poems Volume One: 1375–1650, ed. Priscilla Bawcutt and Felicity Riddy (1987)
Lyndsay, *Selected Poems*, ed. Hadley Williams
        Sir David Lyndsay: Selected Poems, ed. Janet Hadley Williams (Glasgow, 2000)
MÆ   *Medium Ævum*
Maitland Folio MS
        The Maitland Folio Manuscript, ed. W. A. Craigie, 2 vols, STS (1919–27)
MLN   *Modern Language Notes*
MLQ   *Modern Language Quarterly*
MLR   *Modern Language Review*
NAS   National Archives of Scotland
NLS   National Library of Scotland
Palace, ed. Houwen et al.
        A Palace in the Wild: Essays on Vernacular Culture and Humanism in Late-Medieval and Renaissance Scotland, ed. L. A. J. R. Houwen, A. A. MacDonald and S. L. Mapstone (Leuven, 2000)
PBA   *Proceedings of the British Academy*

PQ   *Philological Quarterly*
Riverside Chaucer, ed. Benson
            The Riverside Chaucer, ed. Larry D. Benson, 1987; 3rd edn (Oxford, 1988)
ROSC   *Review of Scottish Culture*
SHR   *Scottish Historical Review*
SHS   Scottish History Society
SLJ   *Scottish Literary Journal*
SSL   *Studies in Scottish Literature*
STC   *A Short-Title Catalogue of Books Printed in England, Scotland, and Ireland, and of English Books Printed Abroad 1475–1640*, ed. A. W. Pollard et al., 2nd edn, 3 vols (London, 1976–91)
STS   Scottish Text Society
TA   *Accounts of the Lord High Treasurer of Scotland*, ed. T. Dickson and J. Balfour Paul, 11 vols (1877–1916)
TLS   *Times Literary Supplement*
Wyntoun, *Original Chronicle*, ed. Amours
            The Original Chronicle of Andrew of Wyntoun, ed. F. J. Amours, 6 vols, STS (1903–14)

Contributors

Priscilla Bawcutt is Honorary Professor in the School of English, University of Liverpool.

Julia Boffey is Professor of Medieval Studies in the School of English and Drama at Queen Mary College, University of London.

John Burrow is Emeritus Professor and Senior Research Fellow in the Department of English, University of Bristol.

Elizabeth Ewan is Professor and University Research Chair, University of Guelph.

R. James Goldstein is Professor of English, Auburn University.

Douglas Gray was formerly J. R. R. Tolkien Professor of English Literature and Language, University of Oxford, and is an Honorary Fellow of Lady Margaret Hall.

Janet Hadley Williams is a Visiting Fellow in English, School of Humanities, The Australian National University.

Roderick J. Lyall is Emeritus Professor of Literatures in English, Free University, Amsterdam, and was previously Professor of Scottish Literature, University of Glasgow.

Anne McKim is Associate Professor of English in the Department of Humanities, University of Waikato.

Joanna Martin is Darby Fellow in English, Lincoln College, Oxford.

Rhiannon Purdie is a Lecturer in Medieval English in the School of English, University of St Andrews.

Nicola Royan is a Lecturer in Medieval and Early Modern Literature in the School of English, University of Nottingham.

Introduction

Poets 'of this Natioun'

PRISCILLA BAWCUTT
JANET HADLEY WILLIAMS

Late medieval poetry is one of the glories of Scottish literature, and the reign of James IV (1488–1513) has sometimes been singled out as a kind of Golden Age. In fact a longer period – extending roughly from the end of the fourteenth century to the first decades of the sixteenth – might better deserve that title. This was an age characterized by increasing literary activity, especially in the second half of the fifteenth century; and its poets showed great self-assurance and originality. In comparison with other medieval literatures (such as those of France or England) the poetic flowering in Scotland occurred late, towards the end of what is conventionally thought of as the Middle Ages. Indeed a few critics have preferred to attach the term 'Renaissance' or 'Northern Renaissance' to some of its later manifestations, such as the rise in classical studies.[1] The term 'Renaissance' is notoriously difficult to define, and is most meaningfully applied to Gavin Douglas, the great translator of Virgil, who was clearly sympathetic to many of the ideals of the humanists.[2] Most Scottish poets of this period, however, display the characteristics of 'late' or 'high' medievalism found throughout western Europe – whether one considers their style and rhetoric, their choice of themes and genres, or their religious beliefs.

The full extent and rich variety of this poetry are not always wholly appreciated, except by Scottish specialists. A handful of Scottish poets – James I, Robert Henryson, William Dunbar and Gavin Douglas – has received justified praise and much critical attention. It is unfortunate, however, that modern bibliographical works with titles such as 'Middle Scots Writers' or 'Middle Scots Poets' are devoted to these poets alone, and thus perpetuate the notion that late medieval Scottish poetry consists solely of this quartet. Far

---

[1] See, for instance, John MacQueen, 'Some Aspects of the Early Renaissance in Scotland', *FMLS* 3 (1967), pp. 201–22; and Roger A. Mason, 'Laicisation and the Law: The Reception of Humanism in Early Renaissance Scotland', *Palace*, ed. Houwen et al., pp. 1–25.
[2] See further, John Durkan, 'The Beginnings of Humanism in Scotland', *IR* 4 (1953), pp. 5–24; Bawcutt, *Gavin Douglas*, pp. 29–36.

wider coverage may be found in William Geddie's *Bibliography of Middle Scots Poets*, which, despite its antiquity, is by no means superseded.[3]

At the opening of the sixteenth century there existed clear recognition of a distinctive native tradition of Scottish poetry, different yet not wholly separate from that of England. In *The Palice of Honour* (c. 1501), Douglas described a procession of the Muses, led by Homer and Virgil, and at its end placed three poets 'Of this Natioun' – Dunbar, Walter Kennedy, and the mysterious 'Quintine' (922–4).[4] Douglas celebrates the Scottish trio, which follows and parallels the famous English poets, Chaucer, Gower and Lydgate; but he also implies that, compared with the great multitude of writers in Latin and Greek, the achievement of vernacular poets is still small. A few years later (c. 1505) Dunbar, in 'I that in heill wes and gladnes' (B 21), lamented the death of twenty-one poets 'of this cuntre' (55).[5] Dunbar here displays an intimate and wide-ranging acquaintance with Scottish poetry, mentioning not only friends and contemporaries but ancient poets such as John Barbour and Andrew of Wyntoun. He shows interest in poets as individuals and also in the genres in which they excelled – 'balat making', tragedy, love poetry and Arthurian romance. A generation later Sir David Lyndsay, in *The Testament of the Papyngo* (c. 1530), listed sixteen poets 'of this land' (15–54).[6] He too, like Dunbar, restricted himself to vernacular poets, and gave the topos a more analytic dimension, singling out some works, such as Dunbar's 'Goldin Targe', for special praise and calling attention to Kennedy's high aureate style.

Other Scottish poets demonstrated a similar sense of allegiance to different branches of this tradition, though in a casual and less formal manner. History-writers, not surprisingly, were particularly conscious of their predecessors. Wyntoun referred flatteringly to 'Maister Iohne Barbour' in his *Original Chronicle*, and also mentioned 'King Robertis buke', substantial extracts from which he incorporated in his own work.[7] Blind Hary speaks with tantalizing vagueness of an earlier time when 'gud makaris' flourished in Scotland. He too mentions 'Brucis buk', and throughout much of *The Wallace* he engages in implicit dialogue with Barbour on the relative importance of Bruce and Wallace

---

[3] See Florence H. Ridley, 'Middle Scots Writers', *A Manual of the Writings in Middle English 1050–1500*, ed. A. E. Hartung, vol. 4 (New Haven, Conn., 1973); Walter Scheps and J. Anna Looney, *Middle Scots Poets: A Reference Guide to James I of Scotland, Robert Henryson, William Dunbar and Gavin Douglas* (Boston, 1986); William Geddie, *A Bibliography of Middle Scots Poets*, STS (1912).

[4] References are to the Edinburgh text of this poem in Douglas, *Shorter Poems*, ed. Bawcutt.

[5] References (by first line and poem number) are to Dunbar, *The Poems*, ed. Bawcutt.

[6] References are to Lyndsay, *Selected Poems*, ed. Hadley Williams.

[7] See Wyntoun, *Original Chronicle*, ed. Amours, vol. 5, pp. 226 and 224; and cf. R. James Goldstein, ' "For he wald vsurpe na fame": Andrew of Wyntoun's Use of the Modesty *Topos* and Literary Culture in Early Fifteenth-Century Scotland', *SLJ* 14.1 (1987), pp. 5–18.

in the Wars of Independence.⁸ It is *The Wallace*, in turn, that seems to be the 'carnicle' or chronicle mentioned by Kennedy in his flyting with Dunbar (B 65, 272). Sometimes a poet acknowledges his debt to tradition more covertly: Dunbar's sole beast fable (B 76) pays oblique tribute to Henryson in its opening line: 'This hindir nycht in Dumfermeling'.

Many of the poets mentioned by Dunbar and Lyndsay are shadowy figures, and others, such as Patrick Johnston, Mersar, Rowle, and Quintin Shaw, are known only for one or two poems. Richard Holland, Sir Gilbert Hay and Walter Kennedy, however, are emerging from the obscurity that once enfolded them. Nonetheless disappointingly little is known in detail about the lives and careers even of the more famous poets. Most were highly educated, the title 'Master' indicating that they held degrees, either from foreign universities or the Scottish universities founded in the fifteenth century. Several held some office in the church or belonged to a religious order: Barbour was archdeacon of Aberdeen, Wyntoun an Augustinian canon and prior of Lochleven, Holland precentor at Moray Cathedral, and William of Touris a Franciscan friar. Douglas rose particularly high in the ecclesiastical hierarchy, becoming provost of St Giles, Edinburgh, and bishop of Dunkeld. Although most of these poets were 'clerkis', it should not be assumed that all were priests. Some ambiguity perhaps attaches to the remark by the author of *Ratis Raving* that he was 'nothir [neither] monk nore frere' (728);⁹ this implies that he was not a member of a religious order, but not necessarily that he was a layman. Some of the poets mentioned by Dunbar, such as 'Schir Mungo Lokert of the Le' (B 21, 63), were laymen. Kennedy was a landowner and a married man, despite holding several benefices, such as a canonry at Glasgow Cathedral. Henryson is believed to have been a schoolmaster at Dunfermline. Nothing in the records or his poetry indicates that he was a priest; but there is evidence to suggest that he was a notary public, as were a number of other Scottish writers, including Holland, Patrick Johnston and Andrew Cadiou. Notaries played an important part in Scottish cultural life, acting as secretaries and copyists of literary manuscripts, as well as carrying out their professional legal duties.¹⁰ Many Scottish poems reveal an intimate acquaintance with legal procedures and terminology; it is known that Dunbar and Douglas occasionally appeared as advocates in the law

---

⁸ See Hary, *Wallace*, ed. McDiarmid, 12:1453; 12:1212; and cf. R. James Goldstein, *The Matter of Scotland: Historical Narrative in Medieval Scotland* (Lincoln, Nebr. and London, 1993), pp. 276–8.
⁹ *Ratis Raving and Other Early Scots Poems on Morals*, ed. R. Girvan, STS (1939).
¹⁰ Two important literary manuscripts copied by notaries are the Asloan MS and the Longleat MS of Douglas's *Eneados*. For detailed information, see John Durkan, 'The Early Scottish Notary', *The Renaissance and Reformation in Scotland: Essays in Honour of Gordon Donaldson*, ed. Ian B. Cowan and Duncan Shaw (1983), pp. 22–40; and R. J. Lyall, 'Books and Book Owners in Fifteenth-Century Scotland', *Book Production and Publishing in Britain 1375–1475*, ed. Jeremy Griffiths and Derek Pearsall (Cambridge, 1989), pp. 239–56 (242–6).

courts, and it seems likely that other authors may have acted similarly.[11] Towards the very end of this period Lyndsay's career, as knight, landowner and Lyon King of Arms, provides a striking illustration of the laicization of culture and transition to a more secular society.[12]

Most of these poets, with the exception of Holland and Kennedy, were associated with the eastern seaboard of Scotland. Their 'mother toung', to adopt Henryson's term (*Morall Fabillis*, 31), was the language of the Scottish Lowlands, which descended from Northern Old English. Linguistic scholars apply the term 'Older Scots' to this language from its beginnings until c. 1700; within it they distinguish different historical stages: 'Early Scots' (until c. 1450) and 'Middle Scots' (c. 1450–1700), which, it should be noted, does not correspond chronologically to Middle English.[13] Lowlanders themselves long employed the term 'Inglis' (English) for their own tongue; this was characteristic not only of early writers, such as Barbour (*Bruce*, 4:253) and the author of *The Legends of the Saints* (18:1471), but also of later ones, including those deeply hostile to the English, such as Hary (*Wallace*, 9:425).[14] Only towards the very end of the fifteenth century did it start to become common to apply the term 'Scottis' to the native language: the earliest recorded uses are in a heraldic manuscript dated c. 1494, and the colophon of Cadiou's *The Porteous of Noblenes*, printed by Chepman and Myllar in 1508.[15] By far the most interesting and self-conscious remarks by a poet about his language occur in Douglas: he proclaims that his translation of the *Aeneid* is 'Writtin in the langage of Scottis natioun', then he terms that language 'Scottis', and contrasts its capabilities with those of French, Latin and English (*Eneados*, I Prol. 103ff.)[16]

Scots, of course, was not the only language employed in Scotland. Latin, which Douglas venerated as the 'maste perfite langage fyne' (*Eneados*, I Prol. 382), had a role similar to its use in other western European countries as the medium for scholarship, education and the services of the church. The theologian John Ireland, who lived abroad for many years, confessed, in *The Meroure of Wyssdome* (completed in 1490), that he knew Latin better than 'the

---

[11] On Dunbar in the law courts, see Bawcutt, *Dunbar the Makar*, p. 6; on Douglas's frequent litigation, see Bawcutt, *Gavin Douglas*, passim.

[12] See Carol Edington, *Court and Culture in Renaissance Scotland: Sir David Lindsay of the Mount 1486–1555* (Amherst, Mass., 1994); and Mason, 'Laicisation and the Law'.

[13] For a detailed account, see 'A History of Scots to 1700' in *DOST*, vol. 12, pp. xxix–clxii. A brief summary is found in *The Concise Scots Dictionary*, p. xiii.

[14] Cf. J. D. McClure, 'Scottis, Inglis, Suddroun: Language Labels and Language Attitudes', *Proceedings of the Third International Conference on Scottish Language and Literature (Medieval and Renaissance)*, ed. R. J. Lyall and Felicity Riddy (Stirling / Glasgow, 1981), pp. 52–69.

[15] See *The Deidis of Armorie*, ed. L. A. J. R. Houwen, 2 vols, STS (1994), vol. 1, pp. xxxix–xl; *The Chepman and Myllar Prints: A Facsimile*, introd. William Beattie (1950), p. 5.

[16] References are to Douglas, *Virgil's Aeneid*, ed. Coldwell.

commoune langage of this cuntre'.[17] A passage in *The Wallace* (9:284–426) illustrates the value of Latin to educated travellers as a lingua franca. Gaelic, then usually called 'Erse', was spoken chiefly in the Highlands and Galloway – the region from which Kennedy came – and was often the object of mockery by Lowlanders (as in *The Howlat*, 795–806). *The Flyting of Dumbar and Kennedie* (B 65) reveals that the language issue was one symptom of the deep cultural divisions between Lowlanders and Highlanders. Dunbar there depicts Kennedy as having an imperfect command of 'Inglis' and ridicules 'Sic eloquence as thay in Erschry vse', that is, the Gaelic poetic tradition (107ff.). Kennedy, in response, champions Gaelic forcefully, saying 'It was the gud langage of this land' (347); nonetheless all his extant verse is in 'Inglis'. Our best source of knowledge about Gaelic verse at this time is the famous manuscript miscellany, compiled in Perthshire (c. 1512–42), known as the Book of the Dean of Lismore.[18]

Much debate has focussed on the place of the royal court in Scottish cultural life.[19] In the reigns of James IV and James V there is abundant evidence of its high literary importance. Kennedy boasted in *The Flyting* (B 65, 417) of being James IV's 'trew speciall clerk', John Bellenden a little later of being James V's 'Clerk of ... comptis' ('Proheme', 31).[20] Dunbar and Lyndsay, like other poets of the time, served in the royal household, both penning vivid vignettes of court life, and Quintin Shaw, a fellow-servitor of Dunbar, wrote a short satire comparing its perils to those of a tempest-tossed ship.[21] Douglas's dedication of *The Palice of Honour* to James IV is considered, very plausibly, to have assisted his promotion to St Giles in 1503.[22] There are many signs too of other cultural activity at the court of James IV, including music and the singing of 'ballatis', the king's acquisition of a 'sang buke' in 1489, and the purchase, binding and illumination of other books, such as an unspecified 'kingis buk'.

---

[17] References are to Ireland, *Meroure*, ed. Macpherson, Quinn and McDonald, vol. 1, p. 164. See also J. H. Burns, 'John Ireland: Theology and Public Affairs in the Late Fifteenth Century', *IR* 41 (1990), pp. 151–81.

[18] See W. Gillies, 'Courtly and Satiric Poems in the Book of the Dean of Lismore', *Scottish Studies* 21 (1977), pp. 35–53; and Donald Meek, 'The Scots-Gaelic Scribes of Late Medieval Perthshire: An Overview of the Orthography and Contents of the Book of the Dean of Lismore', *Stewart Style 1513–1542: Essays on the Court of James V*, ed. Janet Hadley Williams (East Linton, 1996), pp. 254–72.

[19] See Denton Fox, 'Middle Scots Poets and Patrons', *English Court Culture in the Later Middle Ages*, ed. V. J. Scattergood and J. W. Sherborne (London, 1983), pp. 109–27; R. J. Lyall, 'The Court as a Cultural Centre', *History Today* 34 (1984), pp. 27–33; Sally Mapstone, 'Was there a Court Literature in Fifteenth-Century Scotland?', *SSL* 26 (1991), pp. 410–22.

[20] The poem is most easily consulted in the *Bannatyne MS*, ed. Ritchie, vol. 2, pp. 9–20 (fols 4r–8v).

[21] For Shaw's poem, 'Suppois the courte yow cheir and tretis', see *Maitland Folio MS*, ed. Craigie, vol. 1, no. cxlvi (pp. 384–5).

[22] See Bawcutt, *Gavin Douglas*, p. 49.

(Not all of these, however, were necessarily purchased for the king himself.)[23] During the reign of James V were published John Mair's *Historia Maioris Britanniae* (1521)[24] and Hector Boece's *Scotorum Historia* (1527); both were dedicated to the king, who commissioned a translation of the latter work by John Bellenden (c. 1531).[25]

Scantier evidence exists to support the assertion that all early Stewart monarchs were 'keen patrons of literature'.[26] It is true that Barbour, generally regarded as a propagandist for the Stewart dynasty, received a generous pension from Robert II.[27] The chronicler Walter Bower, in a lengthy panegyric of James I, praises his application to 'the art of literary composition and writing', but makes no mention of his support of other poets.[28] One of the most interesting instances of a royal commission is James II's request that a French elegy on his sister Margaret, who died in 1445, should be translated into Scots. Margaret was the wife of the dauphin, later Louis XI; James was perhaps motivated by a mixture of family piety and a desire to enhance the dignity of the Scottish royal house.[29] James III had a youthful taste for exotic travel literature: in 1467 he paid a chaplain for making a copy of 'Mandvile', which unfortunately does not survive; and in 1471 the *Itinerarium*, an account of the travels of his favourite Anselm Adornes in the Holy Land, was dedicated to him.[30] Ireland, who became James III's chaplain and confessor in 1483, testifies to his piety and theological interests. He describes the king's great desire for 'the making' of *The Meroure of Wyssdome* (later dedicated to James IV); he also reports that the king received Ireland's treatise on the Immaculate Conception of the Virgin with 'hertlie deuocioune', and requested a treatise 'maid in Latin' on the doctrine of special grace.[31]

---

[23] See *TA*, vol. 1, pp. 114, 184 and 224. For discussion, see Bawcutt, *Dunbar the Makar*, pp. 79–80; and Sally Mapstone, 'William Dunbar and the Book Culture of Sixteenth-Century Scotland', *Dunbar: Essays*, ed. Mapstone, pp. 1–23 (4–6).

[24] Roger A. Mason, 'Kingship, Nobility and Anglo-Scottish Union: John Mair's *History of Greater Britain* (1521)', *IR* 41 (1990), pp. 182–222.

[25] *TA*, vol. 5, p. 434; vol. 6, p. 37, and Nicola Royan, 'The Relationship between the *Scotorum Historia* of Hector Boece and John Bellenden's *Chronicles of Scotland*', *The Rose and the Thistle: Essays on the Culture of Late Medieval and Renaissance Scotland*, ed. Sally Mapstone and Juliette Wood (East Linton, 1998), pp. 136–57.

[26] David Ditchburn and A. J. MacDonald, 'Medieval Scotland 1100–1560', *New Penguin History of Scotland*, ed. R. A. Houston and W. W. J. Knox (London, 2001), p. 161.

[27] Cf. Goldstein, *Matter of Scotland*, pp. 140–2.

[28] Walter Bower, *Scotichronicon in Latin and English*, ed. D. E. R. Watt et al., 9 vols (Aberdeen and Edinburgh, 1987–98), vol. 8, p. 309 [= bk 16, ch. 30].

[29] On both poems, see Priscilla Bawcutt, 'A Medieval Scottish Elegy and its French Original', *SLJ* 15.1 (1988), pp. 5–13. The Scottish poem is printed in *Liber Pluscardensis*, 2 vols, ed. Felix J. H. Skene (1877–80), vol. 1, pp. 382–8.

[30] *ER*, vol. 7, p. 500, and Alan H. MacQuarrie, *Scotland and the Crusades 1095–1560*, 2nd edn (1997), pp. 97–100.

[31] Ireland, *Meroure*, ed. Macpherson, Quinn and McDonald, vol. 1, pp. 15 and 48; vol. 2, p. 131, and vol. 3, p. 73.

Cultural activity in fifteenth-century Scotland, like political power, seems to have been dispersed rather than highly centralized. It would be an overstatement to say that *The Wallace* was commissioned by Sir William Wallace of Craigie and Sir James Liddale of Halkerstone, yet Hary's conversations with these two southern lairds seem to have played a part in its genesis.[32] One should recall, however, that Hary stoutly proclaimed his independence of patronage: 'For my laubour na man hecht me reward. / Na charge I had off king nor othir lord' (12:1432–3). Henryson teasingly refuses to name the lord at whose 'requeist and precept' he composed *The Morall Fabillis* (34). Other writers, however, received support in some shape or form from lairds and magnates. Wyntoun claimed to have written at the 'instance' and 'bidding' of Sir John Wemyss of Leuchars and Kincaldrum (d. 1428), and Bower likewise mentioned the 'petitions' of another Fifeshire laird, Sir David Stewart of Rosyth (d. 1444).[33] Sir Gilbert Hay's *King Alexander the Conquerour*, according to its Epilogue, was translated 'At the instance of Lord Erskein', probably Thomas, second Lord Erskine (d. 1493).[34] Holland located the composition of *The Buke of the Howlat* (c. 1448) far to the north of Scotland in Darnaway, the seat of the powerful magnate Archibald Douglas, Earl of Moray (see chapter 3). Holland, who later became Archibald's secretary, dedicated the poem to his wife, Elizabeth Dunbar.

Different branches of the Sinclair family, however, were undoubtedly the most significant literary patrons at this time. In 1456 Hay dedicated three prose treatises – *The Law of Armys*, *The Ordre of Knychthede*, and *The Governaunce of Princis* – to William Sinclair, then Earl of Orkney, a title he later surrendered to the crown.[35] Henry, Lord Sinclair (d. 1513), was William's grandson and the friend and patron of Douglas, who in 1513 dedicated his *Eneados* in glowing terms to this 'Fader of bukis, protectour to sciens and lair' (*Eneados*, I Prol. 85). This phrase was no mere piece of flattery, since Henry Sinclair possessed and probably commissioned one of the most important Scottish anthologies of courtly poetry, Oxford, Bodleian Library, MS Arch. Selden. B. 24 (see chapter 4). He was also the likely owner of the Dalhousie Manuscript (NAS, GD 45/31/I–II), containing Norse and Scots historical material.[36] Several other members of the family shared this taste for books: Henry's uncle, Sir Oliver Sinclair, laird of Roslin, possessed the only extant manuscript of Hay's prose

---

[32] Hary, *Wallace*, ed. McDiarmid, 12:1442–4; Introduction, vol. 1, pp. xvi–xxvi.
[33] Wyntoun, *Original Chronicle*, ed. Amours, vol. 2, p. 6; Bower, *Scotichronicon*, ed. Watt, vol. 9, pp. 2 and 354–62.
[34] Hay, *Buik*, ed. Cartwright, 19319–20.
[35] See *Prose Works of Sir Gilbert Hay*, ed. Jonathan A. Glenn, 2 vols, STS (1993–2005), vol. 2, p. 2; also Barbara E. Crawford, 'William Sinclair, Earl of Orkney, and his Family: A Study in the Politics of Survival', *Essays on the Nobility of Medieval Scotland*, ed. K. J. Stringer (1985), pp. 232–53.
[36] See the account by Michael Chesnutt in *Historia Norwegie*, ed. Inger Ekrem and Lars B. Mortensen (Copenhagen, 2003), pp. 28–31.

works and another manuscript that contained John Mirk's *Festial* and *Quattuor Sermones*, both of which were copied by the main scribe of the Selden Manuscript (see chapter 4). A later Henry Sinclair (d. 1565), Oliver's son and bishop of Ross, possessed a remarkably copious and learned library.[37]

No other Scottish family, as far as we know, is comparable to the Sinclairs in their literary interests. But there is plenty of testimony to the growth of a book-reading culture towards the end of the fifteenth century. The major collectors – usually of learned works – were members of the higher clergy, such as Archbishop William Scheves and Bishop William Elphinstone.[38] Another bishop, Robert Maxwell (1470–1540), born about the same time as Gavin Douglas, possessed not only the Latin books relevant to his episcopal office, but a few in the vernacular, such as 'ane Inglis buke of the historeis and sanctis liffis' and 'ane Inglis buke of Goweir'.[39] Douglas envisaged young aristocratic readers of his *Eneados* somewhat similar to Henry, Lord Sinclair:

> Now salt thou with euery gentill Scot be kend,
> And to onletterit folk be red on hight,
> That erst was bot with clerkis comprehend.[40]

Literacy and pleasure in reading were indeed no longer confined to 'clerkis', but spreading among the laity. Small pointers to this are the copy of 'The Siege of Thebes' borrowed by Lord Boyd, Earl of Arran, from Anne Paston in 1472; the three English books – one of which is likely to have been Caxton's print of *The Dicts or Sayings of the Philosophers* – stolen from Robert, Lord Lyle, in 1483;[41] the commissioning of a copy of *Regimen Sanitatis* by John Ramsay, Lord Bothwell, in 1487;[42] the bible, 'ane buke contenand four bukis of the sentence', and three English books owned by William Hay, laird of Ardendracht, in 1492;[43] and the bequest of 'a buk of Gud Maneris' by Sir David Sinclair in 1506.[44] Particularly interesting is the possession of Dunbar's *Goldyn*

---

[37] See Introduction to *Older Scots Literature*, ed. Sally Mapstone (2005), pp. 3–13 (3–5); and A. F. Cherry, 'The Library of Henry Sinclair, Bishop of Ross 1560–1565', *Bibliotheck* 4 (1963), pp. 13–24.

[38] See Lyall, 'Books and Book Owners', pp. 246–50; and Leslie J. Macfarlane, 'William Elphinstone's Library Revisited', *The Renaissance in Scotland: Studies in Literature, Religion, History and Culture Offered to John Durkan*, ed. A. A. MacDonald, Michael Lynch and Ian B. Cowan (Leiden, 1994), pp. 66–81.

[39] William Fraser, *Memoirs of the Maxwells of Pollok* (1863), vol. 1, pp. 409–10.

[40] 'Exclamatioun', Douglas, *Virgil's Aeneid*, ed. Coldwell, vol. 4, p. 193.

[41] See Priscilla Bawcutt, 'The Boston Public Library Manuscript of John Lydgate's *Siege of Thebes*: Its Scottish Owners and Inscriptions', *MÆ* 70 (2001), pp. 80–94 (81–2).

[42] Lyall, 'Books and Book Owners', p. 246.

[43] Margaret H. B. Sanderson, 'The printing and distribution of the Bible and Psalm books in sixteenth-century Scotland: some additional documentation', *Records of the Scottish Church History Society* 29 (1999), pp. 139–49 (149).

[44] F. S. Ferguson, 'Relations between London and Edinburgh Printers and Stationers (–1640)', *The Library*, 4th series, 8 (1927), pp. 145–98 (145).

Targe by Florentine Martin, a small landowner in Fife, some time after 1508.[45] There are indications too that female literacy was becoming more common, at least among the more privileged, and not restricted solely to the pious reading of richly ornamented prayer books, such as the Murthly Hours.[46] It seems not impossible that Elizabeth Dunbar could read *The Howlat* for herself – her signature on an indenture of 1454 is said to be the earliest of a Scotswoman so far recorded.[47]

One challenge facing those interested in this poetry is the difficulty of establishing its chronology. Douglas says that he completed his translation of the *Aeneid* on 22 July 1513,[48] but few other works can be dated with such precision. This is true not only of minor or anonymous writings but of some poetic masterpieces. Despite the quantity of research devoted to Henryson, we are still uncertain as to the exact dates of *The Testament of Cresseid* and *The Morall Fabillis*. The problem is compounded in many cases by the gap, sometimes of more than a century, which exists beween a poem's likely date of composition and the date of its first surviving witness. A striking case is *The Buik of Alexander*, whose colophon says that it was written in 1438 but whose only extant witness is a printed text published c. 1580.[49] Plausible dates for some poems, of course, can be established by their subject matter or topical allusions – instances are Dunbar's two poems on Bernard Stewart, who came to Scotland in May 1508 and died on 11 June (B 23 and B 56). But the dating of many remains highly conjectural – and much debated – and rests on the assessment of a range of factors, such as the life-span of the poet or dedicatee (where these are known), external allusions to the work, and distinctive features in its style and language.

Despite the scattered and fragmentary nature of this evidence, scholars accept that a profound change took place in Scottish poetry around the middle of the fifteenth century. The most important works that can be assigned with some degree of certainty to the early period are the *Legends of the Saints* (a. 1400), Barbour's *Bruce* (c. 1375), Wyntoun's *Original Chronicle* (1408–24), *Ratis Raving* (? c. 1420) and *The Buik of Alexander* (1438). All of these – despite obvious differences of genre – have a great deal in common. They are mostly massive in scale and narrative in mode (apart from the didactic *Ratis Raving*);

---

[45] See *Chepman and Myllar Prints*, introd. Beattie, p. xxi (n. 4); John Durkan and Anthony Ross, *Early Scottish Libraries* (Glasgow, 1961), pp. 129 and 136; Bawcutt, *Dunbar the Makar*, p. 15.

[46] See P. Bawcutt, ' "My bright buke": Women and their Books in Medieval and Renaissance Scotland', *Medieval Women: Texts and Contexts in Late Medieval Britain: Essays for Felicity Riddy*, ed. J. Wogan-Browne et al. (Turnhout, 2000), pp. 17–34; John Higgitt, *The Murthly Hours: Devotion, Literacy and Luxury in Paris, England and the Gaelic West* (London, 2000); and M. H. B. Sanderson, *A Kindly Place? Living in Sixteenth-Century Scotland* (2002), pp. 135–54.

[47] For the signature of 'Elyzabeth contas of Murray' see Sanderson, ibid., pp. 149–51.

[48] 'The tyme, space and dait of the translatioun', *Virgil's Aeneid*, ed. Coldwell, vol. 4, p. 194.

[49] *The Buik of Alexander*, ed. R. L. G. Ritchie, 4 vols, STS (1921–29), vol. 1, pp. xxii–xxv.

they are written in octosyllabic couplets; and, although not lacking in rhetorical skill, they are stylistically plain. The one exception is *The Kingis Quair*, which, if it is (as most critics accept) the work of James I, must have been composed before his assassination in 1437. This poem, in its subjectivity, structural complexity, choice of the theme of love, and elevated style, differs strikingly from the works just mentioned, and might well be regarded not only as a harbinger of the change that occurred in Scottish poetry from the 1440s onwards, but as possibly an actual agent of that change. There was a quickening of literary activity, in prose as well as poetry, in the second half of the fifteenth century. Poets wrote with greater sophistication of style on a much wider range of topics, and they no longer confined themselves to the rather limited octosyllabics, but employed decasyllabic couplets, alliterative verse, rhyme royal and a wide range of other stanzas. To this period are usually assigned not only the poems of Henryson but Hary's *Wallace*, Hay's *King Alexander the Conquerour*, and a number of important anonymous works, including the romances *Lancelot of the Laik* and *Rauf Coilyear*, tale collections such as *The Thre Prestis of Peblis*, and explicitly didactic works such as *De Regimine Principum*. To the very end of this period – roughly co-terminous with the reign of James IV – belong the poems of Dunbar, Kennedy and Douglas, and William of Touris' *Contemplacioun of Synnaris*.

To attribute this remarkable poetic flowering to a single cause would be simplistic. It probably sprang from a complex mixture of factors – the sheer talent of individual poets working in a fruitful literary environment, characterized by increasing literacy and growing national self-confidence. What is striking is the willingness of these poets to experiment with different forms, and their lack of insularity – their openness to new influences, themes, genres and traditions, lying outside the ancient 'matter of Scotland' (as exemplified in Barbour and Wyntoun). In this respect, the long-lasting special relationship between Scotland and France, which originated as a military alliance directed against England, had particular cultural significance. Scotsmen travelled to France not only as soldiers, but as pilgrims, diplomats and students.[50] Many distinguished Scottish scholars, such as John Ireland, Hector Boece and John Mair, first studied and then taught at the University of Paris, which provided the model on which the earliest Scottish universities were founded.

Close literary links between France and Scotland, however, are less plentiful than one might expect.[51] Recent attempts to enrol Dunbar into the ranks of the *Grands Rhétoriqueurs*, for instance, are no more convincing than earlier depictions of him as 'the Scottish Villon'.[52] The most substantial evidence for

---

[50] See, for example, Marie-Claude Tucker, *Maîtres et étudiants écossais à la Faculté de Droit de l'Université de Bourges (1480–1703)* (Paris, 2001).

[51] Janet M. Smith's *The French Background of Middle Scots Literature* (1934) is pioneering but now outdated.

[52] On this topic, see Priscilla Bawcutt, 'French Connections? From the *Grands Rhétoriqueurs* to Clément Marot', *The European Sun: Proceedings of the Seventh International Conference on*

contact lies in the number of translations, particularly in the field of romance: *The Buik of Alexander*, *Lancelot of the Laik*, *Golagros and Gawane*, *Florimond of Albany* and *Clariodus* may all be traced to French originals (see chapter 11). But Scottish translators were active in a variety of other genres. The version of a French elegy on the dauphine Margaret, mentioned earlier, is of special interest. Its elaborate and uncommon ten-line stanza anticipates Henryson's very similar use of the same form for the lament for Eurydice in *Orpheus and Eurydice* (134–73). Residence in France was an important factor promoting awareness of French writing. Hay, the translator of chivalric and didactic prose treatises, lived there for many years and was Chamberlain to Charles VII; John Ireland, whose *Meroure of Wyssdome* is indebted to the sermons of the theologian Jean Gerson, likewise spent many years in France.[53] A less familiar figure is Andrew Cadiou, an Aberdeen merchant and notary, who studied at the University of Paris in 1472; his translation of Alain Chartier's *Le Bréviaire des Nobles*, entitled *The Porteous of Noblenes*, was printed in 1508.[54]

These translators varied greatly in skill. *The Buik of Alexander* has been praised for its fidelity,[55] but the French origins of the over-literal *Deidis of Armorie*, a heraldic treatise, are woefully evident; as its editor comments, 'the Scottification of the text is only thinly applied'.[56] Other translators display little interest in the formal characteristics of their original. The poets of *Clariodus* and *Lancelot of the Laik* substituted five-stress couplets for the prose of the French romances. Cadiou, by contrast, turned Chartier's verse (consisting of twelve *ballades*) into prose. An early sixteenth-century Scottish version of *Le Débat de l'Omme et de la Femme*, written by Guillaume Alexis (d. 1486), retains the metrical form, but abridges the poem considerably and dislocates its neat structural pattern.[57] Scottish authors, it might seem, valued French literature less for its formal qualities than its subject matter; it was, above all, a source of ideas, information and good stories.

Some critics have tried to deny or minimize the extent of English influence upon Scottish poetry at this time.[58] But there can be no doubt that Chaucer – and to a lesser extent the other courtly poets termed 'Chaucerian' – much impressed Scottish readers. This is evident in the glowing and far from

---

Medieval and Renaissance Scottish Language and Literature, ed. Graham Caie, Roderick J. Lyall, Sally Mapstone and Kenneth Simpson (East Linton, 2001), pp. 119–28.

[53] See Ireland, *Meroure*, ed. Macpherson, Quinn and McDonald, vol. 3, pp. xxiv–xlviii.

[54] See *Chepman and Myllar Prints*, introd. Beattie, pp. ix–x; and Harold Booton, 'John and Andrew Cadiou: Aberdeen Notaries of the Fifteenth and Early Sixteenth Centuries', *Northern Scotland* 9 (1989), pp. 17–20.

[55] *Buik of Alexander*, ed. Ritchie, vol. 1, p. xiii.

[56] *Deidis of Armorie*, ed. Houwen, vol. 1, p. xxiv.

[57] See Priscilla Bawcutt, 'An Early Scottish Debate-Poem on Women', *SLJ* 23.2 (1996), pp. 35–42.

[58] See, however, Gregory Kratzmann, *Anglo-Scottish Literary Relations 1430–1550* (Cambridge, 1980), and Priscilla Bawcutt, 'English Books and Scottish Readers in the Fifteenth and Sixteenth Centuries', *ROSC* 14 (2001–02), pp. 1–12.

stereotyped tributes paid to Chaucer by one Scottish poet after another, from James I to Henryson, Dunbar, Douglas and Lyndsay.[59] Less well known, yet of great interest, are the responses of such figures as John Ireland and Hary. Precisely when Ireland – who had travelled in England – encountered Chaucer's writings is uncertain, but he was acquainted with some of *The Canterbury Tales* and 'the buk of Troilus'. Much of what Ireland says is couched in general terms: he praises Chaucer's eloquence, and calls him a good teacher. But he paid particular attention to book IV of *Troilus and Criseyde*, and was clearly uneasy about Troilus's fatalism in the 'predestination soliloquy'.[60] Hary makes no mention of Chaucer, yet his influence may often be detected in *The Wallace*, in the idealized portrait of the hero in book 10, the rather clumsy seasonal and astronomical set-pieces punctuating the action, and the envoi to the whole work, which begins 'Go nobill buk' (12:1449).[61] For Hary, as for his greater Scottish contemporaries, Chaucer was, above all, a model of the high style.

Chaucer's impact upon Scottish poets was complex, and far-reaching. He was the acknowledged master of types of poem that particularly appealed to the late Middle Ages – love stories, allegorical dream poems and love complaints. He also seems responsible for technical innovations in the shape of new verse forms. Rhyme royal, first used in Scotland in *The Kingis Quair*, and the staple form of Henryson's narrative poems, was so strongly associated with *Troilus and Criseyde* that James VI later termed it 'Troilus verse'.[62] The intricate nine-line stanza of the Complaint in *Anelida and Arcite* became phenomenally popular for a while in Scotland. Henryson, in *The Testament of Cresseid*, and the unknown author of *The Quare of Jelusy* followed Chaucer's model closely; both employed the stanza for a woman's love complaint, enclosed within a narrative in a different metre. Later Scottish poets, such as Dunbar and Douglas, used it even more ambitiously for complete poems.[63] Lyndsay chose the stanza to call attention to the most serious parts – the Prologue to *The Testament of the Papyngo* (1–72), and the concluding 'Exhortatioun' to *The Dreme* (1037–1126) – of poems otherwise written in a different metre. Most important of all, for his Scottish and English admirers, was the subtlety of Chaucer's style, enriched with mythological allusions, neologisms and 'flowers' of rhetoric.

[59] See, respectively, *Kingis Quair*, 1373–7; *Testament of Cresseid*, 41–2; *Goldyn Targe*, 253–70; *Eneados*, I Prol. 339–43; *Testament of the Papyngo*, 11–14.
[60] See Ireland, *Meroure*, ed. Macpherson, Quinn and McDonald, vol. 1, pp. 73–4 and 164; and Bawcutt, 'English Books', pp. 6–7.
[61] For brief discussions, see V. Harward, 'Hary's *Wallace* and Chaucer's *Troilus and Criseyde*', *SSL* 10 (1972), pp. 48–50; and Priscilla Bawcutt, 'Writing about Love in Late Medieval Scotland', forthcoming in *Writings on Love in the English Middle Ages*, ed. Helen Cooney.
[62] *Ane Schort Treatise conteining some revlis and cautelis to be obseruit and eschewit in Scottis Poesie, Poems of James VI of Scotland*, ed. James Craigie, 2 vols, STS (1955–58), vol. 1, p. 81.
[63] See *Testament of Cresseid*, 407–69; *Quare of Jelusy*, 191–316; *Goldyn Targe*, and *Palice of Honour* (with a slight variation in part III of the poem).

The imagery in the eulogies penned by Dunbar and other poets suggests that (in the words of Denton Fox) they saw Chaucer as one who 'purified, regularised and clarified English, and so made it possible for highly civilised and highly wrought poetry to be written in the vernacular'.[64] Poets who sought a high style modelled themselves on Chaucer, and tended to use words and grammatical usages characteristic of southern English; and this produced a distinctive, somewhat artificial diction, which differed from that employed in Scottish prose or earlier verse. A. J. Aitken, who had an unrivalled knowledge of the Scots language in this period, concluded that there was 'a good case for applying the designation Scottish Chaucerian, or, still more aptly, Scottish Lydgatian, to this particular branch of Older Scots poetry'.[65] Modern critics who denounce the phrase 'Scottish Chaucerians' seem unaware that when it was coined (apparently by a distinguished Scottish scholar in 1900)[66] it had contrastive significance of a double kind – these Scottish poets differed from the 'English Chaucerians', obviously, but also from the Scottish 'Non-Chaucerians', who wrote the alliterative romances or the plain-style *Ratis Raving*. One should not use it as a blanket term for all Scottish poetry at this time.

The label 'Scottish Chaucerians', as Aitken indicates, contains a grain of truth, but it is nonetheless over-simplified. The phrase is a curious phenomenon: little loved, yet still widely current, it has long had its critics, English as well as Scottish. It tends, when used, to be followed by a ritual disclaimer – the Scottish poets are never mere imitators, but bold, original and innovative. Perhaps the most unfortunate consequence of its over-use has been to distort the picture of Anglo-Scottish literary relations in this period. Chaucer was by no means the only English poet known in late medieval Scotland. Gower and Lydgate were far more than names linked with Chaucer in a formulaic trio; the *Confessio Amantis* and *The Complaint of the Black Knight* were popular with Scottish readers, even if their authorship was not always known.[67] The Scots were also familiar with English poetry in non-Chaucerian traditions. Dunbar is unlikely to have been the only Scottish reader of the romances, outlaw ballads and popular tales that he mentions in 'Now lythis off ane gentill knycht' (B 39). Douglas was not the only Scot to 'flyte' with William Caxton 'of Inglis natioun' (*Eneados*, 1 Prol. 138–72). John Mair, in his *Historia Maioris Britanniae,* pursued a running battle with Caxton, whom he erroneously believed to be not only the printer but the author of *The Chronicles*

---

[64] 'The Scottish Chaucerians', *Chaucer and Chaucerians*, ed. D. S. Brewer (London, 1966), pp. 164–200 (169).
[65] 'The Language of Older Scots Poetry', *Scotland and the Lowland Tongue*, ed. J. Derrick McClure (Aberdeen, 1983), pp. 18–49 (22–3).
[66] G. Gregory Smith, *The Transition Period* (1900), pp. vii and 40.
[67] For discussion, see Bawcutt, 'Boston Public Library Manuscript', pp. 89 and 94, n. 48; Bawcutt, 'English Books and Readers', pp. 7–8.

of England.[68] Scottish readers, around the beginning of the sixteenth century, seem acquainted with the translations of the French or Burgundian works printed by Caxton, such as the *Book of Good Manners*, the *Eneydos*, the *Cordial*, *The Recuyell of the Historyes of Troye*, and *Paris and Vienne*.[69] Continental culture thus came to Scotland not always directly but via English intermediaries.

Many serious and thoughtful Scottish poets justified poetry in terms of its truth-telling. The words 'suthfast' and 'suthfastnes' recur in Barbour's discussion of his purpose in writing *The Bruce* (1:1–36). Henryson too speaks repeatedly of the 'morall sweit sentence' (12) of his fables, their 'gude moralitie' (366 and 1387), and – with particular relish – 'gude morall edificatioun' (1893). A generation later, in words that show the influence of Boccaccio, Douglas defends not only the pagan author Virgil but all poetry in similar terms: 'suythfast materis', or inner truths, are veiled by poets 'vnder the clowdis of dyrk poecy' (*Eneados*, 1 Prol. 193–8).[70] The large quantity of didactic verse still extant from this period suggests that Scottish poets and readers shared such views, and possessed a taste not just for veiled morality, couched in fable, myth or exemplum, but for explicit didacticism. This may be seen in the short 'ballatis of moralitie' that fill approximately a quarter of the Bannatyne Manuscript, and in a number of verse treatises that give advice on personal conduct, such as *Ratis Raving*, poems in 'the Good Wife' tradition, and *The Buke of the Chess*.[71] Many of these have sources or analogues elsewhere in European literature, and this is true of another, more politically focussed type of writing, concerned with justice and good government. This *speculum principis*, or 'advice to princes', theme had a particular resonance for Scottish writers in the later fifteenth century, and may be traced in genres as various as the romance *Lancelot of the Laik*, the framed tale-collection known as *The Thre Prestis of Peblis*, and the devotional *Contemplacioun of Synnaris* by William of Touris.[72] One long poem, *De Regimine Principum*, is wholly devoted to the theme; its continuing popularity in the sixteenth century is suggested by the number of texts that survive, including a print by Chepman and Myllar.

The finest Scottish poets, however, were well aware that it was the traditional office of poetry not only to teach but to delight. Barbour spoke of giving his

---

[68] John Major [Mair], *A History of Greater Britain, as well England as Scotland*, trans. A. Constable, SHS (1892), pp. 145, 191–4.

[69] See Bawcutt, 'English Books', p. 3.

[70] On Douglas's reading of Boccaccio's *Genealogy of the Gods*, see Bawcutt, *Gavin Douglas*, pp. 72–4.

[71] See K. Saldanha, '*The Thewis of Gudwomen*: Middle Scots Moral Advice with European Connections?', *The European Sun*, ed. Caie et al., pp. 288–99; and *The Buke of the Chess*, ed. Catherine van Buuren, STS (1997).

[72] For an authoritative study, see Sally Mapstone, 'The Advice to Princes Tradition in Scottish Literature, 1450–1500', unpublished D.Phil. thesis (Oxford, 1986).

audience 'plesance' (*Bruce*, 1:5), and Henryson was not alone among Scottish poets in recognizing the need to mix 'merines' with more serious matters (*Morall Fabillis*, 26). Indeed, one of the most distinctive features of Scottish medieval poetry is a rich and varied body of comic narrative. *The Freiris of Berwick*, for instance, is a brilliant and sophisticated fabliau.[73] The authors of *The Talis of the Fyve Bestes* and *Colkelbie Sow*, who were possibly Henryson's contemporaries, lacked his genius but were equally alive to the possibilities of the beast fable. One particular comic topos, which might be labelled 'the naming of hens', can be traced from Henryson's Pertok, Sprutok and Coppok (*Fabillis*, 483) through 'The Unicornis Tale' in *The Fyve Bestes* (163–8) and Douglas's Twelfth Prologue (155–60) to its apogee in a twenty-six name list in *Colkelbie Sow* (911–39).[74] A fruitful development in the sixteenth century was the humorous use of animal personae, such as Dunbar's 'auld hors' or Lyndsay's hunting hound Bagsche, to voice complaints.[75] A distinctive and long-lived Scottish tradition of satire and invective was inaugurated by *The Flyting of Dumbar and Kennedie* (B 65).[76] Another low farcical genre, sometimes known as the 'Christis Kirk' tradition, was devoted to the comic description of peasant revelry.[77] Of outstanding interest is a striking group of short fantastic 'eldritch' poems, mostly found in the Bannatyne Manuscript.[78] They include 'The Gyre Carling', 'Fergus Gaist', 'Kynd Kittok', 'King Berdok', Roull's 'Cursing Vpoun the steilaris of his fowlis' and Lichtoun's 'Dreme'. These witty and amusing poems are usually located in a strange topsy-turvy Otherworld, peopled with elves, fairies, etins and other marvellous creatures. Several contain parodic elements – 'Fergus Gaist' is a mock-conjuration and 'The Gyre Carling' plays with familiar romance themes – but many appear to delight in nonsense for its own sake. Dunbar and Douglas

---

[73] The poem is included in *Ten Fifteenth-Century Comic Poems*, ed. Melissa M. Furrow (New York, 1985), pp. 315–62. See R. James Goldstein, 'The Freiris of Berwik and the Fabliau Tradition', *The European Sun*, ed. Caie et al., pp. 267–75.
[74] References are to *'Colkelbie Sow' and 'The Talis of the Fyve Bestes'*, ed. Gregory Kratzmann (New York, 1983).
[75] Dunbar, 'Schir, lat it neuer in toune be tald' (B 66) and Lyndsay, 'Complaint of Bagsche', *The Works of Sir David Lindsay of the Mount*, ed. Douglas Hamer, 4 vols, STS (1931–36). vol. 1, pp. 91–9.
[76] On this tradition see Priscilla Bawcutt, 'The Art of Flyting', *SLJ* 10.2 (1983), pp. 5–24; and Douglas Gray, 'Rough Music: Some Early Invectives and Flytings', *Yearbook of English Studies* 14 (1984), pp. 21–43.
[77] See *The Christis Kirk Tradition: Scots Poems of Folk Festivity*, ed. Allan H. MacLaine (Glasgow, 1996).
[78] See *Bannatyne MS*, ed. Ritchie, vol. 2, pp. 268–305; vol. 3, pp. 10–32. For valuable criticism, see Keely Fisher, 'Comic Verse in Older Scots', unpublished D.Phil. thesis (Oxford, 1999), and 'Eldritch Comic Verse in Older Scots', *Older Scots Literature*, ed. Mapstone, pp. 292–313; and Priscilla Bawcutt, 'Elrich Fantasyis in Dunbar and Other Poets', *Bryght Lanternis: Essays on the Language and Literature of Medieval and Renaissance Scotland*, ed. J. Derrick McClure and Michael R. G. Spiller (Aberdeen, 1989), pp. 162–78.

allude to several of these poems, and Dunbar's dream visions owe much to the tradition.

The preservation of medieval Scottish poetry and its transmission to posterity is a complicated story, of which only a brief account may be given here. It is striking how many poems now survive in unique copies, whether manuscript or printed. This is true not only of love lyrics and other short poems, which one might expect to be ephemeral, but of substantial works, such as *The Kingis Quair* (in Bodleian MS Arch. Selden. B. 24) or the romances *Golagros and Gawane* (printed in 1508) and *Rauf Coilyear* (printed in 1572). Much else must have been lost in the course of time. The Reformers' zeal to weed out papistry certainly played a part in the destruction of religious texts, but many other poems probably perished or were forgotten, because of the growing obscurity of their language and the revolution in literary taste that occurred in the reign of James VI.[79]

The *Legends of the Saints* and other bulky works, such as those of Barbour and Wyntoun, have been preserved in separate manuscripts, chiefly belonging to the fifteenth century. Five sixteenth-century manuscripts exist of Douglas's *Eneados*, one of which (Cambridge, Trinity College Library, MS 0.3.12) has particular value since it was copied, almost certainly in Douglas's lifetime, by Matthew Geddes, his own scribe and secretary.[80] A great mass of early verse, however, is preserved in large manuscript miscellanies.[81] Two of these date from the second half of the fifteenth century: Bodleian Library, MS Arch. Selden. B. 24 is of special interest, both because of its association with the Sinclair family and the richness of its contents (see chapter 4); less is known, unfortunately, about the compilation of Cambridge University Library, MS Kk.1.5. No. 6, which contains *Ratis Raving* and has a narrower, exclusively didactic range of subject matter. Two other important miscellanies, which belong to the pre-Reformation period, are the Asloan Manuscript (National Library of Scotland, MS 16500) and British Library, MS Arundel 285. The Asloan Manuscript (c. 1515–c. 1525) is named after its principal scribe, John Asloan, a public notary active in Edinburgh from the 1490s to c. 1530. The manuscript seems to have originated as a series of semi-independent fascicles, assembled in their present order by Asloan, who also numbered and provided a list of the items. The contents are extremely varied, ranging from prose treatises on penance and historical themes to religious and comic verse.[82] MS Arundel

---

[79] See the useful Introduction to Geddie, *Bibliography*.
[80] On fifteenth-century manuscripts generally, see Lyall, 'Books and Book Owners'; on the texts of the *Eneados*, see Douglas, *Virgil's Aeneid*, ed. Coldwell, vol. 1, pp. 96–106.
[81] For an overview, see Priscilla Bawcutt, 'Scottish Manuscript Miscellanies from the Fifteenth to the Seventeenth Century', *English Manuscript Studies 1100–1700* 12 (2005), pp. 46–73.
[82] See I. C. Cunningham, 'The Asloan Manuscript', *Renaissance in Scotland*, ed. MacDonald et al., pp. 107–35; and Catherine van Buuren, 'John Asloan and his Manuscript: An Edinburgh

285, conjecturally dated c. 1540, is a far more homogeneous work, wholly consisting of devotional prose and verse (see chapter 8).

Two particularly valuable poetic anthologies, compiled in the second half of the sixteenth century, contain much medieval material despite their late date. The Bannatyne Manuscript (National Library of Scotland, Adv. MS 1.1.6), completed in 1568, is the largest and most famous of Scottish manuscript miscellanies, and has prompted much scholarly debate as to its purpose and precise dating.[83] Its most original feature is the fivefold division into 'ballatis of theoligie', 'ballatis of moralitie', 'ballatis mirry', 'ballatis of luve', and 'fabillis'. George Bannatyne, its youthful compiler, had remarkably eclectic tastes: he included poems in different genres, and drew them from many sources – manuscripts and printed books, old and new, Scottish and English. In the section devoted to 'ballatis of luve' Bannatyne included works by Chaucer, Lydgate, Hoccleve and Dunbar, but he saw no incongruity in placing a poem by the Elizabethan ballad writer William Elderton (printed 1560/1) immediately after Henryson's 'Garmont of Gud Ladeis'.[84] The Maitland Folio (Cambridge, Magdalene College, Pepys Library, MS 2553) was compiled in the household of Sir Richard Maitland, probably between 1570 and 1586. It contains many poems by Maitland himself – the origins seem to lie in family piety – but also much undoubtedly early verse, and is the largest single repository of Dunbar's poems.[85]

Printing came late to Scotland. In 1507 James IV issued a patent to Walter Chepman and Androw Myllar, authorizing them to print law books, chronicles and service books 'eftir our awin Scottis use'.[86] Apart from the Aberdeen Breviary (1509–10) there is little evidence that this educational and somewhat nationalistic programme was fulfilled. The most famous prints associated with Chepman and Myllar, several of which are now fragmentary, are literary texts in the vernacular. They illustrate the diversity of Scottish taste around 1507–1508: moral and advisory pieces jostle with comic ones; writings by native

Notary and Scribe in the days of James III, IV, and V (1470–1530)', *Stewart Style 1514–1542*, ed. Hadley Williams, pp. 15–51.

[83] Especially valuable is *The Bannatyne Manuscript: A Facsimile*, introd. Denton Fox and W. A. Ringler (London, 1980). See also A. A. MacDonald, 'The Bannatyne Manuscript: A Marian Anthology', *IR* 37 (1986), pp. 36–47; A. A. MacDonald, 'The Printed Book that Never Was: George Bannatyne's Poetic Anthology (1568)', *Boeken in de late Middeleeuwen*, ed. J. M. M. Hermans and Klaus van der Hoek (Groningen, 1994), pp. 101–110, and Theo van Heijnsbergen, 'The Interaction between Literature and History in Queen Mary's Edinburgh: The Bannatyne Manuscript and its Prosopographical Context', *Renaissance in Scotland*, ed. MacDonald et al., pp. 183–225.

[84] *The Bannatyne Manuscript*, ed. Ritchie, vol. 3, p. 254.

[85] See Julia Boffey, 'The Maitland Folio Manuscript as a Verse Anthology', *Dunbar: Essays*, ed. Mapstone, pp. 40–50.

[86] See Robert Dickson and John P. Edmond, *Annals of Scottish Printing from the Introduction of the Art in 1507 to the Beginning of the Seventeenth Century*, 1890; rpt (Amsterdam, 1975), pp. 7–10; *Chepman and Myllar Prints*, introd. Beattie; and William Beattie, 'Some Early Scottish Books', *The Scottish Tradition*, ed. G. W. S. Barrow (1974), pp. 107–20.

Scottish poets – Hary, Holland, Henryson, Dunbar, and Kennedy – accompany English poems, such as the romance *Eglamour* and Lydgate's *Complaint of the Black Knight*, together with *The Porteous of Noblenes*, a translation from the French. Learned Scottish authors, such as John Mair and Hector Boece, wrote in Latin and usually had their works published in France. Printing does not seem to have flourished in Scotland during the first half of the sixteenth century, but it is probable that many more works were printed than now survive.[87] A fragmentary Scottish edition of Douglas's *Palice of Honour* (c. 1530–40) is the likely source for the London edition printed by William Copland (c. 1553), and it is not improbable that behind Copland's edition of *The Eneados* (1553) there similarly lies a lost Scottish print. In the 1570s there appears something of a revival of interest in publishing earlier poetry, such as *The Wallace* (1570), *The Bruce* (1571), *The Morall Fabillis* (1570 and 1571) Lyndsay, *The Warkis* (1571), and *The Palice of Honour* (1579).[88]

In seventeenth-century Scotland, medieval poetry, apart from *The Bruce* and *The Wallace*, was largely forgotten; Lyndsay was still very popular, but widely regarded as a prophet of the Reformation (see chapter 12). A revival of interest, however, occurred at the beginning of the eighteenth century, inspired in part by antiquarian and patriotic motives. Two landmarks were Thomas Ruddiman's edition of Douglas's translation of the *Aeneid* (Edinburgh 1710) and Allan Ramsay's publication of selections from the Bannatyne Manuscript in *The Ever Green: Being a Collection of Scots Poems Wrote by the Ingenious before 1600* (1724). This is not the place to describe the sometimes piecemeal discovery of texts, and the advances in scholarship and criticism that took place in the nineteenth and twentieth centuries. A concluding tribute, however, should be paid to one of Scotland's greatest scholars – David Laing (1793–1878), bibliophile, antiquary and secretary to the Bannatyne Club, who rescued from neglect and near-oblivion many of the poetic manuscripts and printed texts that are today valued so highly.[89]

---

[87] See Denton Fox, 'Manuscripts and Prints of Scots Poetry in the Sixteenth Century', *Bards and Makars: Scottish Language and Literature: Medieval and Renaissance*, ed. A. J. Aitken, M. P. McDiarmid and D. S. Thomson (Glasgow, 1977), pp. 156–71 (164–6).

[88] See further, H. G. Aldis, *A List of Books Printed in Scotland before 1700* (1904; rev. edn 1970); and P. B. Watry, 'Sixteenth Century Printing Types and Ornaments of Scotland', unpublished D.Phil thesis (Oxford, 1992).

[89] Laing's rich collection of manuscripts was bequeathed to Edinburgh University Library. There is as yet no adequate study of his career, but see D. Murray, *David Laing, Antiquary and Publisher* (Glasgow, 1915).

1

Late Medieval Scotland: a Study in Contrasts

ELIZABETH EWAN

The history of late medieval Scotland is one of contrasts and contradictions. While some historians have seen the period as marked by struggle between kings and over-mighty magnates, others have argued that there was a generally co-operative relationship between monarch and nobles. Architecture, literature and cultural life flourished, despite apparent economic decline and social disruption. Church organization and bureaucracy became increasingly secularized and corrupt, yet popular religious practices and individual piety retained their vitality. Finally, while today the period is best remembered by many for one of the most devastating military defeats in Scottish history, the Battle of Flodden (1513), the era was marked by an unbridled self-confidence as its leaders asserted Scotland's place as a sovereign European power.

At first glance, late medieval Scottish politics appears to be characterized by conflict and instability. The earliest Stewart kings, Robert II (1371–90) and Robert III (1390–1406), both surrendered practical royal authority to other family members during their reigns. Robert III's eldest son died in captivity after being imprisoned by Robert's brother and his younger son was captured by the English. According to the chronicler Walter Bower, Robert III, on his deathbed, assessed himself as 'the worst of kings and the most wretched of men in the whole kingdom' and asked to be buried in a dungheap.[1] After Robert III, no Stewart king died a natural death until James V in 1542 and even his death followed closely on a disastrous military defeat. James I (1406–37) spent eighteen years in captivity in England (1406–24) while his uncle the Duke of Albany, and then Albany's son, ruled Scotland. James II (1437–60), James III (1460–88) and James V (1513–42) each came to the throne as a child, resulting in long periods of minority government when political factions jostled for power. James I and James III died at the hands of certain nobles, James II and James IV (1488–1513) met their deaths while prosecuting war against England on behalf of France. Internal stability was not helped by crown-magnate

---

[1] Walter Bower, *Scotichronicon in Latin and English*, ed. D. E. R. Watt et al., 9 vols (Aberdeen and Edinburgh, 1987–98), vol. 8, pp. 64–5. These reigns are reassessed, however, in Stephen I. Boardman, *The Early Stewart Kings: Robert II and Robert III 1371–1406* (East Linton, 1996).

struggles. James I attacked his cousins, the Albany Stewarts, James II took on the powerful Douglas family, James III attacked his own brothers as well as prominent noble families, James IV waged military campaigns against the MacDonald Lordship of the Isles, and James V began his personal rule in 1528 by attacking the Angus Douglases who had held him captive for the previous two years.

Recent work has revised this picture and suggested that, apart from isolated short periods of friction, the age was marked more by co-operation than by conflict, although the extent of this co-operation is still the subject of debate.[2] Scotland was divided into regional and local power bases, without a strongly developed machinery of central government. In order to rule effectively, kings relied on the authority of nobles over their lands. They also staffed their councils with local lords from throughout the realm, Lowlands and Highlands, suggesting an awareness of the cultural diversity of their kingdom.[3] The periods of minority were useful to the adult kings, who, on coming to power, could forcefully assert their authority. Forfeitures of a few great magnate families allowed the kings to increase their financial resources by taking their lands for the crown and enabled them to reward those who served the crown loyally. Moreover, although individual kings were killed, the dynasty itself was never seriously threatened.[4]

Scotland's foreign policy was dominated by its relationship with its 'auld inimie' England, which still claimed overlordship over its northern neighbour, and its 'auld ally' France. The Scots won a victory at the Battle of Otterburn in 1388, but lost a more significant battle at Homildon Hill in 1402 after Henry IV's invasion of Scotland. The Duke of Albany committed himself to the French alliance, sending a large military force in 1419 to aid France in the Hundred Years War. Despite the defeat of this force in 1424, James I and James II continued to support France and its continental allies, particularly through marriage alliances – four of James I's daughters were married into European families, while James II married Mary of Gueldres, niece of the Duke of Burgundy.[5] The kings also chipped away at the remaining English-held

---

[2] Alexander Grant, *Independence and Nationhood: Scotland 1306–1469* (London, 1984) and Jenny Wormald, *Court, Kirk, and Community: Scotland 1470–1625* (London, 1981). The view of generally harmonious relations is questioned in Michael Brown, 'Scotland Tamed? Kings and Magnates in Late Medieval Scotland: a review of recent work', *IR* 45 (1994), pp. 120–46. Other political studies are Michael Brown, *James I*, rev. ed. (East Linton, 2000); Christine McGladdery, *James II* (1990); Norman Macdougall, *James III: A Political Study* (1982); Norman Macdougall, *James IV* (1989); Jamie Cameron, *James V: The Personal Rule 1528–1542* (East Linton, 1998).

[3] Stephen Boardman and Alasdair Ross, 'Editors' Introduction', *The Exercise of Power in Medieval Scotland c. 1200–c. 1500*, ed. S. Boardman and A. Ross (Dublin, 2003), pp. 15–22 (21).

[4] Grant, *Independence and Nationhood*, pp. 196–9; Wormald, *Court, Kirk, and Community*, pp. 2–26.

[5] Norman Macdougall, *An Antidote to the English: The Auld Alliance, 1295–1560* (East Linton, 2001); Fiona Downie, ' "La voie quelle menace tenir": Annabella Stewart, Scotland, and the

territories in Scotland. James II's siege of Roxburgh in 1460 achieved its goal, but at the cost of the king's death when a cannon exploded. However, his widow, Mary of Gueldres, was able to wring concessions from Henry VI and his queen, refugees from the Wars of the Roses, and by the mid-1460s all of Scotland's conquered territory had been won back from England. James III's marriage to Margaret of Denmark expanded Scotland's borders to their modern form (plus Berwick, which, however, was lost to England in 1482), bringing Scottish control of Orkney in 1468 and Shetland in 1469 when the Danish king pledged them for his daughter's dowry. In the 1470s, James III tried to reverse traditional foreign policy, when he began to explore a rapprochement with England. After almost two centuries of hostilities many Scots found the idea deeply distasteful, which contributed to the king's unpopularity. A rebellion in 1482 and again in 1488, resulting in his death, temporarily ended such moves.

James IV, who took full control of his government in 1495 when he reached his majority, put pressure on the new Tudor dynasty by supporting the pretender Perkin Warbeck,[6] and launching attacks on England in 1496–97. Ironically, this policy led to one of James III's aims, an English marriage alliance – a Treaty of Perpetual Peace was sealed with the king's wedding to Margaret Tudor in 1503. However, traditional loyalties weighed more with James. The navy he built up, which included the largest ship in Europe, the *Great Michael*, showed his determination to be counted as an equal with his Continental counterparts. His attempt to help France by invading England in 1513 led to the decimation of the Scottish leadership and his own death at Flodden. James V's minority (1513–28), opened a new era, with a struggle between pro-English and pro-French parties, complicated by the fact that many of the principal players switched their allegiances between France and England as it suited them. Although James V's adult rule saw the renewal of alliances with France, the struggles between pro-English and pro-French factions, exacerbated by religious factors, recurred after his death.

Government in late medieval Scotland was intensely personal; at the centre it rested largely with the king and his court. The king was the source of justice – the successful Stewart monarchs were those who went on justice ayres (circuit courts) around the country, demonstrating active involvement in maintaining law and order. The chief officers of government were all servants of the king, including the chancellor who presided over the writing office, and the treasurer who looked after the financial affairs of the crown. Relatively infrequent taxes and the lack of a paid army or central judicial system meant that there was no need for permanent institutions, such as an exchequer or treasury, on the

---

European Marriage Market, 1444–56', *SHR* 78 (1999), pp. 170–91; Priscilla Bawcutt and Bridget Henisch, 'Scots Abroad in the Fifteenth Century: The Princesses Margaret, Isabella and Eleanor', *Women in Scotland c. 1100–c. 1750*, ed. Elizabeth Ewan and Maureen M. Meikle (East Linton, 1999), pp. 45–55.
[6] David Dunlop, 'The "Masked Comedian": Perkin Warbeck's Adventures in Scotland and England from 1495 to 1497', *SHR* 70 (1991), pp. 97–128.

English model.⁷ Important decisions were made by the royal council, the king's most trusted advisers, usually drawn from leading magnate families. The king was also assisted, and occasionally opposed, by Parliament, which had developed in the later thirteenth and fourteenth centuries. This was a unicameral body, comprising the prelates, the nobles, and the burgesses (the Three Estates), which passed statutes, and agreed to taxation. It also acted as the highest secular legal court.⁸ The king's council also acted as a judicial body. An increase in judicial business led to the Lords of Council and Session becoming the central court for civil cases from about 1490 until the establishment of the College of Justice with its fifteen permanent judges in 1532.⁹

Central government bureaucracy was relatively underdeveloped in late medieval Scotland because much power rested with local authorities and their courts. The rule of these regions was largely entrusted to local magnates and lords, who comprised roughly two thousand noble families, making up about one per cent of the population of the kingdom. 'Noble' status was defined more broadly in Scotland than in England. At the lower end of the scale, some of these landholders were little wealthier than the peasantry; at the upper end there were about fifty great magnates who dominated national affairs.¹⁰

During the fifteenth century traditional patterns of power shifted. The greatest regional power bases, such as that of the earls of Douglas in southern Scotland, were broken up.¹¹ In the later fifteenth century the one remaining territorial lordship was dismantled by James III and James IV in a series of legal and military actions that culminated in the forfeiture of the Lordship of the Isles in 1493. Most of the earldoms and lordships created in this period were less territorially-based. A new legal distinction marked increasing divisions within the nobility, when individual nobles were made lords of parliament, distinguishing them from lesser lairds.¹² Personal lordships began to take on a new form as bonds of manrent, formal written expressions of lordship, were agreed between individuals, exchanging protection of one party in return for a promise of loyalty by the other.¹³ Local lairds took on greater roles as administrators or military supporters of the magnates, and for those families

---

⁷ Ian D. Whyte, *Scotland before the Industrial Revolution: An Economic and Social History, c1050–c1750* (London, 1995), pp. 83–4; David Ditchburn and Alastair J. MacDonald, 'Medieval Scotland, 1100–1560', *The New Penguin History of Scotland*, ed. R. A. Houston and W. W. J. Knox (London, 2001), pp. 96–181 (162).

⁸ *The History of the Scottish Parliament Volume I. Parliament and Politics in Scotland, 1235–1560*, ed. Keith M. Brown and Roland J. Tanner (2004).

⁹ Ditchburn and MacDonald, 'Medieval Scotland', p. 163.

¹⁰ Grant, *Independence and Nationhood*, pp. 120–2.

¹¹ Michael Brown, *The Black Douglases: War and Lordship in Late Medieval Scotland 1300–1455* (East Linton, 1998).

¹² A. Grant, 'The development of the Scottish peerage', *SHR* 57 (1978), pp. 1–27.

¹³ Jenny Wormald, *Lords and Men in Scotland: Bonds of Manrent 1442–1603* (1985).

wanting to advance further in wealth and standing, crown service became more important than regional power.[14]

The bonds of family and kinship were central to the lives of medieval Scots. The household, made up of a married couple, their children and often servants, was the basic unit of society. Women could marry at twelve, men at fourteen, although it is likely that most, apart from members of the aristocracy, married at a somewhat later age. A woman generally brought a dowry to the marriage, while a man was expected to provide a dower to sustain his wife in her widowhood. For a woman, marriage resulted in a change of legal status, as she came under the authority of her husband. All her property, except for 'paraphernalia' (personal clothing and jewellery), came under the control of her spouse, who was not supposed to alienate it without his wife's consent, but if he did, she could not recover it until after his death. A wife was not allowed to make a will, unless her husband consented. However, it was considered that to give such consent was the right thing for a man to do. Indeed, the restrictive practices suggested by the letter of the law were often bypassed. Marriage contracts could over-ride many of the restrictions on women's freedom, while the daily life of most couples probably involved far more co-operation and negotiation of duties and responsibilities than appears in legal treatises.[15]

The majority of medieval Scots (over 90 per cent of the population) lived in the countryside. Most farmland was worked co-operatively, with families gathered in clusters of farmsteads housing those who jointly farmed the lands. The balance between arable and pastoral varied depending on local conditions – the proportion of pastoral land probably increased in the later Middle Ages as the climate became colder after 1300, while the disturbed conditions of many areas due to war made it easier to raise livestock than crops. The Scottish diet may have become more meat-based, although in the sixteenth century it would return to the more traditional oat-based diet.[16] Below the lords, those at the top of rural society were the husbandmen who rented farm land or shares of it from the local landlord. The Black Death of 1348–50, which probably reduced the population by a quarter or a third from a peak of about one million, resulted in a labour shortage and fall in rents as lords attempted to attract new tenants; many husbandmen increased their holdings. Most leases were short-term, often annual, although it was common for them to be renewed and to pass to the original tenant's kin after his death. Cottars rented small plots of land from the husbandmen in return for labour services. Much less visible were landless

---

[14] Ditchburn and MacDonald, 'Medieval Scotland', pp. 141–2.
[15] Winifred Coutts, 'Wife and Widow: The Evidence of Testaments and Marriage Contracts c. 1600', *Women in Scotland*, ed. Ewan and Meikle, pp. 176–86.
[16] Whyte, *Scotland*, p. 113; Elizabeth Gemmill and Nicholas Mayhew, *Changing Values in Medieval Scotland: A study of prices, money, and weights and measures* (Cambridge, 1995), pp. 380–1.

labourers whose numbers were probably growing in the late fifteenth century as population levels recovered and competition for lands increased.[17]

The late Middle Ages have been seen as a time of population decline and economic recession. Plague returned frequently and war adversely affected overseas trade by cutting off normal markets such as Flanders or by attacks on Scottish shipping (although Scots were not above piracy themselves). Declining foreign markets for wool, the country's most important export, caused a dramatic decline in wool exports from a peak in the 1370s, to about a quarter of that level in the later fifteenth century. A silver shortage led to a devalued currency as the silver content of the coinage decreased. Exchange rates fell, making imports more expensive and inflation added to the country's woes in the later fifteenth and early sixteenth centuries.[18] However, recent research suggests the situation was not as bad as it appeared. Because so few items were subject to export customs, wool revenues give only a partial picture of Scotland's overseas trade. Other exports such as salmon and poor quality cloth may have helped at least partially to offset the decline in the wool trade. Devaluation could stimulate domestic production if it made imports more expensive, as well as making it easier to sell Scottish goods abroad.[19] Moreover, while many prices did rise, those for basic foodstuffs stayed relatively stable. Indeed the price rise may have been partially due to rising demand, implying economic growth.[20] The wide range of building works that characterized fifteenth-century Scotland – palaces, castles, abbeys and cathedrals, bridges and burgh churches – may even imply that late medieval Scotland had 'a slightly more widespread distribution of wealth'.[21] Sumptuary laws, passed in an attempt to restrict the wearing of rich fabrics to the social elite, suggest that a sizeable group could purchase such luxury items.[22]

Responding to rising prices and falling rents, many landholders began to 'feu' their lands, granting them to 'feuars', who became the heritable proprietors, and converting the traditional short-term leases into life or perpetual leases in return for a large entry payment. While of initial benefit to the landholder, inflation ate away at the value of the new rents. It was formerly thought that feuing with its initial high payments led to widespread eviction of sitting tenants, but more recent research has shown over half of the new feuars were the former tenants. However, many were not able to afford the new payments and joined the ranks

---

[17] Whyte, *Scotland*, pp. 46, 88–9.
[18] *Ibid.*, pp. 38–40, 72, 75, 78; Gemmill and Mayhew, *Changing Values*, pp. 116–23, 372–3.
[19] Gemmill and Mayhew, *Changing Values*, pp. 24, 371–5.
[20] *Ibid.*, pp. 374, 378.
[21] Geoffrey Stell, 'Architecture: the changing needs of society', *Scottish Society in the Fifteenth Century*, ed. Jennifer M. Brown (London, 1977), pp. 153–83 (183).
[22] Frances J. Shaw, 'Sumptuary Legislation in Scotland', *Juridical Review* 24 (1979), pp. 81–115.

of the landless labourers.[23] Despite this Scotland appears not to have suffered the peasant unrest common to many medieval societies. It may be that a country with dispersed rural settlements and few large towns lacked the necessary focus for resistance.[24]

Most towns were situated in the south and east of Scotland; they were not a feature of the Highlands. Few burghs (or towns with special trading privileges, incorporated by charter from a royal, ecclesiastical or baronial overlord) had populations over five thousand, the largest by far in the mid-sixteenth century being Edinburgh with a population of perhaps twelve thousand. In the Middle Ages many retained a rural character, with gardens and livestock pens behind the houses and many citizens still engaging part-time in rural activities.[25] The burghs played a central role in the Scottish economy. Royal burghs and some ecclesiastical burghs enjoyed a monopoly over the country's export trade, especially in the wool needed by the cloth-manufacturing towns of the Low Countries. From about 1400, many new baronial burghs were established. Situated mostly inland and without overseas trading privileges, they functioned mainly as local market centres. Many royal burghs were affected by the changing fortunes of overseas trade. Some declined, although others took a larger share of the shrinking market for themselves. Foremost among the latter was Edinburgh – by the 1490s over 70 per cent of Scotland's total wool exports passed through its port of Leith. Other towns responded by diversifying their economies – Perth broadened its manufacturing base, so that by the sixteenth century it was known as a crafts town as opposed to its rival, Dundee, which remained a merchants' town, switching the focus of its export trade from wool to hides and fish.[26]

Towns generally had their own governments, elected by enfranchised citizens, but they were far from democracies. Indeed, their social structure may have become more hierarchical in the later Middle Ages. At the top was a small wealthy elite, generally merchants but also the more prosperous craft masters of the town. This elite dominated the burgh government and also the merchant guild which regulated the overseas trade of many towns. There is some evidence for social tensions from the late fifteenth century onwards. In 1469 Parliament had ordained that the new town council should be chosen by the old council instead of through election by all burgesses, although how far this was followed in practice is not clear. The crafts also won recognition for their own

---

[23] Margaret H. B. Sanderson, *Scottish Rural Society in the Sixteenth Century* (1982); Gemmill and Mayhew, *Changing Values*, pp. 376–7.
[24] Ditchburn and MacDonald, 'Medieval Scotland', pp. 137–9.
[25] For example, E. P. D. Torrie, *Medieval Dundee: A Town and Its People* (Dundee, 1990), p. 85.
[26] M. Lynch, 'Scottish Towns 1500–1700', *The Early Modern Town in Scotland*, ed. M. Lynch (London, 1987), pp. 8–11.

guilds – in Edinburgh from 1474 onwards, fourteen crafts gained town council ratification of their corporate identity.[27]

Most townspeople, however, were neither merchants nor craftsmen. The majority of women were unenfranchised although they could be burgesses and craft guild members in some towns – if married, their status generally depended on that of their husband. Single women usually found employment in domestic service, or for some, in prostitution. Married women often supplemented the family income through such activities as brewing and baking, or selling of other foodstuffs.[28] Men worked as servants or labourers, some rising in status through marriage to burgess daughters or widows. There were also large numbers of poor – in late medieval European towns perhaps one third of the population lived in poverty. By 1500, some local authorities were beginning to feel overwhelmed and responded by passing ever stricter legislation against vagrants. The right to beg was restricted, often to those who had been born in the town; all others were to find work or be expelled.[29] The Christian responsibility of charity for the poor seems to have been breaking down.

There has been much disagreement among historians about the state of Catholicism in late medieval Scotland. Earlier studies stressed the corruption of the church but recent assessments depict a more complex picture. There were certainly aspects of church administration that needed reform; however, there is little evidence of the weakening of conventional piety. Traditional worship continued to the Reformation and beyond, suggesting that the medieval church fulfilled people's sprirtual needs. Since 1192 Scotland (except for the provinces of Galloway and Orkney) had been a 'special daughter of the church', with a direct relationship with the pope. In practice, the church was governed by provincial councils of all the Scottish bishops, the bishop of St Andrews usually taking the leading role. This continued until the late fifteenth century when Scotland received its first archbishopric at St Andrews (1472) and a second one at Glasgow (1492). Relationships between the kings and the papacy were generally cordial; James IV received the Golden Rose, the Sword and the Hat as signs of papal favour.[30]

More direct connections with Rome can be seen in the thousands of petitions to the Roman court, appealing against canon law decisions, seeking marriage dispensations, petitioning for dispensation from illegitimate birth or young age to enter the priesthood, and seeking benefices and clerical offices. The papacy

---

[27] Michael Lynch, 'The Social and Economic Structure of the Larger Towns, 1450–1600', *The Scottish Medieval Town*, ed. Michael Lynch et al. (1988), pp. 261–86 (261).

[28] E. Ewan, 'Crime or Culture? Women and Daily Life in Late-Medieval Scotland', *Twisted Sisters: Women, Crime and Deviance in Scotland since 1400*, ed. Y. G. Brown and R. Ferguson (East Linton, 2002), pp. 117–28.

[29] For example, *Extracts from the Records of the Burgh of Edinburgh AD 1403–1528*, ed. James D. Marwick, Scottish Burgh Records Society (1869), p. 97 (3 January 1503).

[30] James Galbraith, 'The Middle Ages', *Studies in the History of Worship in Scotland*, ed. Duncan Forrester and Douglas Murray, 2nd edn (1996), pp. 17–32 (20–1); Macdougall, *James IV*, p. 218.

was increasingly involved in the provision of clergy to benefices in the fourteenth and fifteenth centuries. The Great Schism (1378–1415), however, weakened papal power, and the Stewarts, like other European kings, began to seek greater say in appointments to high ecclesiastical office.[31] Holders of such offices, the most educated in the kingdom and usually members of the elite families, played a major role in government. In 1487, formalizing what had already been long practice, the pope granted the king an indult (a special privilege) allowing him to fill all major church offices, as well as granting him a period of grace during which he would receive the revenues of the vacant office; this was reconfirmed in 1519 and recognized as a right in 1535.[32]

James IV has been criticized for abusing this privilege in order to replenish his coffers by appointing to the archbishopric of St Andrews first his brother, and then his eleven-year-old illegitimate son Alexander. James V similarly bestowed high monastic office on four of his young illegitimate children in 1534–41, although monastic administrators were appointed to look after the monasteries during their minority. Scotland had fewer of these 'commendator' holders of benefices than many European countries, and safeguards existed so that at least part of the monastic revenues were directed to the maintenance of the house and its monks.[33] The career of Gavin Douglas shows that for some churchmen ambition for church office could co-exist with a desire for church renewal.[34] In the early sixteenth century a number of monastic and friary leaders introduced educational and disciplinary reforms to their houses.[35]

Probably the weakest aspect of the medieval church was the state of its parish clergy, although it is not clear that this situation was worse in the later Middle Ages than earlier. The best-educated clergy would obtain the highest positions in the church. This left the less well-educated in poorly paid positions in parishes, the revenues of which were often appropriated by other religious institutions. By the mid sixteenth century, over 85 per cent of parish churches had been appropriated. Many priests had to do their utmost to exact revenues from their parishioners in order to earn a living, causing no little resentment.[36] There is surprisingly little evidence of heretical beliefs in Scotland, although both government and universities expressed the need to be vigilant against heresy, especially with the rise of Lollardy in late fourteenth-century England.

---

[31] Wormald, *Court, Kirk, and Community*, p. 76.
[32] Mark Dilworth, *Scottish Monasteries in the Late Middle Ages* (1995), pp. 16–18.
[33] Macdougall, *James IV*, pp. 213–4; Dilworth, *Scottish Monasteries*, pp. 20, 22–3.
[34] P. Bawcutt, 'New Light on Gavin Douglas', *The Renaissance in Scotland: Studies in Literature, Religion, History and Culture Offered to John Durkan*, ed. A. A. MacDonald, Michael Lynch and Ian B. Cowan (Leiden, 1994), pp. 95–106.
[35] John Durkan, 'Education: The Laying of Fresh Foundations', *Humanism in Renaissance Scotland*, ed. John MacQueen (1990), pp. 123–60 (125–6); Anthony Ross, 'Some Notes on the Religious Orders in Pre-Reformation Scotland', *Essays on the Scottish Reformation*, ed. David McRoberts (Glasgow, 1962), pp. 185–244 (191–5).
[36] M. Lynch, 'Religious Life in Medieval Scotland', *A History of Religion in Britain*, ed. Sheridan Gilley and W. J. Sheils (Oxford, 1994), pp. 99–124 (109–11).

A statute ordering the execution of heretics was passed in 1425. Only two fifteenth-century executions are recorded. A more obscure episode involves a group of men and women from Ayrshire, apparently charged with Lollardy in 1494.[37]

Traditional practices included pilgrimage and the veneration of relics. Glasgow Cathedral's possessions in 1432 included both Scottish and more cosmopolitan relics, including those of St Kentigern and St Thomas, two fragments of the true cross, the Virgin's hair and milk, and part of the Lord's manger. St Margaret, wife of king Malcolm III, was venerated in Scotland, and her 'sark' or shirt was believed to assist several later queens in childbirth. Such relics drew pilgrims of all classes, from king to peasant.[38] James IV made several pilgrimages to the shrines of the Scottish saints Duthac at Tain and Ninian at Whithorn; the latter had been the site of his mother Margaret of Denmark's pilgrimage in thanksgiving for his safe birth. Scots also made pilgrimages abroad; James IV contemplated first a pilgrimage to the Holy Land, and later a Crusade.[39]

The elite also expressed their piety by founding religious houses and churches. Late medieval Scotland had over one hundred monasteries and friaries. Women's houses were less common – only fifteen were founded, and of these, four had been suppressed by 1500. Notable foundations included Scotland's only Carthusian house, established by James I at Perth in 1429, and the female Dominican house of St Catherine of Siena established in Edinburgh in 1517. Nine houses existed of the Observant Franciscans, a reformed Franciscan order introduced by Mary of Gueldres.[40] The number of hospitals increased in the fifteenth century, with several leper hospitals on the outskirts of towns.[41] Another form of benefaction was the collegiate church, where secular clergy were gathered into a college, often at an existing church. These were promoted by kings, nobles, and towns, and included James III's chapel at Restalrig, the chapel royal at Stirling, William Sinclair, Earl of Orkney's foundation at Roslin, and St Giles, Edinburgh. By the Reformation there were forty-two such foundations.[42] The elite also commissioned the monumental

---

[37] David Ditchburn, *Scotland and Europe: The Medieval Kingdom and its Contacts with Christendom, c. 1215–1545* (East Linton, 2001), pp. 39–40.

[38] Peter Yeoman, *Pilgrimage in Medieval Scotland* (London, 1999), pp. 13, 48–9, 734, 82; Ditchburn, *Scotland and Europe*, pp. 57–61; John Higgitt, *'Imageis Maid with Mennis Hand': Saints, Images, Belief and Identity in Later Medieval Scotland* (Whithorn, 2003).

[39] Lynch, 'Religious Life', p. 121; Macdougall, *James IV*, pp. 196–209.

[40] I. B. Cowan and D. E. Easson, *Medieval Religious Houses: Scotland*, 2nd edn (London, 1976), pp. 86–7, 129–33, 143–56; John Durkan, 'The Observant Franciscan Province in Scotland', *IR* 35 (1984), pp. 51–7.

[41] John Durkan, 'Care of the Poor: Pre-Reformation Hospitals', *Essays on the Scottish Reformation*, ed. McRoberts, pp. 110–28; 'Hospitals', *Atlas of Scottish History to 1707*, ed. P. G. B. McNeill and H. L. MacQueen (1996), pp. 344–5.

[42] R. Fawcett, 'The Churches of the Greater Medieval Cities', *The Architecture of Scottish Cities*, ed. Deborah Mays (East Linton, 1997), p. 16; and Richard Fawcett, *Scottish Architecture from the Accession of the Stewarts to the Reformation 1371–1560* (1994), pp. 142–81.

stone crosses and grave slabs that were a feature of medieval Highland culture, although the crown's political attacks on the Lordship of the Isles led to the decline of the two leading schools of monumental sculpture in the late fifteenth and sixteenth centuries.[43]

The late Middle Ages witnessed an increasing concern for the soul's life after death. Endowments for masses to be said for one's soul could shorten the time spent in purgatory. Wealthy people established altars and priests to serve them and pray for the founder's soul; the less well-off paid for individual masses. Corporate bodies such as craft guilds also established altars where masses could be said for all their deceased brethren. Late medieval churches, especially town churches, contained more and more altars – St Giles in Edinburgh may have had as many as fifty, St Mary's Dundee as many as forty-eight.[44] The altar furnishings, the vestments of the priests, the music and the continuous round of services made for a rich and powerful religious experience for the worshippers.[45]

Medieval religion cannot be divorced from political life. James IV's pilgrimages to Tain and Whithorn helped to bring the largely autonomous regions of Ross and Galloway under greater royal authority. In the later fifteenth century there were attempts to promote a 'national' form of piety, with the encouragement of cults of early Scottish saints. Attempts were also made to introduce a new liturgy replacing the English Sarum use – one purpose of the printing press established by a patent of 1507 was to provide Scottish service books.[46] How much influence all this had on popular belief or practice is hard to gauge. As elsewhere in Europe, new cults associated with Christ and the Virgin Mary became more widespread, with devotional practices such as the Cult of the Holy Blood being introduced from the Low Countries, especially to the towns, in the fifteenth century. Universal saints continued to be popular as hospital dedications, in seals, and in religious literature, and breviaries both of Sarum and Roman use circulated widely in the sixteenth century.[47]

The church, from the twelfth century at least, was the major provider of education in Scotland. However, during the late Middle Ages, an increasing interest in education developed among the laity, perhaps related to the new opportunities that the restructuring of the nobility opened up for lairds and

---

[43] Martin MacGregor, 'Church and culture in the late medieval Highlands', *The Church in the Highlands*, ed. James Kirk (1998), pp. 1–36 (15 and 20); K. A. Steer and J. W. M. Bannerman, *Late Medieval Monumental Sculpture in the West Highlands* (1977).

[44] Torrie, *Medieval Dundee*, p. 89.

[45] For a sense of what was lost: David McRoberts, 'Material Destruction Caused by the Scottish Reformation', *Essays on the Scottish Reformation*, ed. McRoberts, pp. 415–62.

[46] Yeoman, *Pilgrimage*, pp. 14–15; Leslie Macfarlane, *William Elphinstone and the Kingdom of Scotland 1431–1514* (Aberdeen, 1985), pp. 231–46; Galbraith, 'The Middle Ages', pp. 23–8, 31–2.

[47] Ditchburn, *Scotland and Europe*, pp. 50–7; A. A. MacDonald, 'Passion Devotion in Late-Medieval Scotland', *The Broken Body. Passion Devotion in Late-Medieval Culture*, ed. A. A. MacDonald, H. N. B. Ridderbos, and R. M. Schlusemann (Groningen, 1998), pp. 108–31.

burgesses in the service of the king and new magnates. The culmination of such changing lay aspirations was the Education Act of 1496, which decreed that all sons of barons and freeholders of substance should attend grammar schools and learn Latin and law in order to carry out their duties as upholders of justice in the local courts.[48] Its effectiveness can be debated, but there is evidence of spreading literacy from the later fifteenth century.[49] Late medieval Scotland was probably better supplied with schools than once thought; song schools, open to all boys, were attached to most churches of any size, while the number of grammar schools, especially in the towns, was increasing. Noble households, employing their own chaplains, might also provide education for their children and those of kin and favoured tenants. There were some schools for girls, run by women – Edinburgh had such schools by 1499.[50] In the Highlands, education in Latin and Classical Common Gaelic was provided in the schools associated with the learned professions such as poets and physicians.[51] Before 1400 those seeking higher education had to go to England or the Continent, but during the fifteenth century three universities were founded in Scotland – St Andrews (1410–13), Glasgow (1450–51) and King's College, Aberdeen (1495). Most students destined to be leaders in either the church or royal service (or both) continued study abroad, bringing back the new humanist ideals of interest in the classics and the importance of public service. Some graduates, including Hector Boece and John Mair, also returned to take up teaching positions in the Scottish universities, passing along such ideals to a new generation of scholars.[52]

What of the culture of ordinary folk in Scotland? This is an area still under-researched. Few records survive for the countryside, although thanksgiving processions for a successful harvest were probably yearly events.[53] In the towns, people of different social classes intermingled in church, in court, and above all in the marketplace. Local statutes give the impression of well-regulated commerce, but the reality was different. Raucous exchanges, good-natured or not-so-good-natured bargaining, petty thievery and insults – all were to be found in the medieval marketplace. Concerned to maintain the peace, the town authorities brought such disturbances before its court, giving historians

---

[48] R. Mason, *Kingship and the Commonweal: Political Thought in Renaissance and Reformation Scotland* (East Linton, 1998), pp. 108–14; R. Mason, 'Laicisation and the Law: The Reception of Humanism in Early Renaissance Scotland', *Palace*, ed. Houwen et al., pp. 1–25.
[49] Wormald, *Court, Kirk, and Community*, pp. 67–70.
[50] John Durkan, 'Education in the Century of the Reformation', *Essays on the Scottish Reformation*, ed. McRoberts, pp. 145–68; Lynch, 'Religious Life', pp. 115–16; *Extracts from the Records of the Burgh of Edinburgh*, ed. Marwick, p. 76 (8 June 1499).
[51] MacGregor, 'Church and culture', pp. 29–30.
[52] Mason, *Kingship*, pp. 108–10, 115; John Durkan, 'Education: The Laying of Fresh Foundations', *Humanism*, ed. MacQueen, pp. 123–60.
[53] John J. McGavin, 'Robert III's "Rough Music": Charivari and Diplomacy in a Medieval Scottish Court', *SHR* 74 (1995), pp. 144–58.

glimpses of the colourful language and behaviour that characterized social interaction, and perhaps influenced the literature of flyting.[54]

Unlike many European and English towns, each Scottish town had only one parish. The community was united in a *corpus christianum*, with collective worship focussed on one central institution and patron saint, although this began to break down in the later Middle Ages in those churches that became collegiate or had a myriad of craft altars.[55] Important religious festivals began or ended at the town's church. The efforts and expense that went into improving the great burgh churches in the fifteenth and early sixteenth centuries point to their importance to the townspeople. Responsibility for the parish church was often shared between the town, which maintained the nave, and a religious institution outside it, which maintained the choir. In the later fifteenth century, many towns agreed to take over the choir's upkeep,[56] probably increasing the town's identification with the church as a symbol of community.

Religious celebrations such as Corpus Christi processions became popular, although they could lead to tensions as various crafts jostled for precedence. Many communities chose an Abbot of Unreason (or Abbot of Bon Accord in Aberdeen) to organize plays and pageants, but by the early sixteenth century these functions seem to have often been taken over by figures named Robin Hood and Little John. Some towns also had a Queen of May. The tradition began to decline, at least among the town elite who were usually elected to the office, in the sixteenth century. By the 1530s men were being fined for refusing to take it on; the Abbot's office was suppressed in Haddington in 1552, and in 1555 Parliament abolished it nation-wide,[57] authorities having become increasingly concerned with the potential for disorderly behaviour accompanying such festivities.

Was there a 'Scottish identity' in the late Middle Ages? The kingdom was an amalgam of many identities, with different languages, ethnicities and loyalties. As Lowland Scotland focussed on England and Europe, it drew apart from the Highlands. Disparagement of Highland language and culture became more pronounced in the fifteenth century, as Scottish kings tried to enforce their authority there.[58] Orkney, which had had Scottish earls since the thirteenth century and law courts using Scots since the 1430s, was probably more integrated into Scotland than was Shetland. The Borders, faced with constant

---

[54] E. Ewan, ' "Many Injurious Words": Defamation and Gender in Late Medieval Scotland', *History, Literature, and Music in Scotland, 700–1560*, ed. R. A. MacDonald (Toronto, 2002), pp. 163–86; P. Bawcutt, 'The Art of Flyting', *SLJ* 10.2 (1983), pp. 5–24 (7–10).
[55] Lynch, 'Religious Life', pp. 120–1.
[56] Fawcett, 'Churches', pp. 13–17.
[57] Anna Jean Mill, *Mediæval Plays in Scotland* (New York, 1967), pp. 21–30; Keely Fisher, '*The crying of ane play*: Robin Hood and Maying in sixteenth-century Scotland', *Medieval and Renaissance Drama in England* 12 (1999), pp. 19–52 (19–28).
[58] Wormald, *Kirk, Court, and Community*, pp. 61–2.

raids by both Scots and English, and with large parts often under English occupation, developed its own unruly character.[59] Any national identity had to co-exist with strong local identities.

The Wars of Independence (1296–1342) have been seen as the crucible in which the concept of Scottish nationhood was forged,[60] yet the period 1400–1530 witnessed a strengthening of a Scottish identity which, while remaining open to English cultural influences,[61] was increasingly European and anti-English in its political focus. Wyntoun, Bower and other historical writers elaborated on Scotland's long standing as an independent monarchy, while the Scottish monarchs increased their involvement in European politics. Most important, perhaps, was the kings' defence of the realm against the English. With no standing army, the monarch was dependent on men fulfilling their obligation to serve in times of national emergency. Responses to English invasions or the launching of pre-emptive strikes showed to the nation that it had a warrior at its head.[62] Such a military ethos appealed to the chivalric impulses of the nobility, who were part of a European aristocratic world which glorified war. In times of peace, kings met this need by holding tournaments, at which they could also demonstrate their prestige and wealth.[63]

During the fifteenth century, new ideas about kingship began to circulate in Europe. In Scotland, with its background of threats to independence, long minorities or absent kings, debates about kingship took on particular relevance, and a 'mirror of princes' literature developed.[64] From James III on, the doctrine that 'the king is emperor in his own kingdom' was enthusiastically adopted. This fitted well with the expanding royal jurisdiction – the acquisition of Orkney and Shetland, the extension of rule over Ross and the Isles, and the increasing power over the church. The ideology was expressed in various ways – in 1469 Parliament stated that James III had 'full jurisdictione and free impire within his realm'; in the mid-1480s a new silver groat showed the king with a closed imperial crown on his head and in the late 1520s and '30s James V issued a similar coinage. The idea of 'imperium' was also used to demonstrate Scotland's status – among the arms of the rulers on the heraldic ceiling of St Machar's Cathedral, Aberdeen, completed in 1520, only those of the Emperor

---

[59] Ditchburn and MacDonald, 'Medieval Scotland', pp. 152–5.
[60] Grant, *Independence and Nationhood*, pp. 3–31.
[61] Priscilla Bawcutt, 'English Books and Scottish Readers in the Fifteenth and Sixteenth Centuries', *ROSC* 14 (2001–02), pp. 1–12.
[62] Carol Edington, 'Paragons and Patriots: National Identity and the Chivalric Ideal in Late-Medieval Scotland', *Image and Identity: The Making and Re-making of Scotland Through the Ages*, ed. Dauvit Broun, R. J. Finlay and Michael Lynch (1998), pp. 69–81.
[63] Ditchburn, *Scotland and Europe*, pp. 70–3, 96–105; L. O. Fradenburg, *City, Marriage, Tournament. Arts of Rule in Late Medieval Scotland* (Madison, 1991), pp. 153–264.
[64] Sally Mapstone, 'The Advice to Princes Tradition in Scottish Literature, 1450–1500', unpublished D.Phil. thesis (Oxford, 1986).

and the king of Scots bore closed imperial crowns.[65] When in 1540 James V had the crown refashioned in imperial style, he was indicating that Scotland was a worthy marriage partner for France and the equal of any kingdom in Christendom.

[65] Helena M. Shire, 'The King in his House: Three Architectural Artefacts belonging to the Reign of James V', *Stewart Style 1513–1542: Essays on the Court of James V*, ed. Janet Hadley Williams (East Linton, 1996), pp. 62–96 (65–70); Mason, *Kingship and Commonweal*, pp. 104, 126–38.

2

'*I will my proces hald*': Making Sense of Scottish Lives and the Desire for History in Barbour, Wyntoun and Blind Hary

R. JAMES GOLDSTEIN

The three vernacular verse compositions to be discussed in this chapter, John Barbour's *Bruce* (c. 1375), Andrew of Wyntoun's *Original Chronicle* (c. 1408–24), and even Blind Hary's almost entirely fictitious *Wallace* (c. 1476–78), were viewed by early readers as authoritative accounts of Scottish history. Medieval history-writing in general shared a broadly ethical appeal, employing the exemplary life as a principle of narrative structure and thematic organization. Along with the compilers of the two major Latin chronicles of medieval Scotland, John of Fordun's *Chronica Gentis Scotorum* (c. 1385) and Walter Bower's *Scotichronicon* (c. 1445), the three vernacular historians conceived of history-writing as a branch of ethics that preserves the memory of individual lives as models worthy of admiration or admonishment.[1]

Beginnings and endings provide especially opportune moments for authors or their scribes to signal their ethical appeals. The Latin colophon at the end of the only extant manuscript of *The Wallace* demonstrates awareness that the author bases his ethical appeal on the admirable life when the scribe John Ramsay wrote in 1488: 'Here ends the life of the very noble defender of Scotland, the knight William Wallace'.[2] Ramsay is also the scribe of the Latin *incipit* in one of the two extant manuscripts of *The Bruce*: 'Here begins the book composed by Master John Barber, archdeacon of Aberdeen, which is about the deeds, wars, and virtues of Sir Robert the Bruce, the famous king of Scotland, and of

---

[1] See Walter Bower, *Scotichronicon in Latin and English*, ed. D. E. R. Watt et al., 9 vols (1987–98), vol. 9, pp. 12–13. All references, cited by volume and page, are to this edition and appear parenthetically in the text.
[2] Hary, *Wallace*, ed. McDiarmid, Book 12: final note in the textual apparatus (my translation). All references, which are cited by book and line numbers, are to this edition and appear parenthetically in the text; other matter is cited by volume and page. Letter forms u/v/w and yogh are silently modernized, abbreviations expanded, and capitalization normalized. For a student edition, see *The Wallace: Selections*, ed. Anne McKim, TEAMS Middle English Texts (Kalamazoo, Mich., 2003).

his conquest of the Kingdom of Scotland, and of Sir James Douglas'.[3] The ethical appeal of the poem is also implicit in Barbour's prologue when he observes that true ('suthfast') stories offer a double reward of pleasure ('plesance') for the reader: the enjoyment that comes from hearing (or reading) stories, and the special satisfaction of knowing it is true.[4] Writing enables the memory of 'stalwart folk' (19) to endure as a living 'presence' (20). When Barbour describes Robert Bruce and Sir James Douglas as 'wycht and wys' (22), his pairing the classical virtues of *fortitudo* and *sapientia* helps convey the poem's function as *speculum principis*, a mirror for the reigning monarch Robert II (the first Stewart king) and his descendants.

When one such descendant, James III, pursued a marriage allegiance with the English in the mid-1470s, Blind Hary responded with an ethical appeal by asking his compatriots to remember their ancestors' 'nobille worthi deid' instead of forging alliances with the old enemy, England (1–5). However unattractive Hary's belligerent attitude may seem to modern readers, the ethics of his opposition to the king's conciliatory foreign policy were evidently shared by the two Border lairds whom he names as intended readers (12:1443–4), men whose livelihood depended on a perpetual state of hostility with the more powerful southern neighbour.[5] *The Bruce* appeals to the reigning monarch after narrating the dramatic victory of Bannockburn, a useful enough moment of closure for the poet to insert a direct genealogical link between Robert Bruce and Robert II, son of Walter Stewart and Bruce's daughter Marjory.[6] Thus he records for posterity that 'in the tyme of the compiling / Off this buk this Robert wes king' (13:709–10), before praying for the successful governance by the Stewart line in the future:

> God grant that thai that cummyn ar
> Off his ofspring manteyme the land
> And hald the folk weill to warand
> And manteyme rycht and leawté
> Als wele as in his tyme did he.   (13:718–22)

---

[3] The standard scholarly edition, Barbour, *Bruce*, ed. McDiarmid and Stevenson, does not print the incipit; for the Latin and English translation see *The Idea of the Vernacular: An Anthology of Middle English Literary Theory, 1280–1520*, ed. Jocelyn Wogan-Browne, Nicholas Watson, Andrew Taylor and Ruth Evans (University Park, Pa., 1999), p. 25. Ramsay copied both poems, now bound together in Edinburgh, National Library of Scotland, MS Advocates 19.2.2.

[4] John Barbour, *The Bruce*, ed. and trans. A. A. M. Duncan, Canongate Classics 78 (1997), 1:1–10. Subsequent references, which are cited by book and line numbers, are to this edition and appear parenthetically in the text. Duncan's edition and facing-page translation provides a convenient text based on McDiarmid and Stevenson, though with modernized letter forms and silent expansion of scribal abbreviations.

[5] See *Wallace*, ed. McDiarmid, 1, pp. xvi–xx; li–lvi. One of the knights, James Liddale, was steward to Alexander duke of Albany, the king's brother, who was to lead a rebellion against him in the early 1480s. It is possible that Albany was the poet's patron.

[6] On Barbour's lost 'Stewartis Orygenale': Stephen I. Boardman, *The Early Stewart Kings: Robert II and Robert III 1371–1406* (1996), pp. 59, 69–70, nn. 78, 79.

By emphasizing the art of governance, the ethical appeal proclaimed by medieval history-writing is inseparable from an avowed political one; indeed, the three Scots verse narratives and the two Latin prose compilations are concerned not just with the lives of rulers and their narrow circle of supporters but the collective life of the Scottish nation.[7] As Bower exclaims at the end of his massive work: 'Christ! He is not a Scot who is not pleased with this book' (vol. 8, p. 341).

The appeal of exemplary deeds led medieval writers and their audiences to turn to chronicles to satisfy the desire for 'suthfast' narrative and to address a compelling need to make sense of Scottish lives. Yet within the broadly shared parameters of ethical and political guidance, these works of late-medieval historical writing from Scotland are based on many principles of selection and arrangement, which in turn suggest a variety of strategies for interpreting history. One important reason for the variety of perspectives that they offer lies in the standard methods for creating such compositions in an age before modern regimes of authorship and copyright had taken root. The production of medieval historical texts was truly a collaborative enterprise, even in those cases when an individual author (or his scribe) 'signs' the work, though like Bower, he may eschew the name of 'author' (an honorific term Bower reserved to describe Fordun, preferring to designate himself more modestly as 'scriptor').[8] Yet even Fordun depended on the labours of many earlier Scottish writers whose names and separate texts have been lost.[9] Wyntoun honours his vernacular predecessors by drawing attention to their contributions. In addition to following Barbour in employing the octosyllabic couplet, Wyntoun inserts substantial portions of *The Bruce* into his work; he also uses an anonymous chronicle from shortly after 1390 as his main source for the reigns of David II (1329–71) and Robert II (1371–90).[10]

Bower offers an especially revealing idea about how history ought to be properly written so that it never becomes the preserve of an individual author. He suggests a plan for each monastery to appoint a writer to record 'all

---

[7] See R. James Goldstein, *The Matter of Scotland: Historical Narrative in Medieval Scotland* (Lincoln, Nebr. and London, 1993).
[8] *Scotichronicon*, vol. 9, p. 4. See the indispensable study by Alastair J. Minnis, *Medieval Theory of Authorship: Scholastic Literary Attitudes in the Later Middle Ages*, 2nd edn (Aldershot and Philadelphia, 1988); see also *Idea of the Vernacular*, ed. Wogan-Browne et al.
[9] On Fordun's lost sources for legendary material, see Dauvit Broun, *The Irish Identity of the Kingdom of the Scots* (Woodbridge, 1999); contrast Goldstein, *Matter of Scotland*, pp. 121–2. For other lost sources, see Dauvit Broun, 'The Birth of Scottish History', *SHR* 76 (1997), pp. 4–22; Dauvit Broun, 'A New Look at *Gesta Annalia* Attributed to John of Fordun', *Church, Chronicle and Learning in Medieval and Early Renaissance Scotland: Essays Presented to Donald Watt on the Occasion of the Completion of the Publication of Bower's 'Scotichronicon'*, ed. Barbara E. Crawford (1999), pp. 9–30.
[10] See R. James Goldstein, ' "For he wald vsurpe na fame": Andrew of Wyntoun's Use of the Modesty *Topos* and Literary Culture in Early Fifteenth-Century Scotland', *SLJ* 14.1 (1987), pp. 5–18; Stephen Boardman, 'Chronicle Propaganda in Fourteenth-Century Scotland: Robert the Steward, John of Fordun and the "Anonymous Chronicle" ', *SHR* 76 (1997), pp. 23–43.

noteworthy things during a king's reign'. At the first parliament after the king's death, wise men would be chosen to compile a chronicle from these annals, which would be stored 'in monastic archives as authenticated chronicles which can be trusted, lest by the passing of time memories of happenings in the kingdom perish' (vol. 8, p. 339). Bower views the writing of history as a collaborative effort, one that implies 'an idea of a chronicle as both fixed and adaptable, representing an ideological *status quo*, a collectively agreed and interpreted record of events'.[11] Even more striking is Bower's notion that his death need not prevent the continuation, in both senses, of his work. These instructions to his readers, directed in the first instance to the monastic community of Inchcolm where he served as abbot until his death in 1449, are the moving response of an old man to his sense of impending mortality; his plan for filing duplicate copies in scattered monastic archives provides an answer to the ever-threatening danger of oblivion. So long as the recorded lives provide 'a stimulus to virtue and a warning of wrongs' (vol. 8, p. 341), history will never be devoid of ethical meaning.

Yet despite his anxieties about the future, the abbot of Inchcolm shares a general Christian understanding of the providential design for human history with that of the other chroniclers. According to this understanding, most details of which were worked out by such early Christian authors as St Augustine and Boethius, the broad pattern of historical events makes sense by reading retrospectively from an end-point that has been revealed in advance in the closing book of Scripture, which narrates how human history will come to a close at a date known in advance only to God, when the quick and the dead will receive final judgement. In the forward progression of time since the Creation, everything necessarily leads up to that end – each individual life, the communal lives of nations large and small, the universal church, ultimately the entire world. It is of course true that readers of any kind of narrative will experience a small segment of the inexorable forward march of time during whatever hours they spend reading; nevertheless, stories purporting to be 'suthfast' representations of history make especially strong claims that our sense of time receding as we read a text from beginning to end is directly linked to our larger temporal experience of life as unidirectional. Moreover, just as individually we can always repeat a reading but can never read a historical narrative again for the first time, individually or collectively we can always remember the past (which is the main purpose of writing history), but we can never relive the past in the present, only experience it as a present memory, given the forward movement of individual and historical time, as St Augustine suggests at the end of his *Confessions*.

The individual human life as a measure of historical time exerts such a powerful draw that the providential view of history divides the ages of the

---

[11] Sally Mapstone, 'The *Scotichronicon*'s First Readers', *Church, Chronicle and Learning*, ed. Crawford, pp. 31–55 (quotation, p. 34).

world according to the lives of prominent men in sacred history. The attractions of such a scheme are evident in Fordun's account of the five ages of the world before Christ, which Bower copies in *Scotichronicon*, vol. 1, pp. 18–29.[12] Not content to leave Christian time in suspension, Bower extends the narrative frame of providential history to include all seven ages, bringing it to the very end of time itself (vol. 9, pp. 62–5). The scheme of seven ages thus provides the most inclusive frame possible for the process of human time plotted in historical narrative. Andrew of Wyntoun's *Original Chronicle* is the only Scottish chronicle that attempts to comprehend all the time that has elapsed since the very beginning, even before the creation of man, and so his work takes its name from the desire to begin with the absolute origin:

> The titill of this tretise haill
> I will be callit Originall,
> For that begynnyng sall mak cleire
> Be plane procese oure matere. (vol. 2, p. 8:95–8)[13]

Clear traces of the providential scheme of the ages of the world are evident in the structure of Wyntoun's work in the earlier Wemyss version, which associates the seven-book scheme with the seven 'eldis' (ages) of the world.[14] The first book takes us through the entire second age until the time of Abraham.

Yet Wyntoun does not sustain the effort to map the seven ages directly onto his seven-book structure, since he finds other ways of plotting history that intermingle with the one derived from biblical events. In book two Wyntoun begins to follow the universal history of Orosius, which keeps the providential meaning of history in clear view as the pagan kingdoms of Babylon, Greece, and Rome, are placed side by side with events from Old Testament history. Wyntoun also provides an account of the origin of the Scots, in preparation for his increasingly narrow focus on local events of Scottish history, organized for the most part according to the life spans of the nation's kings.[15] In both the vernacular and Latin traditions of chronicle writing in Scotland, then, the

---

[12] Johannis de Fordun, *Chronica Gentis Scotorum*, ed. William F. Skene (1871), 1:8; cf. Bower, *Scotichronicon*, ed. Watt, vol. 1, p. 100, notes at 1–2.

[13] All references are to Andrew of Wyntoun, *The Original Chronicle of Andrew of Wyntoun*, ed. F. J. Amours, 6 vols, STS (1903–14), by volume, page and line numbers, which appear parenthetically in the text. Letter forms are silently modernized and abbreviations expanded. Unless otherwise stated, I cite the 'Wemyss' version (c. 1408), the earliest of the three editions produced by Wyntoun, an Augustinian canon regular of St Andrews who was prior of the dependent monastery of Loch Leven island. Amours also prints the last version, the 'Cottonian', which must have been completed before the return of James I from captivity in 1424. See Broun, 'A New Look at *Gesta Annalia*', p. 24, n. 39.

[14] *Wyntoun*, ed. Amours, vol. 2, p. 10:129–32 (accepting the editor's emendation of the reading in MS W, 'eldest'). The seven-book scheme was revised in the Cottonian version to a nine-part one, after the number of angelic orders.

[15] See Broun, *The Irish Identity of the Kingdom of the Scots* for analysis of the origin legends and the early king lists on which they were ultimately based.

genealogy of kings adapted from older king lists creates a continuous chain of links in the unfolding of history in a unidirectional narrative. For example, Wyntoun traces 'Sir Newill', a lineal descendant from Noah by twenty generations, a Scythian who won 'gret lordschip' in Greece; his son 'Gadeill-Glaiss' married Scota, the daughter of the Pharaoh, and 'gat on Scota barnis faire'.[16] Eventually reaching Spain, Gaythelos (to assign this figure his more usual name) builds Brigantia, whence he sights an island in the distance and sends three ships with armed men to find out more about the unknown land, which eventually will be settled and named Ireland. Thus the drive for knowledge and conquest propels the legendary narrative forward. But death comes unexpectedly to Gaythelos before his scouts return, though his sons live on to continue the project and fulfill the leader's desire to establish a permanent homeland, which eventually leads to the settlement of Scotland and the foundation of the kingdom.

Placed within the framework of providential history, the kingdom of the Scots might have seemed to Wyntoun divinely appointed to last until the end of time. Indeed, the more he focuses on the details of Scottish history, the clearer it becomes that he writes in response to the desire of his fellow Scots to make sense of the more local destiny of his kingdom within this larger providential framework. As long as the lineage of Scottish kings remained unbroken, Scottish historiographers could project a hopeful future for their nation. Yet without the certainties about the end of history that providential narratives offer, the future shape of secular history remained open and subject to anxiety. For this reason, the most important historical contexts for reading Scottish historical verse (and the parallel Latin tradition) are the periodic threats to Scottish independence from English imperialist ambitions, and the internal divisions that frequently plagued medieval Scotland. Without the wars of independence and the continuing possibility of hostile relations with England throughout the later Middle Ages, Barbour's *Bruce* and Hary's *Wallace* would scarcely have been written from the same sense of urgency, nor would the chronicles of Fordun, Wyntoun, or Bower have taken anything like their present shape. When one chronicler leaves his work incomplete upon his death, it remains for others to take up the burden of writing, just as it is left up to the next generation of Scots to preserve the fragile inheritance of political independence and to maintain the kingdom's welfare.

Because human beings are endowed with free will and are thus capable of changing the direction of their lives, the moral pattern of any individual life is only completed at death. By creating closure, death allows the life to make sense retrospectively, when it becomes available for plotting out as 'a life written backwards ... constructed to make sense of the death that is required by

---

[16] *Wyntoun*, ed. Amours, vol. 2, p. 190:635–53.

the larger narrative'.[17] This retrospective sense of meaning is especially evident in the frequent moments where the chronicler breaks the narrative progression to eulogize the dead. Bower ends his *Scotichronicon* by praising the virtues of James I (d. 1437), the most recent king whose life could now fit into its final moral pattern (vol. 8, pp. 302–25). With the exception of a fragmentary song composed soon after the death of Alexander III in 1286, Barbour provides the earliest surviving vernacular remembrances of the Scottish dead.[18] Walter Stewart, whose importance as father of the first Stewart monarch was retrospectively clear to Barbour, is mourned by many a knight and lady, 'For off his eild he wes worthy'.[19] Even more striking is the major role Barbour assigns to James Douglas, whom he eulogizes as 'honest lele and worthy' (20:576). Again, his importance could only be understood retrospectively, by reading backwards from the moment of his chivalric death on crusade against the Muslims in Spain while carrying Bruce's heart in a sealed casket, and also by reading backwards from the vantage of the intervening years, since by the time of Barbour's composition the Douglas family had risen to a national prestige and power it did not enjoy at the time of the war itself. Sir James Douglas, in other words, did not have as important a role in Bannockburn and elsewhere as Barbour claims.[20]

The chroniclers' eulogies are frequently accompanied by accounts of the moment of death, and, almost as often, by descriptions of funerals and monuments.[21] Typically the writer will offer a brief prayer for the hero's soul. *The Bruce* understandably devotes the fullest account to the funeral of Robert I (20:254–308) but also describes Walter Stewart's interment at Paisley Abbey (19:224–8) and the funeral and alabaster tomb of Douglas (20:579–600). Reading a historical narrative of another person's death provides some sense of how it seals the meaning of life, a sense that works more powerfully in a 'suthfast' story than in a work of fiction. That the narration of death is linked to anxieties arising from one's own sense of mortality is suggested by the tendency in medieval chronicles to evoke the topos of *memento mori*, inviting contemplation of the ultimate destiny of the individual soul, for the person

---

[17] Felicity Riddy, 'Contextualizing *Le Morte D'Arthur*: Empire and Civil War', *A Companion to Malory*, ed. Elizabeth Archibald and A. S. G. Edwards (Cambridge, 1996), pp. 55–74 (quotation p. 61). Riddy draws on Peter Brooks, *Reading for the Plot: Design and Intention in Narrative* (Cambridge, Mass., 1992); I am generally indebted to both.
[18] A stanza of the song is preserved in *Wyntoun*, vol. 5, pp. 144–5; Barbour alludes to the song: 1:37–8.
[19] *Bruce*, ed. Duncan, 19:222; there is a preliminary eulogy at 17:927–35; Duncan ties Barbour's conspicuous praise for Walter Stewart, though he 'remains a minor character' (p. 14), to the virtual certainty that the poet composed the poem for Robert II.
[20] See *Bruce*, ed. Duncan, pp. 25–8 for discussion of evidence that Barbour used a lost source that focused on the life of James Douglas.
[21] The brief Latin epitaph written in the margin of *Scotichronicon* MS C may well have been inscribed on Bruce's tomb at Dunfermline Abbey (see vol. 7, pp. 51 and 191, note at 90–4). In addition, Bower copies a longer verse epitaph to mark Bruce's death (vol. 7, pp. 46–51).

whose life has been plotted, for the author who narrates that life, and ultimately for the individual reader. With the death of James I, Bower quotes from a psalm: 'What man alive will not see death?' before turning from this grim awareness to the hopeful providential understanding of history, which offers Christian consolation: God 'in his indescribable providence has arranged for the king ... to leave behind a son to be a similar king in the future'.[22] What Bower did not live long enough to understand was how disappointing the future of Scottish kingship was to prove, as the next four Stewart kings died prematurely, mostly from violent deaths. Like an individual life, the forward direction in the 'proces' of Scottish history had an alarming tendency to succumb to unexpected interruptions and apparently abrupt ends, often in the most traumatic circumstances.

Given the generic constraints of *The Bruce* and *The Wallace* as chivalric biographies, both works are almost entirely devoted to a sequence of violent acts ostensibly committed in the name of defending Scotland against unjust English aggression. As Barbour shows, Bruce's life takes on a meaningful pattern because of his selfless and untiring dedication to the cause of Scottish 'freedom', which after a long struggle he manages to vindicate because he is 'hardy' and because God is on his side:

> The romanys now begynnys her
> Off men that war in gret distres
> And assayit full gret hardynes
> Or thai mycht cum till thar entent.
> Bot syne our Lord sic grace thaim sent
> That thai syne throu thar gret valour
> Come till gret hycht and till honour,
> Magré thar fayis everilkane.   (1:446–53)

As Barbour presents Bruce's story, the king's ambition to possess 'his' kingdom is legitimized by proclaiming his cause as unequivocally just, though in fact Bruce's right was disputed by Scottish allies of the deposed king, John Balliol, as well as by those who accepted Edward I's claim to the overlordship of Scotland.[23] Even when Barbour's account reaches the point where the Scottish invasion of Ireland expands the theatre of war, the poet never questions the legitimacy of his hero's participation in the invasion, though he assigns considerable blame for that failed mission to the king's brother, Edward Bruce, whose ambition led him to seek territory in Ireland. In the Irish episodes, the apparent contradiction beween what looks like imperialist aggression and Barbour's justification of the invasion as an act of self-defence may in part be a result of the poet's weaving together material from earlier accounts.[24]

---

[22] *Scotichronicon*, vol. 8, p. 335; Bower quotes Psalm 88:49 (Vulgate).
[23] See Goldstein, *Matter of Scotland*, pp. 150–204 for fuller discussion.
[24] *Bruce*, ed. Duncan, p. 22.

Barbour is especially eloquent about the pains the king endures in the early stage of his career as king, when he eludes capture shortly after the murder of John Comyn. As the king and his small band of followers journey through the southwest of Scotland, he defends himself from a series of ambushes by traitors and enemies, wandering through the rugged terrain 'emang the hey montanys, / Quhar he and his oft tholyt paynys', such as extreme hunger and winter 'cauld with schowris snell / That nane that levys can weill it tell' (3:371–2, 377–8). Such are the personal sacrifices necessary to defeat the foreign oppressor. As Bruce gradually consolidates his power and begins to gain territory from the English, however, Barbour eventually reaches a major turning point with the battle of Bannockburn, the narrative climax of the poem, in an extended sequence that provides some of the clearest indications of what readers anticipate as the retrospective meaning of his life. In short, Bruce will prove himself as both an excellent warrior and an inspiring leader. We witness his stunning self-defence in a preliminary skirmish the day before the great battle, when Henry de Bohun rushes to attack the king, whose response is swift and deadly:

> With the ax that wes hard and gud
> With sua gret mayne raucht him a dynt
> That nother hat na helm mycht stynt
> The hevy dusche that he him gave
> That ner the heid till the harnys clave.   (12:52–6)

Moreover, he boosts his men's morale in his famous speech on the eve of battle, reminding them of the justness of their cause: 'Ye mycht have lyvyt into threldome, / Bot for ye yarnyt till have fredome / Ye ar assemblyt her with me' (12:281–3). The spectacular victory is followed by several more years of war; when the English are forced to endure devastating invasions, they finally lose the will to fight.

As his life draws to a close, Bruce has succeeded in forcing the enemy to agree to 'a perpetuale pes' (20:35) and in securing a stable succession for his son David, while making provisions for the future if his son dies without an heir (20:119–52). When Bruce succumbs to his final illness, he makes his will and testament and instructs James Douglas to carry his heart on crusade 'apon Goddis fayis' (20:185). As the life of good king Robert comes to its appointed end, he dies in 'verray repentance' and God welcomes his soul to heaven, to be among 'his chossyn folk' (20:259, 261). By sequentially joining Bruce's violent life and political ambitions to this joyful eternal reward, the poet makes final sense of his hero's life, which has reached its narrative closure. Yet the process of history remains open-ended, in ways that leave some anxieties for the future of Scotland. When the poem concludes, Barbour expresses his wish that God 'graunt his grace that thar ofspring / Leid weill the land', that Robert II and his successors take care 'to folow in all thar lyve / Thar nobill eldrys gret bounte'

(20:624–7). Thus the poet ends with another ethical appeal that suggests the final meaning of the lives still in process or yet to come remains an open question to all but the deity.

Blind Hary arranges his hero's life in a sequential form whose final meaning is sealed with his martyrdom. The poet announces the unidirectional movement of his narrative in the prologue: 'hensfurth I will my proces hald / Of Wilyham Wallas' (1:19–20). The narrative 'proces' drives relentlessly towards his voluntary self-sacrifice, but along circuitous routes whose details no reader can fully anticipate, yet whose full meaning, the narrative implicitly assures us, will be clear at the end. Until then, Wallace spends his time 'cutting throats, dashing out brains, shattering bones, striking out eyes and tongues, and beheading others in an orgy of violence described with a relish some readers have found distasteful'.[25] Yet his entire bloody career will make retrospective sense in the light of his death. Thus the poem legitimizes Wallace's acts of violence, which are plotted in a linear pattern structured on the hero's need to rescue Scotland three times, until the seeds are planted in Bruce's mind to lead the national struggle himself and Wallace can die at inner peace.[26]

Hary shows no qualms about taking events that were well known to Scottish readers from *Gesta Annalia* and the chronicles of Wyntoun and Bower and rearranging them into a fictitious chronology. He postpones the battle of Falkirk from 1298 to 1303–04 (Book 11), invents a conflict that never took place with the battle of Biggar (Book 6), and associates Wallace with a battle actually fought by Bruce at Loudon Hill (Book 3), all so the poet can structure his narrative into a more meaningful pattern.[27] Early in the work the poet makes clear through the formal device of prophecy that – if we consent to read the narrative through to the end – its structural pattern will be fulfilled, allowing its retrospective sense finally to be clear. The central structural pattern is revealed in advance, though in the vague and general language typical of prophetic speech, when Thomas Rymour foretells that Wallace will thrice bring peace to Scotland, though many thousands must die in battle (2:346–50).

By the time Hary composed his work Wallace had long been the subject of many legends circulating in Scotland. Andrew of Wyntoun earlier in the century refers to 'gestis and sangis' about Wallace's 'gud deidis and his manheid', sources on which Bower evidently drew as well.[28] Despite some moments of lively dialogue, however, Wyntoun cannot pause for long in

---

[25] *Wallace: Selections*, ed. McKim, p. 7.
[26] See Hary's elaboration (11:442–96) of a scene from *Scotichronicon* [vol. 6, pp. 94–5]; see also Goldstein, *Matter of Scotland*, pp. 245–6; Mapstone, '*Scotichronicon*'s First Readers', p. 42.
[27] See discussion in *Wallace*, ed. McDiarmid, 1, pp. lxxviii–lxxxvii.
[28] *Wyntoun*, ed. Amours, vol. 5, p. 318:2257–8; see discussion in *Scotichronicon*, vol. 6, p. 234. On Hary's adaptation of Bower's material, see Mapstone, '*Scotichronicon*'s First Readers', pp. 41–2. See also James E. Fraser, ' "A Swan from a Raven": William Wallace, Brucean Propaganda, and *Gesta Annalia* II', *SHR* 81 (2002), pp. 1–22.

narrating the events of Wallace's life, and he acknowledges that 'Quha his worschip all wald write, / He suld a mekle buke endite' (vol. 5, p. 319:2261–2). Yet we catch a faint glimmer of the earlier legends as Wyntoun provides the earliest surviving account of the hero's personal sorrow when he witnesses the murder of his 'lemman' at the order of the sheriff of Lanark (voL 5, pp. 302, 304:2035–52). For Blind Hary, such details clearly hinted at potentially greater narrative meanings as he plotted out Wallace's life.[29] Thus Hary elevates the woman's status to 'a gentill woman' (5:579), whose parents are dead and whose brother has been slain by the evil sheriff of Lanark, Hesylryg (5:595). Having established her gentle lineage and good character, Hary recreates a scene out of courtly romance, where the hero falls in love at the first sight of the lady in church: 'The prent off luff him punyeit at the last' (5:606).[30]

Having fallen in love, Wallace (like many other hypermasculine warrior figures) initially resists eros as a dangerous distraction from his true mission: 'This will nocht graithly be, / Amors and wer at anys to ryng in me' (5:633–4). But he finds the power of love difficult to resist and so decides to meet her in person. Rewriting the earlier legend, Hary elevates the heroine's moral status by having her insist on maintaining her sexual honour: 'I wyll no lemman be' (5:693). In reply Wallace makes a conditional offer of marriage in the future with what the canonists might identify as a *sponsalia per verba de futuro*: 'Gif it mycht be / Throuch Goddis will that our kynryk war fre, / I wald yow wed with all hartlie plesance' (705–7), but in the meantime his greater purpose must deter him from seeking his personal 'plesance' (710). As Book 6 opens, Hary plunges the narrative even further into the artificial world of courtly love, shifting to eight-line stanzas to describe the coming of April and the effect of spring upon the hero. Under these pressures Wallace can no longer resist the sexual instinct and reluctantly follows its direction. The poet shares that reluctance by indirectly referring to their marriage: 'Myn auctor sais scho was his rychtwys wyff' (6:48). But Wallace's marital bliss is entirely short-lived. Soon after, when he finds himself taunted by the English in Lanark, he responds with deadly force in a scene that provides a good example of the brutal violence the poet clearly enjoys. We see how the hero 'smat [smote] off the rycht hand' of 'a Sotheroune' (Hary's favourite ethnic slur), who now unable to fight, must hold his buckler in his left hand while 'fra the stowmpe the blud out spurgyt fast' (6:164, 167).[31] Although Wallace escapes, the English capture his wife and immediately put her to death (193), leading him to vow in a moment of overpowering grief that he will not rest until he avenges her death on every able-bodied Englishman he can get his hands on (unlike his enemy, Wallace is

---

[29] Recent scholarship rejects Hary's claim to be translating from a Latin book, an eye-witness account by John Blair (see 5:533–42; 12:1410–15); see McDiarmid's discussion, 1, pp. lx–lxii.
[30] See Vernon Harward, 'Hary's *Wallace* and Chaucer's *Troilus and Criseyde*', SSL 10 (1972), pp. 48–50.
[31] On Hary's use of racist language see Goldstein, *Matter of Scotland*, pp. 222–3.

scrupulous about not killing priests and women [6:212–20]). Within a few dozen lines Wallace slices cleanly through the sheriff's skull (245–7).

In the next book, the divinely sanctioned nature of Wallace's struggle is suggested in a dream sequence (7:68–152) inspired in part by a passage from the Coupar Angus MS of *Scotichronicon*.[32] In Hary's far more imaginative version, Wallace has a vision of St Andrew, the patron saint of Scotland and himself a martyr, who entrusts him with a sword. Unlike Bower's earlier version, however, the poem then has Wallace encounter the Virgin Mary, who welcomes him as her 'luff' (7:95) and prophetically states that God has chosen him to redeem Scotland. Though his 'last reward in erd sall be bot small', as Mary predicts in a cryptic understatement, he 'sall haiff lestand blys' (102, 104). Newly endowed with a greater sense of spiritual legitimacy, Wallace is now prepared to continue his military career with strengthened zeal. Within a few dozen lines (one can only admire the poet's control of structure) the narrative unfolds in one of its most powerful sequences, the entirely fictitious account of the atrocity at the Barns of Ayr where the English treacherously hang Wallace's uncle and numerous other innocent Scots, quickly followed by Wallace's horrific revenge, when he burns alive the entrapped garrison.[33] Powerful psychic energies are indeed at work not far below the surface of the narrative.

There is no space to follow any more of the detours that lead the narrative inexorably to its end with Wallace's death. Instead, we may conclude with a brief look at Hary's representation of the hero's martyrdom after his betrayal to the English by the false earl of Menteith and his imprisonment in London. Unlike the recent version in the film *Braveheart*, the poem is reluctant to dwell on Wallace's agonies. Indeed, the narrator resorts for over a hundred lines to various tactics to delay the unpleasant task of recounting the hero's death while signalling his awareness that time is passing when he calls the digressions to a halt with this observation: 'Tharoff I mak no langar contenuans. / Bot Wallace end in warld was displesans, / Tharfor I ces and puttis it nocht in rym' (12:1229–31). Instead, he assures us, Wallace is now in heaven, which leads to another digression, on a recently dead monk of Bury St Edmunds (no political partisanship allowed in heaven!) who prophesied that because Wallace defended Scotland in a just war, the man who killed more enemies than anyone else alive was to be rewarded in heaven (12:1278–88). Finally reaching the scene of martyrdom, Hary reveals that King Edward orders the archbishop of Canterbury not to administer the sacrament of confession to the condemned prisoner, only to have his command disobeyed. On the scaffold, a priest instructs Wallace to remember his misdeeds, but having already confessed to the archbishop, the hero's conscience is clean: 'I grant ... part Inglismen I slew, / In my quarell me thocht nocht halff enew' (1385–6), he replies in one of the

---

[32] See *Scotichronicon*, vol. 6, p. 236, notes 35–7.
[33] For further discussion, see *Matter of Scotland*, pp. 224–9.

most chilling couplets in literary history. With self-assurance, Wallace requests that the psalter he has kept with him since childhood be held open so that he may pass the final moments of his life in reverent devotion, until 'thai till him had done all at [that] thai wauld' (1400). Thus, the poet observes, 'fair was his endyng' (1404), and though they divided his corpse into five parts, 'his spreyt be liklynes was weill' (1409).

The religious colouring to the end of the narrative casts a long retrospective shadow over the thousands of lines of violence and destruction that precede it, shrouding Wallace's life in the aura of sanctity, even placing him in the holy company of the martyred English saints Oswald, Edmund, Edward, and Thomas Becket (12.1308). For Blind Hary, the suggestion of heavenly trumpets seals the ultimate meaning of the worthy life his narrative fashions; honouring the memory of such ancestors as William Wallace, this weirdly seductive poet would have his Scottish readers believe, means never forgetting that the English are 'our ald ennemys cummyn of Saxonys blud' (1.7). These narratives of war and death deserve our attention not only for what they can help us understand about the past, but also for what they might help us to understand about ourselves. If Blind Hary's carefully confected brew of bloody fanaticism asks us to reconsider the meaning of sacrificial desire, now more than ever we are under no compulsion to accept his answers.

3

'Mark your Meroure be Me':
Richard Holland's Buke of the Howlat

NICOLA ROYAN

The *Buke of the Howlat* by Richard Holland might be described as the quintessential medieval Scottish poem.[1] Firstly, it incorporates many of the poetic influences current in fifteenth-century Scotland. Its central passage clearly responds to Barbour's *Bruce* and the model of Scottish freedom presented there, and it demonstrates familiarity with a Latin fable collection, Chaucer's *Parliament of Fowls*, and Northern Middle English alliterative verse. It also shows a knowledge of Gaelic culture, although it does not present this in a particularly flattering manner. Secondly, the poem was written for Elizabeth Dunbar, wife of Archibald Douglas, Earl of Moray. This in part explains the core of the poem, a heraldic account of Douglas history from the Wars of Independence, stressing the essential contribution of the kin to the Scottish realm's independence and success. The poem's topic, advice to princes, and its patrons, a magnate and his wife, rather than the king, are typical of medieval Scottish practice. While these diverse elements would mark the poem as Scottish, however, taken together they make its ultimate purpose harder to decipher.

Richard Holland was a priest and notary public, and by 1449 secretary to Archibald Douglas. His career thereafter seems to have been tied to Douglas success, for his fortunes in Scotland failed after the battle of Arkinholme in 1455, when Archibald was killed, and in the 1480s he was in exile with other members of the Douglas family in England.[2] Like many of his clerical contemporaries, Holland is easiest to trace when involved in the pursuit of various church appointments, such as the precentorship of Moray cathedral. His attempts to gain these posts frequently involved him in legal disputes, sometimes taken as far as the papal courts. As a result of this, and perhaps also his links with the Douglas kin, we know far more about his life than we do of

---

[1] References to the *Buke of the Howlat* are from the text in *Longer Scottish Poems, Vol. 1*, ed. Bawcutt and Riddy, pp. 43–84. This essay is indebted to Sally Mapstone's chapter 'Richard Holland and *The Buke of the Howlat*', in her forthcoming book, *The Wisdom of Princes*. I am very grateful to Dr Mapstone for giving me access to it.
[2] On Holland's career, see Marion Stewart, 'Holland of the *Howlat*', *IR* 23 (1972), pp. 3–15.

other Scottish poets'. *The Buke of the Howlat* was written in the late 1440s (its precise date will be discussed later) and is the only testimony to Holland's poetic skill. Nevertheless, the poem seems to have been popular and widely read. It was printed by Chepman and Myllar (c. 1508),[3] and also transcribed into two major Scottish manuscript miscellanies, the Asloan Manuscript (c. 1515–c. 1525) and the Bannatyne Manuscript (c. 1568). Holland was known to later poets, including William Dunbar and David Lyndsay, both of whom include him in lists of poets.[4] While to a modern reader the central concern with Douglas endeavours might seem to limit the audience of the work, clearly *The Howlat* found an audience far beyond its first patrons.

The Buke of the Howlat has a complex structure, consisting of a frame narrative, where the narrator recounts his own actions; a fable, which is the story of the howlat, or owl, and his borrowed feathers; and a central divertissement, describing the achievements of the Douglas family against the backdrop of the bird parliament summoned to decide the response to the owl's complaint. Each part is richly detailed, making best use of a rhymed alliterative stanza, and displaying the same exuberant delight in ornateness that can be seen later in Gavin Douglas's *The Palice of Honour*. While the frame, the fable and the centre are straightforward in isolation, they do not immediately seem to mesh, when taken together, since the fable warns against pride, and the centre glorifies the Douglases' martial prowess. Before attempting to analyse the cumulative effect of the poem, however, this chapter will consider various aspects of the work separately. These include the stanza form and language, the frame narrative and the fable, the heraldic core and the structure, and finally its likely date of composition, together with the implications of that date for our interpretation of the poem. Despite difficulties in bringing together all aspects of the poem, *The Buke of the Howlat* is more than a sum of its parts.

Stanza Form

The Howlat's complexity is evident even in its form. Holland chose a thirteen-line stanza that both alliterates and rhymes. The first nine lines have four alliterating stressed syllables; the last four lines have two stressed syllables, which alliterate in all but the last line. The stanza rhymes thus: $ababababc^4dddc^2$, neatly tying the end of the 'wheel' – the shorter lines – to the main body of the stanza. In addition, there is concatenation between many of the stanzas, where a significant word from the last line of one stanza appears in the first line of the next. Holland is not consistent in his practice, as the

---

[3] Two fragments of this print exist: one in Cambridge University Library (Sel.1.19) and the other with Dundee City Archives, burgh protocol book 19 November 1526–12 July 1528. See William Beattie, 'An Early Printed Fragment of the *Buke of the Howlat*', *EBST* 2 (1938–45), pp. 393–7, and Robert Donaldson, 'An Early Printed Fragment of the *Buke of the Howlat* – Addendum', *EBST* 5.3 (1980–83), pp. 25–8.

[4] See 'I that in heill wes and gladnes' (B 21), 61, Dunbar, *The Poems*, ed. Bawcutt, and *The Testament of the Papyngo*, 19, Lyndsay, *Selected Poems*, ed. Hadley Williams.

concatenation is stronger in the first section of the poem, the formal description of the May morning and the bird parliament. What is initially surprising, perhaps, is that the regular concatenation does not return at the end of the poem, although its last lines echo the first ones. However, since part of the moral is the howlat's disruption of Nature's ordained order, the slight breakdown in form mirrors the conclusions of the fable.

This metrical form, with a long ninth line instead of a 'bob', is usually identified with that of the Northern Middle English poem, *The Awntyrs off Arthure*, where it first occurs.[5] Holland's use of the stanza is significant for two reasons. Firstly, *The Buke of the Howlat* is the earliest datable text in which the form is recorded in Scotland. As a result, the poem is sometimes taken as the beginning of a revival of alliterative metres in Scotland, in response to their popularity in England in the fourteenth century.[6] While the English fashion faded in the fifteenth century, Scots writers seemed to find alliteration, both as a structural and an ornamental device, to their taste well into the sixteenth century. Holland is proficient in his use of the stanza, suggesting that, although *The Howlat* is probably the first surviving Scottish poem to employ it, the stanza was nevertheless familiar to earlier Scottish poets. This suggests in turn that *The Awntyrs*, possibly with other poems in its stanza, was circulating in Scotland well within fifty years of its composition.

Secondly, the form seems to support the structural pattern of *The Howlat*. The precedent for the stanza is an Arthurian romance and indeed two fifteenth-century Scottish poems in this stanza are also romances, one serious and Arthurian (*Golagros and Gawain*) and one humorous about Charlemagne (*Rauf Coilyear*). In *The Howlat*, the stanza form might seem to sit most comfortably with the chivalric core, describing the martial prowess of the Douglas family. Yet *The Awntyrs* is also a text in two halves, where one is moral and one is chivalric. In *The Awntyrs*, Guinevere and Gawain encounter the ghost of Guinevere's mother, who warns them against the sin of pride; subsequently, Gawain is required to fight Galeron, an apparently Scottish knight who arrives at court to reject Arthur's authority to give his lands to Gawain. Precisely the same themes are addressed in *The Howlat*, albeit in a different way. It is sometimes said that the *The Awntyrs* is broken-backed, that one half of the poem does not relate to the other half. Holland, in contrast, embeds his chivalry within the frame narrative, thereby insisting on a connection between the sections. Such a link seems reinforced by a consideration of *Golagros and Gawain* and *Rauf Coilyear*, for both these poems also present their narrative in two halves and offer morals regarding pride. It is possible, therefore, that

---

[5] See Thorlac Turville-Petre, *The Alliterative Revival* (Cambridge, 1977), pp. 35, 65–6, and Susanna Greer Fein, 'The Early Thirteen-Line Stanza: Style and Metrics Reconsidered', *Parergon* n.s. 18.1 (2000), pp. 98–126. For the suggestion that the stanza form was as likely to have 'drifted southwards across the border ... as northwards', see F. Riddy, 'The Alliterative Revival', *History*, ed. Jack, pp. 39–54, especially 42–3.

[6] Turville-Petre, *Alliterative Revival*, pp. 115–16.

Holland and these other writers understood the stanza form as having a certain moral resonance and association.

Holland stretches the stanza to its full range. At one extreme is the prayer to the Virgin Mary, a high-style list of her attributes (716–54); at the other is the mobbing of the Gaelic bard, in the form of a rook (794–832). While the utterances of the rook look like nonsense, it is possible to reconstruct them as representing real Gaelic words, and it is likely that Holland, largely working in the North-East of Scotland, might have been familiar with some Gaelic, although not, perhaps, its spelling systems. Such a range contributes to the comedy of the poem, obviously in the knockabout farce around the rook, but also through the contrast with the ritual prayer to the Virgin. The comic element of the poem might point forward to later uses of the stanza in the fifteenth and sixteenth centuries, where it is used for more overt satire, such as Henryson's *Sum Practysis of Medecyne*, or burlesque comedy, such as *The Gyre Carlyng*.[7] However, while comic and light-hearted in places, *The Buke of the Howlat* is a poem with serious intent.

The Frame Narrative and The Fable

The *chanson d'aventure* motif of a narrator walking out on a beautiful May morning is common in medieval writing; here he does not dream the events, but ostensibly witnesses them and then records them for his patrons. Although the narrator is the medium for the fable, he does not in fact interpret the fable's moral at the end. Instead, the moral is delivered by the owl, speaking directly to the wider audience; the narrator concurs with commonplace piety (986–8) before moving on to his dedication.[8] As a result, the interpretation of the fable itself is presented as straightforward, for not only does the howlat realize the dangers of pride, but in his return to his initial state, he recognizes his lowly place in the world, thus reinforcing the notions of earned nobility presented in the heart of the poem.

The fable of the howlat probably derives from Odo of Cheriton's *Fabulae*, a collection known to have circulated in fifteenth-century Scotland.[9] Holland makes some changes, replacing Odo's crow with an owl, and invoking Nature as ultimate authority. The narrator overhears 'ane petuos appele' (41) and then sees the howlat lamenting his appearance while considering his reflection in the lake. The howlat takes his plea to the pope, a procedure with which Holland

---

[7] See Henryson, *Poems*, ed. Fox, note on 'Sum Practysis of Medecyne', pp. 475–6; J. E. H. Williams, 'James V, David Lyndsay, and the Bannatyne Manuscript Poem of the Gyre Carling', *SSL* 26 (1991), pp. 164–71.

[8] For discussion of the framing narrative: Judith M. Davidoff, *Beginning Well: Framing Fictions in Late Middle English Poetry* (London and Toronto, 1988), pp. 87–8.

[9] See Matthew P. McDiarmid, 'Richard Holland's *Buke of the Howlat*: An Interpretation', *MÆ* 38 (1969), pp. 277–90 (281–2). For Odo's fable, see *Les Fabulistes latins*, ed. Léopold Hervieux, 5 vols (Paris, 1893–99), vol. 4, pp. 180–1; also the *Fables of Odo of Cheriton*, trans. and ed. John C. Jacobs (Syracuse, 1985), pp. 74–5.

would be very familiar, who calls a council firstly of the clerical class and then of the political class. The parliament recommends to Nature that the howlat be helped; she requires each bird to give up one of its feathers so that she can make a new coat for the owl. Once this is done, the howlat begins to act arrogantly, claiming the status due to the feathers rather than to him. The other birds complain, and Nature strips the howlat of its new glory, saying 'My first making ... was unamendable' (928). The howlat and the narrator are left alone again as the bird parliament disperses, and the howlat both laments and delivers the lesson he has learned about unwarranted pride.

The lamentation also acts as the moral for the fable, since the howlat addresses his lesson to the widest audience: 'mark your merour be me, all maner of man' (970). Both this line and its implication – the transformation of the subject of the story into its interpreter – can be paralleled in other medieval texts.[10] In a Scottish context, the most interesting parallel occurs in *The Testament of Cresseid*, where Cresseid laments her change in worldly status and urges 'in your mynd ane mirrour mak of me' (457).[11] Her warning is addressed specifically to 'ladyis fair of Troy and Grece' (452). The similarity extends further, however. As Cresseid learns to modify her lament about the transitoriness of human life with an acknowledgment of her own previous wrongdoing (540–74), so too does the howlat warn of the dangers of misgovernment (984). In both cases, the recognition of agency forms a crucial part of the overall moral, necessary for a full appreciation of the whole poem.

The nearest parallel to this combination of frame and fable is another of Henryson's poems, *The Preaching of the Swallow*; but whereas Henryson's fable works in part by playing the allegorical message against natural bird behaviour, Holland's birds are much closer to their human equivalents. Where Henryson's birds flit away from the swallow's preaching ('The foulis ferlie tuke thair flicht anone', 1770), Holland's rarely seem to fly. The greater similarity between the poems comes in the representation of the narrator, for Holland's narrator, like Henryson's, is not involved in the action and therefore the fable does not relate directly to his state of mind or connect to any prior reading. Instead, in his appreciation of both the setting and the moral, he is placed in opposition to the howlat, and in consequence, forms a pair with the howlat in the guidance of the reader. The narrator's acceptance of divine order is most obvious at the end, where he receives the moral with a prayer that God might 'Set our sawlis in sicht / Of sanctis so sere!' (987–8). This response is, however, prefigured in the opening, when the narrator walks out into the May morning. The season is presented as a direct gift from God: 'So soft was the sessoun our soverane doune sent / Throw the greable gift of his godhed / That

---

[10] See line 120 of 'The Three Dead Kings', *Alliterative Poetry of the Later Middle Ages: An Anthology*, ed. Thorlac Turville-Petre (London, 1989), pp. 148–57; also Riddy, 'Alliterative Revival', pp. 44–5.
[11] References are to Henryson, *Poems*, ed. Fox.

all was amyable owr the air and the erd' (7–9). This is reinforced in the third stanza, where the narrator presents the season as beneficent to men:

> The birth that the ground bure was browdin on breidis,
> With gers gaye as the gold and granes of grace;
> Mendis and medicyne for mennis all neidis,
> Helpe to hert and to hurt, heilfull it was.   (27–30)

Clearly this puts humanity at the centre of the universe, but it also indicates the divine nature of such a gift. The word 'grace' indicates the power of the gift, which is concerned with both physical and spiritual well-being. Even here there is an implied contrast between natural goodness, exemplified by the beautiful landscape, and worldly goodness, for the herbs are described as being like gold, but have more long-term value than the precious metal. In this environment, it is not surprising that the narrator is able to sit 'in solace, sekerly and sure' (22).[12]

Into this perfect scene breaks the unhappy owl. The horror of the owl's appearance is at odds with the May setting, and the initial complaint against Nature seems understandable: 'Quhy is my fax ... fassonit so foule, / My forme and my fetherem unfrely, but feir? / My neb is netherit as a nok, I am bot ane owle!' (55–7). Other than his owlishness, there is no apparent reason for him to be so ugly. Yet, though the reader's sympathy is apparently invited, criticism of the howliat is embedded in the text. His complaint is described as 'churliche' (54) and he himself is described as 'vylest in vyce' (88). Futhermore, the disorder of the howlat contrasts with the well-ordered May morning surrounding him, and in making his complaint, the howlat is arguing against the very order that God has instituted. These features point forward to Nature's final judgement, where she indicates that the owl's appearance was from the beginning representative of his character.

In this poem, Nature is the ultimate authority, God's deputy. This is as true of the narrator's world, where 'thir savorus seidis / War nurist be dame Natur, that noble mastres' (31–2), as it is of the howlat and the other birds. Nature gives order to the living universe, and her judgement is final. This representation of Nature is probably drawn from Alan of Lille's *De Planctu Naturae*; the same work also underpins Chaucer's *Parliament of Fowls*.[13] Chaucer's Nature, whom he calls 'the vicaire of the almyghty Lord' (379), is more proactive than Holland's in calling the parliament; in Holland's poem, she responds to a plea

---

[12] The frame of beneficent May contradicts Davidoff's view of the poem's movement from ugliness to triumph to ugliness (*Beginning Well*, p. 192). Rather the narrator's movement away from the owl suggests that for those obedient to the natural order rewards will follow.

[13] See McDiarmid, '*Buke of the Howlat*', pp. 280–1; also Nick Havely's introduction to *The Parliament of Fowls* in *Chaucer's Dream Poetry*, ed. Helen Phillips and Nick Havely (London, 1997), pp. 219–32. For references to the text of *The Parliament of Fowls*, see *Riverside Chaucer*, ed. Benson, pp. 385–94.

from her realm. Her purpose in both is to enforce order: in Chaucer's poem, her task is to ensure the continuation of life, while in *The Howlat*, she demonstrates the rightness of natural order and God's original creation. In her support of order, Nature has the potential to be read as a political figure. In *The Parliament of Fowls*, for instance, she permits the formel to defer her decision regarding a mate, which both underscores the formel's rank as a noble bird but also the limitations on feminine self-government – the formel is not able to refuse a mate altogether. In *The Buke of the Howlat*, the political reading is far more evident because of the nature of the councils of birds, and because of the specifically political authority and kingship the howlat claims in his new feathers (906–14).

Compared to *The Parliament of Fowls*, *The Howlat* is far more detailed in its representation of the bird council. There is a similar division of bird classes, raptors, worm-eaters, seed-eaters and water fowl, but Holland presents a council where the birds gather to talk and make a decision, rather than simply to 'take hire [Nature's] dom and yeve hire audyence' (308). Holland's birds have clear functions, instead of simply being part of a list. Thus, the capon, 'a clerk under cleir weidis / ... / Was officiale ... that the law leidis / In causis consistoriale' (222–5), and able to punish the sparrow, who lay 'in lichory' (227), a nice touch of irony since the capon is neutered. In *The Parliament of Fowls*, in contrast, no such drama is implied, for the sparrow is simply 'Venus sone' (351).

Such dramatic details contribute to the richness of Holland's poem, and form part of its comic strength. The classes of birds are carefully distributed between the estates: sea fowl and seed fowl form the papal court, and the raptors and the worm-eaters form the secular court. In this division, there is also a parallel with *The Parliament of Fowls*, but while Chaucer's comedy is limited to mockery of the lower-class birds, such as the goose, Holland's comedy is wittier and more complex. Species are tied to particular roles. Sometimes the link rests primarily on appearance: for instance, gulls, both black and white, represent the Benedictine and the Cistercian monks, according to their habits (178). At other points, the association is proverbial, such as the swallow – known for its swiftness – being used as a courier (289–91). Sometimes the link is a mixture of the two: the curlew is chancellor, 'For he couth wryte wounder fair / With his neb ... / Apon the se sand' (206–8). While the curlew's bill seems appropriate enough as a writing instrument, his choice of material nicely points up the distance between human affairs and this parliament. The sea sand is by no means a permanent record of events; likewise, this parliament is also a momentary diversion. Occasionally, there is a slight hint of satire in the bird portraits: for example, the only exception to the division of bird classes in *The Howlat* is the raven, the rural dean (215–20). Both as raven and as rural dean, this figure scavenges food, possibly a comment on the deans of Holland's acquaintance.

The pope and the emperor are not exempt from such treatment. The pope is the peacock, a bird often used to symbolize pride; the contrast between his beauty and the owl's ugliness mirrors their difference in power.[14] Moreover, the gathering that the peacock calls is not a small advisory panel, for it includes 'cardinallis and ... counsall,/ Patriarkis and prophetis, of lerit the laif' (121–2), so his own glory is increased by the glory of those around him. The emperor is an eagle, a familiar image of martial monarchy, replicated on the emperor's shield in this poem, and employed by Dunbar in 'Quhen Merche wes with variand windis past' (B 52).[15] Even though they are so common, some ambivalence must attach to visions of kingship which present the monarch as a raptor, for he survives through consuming some of his lesser subjects.[16] While strong and often violent kingship was a necessity in medieval politics, nevertheless it was successful only through the suffering of others. However, Holland goes further with his criticism of the emperor, since in order to summon him, the messenger (the swallow) has to travel to Babylon, associated with Babel (293, 302). The emperor therefore has his seat in an oppressive city (Babylon being the place of exile of the Jews in the Old Testament) and a tower built by men seeking to reach heaven and challenge God, an act of overweening pride.[17] It is perhaps not surprising, therefore, that courts headed by these birds are sympathetic to the owl's plea, and take it on his behalf to Nature. The referral to a higher authority – requested right at the beginning by the owl – seems a rather feeble end to such grand negotiations, particularly since the debate regarding this decision has been long and scholarly; the poem does not seem to support an enthusiastic view of such Babel parliaments and councils.

The Heraldic Core

The Buke of the Howlat is not simply estates satire. Through the use of heraldic devices, which begin the central section of the poem, Holland ties his bird figures closely to contemporary figures. The arms of the pope and the emperor, borne by the woodpecker pursuivant, are both real (339–59). The pope's arms are those of Felix V, the last anti-pope (1439–49), elected by the Council of Basle.[18] Although the Douglases had been supporters of the Church Council in its early stages, by the time of the composition of the poem, their allegiance – and Holland's – had been transferred to Nicholas V. The emperor's arms are those of an emperor-elect rather than an emperor crowned, for Frederick III

---

[14] Regina Scheibe argues for a positive interpretation of the peacock in 'The Major Professional Skills of the Dove in *The Buke of the Howlat*', *Animals and the Symbolic in Medieval Art and Literature*, ed. L. A. J. R. Houwen (Groningen, 1997), pp. 107–37 (118–19).

[15] See Dunbar, *The Poems*, ed. Bawcutt, pp. 163–8.

[16] For other ambivalent references to meat-eating nobility in similar contexts: Chaucer, *Parliament of Fowls*, 330–6; Henryson, *Lion and the Mouse*, 1510–15. However, for a different bestiary view: William Dunbar, 'Schir, yit remember as befoir' (B 68), 26–30.

[17] See Felicity Riddy, 'Dating *The Buke of the Howlat*', *RES* n. s. 37 (1986), pp. 1–10 (5).

[18] See McDiarmid, '*Buke of the Howlat*', pp. 278–9 and Riddy, 'Dating *The Buke*', pp. 3–4.

adopted the double-headed eagle on his coronation in 1452.[19] As a result, the heraldry subverts these figures of worldly authority, in a different way. The peacock may not be the most respectful symbol of the papacy, nor Babel the most admirable seat for an empire, but such subversion touches the institutions as a whole. The identification with individual political figures on the contemporary stage makes a closer link with the owl, for, particularly in the case of the anti-pope, arguably their feathers are also inappropriately borrowed.

Associated with the papal and imperial arms are those of the royal houses of France and Scotland (360–77). The link between Scotland and the rest seems to be marriage alliances sought by James II for his sisters in the house of Savoy (from which Felix came) and the imperial house.[20] Given the queries raised by the other shields, it is pertinent to ask similar questions about the representation of the kings of France and Scotland. The French king, Charles VII, had defeated the English to gain his throne, overcoming accusations of illegitimacy on the way. By the 1440s, however, Charles VII was a strong monarch, fully in control of his realm; the English continued to exercise authority only over Normandy and Gascony. Although the fourth Earl of Douglas (the great-uncle of the Douglas earls of *The Howlat*) had fought for Charles VII and been rewarded with a dukedom, after his death at the battle of Verneuil (1424) the Douglases had been unable to hold onto that possession, possibly leaving them with some residual resentment towards the French king.[21] The last shield to be described is that of the king of Scots: like the emperor, at the time of writing, James II was not quite a king, since he was emerging from his minority. The common theme of these arms is a weak or contestable claim to power, be that royal or imperial, in contrast to the rights of the Douglases. Association with that theme rather diminishes the man to whom the poet then claims the Douglases owe all allegiance.

At the very heart of *The Buke of the Howlat* lie the Douglas shields, together with the narratives that justify their possession (378–631). If the beginning and end of the poem stress the dangers of false pride and rebelling against the natural order, then the centre of the poem celebrates earned power and virtue, exemplified by the Douglas family. Four Douglas shields are described, matching the four in the previous section. They are the arms of the Earl and Master of Douglas (408–20), the Earl of Moray, Holland's employer (586–98), the Earl of Ormond and Lord Balvenie (599–603), all sons of James 'The Gross'. The weight of the shields is impressive enough, but the narrative of Douglas service that supports them is even more striking. The key story belongs to their ancestor, 'the Good Sir James', the 'Black Douglas', who was one of Robert Bruce's lieutenants.

---

[19] See Riddy, 'Dating *The Buke*', pp. 4–5.
[20] See Riddy, 'Dating *The Buke*', pp. 7–9.
[21] Michael Brown, *The Black Douglases: War and Lordship in Late Medieval Scotland 1300–1455* (East Linton, 1998), pp. 214–24.

Bruce and Douglas already have a literary history together in Barbour's *Bruce* (c. 1375), where Barbour presents Bruce as the ideal king and Douglas as the ideal and loyal lieutenant.[22] In *The Bruce* Douglas is a supporting actor, who is dependent on Bruce as ultimate leader, right to the very end. Here Holland changes the emphasis. Whereas in Barbour's poem, Bruce is in control of events, both making provision for his succession and commissioning Douglas to take his heart on crusade (20:153–248), in Holland's poem, Douglas takes centre stage. Even at the deathbed, Douglas does all the talking – the king says nothing – and thereafter his adventure takes priority. Indeed, Holland extends the narrative beyond Barbour's, so that Douglas takes the heart to the Holy Land (in *The Bruce* he only gets as far as Spain, 20:309–479), and there perishes in battle against the Saracens, where he has urged himself onwards by hurling Bruce's heart, in its case, ahead of him. This narrative sits right at the midpoint of the poem, stressing Douglas courage, determination and loyal sacrifice for the king.

While it is possible to argue that it is natural for Holland to put his patron's family at the centre of his text, the way he chooses to do so seems pointed. Barbour's Douglas is very clearly subordinate to Bruce, but Holland's seems able to manage well by himself. For instance, Douglas is described as 'lelest all Scotland fra scaith to reskewe' (433), implying that his loyalty is to the realm rather than to Bruce, and that his skill in war is deployed for the benefit of Scotland rather than the royal house as a feudal superior; shortly after, his valour is recognized by his peers rather than simply by his king. This appears to be an assertion of James Douglas's worth as first among equals, and favours strongly the lieutenant over the king.

While the narrative of the heart is central to this image, the importance of the realm and the nobility and the significance of the Douglas kin to the preservation of both is stressed throughout this section. The Douglas arms are described thus:

> Next the soverane signe was sekerly sene
> That servit his serenite ever servabile,
> The armes of the Dowglas, douchty bedene,
> Knawin throw all Cristindome be conysance able,
> Of Scotland the werwall, wit ye but wene,
> Our fais force to defend and unfalyeable,
> Baith barmekyn and bar to Scottis blud bene,
> Our lois and our lyking, that lyne honorable.   (378–85)

Notwithstanding the previous stanza with its summary of the royal arms of Scotland and the opening statement of service to the Scots' king, here the emphasis is clearly on the impressions of the realm not on the ruler. The

---

[22] All references are to Barbour, *Bruce*, ed. McDiarmid and Stevenson.

Douglases are the 'werwall' of Scotland, not the king or his kin, and in so being they defend 'Scottis blud' and 'our' blood, not only the king's. The Douglas service thus follows a model set out in the Declaration of Arbroath, where the realm is separable from the king. The reader and the speaker are identified as sharing an identification with the Scottish realm. While the main example of these Douglas traits is the good Sir James, Holland transfers them to his descendants by two methods. Firstly he associates the Saxons – the English – with the Saracens (482–5). As a result, the crusade with Bruce's heart both replicates Bruce's campaigns against the English and also endorses both of those wars as being against an entirely alien enemy. This means that later campaigns of Douglas kin can carry the same associations and attract the same glory as that of the first Douglas, even though their campaigns are generally limited to the Anglo-Scottish border. The second technique is more straightforward, relying on the chains of inheritance. Dotted throughout the account of the Douglases are references to hereditary virtue, for instance 'that lyne honorable' (385), 'honorable ay' (392). This is developed further when Holland ascribes to them ancestral rights in Galloway (563), in fact a title that the kin had only just recovered in the 1440s. The virtue of the good Sir James becomes indistinguishable from that of his descendants. Most significantly, this is virtue justly rewarded, as Holland points out: 'sa throw Goddis forsicht / The Douglas succedis' (558–9).

The Douglas kin dominate this section of the poem. Apart from Bruce, no other king is named, nor any other family. Moreover, the Douglases stand in marked contrast to the howlat, whose outward appearance reflects the poor spirit within, whereas the Douglas rights and powers are divinely ordained and thus reflect natural order. Their virtue is affirmed by the punning identification of Elizabeth Dunbar with a dove (989–90). This unexpected association is also found earlier in the poem, when the Douglases are described as 'Tender and trewe' (403), epithets applied to the turtle dove (127, 135, 287). Any complete reading of the poem must therefore reconcile the fable to the core in order fully to appreciate the praise being offered to the Douglases and the condemnation given to the howlat. For while the moral of the fable by itself has a general application, the links with the bird parliament rather suggest the intent of a more particular political reading relating to the circumstances of the 1440s. For this reason the dating of the poem is crucial.

The Historical Context and the Date of the Poem

The precise date of *The Howlat* has implications for its wider interpretation because of the close links of the poem and its author to the Douglas fortunes. Using the evidence of the arms described in the poem, it is possible to date its composition to summer 1448, possibly even May 1448, which would fit with the setting of the poem.[23] Such a date places the composition at the height of Douglas power, when the family had obtained, not without some dispute, a large power base across Scotland. In the first half of 1448, in the last months of James II's minority, the Douglases were still a rising force. One of the other influential families who had risen to power in the minority had already largely had its power dismantled, in part by the Douglas kin, while another was about to fall.[24] Previous readings of the poem have thus suggested it may serve to glorify the Douglases at the expense of other noble houses, and to warn of the doom of those who cannot, in the words of the howlat, rule themselves 'richtwis'.[25] While such readings are tempting, it is remarkable that Holland does not juxtapose the Douglases with their magnatial peers, but only with the royal house: only the royal arms of Scotland are described, only Robert I is mentioned by name and his son by implication. Even Robert I, moreover, required lieutenants to support his claims, and thus borrowed might from James Douglas as well as from others. One further possibility might therefore be to read *The Howlat* as critical of the Stewart dynasty.

This seems a little far-fetched, since the poem consistently emphasizes the loyalty of the Douglases. Yet, apart from the relationship between Bruce and Douglas, that loyalty seems as often directed towards the realm or Scotland as it ever does towards the king who embodies the nation. Robert I, of course, justifies his position as king by his struggles, his victories and his hold on the crown: he is marked out for kingship. The Stewart claim was based on their descent from Robert I but, as a kin, they did not have such a dazzling history of courage and warfare; despite Barbour's attempts to provide a history of the Stewart family, most of the Stewart kings seemed content to rest on the authority of their distinguished ancestor.[26] Furthermore, as kings, the Stewarts

---

[23] The *terminus a quo* is July 1445, when Archibald first became Earl of Moray and his younger brother, Hugh, Earl of Ormond, the titles under which they appear in the poem; the *terminus ad quem* is 1452, when the young James II killed the Earl of Douglas at Stirling Castle. Furthermore, the description of only four coats of arms when there were five Douglas brothers suggests that the poem was written after 1447, when James Douglas became Master of Douglas and held identical arms to his elder brother, Earl William. The arms of the anti-pope, Felix V, and the imperial arms of Frederick III when he was emperor-elect support a date before April 1449, when Felix resigned. In addition, missing from the list of arms is any reference to Mary of Gueldres, to whom King James became betrothed in September 1448, and from the list of achievements of the Earl of Ormond his glorious victory at the Sark, in October of the same year; these omissions suggest a date prior to September 1448. The most likely date thus seems to be summer 1448. For full discussion of the dating issues: Riddy, 'Dating *The Buke*'; Brown, *Black Douglases*, pp. 278–9; and Marion Stewart, 'Holland's *Howlat* and the Fall of the Livingstones', *IR* 26 (1975), pp. 67–79.

[24] For the Douglases' part in these events: Brown, *Black Douglases*, pp. 256–311. For a reading linking *The Howlat* and a particular downfall: Stewart, 'Holland's *Howlat* and the Livingstones'.

[25] See McDiarmid, '*Buke of the Howlat*'; Stewart, 'Holland's *Howlat* and the Livingstones', and Riddy, 'Dating *The Buke*', for readings along these lines.

[26] Stephen I. Boardman, *The Early Stewart Kings: Robert II and Robert III 1371–1406* (East Linton, 1996), p. 59.

had proved to be rapacious: Robert II had sought to provide for his large number of sons; on his return from captivity, James I had adopted English models of royal economic interest unwelcome to his nobility. Clearly, the interests of the sovereign might here clash with the interests of the Douglas affinity; such unease among the Douglas kin might only be strengthened by a sense that the Stewarts, as an affinity, are not so distinct from their Douglas lieutenants.

Here the precise dating of the poem becomes most significant. If the date of summer 1448 is accurate, then the poem was composed just before James II came into his full majority, and thus just before he would confirm the grants made in his name in his minority. It would be an opportune time to remind the king both of the Douglas power and of their loyalty to the realm. The fable of the dangers of pride and fortune, that 'We cum pure, we gang pure, baith king and commoun. / Bot thow reule the richtwis, thi roume sall orere [decline]' (983–4), is also applicable to the Stewart king. Such oblique warning and criticism directed towards a monarch is not unusual in Older Scots literature and, as mentioned above, the relationship between magnates and king had been presented as a negotiated one from the Declaration of Arbroath in 1320. What is less common is the overt celebration of a magnatial family, particularly in opposition to the crown; such atypicality is what has made *The Buke of the Howlat* hard to interpret without its political context.

Conclusion

Whatever the intent and circumstances of composition, however, subsequent readings of the poem are necessarily conditioned by knowledge of the spectacular fall of the Black Douglases in the 1450s.[27] The power base that Holland celebrates as deserved reward, James II clearly saw as a threat and consequently removed. Thus, the pride of the Douglases is open to be read as being as hollow as the howlat's, and the Douglases themselves as every bit as subject to the vagaries of Fortune.

The Buke of the Howlat therefore demands a layered reading. Its original intent must have been to separate the achievements of the Douglases from birds with false feathers, be they rival families, or the royal house itself. Holland makes clear both that his patron and his family were to be included in the application of the howlat's morals, through his address of them as birds, and that they are to be contrasted with the howlat, since they deserve their feathers. In making this distinction, Holland contributes a notable strand to Douglas mythology, one which reappears in later chroniclers as fact rather than as literary elaboration.

The fall of the Black Douglases contributed another strand to Douglas mythology and another layer of meaning to *The Buke of the Howlat*. Although Holland's intent is evident, still an alternative reading presents itself. All are

---

[27] Brown, *Black Douglases*, pp. 283–334.

subject to the howlat's first moral: 'we cum pure, we gang pure', so even Douglas worldly glory is finite, and that is without the intervention of James II. This commonplace makes it easier to compare the Douglases with the howlat, for in full knowledge of their ultimate fall, the limits of self-government and the possible misinterpretation of Nature's support of their situation stand out.

Either of these readings is defensible. To attempt to retrieve the first context of the poem is to support the first; while to acknowledge subsequent events may be to champion the second. The conflict between these readings is evident in an early response to *The Howlat* in Hary's *Wallace*. Towards the end of that poem, Stewart of Bute tells the howlat's story to Wallace in response to Wallace's refusal specifically to allow Stewart to command the vanguard, but more generally to cede power to the aristocracy.[28] Stewart's implication is that Wallace, like the howlat, is suffering from delusions of grandeur; Wallace's response is consistent with the line taken through the rest of the poem, namely that Wallace acted in defence of the realm, when the aristocracy and the rightful sovereign hid themselves away. Wallace's view is akin to Holland's presentation of the Douglases, and hence the first reading of *The Howlat*, suggested above; Stewart offers a warning of over-ambition and might thus speak to the second reading of Holland's poem. While usually Wallace's view would be the view of his eponymous poem, on this occasion Hary seems less sure: he writes that Wallace responded over hastily to 'thir wordis gud' (11:143–4). The Scots lose the battle, and this defeat leads ultimately to Wallace's betrayal and death. Hary, therefore, may point to the second reading of the poem, implying that notwithstanding the greatness of Wallace – or indeed of the Douglases – he and they are still subject to the same dangers of arrogance as anyone else.

Such ambivalence lies at the heart of *The Howlat*, a result of its intricate structure and exuberant style. The fairest interpretation of the text is probably to accept the first reading, for this is where the poem's argument leads, but it is impossible to forget altogether that not even the Douglases were entirely masters of their own fate. Even so skilled a poet and propagandist as Holland could not foresee that.

---

[28] Hary, *Wallace*, ed. McDiarmid, 11:105–58. See also R. James Goldstein, *The Matter of Scotland: Historical Narrative in Medieval Scotland* (Lincoln, Nebr. and London, 1993), p. 245.

4

The Kingis Quair
and the other poems of
Bodleian Library MS Arch. Selden. B. 24

JULIA BOFFEY

The Manuscript

Oxford, Bodleian Library MS Arch. Selden. B. 24 associates Chaucer's *Troilus and Criseyde* (*IMEV* 3327)[1] with dream visions, poems on love, and further texts – anonymous or by authors other than Chaucer – in the same broadly courtly tradition. Chaucer's *Parliament of Fowls* (*IMEV* 3412), his *Legend of Good Women* (*IMEV* 100), and several shorter poems ('The Complaint of Mars', 'The Complaint of Venus', and 'Truth', *IMEV* 913, 3542, 809 respectively) accompany Lydgate's *Complaint of the Black Knight* (*IMEV* 1507), Clanvowe's *Book of Cupid* (*IMEV* 3361; also known as *The Cuckoo and the Nightingale*), and Hoccleve's 'Mother of God' (*IMEV* 2221). Groups of short lyrics serve as fillers between these longer texts. One main hand completed the copying, and supplied also lines 1–1239 of *The Kingis Quair* (*IMEV* 1215), before a second scribe took over to complete this text and to add Hoccleve's *Letter of Cupid* (*IMEV* 666), *The Lay of Sorrow* (*IMEV* 482), *The Lufaris Complaynt* (*IMEV* 564) and *The Quare of Jelusy* (*IMEV* 3627.5).[2] A seemingly slightly later hand added two lyrics on blank leaves at the end of the volume (*IMEV* 2478, *4284.3). The collection is a curious amalgam of poems whose language (and often patterns of circulation) indicate Scottish origins, and of widely-transmitted texts from an English Chaucerian tradition, here given a Scottish flavour in copies made by Scottish scribes.[3]

---

[1] References are to Carleton Brown and Rossell Hope Robbins, *The Index of Middle English Verse* (New York, 1943), and Rossell Hope Robbins and John L. Cutler, *Supplement to the Index of Middle English Verse* (Lexington, Ky, 1965).
[2] It has been suggested that the first scribe is one James Graye and the second the 'V. de F.' responsible for parts of Cambridge, University Library MS Kk.1.5, but these identifications seem unlikely; see *The Works of Geoffrey Chaucer and 'The Kingis Quair': A Facsimile of Bodleian Library, Oxford, MS Arch. Selden. B. 24*, with an introduction by Julia Boffey and A. S. G. Edwards, and an appendix by B. C. Barker-Benfield (Cambridge, 1997), pp. 6–10.
[3] Scholarship on this is summarized in C. D. Jeffery, 'Anglo-Scots Poetry and *The Kingis Quair*', *Actes du 2e Colloque de Langue et de Littérature Ecossaises (Moyen Age et Renaissance)*, ed. Jean-Jacques Blanchot and Claude Graf (Strasbourg, 1978), pp. 207–21; see

In material terms, the manuscript is not particularly fine, even though recent conservation has improved its somewhat worn state and revealed new information about its structure. It is made of paper rather than parchment or vellum, and is not unusually large (most of the 231 leaves measure approximately 260 x 175 mm). Its writing and illumination, although fairly carefully executed, are not ornate and lavish. Visible evidence of the circumstances of its compilation is sparse: the arms represented on fol. 118v have been identified as those of Henry, Lord Sinclair, assumed after 26 January, 1488/9, and together with the note 'liber Henrici domini Sinclar' (fol. 230v), and other names, suggest a provenance; but it is not clear how long the manuscript remained with the Sinclair family, or indeed why or how they might have come to own it.[4] Physical evidence of other kinds, however, indicates that the volume underwent successive stages of enlargement and upgrading. It seems to have begun life (presumably in or shortly after 1488/9) as a copy of Chaucer's *Troilus and Criseyde* (fols 1–118v); to have been extended at various times with the addition of *The Kingis Quair* and other poems; and to have been enhanced with a programme of decoration that included the recopying of the opening stanzas of *Troilus and Criseyde* to accommodate an historiated initial. Still later in its existence successive readers added copies of short verse texts and other notes on the final leaves.

As a collection it evokes much more than the tastes of specific readers at a particular moment. Its contents stretch back to include texts first conceived a century before its compilation, and some have an afterlife in their emergence in later sixteenth-century Scottish manuscripts and printed books in forms closely related to their states in this manuscript. If on the one hand its nature as a Sinclair 'family' book is defined by its inclusion of the unique surviving copy of *The Kingis Quair*, the book of a king (James I) who was brother to Henry Sinclair's grandmother, on the other hand it may also have had a more public

---

also Julia Boffey and A. S. G. Edwards, 'Bodleian MS Arch. Selden. B. 24 and the "Scotticization" of Middle English Verse', *Rewriting Chaucer: Culture, Authority, and the Idea of the Authentic Text, 1400–1602*, ed. T. A. Prendergast and B. Kline (Columbus, OH, 1999), pp. 166–85.

[4] The first scribe's work also appears in three other manuscripts connected with members of the Sinclair family: Edinburgh, National Library of Scotland MS Acc. 9253 (prose translations by Gilbert Hay); Cambridge, St John's College MS G.19 (187) (Mirk's *Festial* and *Quattuor Sermones*); and Edinburgh, National Archives of Scotland, MS GD 45/31/I–II (deposited there by the Earl of Dalhousie). On the manuscript's history, see further, A. S. G. Edwards, 'Bodleian Library MS Arch. Selden B.24: A "Transitional" Collection', *The Whole Book: Cultural Perspectives on the Medieval Miscellany*, ed. Stephen G. Nichols and Siegfried Wenzel (Ann Arbor, 1996), pp. 53–67; Julia Boffey, 'Bodleian Library, MS Arch. Selden. B. 24 and Definitions of the "Household Book" ', *The English Medieval Book: Studies in Memory of Jeremy Griffiths*, ed. A. S. G. Edwards, Vincent Gillespie, and Ralph Hanna (London, 2000), pp. 125–34; Julia Boffey and A. S. G. Edwards, 'Bodleian MS Arch. Selden. B. 24: The Genesis and Evolution of a Scottish Poetical Anthology', *Poetica* 60 (2003), pp. 31–46.

significance.⁵ The manuscript thus interestingly represents both the range of courtly reading matter available in Scotland at the close of the fifteenth century, and the nature of Scottish literary tradition over some considerable time.

The Short Verse Texts

Most of the short items in the manuscript fill blank space between longer texts (which routinely start at the top of a page) in the first and predominantly Chaucerian section. The clearest example of this, a single rhyme royal stanza following the representation of Henry Sinclair's arms after the end of *Troilus and Criseyde* (fol. 118v), comments on the appropriateness of mourning dress for such a 'soroufull book' ('Blak be thy bandis and thy wede also', *IMEV* 524), and was inserted quite possibly with reference to an early binding of the manuscript, which seems originally to have ended at this point. Outside Scotland the stanza circulated with Lydgate's *Fall of Princes* as part of a longer poem entitled 'Greneacres A Lenvoye vpon John Bochas', and was also printed at the end of Richard Pynson's 1494 edition of that text (*STC* 3175).⁶ In what form it came the way of the Selden scribe is not clear.

The gathering that follows this presumably represents the start of the first process of extension undergone by the manuscript. Its first main text, *The Parliament of Fowls*, is preceded by a small group of fillers, all attributed to Chaucer as if designed to effect a smooth transition after *Troilus*, and concluding with a Latin note on the nativity of James IV. Chaucer's 'Truth' (fol. 119) ends with the words 'Explicit chauceres counsaling'; a single-stanza extract on the evils of prosperity, actually from John Walton's verse translation of Boethius (*IMEV* 2820, fol. 119), concludes 'Quod Chaucere'; and an anti-feminist poem of seven rhyme royal stanzas, beginning 'Deuise prowes and eke humylitee' (*IMEV* 679, fols 119v–120r), is rounded off with the statement 'Quod chaucere quhen he was rycht auisit'. The Walton extract evidently had quite a wide independent circulation. Its attribution to Chaucer in MS Arch. Selden. B. 24 is repeated in two other Scottish contexts: in fragments bound with John of Fordun's *Chronica gentis Scotorum* (London, British Library MS Cotton Vitellius E. XI), and in the Bannatyne manuscript (Edinburgh, NLS MS Advocates 1.1.6).⁷ The circulation of 'Deuise prowes and eke humylitee' was apparently more limited. Like Lydgate's *Complaint of the Black Knight*, it was

---

⁵ The main scribe noted details of the nativity of James IV on fol. 120, and it is possible that the upgrading of the manuscript was designed to celebrate events of royal or court significance; see Louise Olga Fradenburg, 'Sovereign Love: The Wedding of Margaret Tudor and James IV of Scotland', *Women and Sovereignty*, *Cosmos* 7 (1992), pp. 78–100; Boffey and Edwards, 'Genesis and Evolution', pp. 40–2.
⁶ See further *The Quare of Jelusy*, ed. J. Norton-Smith and I. Pravda, Middle English Texts 3 (Heidelberg, 1976), pp. 18–19, and C. Peterson, 'John Hardyng and Geoffrey of Monmouth: Two Unrecorded Poems and a Manuscript', *Notes and Queries* n.s. 27 (1980), pp. 202–4.
⁷ Julia Boffey, 'Proverbial Chaucer and the Chaucer Canon', *Huntington Library Quarterly* 58 (1996), pp. 37–47.

printed in Edinburgh by Chepman and Myllar in 1508 (*STC* 7348).[8] It also appears (probably copied from the print) in the Bannatyne manuscript.

Although fillers of this sort are often of a random nature, this little selection seems quite carefully related to the texts that surround it. A poem on truth, an extract from Boethius, and a castigation of women are all appropriate company for *Troilus and Criseyde*. It is harder to find a thread to link Chaucer's 'Complaint of Venus' (fols 136r–137r) and Clanvowe's *Book of Cupid* (fols 138v–141v) with the Marian lyric 'O hie emperice and quene celestiall' (fols 137v–138r; *IMEV* 2461) and the stanza beginning 'This warldly Ioy is onuly fantasy' (fol. 138r; *IMEV* 3660), which come between them, although the attribution here of 'O hie emperice' to Chaucer attempts to forge one. Like 'Deuise prowes and eke humylitee', these two pieces have a uniquely Scottish circulation, in witnesses that all postdate MS Arch. Selden. B. 24. The Marian lyric appears in the Asloan manuscript (Edinburgh, NLS MS 16500), 'This warldly Ioy' in the Bannatyne manuscript and in the later Maitland Folio (Cambridge, Magdalene College, Pepys MS 2553) and Reidpeth manuscript (Cambridge, University Library MS Ll.5.10). Preservation in these two late witnesses, together with poems by Kennedy and Dunbar, suggests an early court circulation.[9] Such a context would also be entirely appropriate for the brief instructions to serving men ('My frende gif thou will be a seruitur', fol. 229; *IMEV* 2242), preserved in the main scribe's hand on a misplaced leaf now at the end of the collection.

Physical damage has rendered partly fragmentary the remaining short poems. Two rhyme royal stanzas copied by the main scribe, with the opening 'Thy bagynyng Is barane brutulnesse' (fol. 229v; *IMEV* 3727), constitute a short moral poem, also surviving in the Bannatyne manuscript. A further poem of twelve lines, beginning 'Man be als mery as tho ...' (fol. 229v; *IMEV* 2043) and probably made up of one eight-line stanza and a fragment of another, is not extant elsewhere.[10] Two love lyrics added on the final leaves are the work of a later hand. Although unique survivals, they conform to the general flavour of the rest of the manuscript in their concentration on courtly forms: 'O lady I shall me dress with besy cure' (fol. 231r, 230r; *IMEV* 2478) is the complaint of a prisoner of love, and 'Go go fro my window' (fol. 230r; *IMEV* *4284.3) a dialogue on a night visit.[11]

---

[8] *The Chepman and Myllar Prints: A Facsimile*, introd. William Beattie (1950).

[9] 'This warldly Ioy' has much in common with Dunbar's 'Be mery, man, and tak nocht fer in mynd' (B 6), and with 'Quhat is this lyfe bot ane straucht way to deid' (B 51), while 'O hie emperice' can be compared to 'Hale, sterne superne' (B 16) and 'Done is a battell on the dragon blak' (B 10); see Dunbar, *The Poems*, ed. Bawcutt.

[10] Both may be extracts from longer works, like the stanza from Walton's Boethius.

[11] For the first, cf. Dunbar's 'Sen that I am a presoneir' (B 69); for the second, see P. J. Frankis, 'Some Late Middle English Lyrics in the Bodleian Library', *Anglia* 73 (1956), pp. 299–304.

The Kingis Quair

The Kingis Quair has long been recognized as both vitally illustrative of Scottish literary traditions and yet in some sense outside them, since its linguistic forms reflect both English and Scots usage.[12] A note in the scribe's hand at the end of the text, 'Quod Jacobus primus scoto*rum* rex Illustrissimus' (fol. 211r), attributes it to King James I of Scotland (1394–1437), and a later hand extends this information just before the start of the poem: 'heirefter followis the quair maid be / King James of scotland ye first / callit ye kingis quair and / maid q*uhe*n his ma*jestie* wes in / Ingland' (fol. 191v). That the poem refers to the contours of James's young life is clear, but whether it was in fact written 'in Ingland' at the end of his years of imprisonment there, or after his return to Scotland (1424), or indeed by James himself at all, is less certain.[13] Whoever its author, the poem contrives an arresting conjunction of biographical detail and literary tropes and allusions, tracing the facts of James's imprisonment, liberation, and marriage through a series of figures drawn from sources which include Boethius's *Consolation of Philosophy*, Chaucer's *Troilus* and *The Knight's Tale*, and very probably works by Gower, Lydgate, and Deguileville as well.[14]

In the context of MS Arch. Selden. B. 24, this tissue of references is particularly striking. It is almost as if the author of the *Quair* ('quire' or 'book') produced his poem with something like the first fifteen gatherings of this manuscript fresh in his mind, and it has been suggested more than once that Selden. B. 24 may be a copy of an anthology compiled in England and then brought back to Scotland by James.[15] The recurrent interests that dominate the texts of the first part of the collection – love and fortune – become the matter of the *Quair*, and the poem's sources in other texts are artfully flagged by various devices. Analogues of the metaphors used of Troilus's love, of the delicious landscape of *The Parliament of Fowls*, the complaint uttered by Lydgate's Black Knight, the avian advice of Clanvowe's *Book of Cupid*, all find their way in, with a complexity of association controlled with deft humour. Just as the English poems of Charles d'Orléans occasionally hint at a sense of comic

---

[12] See Jeffery, 'Anglo-Scots Poetry', p. 217.
[13] Full biographical details are in E. Balfour-Melville, *James I, King of Scots, 1406–1437* (London, 1936), and Michael Brown, *James I*, rev. ed. (East Linton, 2000). Attempts to attribute other works to James are unconvincing: see also *The Kingis Quair together with A Ballad of Good Counsel*, ed. W. W. Skeat, STS (1911), pp. 51–4, 99–101.
[14] The most recent discussion of sources is that of Alessandra Petrina, *The Kingis Quair of James I of Scotland* (Padova, 1997).
[15] See *Quare of Jelusy*, ed. Norton-Smith and Pravda, p. 18, and Edwards, 'Bodleian Library MS Arch. Selden B.24', p. 64. See *The Kingis Quair*, ed. John Norton-Smith, 2nd edn (Leiden, 1981), introduction. The fact that the manuscript's text of Lydgate's *Complaint of the Black Knight* seems closely related to that of the metropolitan scribe John Shirley in London, British Library MS Additional 16165 (see Boffey and Edwards, 'Scotticization', pp. 179–80) may support this possibility.

triumph in the mastery of Chaucerian and Lydgatian modes, so the author of the *Quair* seems to revel in his poem's allusiveness.[16]

The Boethian framework of the *Quair* has attracted much critical attention, including some suggestions that it is designed to prompt an ironic reading of the poem, and adverse criticism of what has been seen as trivialization of Boethian philosophy.[17] While the form and length of the *Quair* hardly allow for the extended development of the arguments of the *Consolation*, much is nonetheless contrived through summary, or through deft allusions. Routes to Boethius are also opened through echoes of *The Knight's Tale* and *Troilus*, Chaucer's own most deeply Boethian works. Boethianism of yet another kind has been noted in the formal properties of the poem, whose emphases on prime and other significant numbers may reflect observance of arguments about harmony and numerical ratios in Boethius's treatise *De musica*.[18]

A related aspect of the *Quair*'s construction is the incorporation of several potentially free-standing lyrics within its 197 rhyme royal stanzas. The most obvious of these is the birds' welcome to May ('Worschippe, ye that loveris bene, this May', 232–8),[19] described twice in the text as a 'song' (231, 239), and signalled in the manuscript by the marginal note 'Cantus' (fol. 195). Several more single stanzas or sets of stanzas function in a self-contained way.[20] It would be possible to argue that these portions of the poem are simply characteristic of its somewhat episodic construction, and that there is little to

---

[16] *Fortunes Stabilnes: Charles of Orleans's English Book of Love*, ed. Mary-Jo Arn, Medieval and Renaissance Texts and Studies (Binghampton, NY, 1994). Fragmentary evidence suggesting that the French and Scottish prisoners may have known each other's work may indicate that their poems were conceived as rival attempts at cultural appropriation; see Julia Boffey, 'Charles of Orleans Reading Chaucer's Dream Visions', *Medievalitas: Reading the Middle Ages. The J. A. W. Bennett Memorial Lectures, Perugia, 1995*, ed. Piero Boitani and Anna Torti (Cambridge, 1996), pp. 43–62.

[17] See Lois Ebin, 'Boethius, Chaucer, and *The Kingis Quair*', *PQ* 53 (1974), pp. 321–41; ironic readings are suggested by Vincent Carretta, '*The Kingis Quair* and *The Consolation of Philosophy*', *SSL* 16 (1981), pp. 14–28, and Clair F. James, '*The Kingis Quair*: The Plight of the Courtly Lover', *New Readings of Late Medieval Love Poems*, ed. David Chamberlain (Lanham, Md., 1993), pp. 95–118.

[18] John MacQueen, 'Poetry – James I to Henryson', *History*, ed. Jack, pp. 55–71 (59–60); and Alice Miskimin, 'Patterns in *The Kingis Quair* and *The Temple of Glas*', *Papers on Language and Literature* 13 (1977), pp. 339–61. The attribution of *The Kingis Quair* to King James I has sometimes been connected with the coining of the term 'rhyme royal' for the seven-line stanzas used in this poem (and in much Chaucerian and post-Chaucerian verse); see further, Eric Stanley, ' "Rithme royall, & surely it is a royall kinde of verse, seruing best for graue discourses": but not always best in Bodleian MS Arch. Selden B. 24, and not always best transmitted in *The Kingis Quair*', *Poetica* 50 (1998), pp. 29–62.

[19] References are to James I of Scotland, *The Kingis Quair*, in *Fifteenth-Century English Dream Visions: An Anthology*, ed. Julia Boffey (Oxford, 2003), pp. 90–157.

[20] Examples include the narrator's prayer to Venus ('O Venus clere, of goddis stellifyit', 358–64, described at 365 as 'this orisoun'); his prayer to the lady for mercy ('Quhen sall your merci rew upon your man', 435–41, termed a 'ditee' at 429), and his five-stanza dream salutation of Venus ('Hye quene of lufe, sterre of benevolence', 687–721, characterized at 684 as a complaint).

distinguish them from other rhetorical set-pieces such as the invocation of the muses (127–33), or the list of animal inhabitants of Fortune's domain (1079–99), or the closing thanks and blessings (1316–37). But the demonstration of expertise in the favourite fifteenth-century courtly forms of supplication and complaint aligns the *Quair* with other early fifteenth-century lyrico-narratives such as Lydgate's *Complaint of the Black Knight* (included in this manuscript), his *Temple of Glass*, and of course the sequence of English poems attributed to Charles of Orleans, probably the most elaborate English experiment with this genre. Poems such as these were almost certainly known to the author of the *Quair*, who may also have found some inspiration in Lydgate's Boethianism.[21] The *Temple of Glass*, for example, explores the influential Boethian doctrine of contraries (the alternation of joy and sorrow, and the enhancement of one through comparison with the other), and concludes with an episode in which the dream petitioners are encircled in Venus's chain of love.[22]

The dazzling intertextuality of the *Quair* is matched by inventive experiments with the conventions of dream vision. The dream here is only one element of the poem (526–1204), whose scheme is shaped as a retrospective account of part of the narrator's life-history, prompted by reading Boethius in bed at night. The recollections of past experience, framed by reference to the present time in a structure whose circularity is reinforced by the repetition of the poem's opening line just before the conclusion (1372), do of course themselves take on something of the flavour of a dream, and readers are often confused by the complex layers of the poem's chronology.[23] This blurring of boundaries between dream and waking worlds is further intensified in moments that seem designed to evoke both at once; when a dove brings a hopeful written message to the newly awakened dreamer, for example, it is hard to know quite which world we are in. Structural complexities of these kinds are frequent in French fourteenth- and fifteenth-century poetry, where poems such as Machaut's *Dit de la fonteinne amoureuse* weave in and out of waking and sleeping worlds to potent effect.[24]

---

[21] The lyrico-narrative structure of the *Temple* is carefully signalled in one early copy, London, British Library Additional MS 16165, whose scribe announces such sections as 'the supplicacion of the Louer', and 'Balade of the lover'; see *Fifteenth-Century English Dream Visions*, ed. Boffey, pp. 15–89. The date of Lydgate's poem is unclear, although it seems likely to have been completed by 1425, the approximate date of the copy in this manuscript.
[22] Lydgate is not mentioned in the envoy to the *Quair* where Chaucer and Gower are named (1374), possibly because he was still alive at the time of the poem's composition.
[23] For further discussion, see William Quinn, 'Memory and the Matrix of Unity in *The Kingis Quair*', *Chaucer Review* 15 (1980–81), pp. 332–55.
[24] A point explored by Karin E. C. Fuog, 'Placing Earth at the Center of the Cosmos: *The Kingis Quair* as Boethian Revision', *SSL* 32 (2001), pp. 140–9, and further contextualized by Peter Brown, 'On the Borders of Middle English Dream Visions', *Reading Dreams: The Interpretation of Dreams from Chaucer to Shakespeare*, ed. P. Brown (Oxford, 1999), pp. 22–50, and Helen Phillips, 'Frames and Narrators in Chaucerian Poetry', *The Long Fifteenth Century: Essays for Douglas Gray*, ed. Helen Cooper and Sally Mapstone (Oxford, 1997), pp.

There are similarities between the processes of some of the French poems and the *Quair*'s poetic interlace of experiences, memory, and imagination; recent crticism has been much concerned with these aspects of the poem, and with the issue of whether or not it succeeds in evoking an individual sensibility. Dreaming, imprisonment, and love have all figured in recent psychoanalytical approaches to the poem as states with special potential for the construction of subjectivity.[25] Interestingly, much of this discussion is able to build on what have been recurrent issues in scholarship and writing about the *Quair*, since earlier critics were also absorbed (if for different reasons) by the facts of its authorship, and by such matters as the identification of the anonymous lady with James's wife, Joan Beaufort. C. S. Lewis's assessment of it as 'the first modern book of love',[26] made in the context of a discussion of whether it is a 'literal' or an 'allegorical' story, in essence addressed similar issues, and many subsequent discussions of the poem's Boethianism, its relationship to Chaucerian modes of writing, and its formal and stylistic qualities have hinged on the overlap of allegorical and literal levels. Sally Mapstone's fruitful exploration of the *Quair* as a text on kingship extrapolates its concern with 'public' love and self-government from the same autobiographical / allegorical combination.[27]

Most analyses of the poem either ignore or carefully skirt around questions of its textual integrity. Local textual difficulties have been recognized readily enough in successive editions, with a steady flow of articles suggesting supplementary emendations,[28] but the larger problem posed by the division of the copy between two scribes has not been explored. The main scribe seems to have known that he was going to finish his stint part of the way down fol. 209v, since he ended his red marginal ruling there, and it is conceivable that he finished his copy there (at line 1239) because he thought he had reached the end

---

71–97. A useful introduction to some of the French poems is William Calin, *The French Tradition and the Literature of Medieval England* (Toronto, 1994).

[25] See R. James Goldstein, 'Writing in Scotland, 1058–1560', *The Cambridge History of Medieval English Literature*, ed. David Wallace (Cambridge, 1999), pp. 229–55 (236–7); A. C. Spearing, 'Dreams in *The Kingis Quair* and the Duke's Book', *Charles d'Orléans in England*, ed. Mary-Jo Arn (Cambridge, 2000), pp. 123–44; Robert Epstein, 'Prisoners of Reflection: The Fifteenth-Century Poetry of Exile and Imprisonment', *Exemplaria* 15 (2003), pp. 159–98; Joanna Summers, *Late Medieval Prison Writing and the Politics of Autobiography* (Oxford, 2004), pp. 60–89; Michael R. G. Spiller, 'The *donna angelicata* and *The Kingis Quair*', *Scottish Language and Literature, Medieval and Renaissance: Fourth International Conference 1984 Proceedings*, ed. Dietrich Strauss and Horst W. Drescher (Frankfurt am Main, 1986), pp. 217–27.

[26] *The Allegory of Love. A Study in Medieval Tradition* (Oxford, 1936), p. 237.

[27] Sally Mapstone, 'Kingship and *The Kingis Quair*', *The Long Fifteenth Century*, ed. Cooper and Mapstone, pp. 51–69.

[28] The following articles postdate published bibliographies: Priscilla Bawcutt, ' "The copill": A Crux in *The Kingis Quair*', *Review of English Studies* n.s. 38 (1987), pp. 211–14; A. S. G. Edwards and Elizabeth Robertson, '*The Kingis Quair*, 402', *Notes and Queries* 41 (1994), p. 307; Nicholas Jacobs, '*The Kingis Quair*, lines 1188–90', *Notes and Queries* 30 (1983), pp. 392–4.

of the poem. The narrator has recalled waking from his prison dream, has reflected on it, and has received 'kalendis of confort' from a dove. In relation to his claims at the start of his poem that his own 'aventure' would reverse the trajectory of Boethius's, we have been told all we need to know. The poem could quite plausibly end here, and indeed at some stage possibly did so. It is tempting to speculate that the second scribe's portion, a series of concluding gestures (prayers, praise and an envoy), which offer little further development,[29] may somehow represent a conclusion found or confected at a later stage.[30]

The Complaints

The remaining texts in the portions of the manuscript copied by the second scribe – *The Lay of Sorrow* (fols 217r–219r), *The Lufaris Complaynt* (fols 219r–221v), *The Quare of Jelusy* (fols 221v–228v) – have a striking homogeneity, apparently building on the concern with women's experiences in love which surfaces in the first scribe's copy of *The Legend of Good Women*, and is treated with varying degrees of equivocation in *Troilus and Criseyde* and the short 'Deuise prowes and eke humylitee'. Almost all represent women's opinions and give space to women's voices (the single exception, *The Lufaris Complaynt*, represents the view of a jilted man as if to play some variation on the usual theme.) All, including *The Letter of Cupid*, which Hoccleve translated from the French of Christine de Pizan, display a perceptible interest in the mode of complaint. The poems share with *The Kingis Quair* a thorough acquaintance with Chaucerian models, acknowledged in their modes, their frames of reference, occasionally also in overt allusions.[31] Interestingly and perhaps significantly, though, no attempts are made to claim Chaucerian authorship for them. This is a remarkable departure from the first section of the manuscript, which bristles with titles and *explicits* into which Chaucer's name is dropped. Thus, not only are *The Parliament of Fowls*, *The Legend of Good Women*, 'The Complaint of Venus' and 'Truth' attributed to Chaucer, but Lydgate's *Complaint of the Black Knight* becomes 'The maying and disport of Chaucere' (fol. 129v), Hoccleve's 'Mother of God' is termed 'Or*acio* galfridi Chaucere' (fol. 131v), and a number of the short items are associated with Chaucer's name.[32] The only two attributions in the second scribe's portion of the manuscript are his subscription to *The Kingis Quair* (see p. 67 above), and a

---

[29] See also Alan MacColl, 'Beginning and Ending *The Kingis Quair*', *Bryght Lanternis: Essays on the Language and Literature of Medieval and Renaissance Scotland*, ed. J. Derrick McClure and Michael R. G. Spiller (Aberdeen, 1989), pp. 118–28.
[30] The manuscript's text of *The Parliament of Fowls* has its own specially made conclusion; see Boffey and Edwards, 'Scotticization', pp. 169–70.
[31] *The Lufaris Complaynt*, 29–35; possibly *The Lay of Sorrow*, 184–5.
[32] 'Deuise prowes and eke humylitee', 'O hie emperice and quene celestiall', and the Walton extract conclude with 'Quod Chaucere'. Clanvowe's *Book of Cupid* ends imperfectly; but could originally have concluded with an attribution.

note at the end of *The Quare of Jelusy* (fol. 228v), now virtually illegible because of damage to the leaf, which reads 'Explicit q*uod* ?a[...]'.[33]

Apart from Hoccleve's *Letter of Cupid* (fols 211v–217r), all the texts in this section (even *The Kingis Quair*, which the scribe finished) appear to have had no wider circulation outside this anthology, and it is possible that their transmission was confined to a small circle. *The Lay of Sorrow* concludes with an unusually personal address to an unnamed 'Princes, full graciouse and excellent' (176), at whose command it was apparently produced. If these are indeed coterie poems, and if they originated in Scotland (as has been argued on the basis of the rhymes and lexis),[34] then it is possible that their conjunction with the more studiedly 'English' Chaucer anthology that precedes them was designed to make a statement about Scottish mastery of English forms. Even so, the Scottish cast lent by scribal forms to genuinely Chaucerian works in the collection serves to blur differences between these and what have been defined as the Scottish texts.

The compilation of the second portion of the manuscript might equally plausibly have been driven by efforts to extend the experimentation with themes and forms opened up in the preceding texts. Continuity of this kind can be demonstrated, for example, in the provision of the seemingly pro-feminist *Letter of Cupid* as a sequel to *The Legend of Good Women*, a text which Hoccleve's translation actually names (at line 316).[35] *The Quare of Jelusy* also shares a number of features with the poems of the first section. Like *The Complaint of the Black Knight*, or the individual stories of *The Legend of Good Women*, or the spurious combination of Chaucer's complaints of Mars and Venus, it offers framed complaints: its narrator overhears a lady complaining of her unkind treatment, and takes up her case with his own diatribe against the forms of jealousy by which women are oppressed. Like some of these poems, it too explores a variety of verse forms, with a framework in couplets enclosing groups of stanzas of different lengths, presumably thus justifying its status as a mini-compilation or 'quare'. *The Lay of Sorrow*[36] similarly uses a variety of stanza forms to construct a woman's lament, and with *The Lufaris Complaynt* –

---

[33] On the basis of a partly-visible ascender, which could be a part of the scribe's form of 'ch', attempts have been made to read the name as 'Auchen' and even as 'Auchinleck', but (beyond recognizing that it is unlikely to be 'Chaucer') it is impossible to reconstruct what is missing with any certainty. See *Quare of Jelusy*, ed. Norton-Smith and Pravda, pp. 14–17.

[34] See Kenneth G. Wilson, '*The Lay of Sorrow* and *The Lufaris Complaynt*: An Edition', *Speculum* 29 (1954), pp. 708–26, and P. J. Frankis, 'Notes on Two Fifteenth Century Scots Poems', *Neuphilologische Mitteilungen* 61 (1960), pp. 203–13.

[35] See *Poems of Cupid, God of Love*, ed. Thelma S. Fenster and Mary Carpenter Erler (Leiden, 1990), pp. 176–202.

[36] The title is editorial, suggested by the first line: 'befor my deth this lay of sorow I sing'.

not an answer, but a parallel male-voiced outpouring of 'teres, weymenting, and playntee' – demonstrates the potentialities of unframed lyric forms.[37]

The directions in which these experiments move may draw on a number of Chaucerian precedents. Chaucer's interest in Ovidian models for abandoned women, specifically those of the *Heroides*, finds its way not only into *The Legend of Good Women* but also into *The Squire's Tale*, *The House of Fame*, *The Complaint of Mars* (whose speaker is of course male), and *Anelida and Arcite*. The artfully varied stanza forms and the rhetorical strategies used in *Mars* and *Anelida* are echoed in a number of fifteenth-century English poems, whether lyrico-narrative (like Lydgate's *Temple of Glass*, or the anonymous *Assembly of Ladies*) or in shorter pieces.[38] But it is worth remembering that *The Quare of Jelusy*, *The Lay of Sorrow*, and *The Lufaris Complaynt* are by no means the only fifteenth-century Scottish poems to explore these modes – Henryson's *Testament of Cresseid* and *Orpheus and Eurydice* include inset complaints and varied stanzas-forms;[39] *Lancelot of the Laik* includes a short prison complaint[40] – and all engage with precedents from a wide European context.

The poems of the second portion of MS Arch. Selden. B. 24 are something more than isolated attempts at aping Chaucerian models, and are perhaps best defined as instances of experiment with a lively European tradition of writing about love, and by implication, of writing about desire, imagination and rhetoric. The significance of such a conjunction for the writing of poetry is explored not just in Chaucer's work but in poems such as Machaut's *Remède de Fortune* or Dunbar's *The Goldyn Targe* or Douglas's *Palice of Honour*. Many of the poems in MS Arch. Selden. B. 24 relate to these same themes, whether longer texts like *Troilus and Criseyde* or *The Kingis Quair*, or the shorter complaints and lyrics. That the manuscript includes *The Letter of Cupid* seems significant, for the affiliations of this work take in not just Hoccleve and Chaucer, but Christine de Pizan and the *querelle des femmes*, with its influential codification of documentary practice for defending one's sex or lodging a plea at the court of love. The contents of MS Arch. Selden. B. 24, like those of a number of fifteenth-century manuscript anthologies produced in England, draw on these same traditions of writing. All contain selections of Chaucer's poems, and samples of writing conventionally defined as 'in the Chaucerian tradition'.

---

[37] On these genres, see W. A. Davenport, *Chaucer: Complaint and Narrative* (Cambridge, 1988), and John Kerrigan, *Motives of Woe: Shakespeare and 'Female Complaint'. A Critical Anthology* (Oxford, 1991).

[38] For the *Assembly*, see *Fifteenth-Century Dream Visions*, ed. Boffey, pp. 195–231. For a convenient short lyrics selection: *Women's Writing in Middle English*, ed. Alexandra Barratt (London, 1992).

[39] Henryson, *The Poems*, ed. Fox: Cresseid's complaint (in 9-line stanzas), 407–69; Orpheus's complaint (in 10-line stanzas), 134–73.

[40] *Lancelot of the Laik*, ed. M. M. Gray, STS (1912), 698–717; see also *Ballatis of Luve*, ed. John MacQueen (1970), pp. 9–10.

But this tradition (as reflected in the French sources and titles of some of these anthologized poems) drew on a wider context of European courtly writing in which the significance of national borders may have been overestimated.[41]

---

[41] See, for example, Bodleian MS Fairfax 16 and its relatives: John Norton-Smith's Introduction to *Bodleian MS Fairfax 16* (London, 1979).

5

'Of Wisdome and of Guide Governance':
Sir Gilbert Hay and
The Buik of King Alexander the Conquerour

JOANNA MARTIN

The Buik of King Alexander the Conquerour (hereafter *Alexander the Conquerour*) is the most detailed version of the Alexander legend to survive from late medieval Britain.[1] Despite the fact that its prologue and part of the narrative of Alexander's conception are missing in both witnesses, the poem still runs to over 19,000 lines of decasyllabic couplets. It handles its sources with considerably more freedom than most of the Middle English accounts of Alexander's life, responding to the conqueror's contested reputation by drawing together a surprisingly wide range of prior texts in the Alexander tradition as well as other material from its wider Scots literary heritage. Furthermore, while it is not unusual for writing on Alexander the Great to become the occasion for reflections on the exercise of power, *Alexander the Conquerour* is emphatically presented as a 'mirrour' or exemplary 'storie' that 'treittis of wisdome and of guide governance' (271, 19331, 19339). However, despite its imaginative reworking of inherited material, *Alexander the Conquerour* is perhaps the least well known of the insular Alexander texts and important questions remain unanswered about the circumstances of its composition and transmission. This chapter reviews these questions, and also examines the poem's distinctive and at times troubled discussion of Alexander's kingship as he attempts to order the wildernesses of the unknown world and of his own youthful and amorous self.

I

Alexander the Conquerour has been conventionally attributed to Sir Gilbert Hay, who, in his own words, was a 'knycht / maister in arte and bachilere in decreis / Chaumerlayn vmquhile to the maist worthy king Charles [VII] of ffraunce'.[2] Hay gives these details while identifying himself as the translator of

---

[1] References are to Hay, *Buik*, ed. Cartwright.
[2] *The Buke of the Law of Armys* in *The Prose Works of Sir Gilbert Hay*, ed. Jonathan A. Glenn, 2 vols, STS (1993–2005), vol. 2, p. 2. Hay probably graduated from the University of St

The Buke of the Law of Armys, a version of Honoré Bonet's *L'Arbre des Batailles*. It is also likely that he was responsible for two other prose texts, *The Ordre of Knychthede* (from a French version of Raymond Lull's *Libre de Caballeria*), and *The Buke of the Governaunce of Princis* (based on the *Secretum Secretorum*).[3] He tells us that this work was undertaken 'at the request of ane hye and mychty prince and worthy lord williame [Sinclair] erle of Orknay – and of Cathnes', and completed in 1456.[4]

These works survive in a single manuscript, probably copied for William Sinclair's son Oliver Sinclair of Roslin in the 1480s.[5] It is consequently difficult to gauge the extent of their circulation. Nevertheless, Hay's literary reputation was well established by the opening of the sixteenth century. He is named as a 'makar' or poet in Dunbar's 'I that in heill wes and gladnes',[6] and David Lyndsay's *Testament of the Papyngo*.[7] In addition, the original contents list of the Asloan MS (c. 1515–c. 1525) includes a work, now lost from the codex, entitled the 'document of Sir gilbert hay'. As Mapstone has pointed out, this 'document', and the intriguingly entitled 'buke of curtasy and nortur' and 'the Regiment of kingis with the buke of phisnomy' mentioned with it, would have been found in the poetry, rather than the prose, section of the anthology, lending weight to the possibility of Hay's reputation as a verse writer.[8]

However, the main evidence for the association of *Alexander the Conquerour* with Hay is far from conclusive, resting as it does on the rather disjointed epilogue that survives in the poem's two witnesses, both of which were copied in the sixteenth century.[9] These are British Library, Additional MS 40732 (c. 1530) and National Archives of Scotland MS GD 112/71/9 (c. 1580–90). Although there is no break in the manuscripts, the epilogue seems to shift in tone and direction after the sequence of leave-taking devices that precede line 19310. The first part of the epilogue contains the promise of the narrative voice to again rehearse, as he had apparently done in the missing prologue, his 'awin

---

Andrews in 1418–19. See further, Sally Mapstone, 'The Advice to Princes Tradition in Scottish Literature, 1450–1500', unpublished D.Phil. thesis (Oxford, 1986), pp. 48–53.

[3] For an edition of the other translations: *Prose Works*, ed. Glenn.

[4] *Prose Works*, ed. Glenn, vol. 2, p. 2. On the connection between the Sinclairs and the later owners of *Alexander the Conquerour* manuscripts, the Campbells of Glenorchy, see Mapstone, 'Advice to Princes Tradition', p. 45.

[5] Edinburgh, NLS, Acc. 9253.

[6] Dunbar, *Poems*, ed. Bawcutt (B 21), 67.

[7] Lyndsay, *Selected Poems*, ed. Hadley Williams, 19.

[8] Mapstone also considers the possibility that 'the Regiment of kingis with the buke of phisnomy' was a version of the advisory episode that appears half way through *Alexander the Conquerour*: 'The Scots *Buke of Phisnomy* and Sir Gilbert Hay', *The Renaissance in Scotland: Studies in Literature, Religion, History and Culture Offered to John Durkan*, ed. A. A. MacDonald, Michael Lynch and Ian B. Cowan (Leiden, 1994), pp. 1–44.

[9] For a controversial view on the poem's authorship see Matthew P. McDiarmid, 'Concerning Sir Gilbert Hay, the Authorship of *Alexander the Conquerour* and *The Buik of Alexander*', *SSL* 28 (1993), pp. 28–54. Contrast Gerrit H. V. Bunt, *Alexander the Great in the Literature of Medieval Britain*, Mediaevalia Groningana 14 (Groningen, 1994), p. 64.

excusatioun' (19300) for writing the poem. However, the last section of the epilogue seems more objectively to identify Hay with 'him that maid the first translatioun' (19312), while also stating that the present writer, who refers to himself in the first person, 'endit' the poem and 'of faltis mendit' it (19342–3), completing his work on the twenty-first of August 1499.[10] Although the narrative voice of the epilogue promises to reveal 'Quha causit this buike agane to wreittin be' (19314) this information is never divulged.

Given the date of Hay's prose translations, it is likely that his version of the subsequently 'endit' and 'mendit' romance was written some considerable time before the 1499 date given in the witnesses, perhaps in about 1460.[11] This, and the epilogue's apparent distinguishing of an original translator and a reviser, suggest that *Alexander the Conquerour* as it survives does not represent Hay's original work.[12] Although there is no reason to doubt that Hay was connected with an earlier version of the poem, the problematic evidence for authorship means that this essay does not attribute the poem to him, but simply to an anonymous Scottish poet.

II

The narrator of *Alexander the Conquerour* both defends the poem's fidelity to a 'Lateine buik' (18561) and claims that the work has been 'translaittit ... / ... out of the Frensche leid' (19333–4). The sources referred to here are the twelfth-century J2 recension of the *Historia de Preliis*, and the thirteenth-century *Roman d'Alexandre* of Alexandre de Paris, including the poems often interpolated into the French work, *Li Fuerre de Gadres* and *Les Voeux de Paon*.[13] These works are treated with considerable freedom, the narrator asking on one occasion to be excused for not relating 'all the dedis ... / Quhilk wther

---

[10] Sally Mapstone (*pers. comm.*) has drawn attention to the similar wording of the colophon to the copy of Lydgate's *Troy Book* and Scottish *Troy Book* fragments in Oxford, Bodleian Library, MS Douce 148, which states that the work has been 'writtine and mendit at the Instance of ... Thomas ewyne'. See *Barbour's des Schottischen Nationaldichters Legendensammlung nebst den Fragmenten seines Trojanerkrieges*, ed. C. Horstmann, 2 vols (Heilbronn, 1881–82), vol. 2, p. 304.

[11] There are similarities between the accounts of Aristotle's bridling in *The Spectacle of Luf* (c. 1492) and *Alexander the Conquerour* (7163–247), but this is of little help in establishing the romance's date. See Kathryn Saldanha, '*The Thewis of Gudwomen*: Middle Scots Moral Advice with European Connections?', *The European Sun: Proceedings of the Seventh International Conference on Medieval and Renaissance Scottish Language and Literature*, ed. Graham Caie, Roderick J. Lyall, Sally Mapstone and Kenneth Simpson (East Linton, 2001), pp. 288–99 (297–8).

[12] Compare Mapstone, 'The Scots *Buke of Phisnomy*', p. 2.

[13] See John Cartwright, 'Sir Gilbert Hay and the Alexander Tradition', *Scottish Language and Literature, Medieval and Renaissance: Fourth International Conference 1984 Proceedings*, ed. Dietrich Strauss and Horst W. Drescher (Frankfurt am Main, 1986), pp. 229–38. For the sources, see *Historia Alexandri Magni (Historia de Preliis) Rezension J2*, ed. A. Hilka (Meisenheim am Glan, 1976); *The Romances of Alexander*, trans. D. M. Kratz (New York and London, 1991); Alexandre de Paris, *Le Roman d'Alexandre*, trans. Laurence Harf-Lancner (Paris, 1994).

buikis in thare ditis recordis' (6024–5). These sources are also combined with others such as the *Secretum Secretorum*, the *Epistola Alexandri ad Aristotelem*, *Le Voyage d'Alexandre au Paradis Terrestre*, and materials from the exemplum tradition. The incorporation of sections from a mid-fifteenth-century Scots parental advice text contributes to the distinctive intertextuality of the work, which is rich in original speeches and passages of description and comment.[14]

In his use of the *Historia de Preliis*, *Roman d'Alexandre* and *Secretum Secretorum*, the Scottish poet drew on a tradition that, although not without its ambiguities, was largely positive about Alexander, presenting him as a model of chivalry and *courtoisie*. Nevertheless, the poet takes every opportunity to increase the exemplary potential of his material and its ability to sustain serious reflections on the nature of good kingship: the romance, the narrator says, is not merely concerned with 'worthie deidis' but also with 'the wayis of virtue and valieance, / Rycht reull and ordour of kingis gouernance' (2057–8). Although a subtle realignment of the poem with more negative aspects of the Alexander tradition is evident in the later stages of the text, for much of the narrative Alexander is an embodiment of 'wisdome and prudence' (4355) who conquers through the 'renoun of gentrice and larges' (3063). Unlike the acquisitive Alexander of the exemplum tradition, he only requires the love of the people he conquers as a tribute, not their 'tressoure' (12539). In contrast, Alexander's avaricious adversaries remind the reader that 'punycioun and vengance / Cumyis oft to kingis for thare mysgouernance' (9939–40). Nicholas, Darius and Porrus meet their ends desiring Alexander's favour, and with belated self-knowledge figure themselves as 'myrroure[s]' (6826) of folly.

Almost half the Scottish poem is devoted to describing Alexander's triumph over the exotic regions of the world, often magnifying the marvellous encounters he has in this 'wildernes' (10831).[15] However, where some versions of Alexander's exotic travels, including the *Alexandri Magni Iter ad Paradisum*, depict him as beguiled by the orient's riches, *Alexander the Conquerour* preserves his exemplariness. Alexander quickly recognizes the faults of the 'barbarianis' (7287), and desires to 'convert thame fra ydolatrie' (7289):

> For thai ar ay creuel folk and but ressoun,
> And werst to reule of any natioun:
> Thay war presumpteous and rude and vnhonest.   (11365–7)

Yet he also accepts the limits of his power, treating with 'grete pite' (13287) the wild people 'Quhilkis nowtherane witt na governance has' (15934) and of whom 'he couth neuer be maister' (11684). He defends the extension of his rule

---

[14] See Deborah E. Van Duin, ' "Na Man Micht Noumber þe Riches": The City of Segar in Gilbert Hay's *Buik of King Alexander*', *English Studies* 77 (1996), pp. 517–29.
[15] For original descriptions of Alexander's monstrous adversaries see 11451–68, 11607–54 and 14558–97.

by insisting that it is beneficial for the 'commoun proffitt', which would otherwise perish through the division that occurs when there are 'sundry kingis' (16352–7) in the world. Furthermore, Alexander is presented as a monotheist who attributes his success solely to the 'mekill God that governis all' (11359). It is telling that his spirit is ravished by a glimpse of the Earthly Paradise, the like of which he is not permitted in any of the sources.[16] 'No wounder', the narrator says, 'thocht he be a conquerour' (2048).

The seal on Alexander's exemplariness is his ability to act as an adviser to his adversaries, and much of the counsel that he offers them with 'ane mesure and a sobernes' (739) is the invention of the Scottish poet. Some of the wisdom he imparts, such as his original speech on the 'vanetie' (6928) of temporal lordship following the murder of Darius of Persia, reworks perennial moral themes. But other counsels, such as his warning to the oriental prince Caractor on the king's obligation to protect those he summons to his presence, has greater political resonance. In his speech, which is not paralleled in the sources, Alexander uses the phrase 'assoverit of the law' to express the guarantee of safe conduct that Caractor is obliged to give even to an outlaw or 'banist man' (15284–8). Forms of the verb 'assover' ('to assure') appear with this meaning in fifteenth- and sixteenth-century legislation,[17] and the Auchinleck Chronicler records that James II had given 'speciale assouerans' to the Earl of Douglas when he arrived at Stirling Castle on 21 February 1452.[18] On this occasion, James broke his word, and Douglas was slain at the king's own hand. Alexander's warning to Caractor that 'in youre persoun suppois ye me sla, / It wilbe reput to yow welany' (15278–9) seems to recall this distasteful act of Scottish royal tyranny in a way that would have been meaningful for fifteenth-century readers.

Alexander's wisdom is all the more extraordinary because of his tender age, and his status as a *puer senex* is particularly important to the Scottish poet. The romance's consideration of young kingship is a powerful reminder of its genesis in fifteenth-century Scotland, a period in which the Stewart dynasty endured a succession of royal minorities. Hay's version of the romance may well have been written during the minority of James III (1460–59), and the revised version of the poem dates from the years immediately following the minority of James IV. Its discussion of young rule is also perhaps one of the reasons why the poem retained significance for sixteenth-century readers who witnessed the long minorities of James V, Mary, and James VI.[19]

---

[16] See John Cartwright, 'Sir Gilbert Hay's *Alexander*: A Study in Transformations', *MÆ* 60 (1991), pp. 61–72.

[17] *DOST*, v. 'assover', sense 3.

[18] See *Asloan Manuscript*, ed. Craigie, vol. 1, pp. 239–41 (240). See also Ranald Nicholson, *Scotland: The Later Middle Ages* (1974; repr. 1997), pp. 358–9.

[19] The subject would have had relevance for contemporary aristocratic families such as the Campbells, for whom the succession of a minor to an earldom could have serious implications. See Jenny Wormald, *Lords and Men in Scotland: Bonds of Manrent, 1442–1603* (1985), pp. 101–2.

In the opinion of his opponents Alexander is 'bot ane young folt and a page' (1025), a 'conterfete' (4518) king whose youth can only result in misrule. To rebut such accusations the poet describes how Alexander 'began sone in youthed to be wys' (248), inclining to innate moral as well as physical 'conditionis' (267) that make him a conquerour. Even as an untutored child he is depicted as an ideal prince who puts from him traitors, protects the church, and succours the poor.[20] Indeed, the poem's discussion of minority rule is largely optimistic in a way that some fifteenth- and sixteenth-century Scottish writing on the subject is not. For example, *Lancelot of the Laik*, a reworking of a French prose romance, adds to its source a warning that when kings reach their 'yheris of Resone' (1660) they must make amends for the injustices committed during their minorities.[21] In the later fifteenth-century poems *King Hart* and *The Thre Prestis of Peblis*, the youthful royal protagonists go astray under the influence of their vibrant but irresponsible courts, and only after some difficulty are brought in hand.[22]

Yet, *Alexander the Conquerour*'s examination of minority is not without a trace of anxiety. One striking episode that exemplifies this comes at the moment of Alexander's accession, and is almost entirely the invention of the Scottish poet. Although Philip has bequeathed his crown to Alexander, the poem departs from the Latin source to have the young king call a parliament and request that his lords 'cheis ane king with haill consent, / To quhome thair is baith wit and wisdome lent' (2437–8). Alexander presents himself as 'bot ane childe heir' (2449) and places himself in the judgement of these men of 'perfyte age' (2447). The moment he steps from the throne to the parliament makes him governor and protector. But still Alexander asks them for 'counsall, / Sen he was young' (2477–8) and in view of the responsibility imposed on him by his office:

> Yit am I nothing bot a man as ye,
> And rycht as I haue greter gouernall,
> I haue mare charge, vexatioun, and travell.   (2480–2)

Alexander's astute request for counsel thus becomes an opportunity for him to remind his lords that 'euirie man his awin charge [responsibility] mon bere' (2503). The lasting importance of this scene resides in its demonstration of the young king's worthiness to rule both in his voluntary submission to counsel and his own innate wisdom. However, it inevitably raises the possibility of the replacement of an unfit child king when a realm is under threat. Although this remedy for minority rule is not revisited in such explicit terms, the importance

---

[20] Lines 245–67. For similar injunctions in *The Ordre of Knychthede*, see Hay, *Prose Works*, ed. Glenn, pp. 20, 38.
[21] *Lancelot of the Laik*, ed. Margaret M. Gray, STS (1912).
[22] For editions see Douglas, *Shorter Poems*, ed. Bawcutt; *The Thre Prestis of Peblis*, ed. D. Robb, STS (1920).

of kings earning their office through public consent as well as inheritance and conquest remains a strong theme in the poem.[23]

Furthermore, nothwithstanding the poem's attempts to show that Alexander is wise beyond his years, the role of Aristotle as 'evir chief of his [Alexander's] governyng' (7272) is significantly extended in comparison with the sources and analogues. Despite the popularity of the *Secretum Secretorum*, Aristotle is usually a minor figure in the medieval romances of antiquity that deal with Alexander's life.[24] In contrast, the Scottish poet makes the philosopher a guiding presence throughout the first half of the poem, expanding the account of his spiritual and political instruction of Alexander in Athens (338–480) and his reiteration of these lessons after the conquest of Persia (7249–396). These episodes anticipate the formal Regiment and Physiognomy composed by Aristotle on the eve of Alexander's departure for the East,[25] which again mark a major divergence from the *Historia de Preliis* and *Roman d'Alexandre*.[26]

The Regiment is characteristically independent of its ultimate source, the *Secretum Secretorum*, but its most original passage is a complex allegory that makes explicit the connection between good self- and political rule. The allegory employs corporeal and political imagery to describe how 'A realme ... to ane man may liknit be' (9659).[27] Aristotle first compares the soul 'to ane king, / Quhilk hes ane kingrik in his governing' (9707–8). However, the heart, which is described as 'the corage' (9759) or 'ane disire and a will' (9719), is also likened to a king. Although this king's 'portaris', the five wits, guard his 'palais' (9730–1), he has enemies within his household that include 'Yewthhed', 'Ydilnes', 'Lust', 'Wantones', 'Glutoney' and 'Covarese' (9761–3). These, the king complains,

>   ... blyndit me, quhen I was myne allane,
>   And all my counsallouris was fra me tane,
>   And braik my purpusis, and changit myne entent,
>   And to thare folyis gart me thus consent.   (9765–8)

---

[23] Compare 9425–8, and see Mapstone, 'The Advice to Princes Tradition', p.109

[24] See Catherine Gaullier-Bougassas, 'Alexander and Aristotle in the French Alexander Romances', *The Medieval French Alexander*, ed. Donald Maddox and Sara Sturm Maddox (Albany, NY, 2002), pp. 57–73.

[25] On the possibility that these sections originated as independent pieces by or thought to be by Hay, see Mapstone, 'The Scots *Buke of Phisnomy*', pp. 21–3.

[26] A similar reworking of source material to include a *speculum principis* is found in *Lancelot of the Laik*, Book II.

[27] See further, Joanna Martin, ' "Had the Hous, for it is myne": Royal and Self-Reform in Older Scots Literature from *King Hart* (c. 1500) to Lyndsay's *Ane Satyre of the Thrie Estaitis* (c. 1552)', *The Medieval Household in Christian Europe, c. 850–c. 1550: Managing Power, Wealth, and the Body*, ed. Cordelia Beattie, Anna Maslakovic, and Sarah Rees Jones (Turnhout, 2003), pp. 137–54 (145–50) and, on the theological background, Priscilla Bawcutt, '*DOST* and the Literary Scholar', *Perspectives on the Older Scottish Tongue*, ed. Christian J. Kay and Margaret A. Mackay (2005), pp. 5–17 (14–15).

Inside the palace also sit the 'Grete Counsale' (9732) comprised of the regulatory figures Understanding, Reason and Memory. In conjunction with them, Conscience 'schawis the hart that he hes done erroure' (9751), calling him 'before his Parliament', where 'Discretioun' is summoned 'for to reprufe the king', and where 'Ressoun' then passes 'furth his iugment' (9753–6). With their counsel the king is able to reform, promising to become 'wourthy to haue the governance' (9774).

Although the allegory specifically identifies the enemies of good governance as youth and its attendant follies of lust and wantonness, it concludes optimistically. It is a fitting preface to Alexander's travels to the East during which the poet continues to present the king as well counselled, altering his sources to make more advisory many of the epistles Alexander receives during the period. Thus the letter of the queen of the Amazons is rewritten to remind Alexander of his duty to 'succoure, favore, and defend' (11828) women, and the first epistle of Dindimus of the Brahmins includes original advice on the nature of true sovereignty. Even Alexander's mother writes to remind her son that 'Now war it tyme a king him-selff to knaw' (17579), where the sources only mention her warnings about Antepater's treacherousness.

However, despite these extensive attempts to depict Alexander as well advised, the poet gives considerable attention to another problematic corollary of young kingship, and a subject that troubled the Older Scots writers: royal amorousness. As well as incorporating many of the amatory elements from the French Alexander romances, the Scottish poet presents his protagonist as rather more amorous than his antecedents, and increases the opportunities offered in the sources to discuss love. The poem's treatment of love is typically distinctive, making amorousness the occasion for further examination of the theme of self-restraint and thus fundamental to its advisory agenda. In some respects the poem's conclusions are again optimistic, showing that if love does lead to unwise behaviour it can be corrected. The interpolation of the popular exemplum of the bridling of Aristotle by a woman 'belouit' (7167) by Alexander thus becomes the occasion for the philosopher's composition of a 'buke' on 'how lufe ourcummys all thing' (7230–1), and Alexander's unequivocal rejection of his beloved. Even the poem's longest advisory section, Aristotle's Regiment, is precipitated by an amorous encounter associated with the king. Just before the Regiment, the poet inserts the well-known exemplum of the Poisoned Maiden. It is not found in the *Historia de Preliis* or *Roman d'Alexandre*, but is included in the *Gesta Romanorum* and some versions of the *Secretum Secretorum*, though not Hay's translation. The Scottish poet tells how the maiden is sent by the sister of Duke Melchis, who 'wist that Alexander was / Richt amorus of ladyis fare of face' (9291–2), to avenge the death of her cousin Clarus. The maiden is exceptionally beautiful and Alexander does indeed desire her. However, Aristotle urges him to observe 'hir maner of lyving' (9312) and the king is both saved from his desires and inspired to request more counsel from his teacher.

One of the most striking episodes where love is placed in an advisory framework is a section based on, but remodelled from, *Les Voeux du Paon*. Here Alexander's lifting of the Siege of Effesoun is celebrated by the young nobles of the city with the election of a King of Love to partake in a playful love debate. Duke Betis is elected to this office and swears to give 'richtwis iugment' (7959) on all questions pertaining to love, many of which are not found in the French source. Much of the debate in the Scottish text addresses love from a moral perspective. The players discuss the dangers of jealousy and 'fals sembland' (8269), how women should show 'piete' (8372), while preserving their honour, and the nature of 'wise luffe' (8211). During the debate Dame Ydory asks the King of Love, 'Quhilk ar the thewis of ane gud women' (8478). Betis's reply is in fact largely taken from a mid-fifteenth-century Scottish parental advice text, *The Thewis of Gudwomen*.[28] As Saldanha has pointed out, there is some inconsistency in having a festive king of love recommending that young women abstain from 'sangis of plesance' (8510), and something rather comic about the injunction that his gentle audience avoids gossiping on street corners.[29] But even if meant lightheartedly this interpolation from an advice text that is itself inculcating virtue in the young is hardly at odds with the romance's concern with self-mastery.

Yet despite such attempts to view desire as governable, Alexander's own amorousness does become more problematic. According to the medieval Alexander tradition, Queen Candace was the most important object of the king's own passions. In an addition to his sources, the poet describes how Alexander places himself in 'danger' (15154) of the queen, because he 'euer was to wemen swete' and 'knew of lufe the maledy' (15162, 15164). By this point Alexander is married to Roxane, so the episode sits at odds with the poem's several lessons on the dangers of adultery. Nectanabus's dying speech, which is unique to the Scottish text, includes a lesson on how adultery is 'tressoun of thi self' (342) and this is later echoed in Alexander's own rebukes of other adulterers.[30] At the end of the poem, the narrator also blames the discord that follows Alexander's death on misplaced passions – implicitly those of Alexander, as well as his parents:

> For oftymeis wrangous love againis the law
> Garris monie ane guide man to thair ending draw,
> Bot namlie of forceing and adultre
> Garris mekle sorrow happin commounlie. (19163–6)

The Scottish poet makes no attempt to excuse Alexander's adultery by laying the blame for it solely on Candace. The magnificent queen of the *Historia de*

---

[28] On the romance's use of other texts in MS Kk.1.5, see Mapstone, 'The Scots *Buke of Phisnomy*', pp. 19–20.
[29] Saldanha, '*The Thewis of Gudwomen*', pp. 295–6.
[30] Compare 2216–22; 14987–15002.

Preliis and *Roman d'Alexandre*, and the manipulative Candace of the *Roman de Toute Chevalerie*, becomes in *Alexander the Conquerour* less calculating and more troubled. In the sources it is made clear that when Alexander visits Candace in disguise she immediately recognizes his true identity and informs him of this, rejoicing that she has single-handedly captured the most powerful man in the world. In the Scottish romance she only gradually sees the likeness of her visitor to the portrait she has had made of the king and then, in an interior monologue, admits her cowardice in concealing the knowledge for fear that the king will never love her as a result. Seeing her distress, Alexander promises that she is 'assoverit now' (15191) – a word that, as discussed above, he uses to remind Caractor of his royal obligations soon after this scene. But when he hears that Candace has secretly had a portrait made of him he forgets this promise and threatens to kill her. In another departure from the sources Candace falls at his feet with 'sob and grete' (15213) and he eventually forgives her. The changes to this scene seem designed to convince us of the sincerity of Candace's affection, and perhaps to prepare us for the eventual succession of her child as Alexander's heir. Yet it is still difficult to escape the conclusion that Alexander has been overwhelmed by his desires and made careless of his royal integrity.

The inclusion of two popular Alexander anecdotes, not found in the *Historia de Preliis* or *Roman d'Alexandre*, contributes to the increasingly ambiguous presentation of the protagonist.[31] Immediately before the omens that presage Alexander's death, the poet interpolates the story of Alexander's meeting with Diogenes in which the philosopher responds to the king's request for counsel by accusing him of having 'reft with wrang and wikkitnes' (17703). At the end of Diogenes's reprimand, which is longer than in most versions of the exemplum, Alexander sees that the philosopher has spoken 'soith and fare' (17726) but makes no other response than to go on his way. This is followed by an exemplum in which Alexander accuses a pirate of oppressing his people only to be again confronted with criticism of his own conduct. The pirate claims that Alexander has 'heryit' (17742) his kin, and that such aggression 'giffis exampill' that 'reif' can bring 'grete honoure' (17746–8) to its perpetrators. He also points out the essential difference between his situation and Alexander's: 'For nede garris me, and falt of my liffing, / Quhilk thow has nocht, for thow art borne a king' (17754–5).

Alexander takes the pirate into his service, recognizing his self-knowledge, and also the 'grete necessetie' (17788) that motivated his actions. However, he does not respond to the pirate's contention that kings do not have any need to take from others. Neither story is consistent with the emphasis of much of the poem that Alexander is a liberal and just conqueror. And although both episodes again show that Alexander is capable of recognizing wise counsel,

---

[31] See George Cary, *Medieval Alexander* (Cambridge, 1956), pp. 83–95, 146–9, 253–6.

they do not show him either modifying his behaviour or fully responding to the charges levelled against him.

The questions raised by these parts of the poem are compounded in the sequence that deals with Alexander's death and its aftermath. Just before the feast at which Alexander is murdered, the narrator charges his hero with dissoluteness more explicitly than at any other point in the text:

> And commounly before ane grete myschance
> Thare cummys ane blythnes, with ane arrogance,
> And tharewith cummys a welthful wantones withall,
> And commounly sone eftir cummys ane fall. (17946–9)

The poet then extends Alexander's dying speeches into *ubi sunt* laments full of unprincely self pity for the loss of his 'robis ryall' (18065) and sensual 'plesance' (18071). Alexander's earlier complaints in the 'Wale Perrelus' and Garden of the Trees of the Sun and Moon demonstrated his ability to move from hopelessness to self-knowledge (13669–94 and 14117–19). However, his despair here is only ameliorated with the help of his queen, who is a far wiser and more resourceful consort than the insubstantial Roxane of the sources.[32] The Scottish Roxane is given six highly rhetorical addresses to her husband in place of the brief, rather reproachful lines she utters in the *Historia de Preliis* and *Roman d'Alexandre*. Her laments urge the king to confront his tribulations with patience and remember his royal obligations:

> ... 'Suete lord, think how ye ar a king –
> ...
> Ye haue sic witt and knawlege of ressoun –
> Now at a nede schaw youre discretioun.' (18111, 18114–15)

In another change to the endings of the main sources the Scottish poet focuses on the political upheaval that follows Alexander's death.[33] Alexander's principal heir Alior is a child who must be placed in the charge of Tholome as 'governour and tutour' (19232), and though the poem shows him heeding counsel and participating in the punishment of those who betrayed his father, a return to the earlier more optimistic account of minority rule is not to be. Rather, the regency government causes 'great invy' (19237) amongst Alexander's lords, and when the rest of the empire hears that both Alior and

---

[32] See Gerrit H. V. Bunt, 'A Wife There was for Alexander the Great', *A Wyf Ther Was: Essays in Honour of Paule Mertens-Fonck*, ed. Juliette Dor (Liège, 1992), pp. 41–8 (46–3); Jane H. M. Taylor, 'Alexander Amoroso', *The Medieval French Alexander*, ed. Maddox and Sturm Maddox, pp. 219–34.
[33] On the sparse account of this discord in an English analogue, see G. V. H. Bunt, 'Alexander's Last Days in the Middle English *Kyng Alisander*', *Alexander the Great in the Middle Ages: Ten Studies on the Last Days of Alexander in Literary and Historical Writing*, ed. W. J. Aerts, Jos. M. M. Hermans, and Elizabeth Visser (Nijmegen, 1978), pp. 202–29.

Alexander's half-brother Phillipone 'war young of age and tender' (19256), each land withdraws its tribute and adopts its own means of government: 'And thus the warld rais in divisioun' (19263). The poem ends with a bleak assessment of the double blight of regicide and ensuing royal minority, a predicament that became reality more than once in fifteenth-century Scotland.

III

Like much fifteenth-century Scottish literature *Alexander the Conquerour* is not directed at an exclusively courtly audience.[34] The work, the narrator tells us, is 'not compyillit' only for 'kingis and princeis and lordis that ar mychttie' but for 'all men that richteouslie wald life' (19275–7). Nevertheless the early readers of *Alexander the Conquerour* were well placed to appreciate its distinctive politicization of the Alexander legend. The poem's epilogue informs us that Hay wrote the 'first translatioun' 'At the instance off Lord Erskein' (19312, 19320), who is likely to have been Thomas, second Lord Erskine (d. 1493). Erskine's family had a history of royal service, although he does not seem to have played a major role in Scottish political life.[35]

The two manuscripts of the poem belonged in the late sixteenth century to the Perthshire landowner and book collector Duncan Campbell, seventh laird of Glenorchy (d. 1631), who rose to prominence during the minority of James VI.[36] It is generally accepted that the later copy of the poem was made for Campbell from the earlier text already in his possession, although significant differences in the rubrication of the manuscripts may suggest that the Campbell scribe had access to another witness.[37] The Glenorchy family was a cadet branch of the powerful Campbell clan, but they nevertheless had an acute sense of their own importance, and had been crucial to the crown's control over the rebellious western highlands since the reign of James IV.[38] A century separates Erskine and Campbell as readers of *Alexander the Conquerour*. The political fortunes of the latter flourished where the Erskines had a more troubled relationship with the crown, experiencing, like other fifteenth-century noble families, the Stewart dynasty's rapaciousness. In some respects however the two families were not dissimilar. Their interests were located on the geographical boundaries of Scotland's Gaelic and Lowland cultures and both

---

[34] See Sally Mapstone, 'Was there a Court Literature in Fifteenth-Century Scotland?', *SSL* 26 (1991), pp. 410–22.
[35] See *The Scots Peerage*, ed. J. Balfour Paul, 9 vols (1904–14), vol. 5, pp. 601–7.
[36] On Campbell's books see Priscilla Bawcutt, 'The Boston Public Library Manuscript of Lydgate's *Siege of Thebes*: its Scottish Owners and Inscriptions', *MÆ* 70 (2001), pp. 80–94.
[37] The later manuscript (see above, p. 76) contains over twenty rubrics not present in the earlier one. They may be the invention of the scribe, but considerable planning and knowledge of the poem would have been required by him or his patron.
[38] William A. Gillies, *In Famed Breadalbane: The Story of the Antiquities, Lands and People of the Highland District* (Perth, 1938), pp. 135–42; Julian Goodare, *State and Society in Early Modern Scotland* (Oxford, 1999), pp. 254–85.

were therefore naturally concerned with the extension of royal power into the uncivilized regions of the nation, preoccupations to which *Alexander the Conquerour* speaks articulately.

Apart from the interest of these two families the extent of *Alexander the Conquerour*'s circulation is unclear, although sections from it may have had a wider readership. John Rolland's *The Court of Venus*, composed c. 1560, contains echoes of *Alexander the Conquerour*'s Physiognomy, and this section of the poem survives excerpted in two seventeenth-century manuscripts.[39] Other Alexander literature was well known in fifteenth- and sixteenth-century Scotland. For example, a copy of the Latin *Historia Alexandri* was in the possession of Henry Barry, rector of Collace (fl. 1475) in the late fifteenth century.[40] *Alexander the Conquerour*'s narrator notes that the Alexander legend 'has oft tymes bene sene' in 'buikis of the auld translatioun' in 'this cuntrie' (6027, 6029–30). The identity of this text is unclear, especially as it is later asserted that the Alexander story was 'neuir befoir translaittit in this land' (19333), but it may be that it is a French work.[41] Indeed *Li Fuerre de Gadres* and *Les Voeux du Paon* were closely followed in *The Buik of Alexander*, c. 1438, another long poem on the Alexander theme, written in octosyllabic couplets.[42] Furthermore, when writers such as Andrew of Wyntoun,[43] and Barbour and Hary refer to Alexander they often show specific knowledge of episodes such as the Siege of Tyre and the Foray of Gadres.[44]

At about the same time as the second manuscript of *Alexander the Conquerour* was being copied, *The Buik of Alexander* was selected for publication by Alexander Arbuthnet, and now survives uniquely in his print of c. 1580. A 1578 inventory of books in Edinburgh Castle includes a volume of 'Thre Lyves of Alexander the Greit & utheris nobles'.[45] Copies of the 'Vowis of Alexander' (perhaps the Arbuthnet print) are recorded amongst the possessions of the Edinburgh bookbinder, Robert Gourlaw, in his will of 1586 and in that of the printer Henry Charteris, who died in 1601.[46]

---

[39] Mapstone, 'The Scots *Buke of Phisnomy*', pp. 5–7.
[40] John Durkan and Anthony Ross, *Early Scottish Libraries* (Glasgow, 1961), p. 75.
[41] French Alexander romances may have reached Scotland in printed editions. See generally, D. A. J. Ross, 'The Printed Editions of the French Prose Alexander Romance', in his *Studies in the Alexander Romance* (London, 1985), pp. 194–7.
[42] See *The Buik of Alexander*, ed. R. L. Ritchie, 4 vols, STS (1921–29).
[43] Wyntoun, *Original Chronicle*, ed. Amours, vol. 2, pp. 83, 151; vol. 3, pp. 95–7, 149; vol. 6, p. 433.
[44] See Barbour, *Bruce*, ed. McDiarmid and Stevenson, 1:529–36; 3:71–87 and 10:706–11; Hary, *Wallace*, ed. McDiarmid, 10:342–4 and 11:1242. The 'Boar's Tale' in *The Talis of the Fyve Bestes* (preserved in the Asloan MS) is a reworking of a popular exemplum about Alexander's readiness to spare a besieged city at the request of his tutor. For an edition see *'Colkelbie Sow' and 'The Talis of the Fyue Bestes'*, ed. Gregory Kratzmann (New York and London, 1983).
[45] *Buik of Alexander*, vol. 1, p. xxvi, n. 2.
[46] *The Bannatyne Miscellany*, vol. 2, ed. D. Laing, Bannatyne Club 19 (Edinburgh 1836), pp. 210, 224.

This continued interest in Alexander literature speaks of the cultural importance of the hero in late medieval and early modern Scotland. The nature of the extensive reworking and synthesis of materials from this vast tradition in *Alexander the Conquerour* gives us an intriguing indication of the reasons for that response. With its complex treatment of minority rule and royal amorousness, the poem resists clear alignment with either the wholly positive or negative aspects of the Alexander tradition. It is by turns optimistic and admonitory, and surely one of the most fascinating, if elusive, of Older Scots texts.

6

Henryson's Morall Fabillis: *Structure and Meaning*

RODERICK J. LYALL

Nowhere has the rapid development in Older Scots studies been more apparent than in the transformation which has taken place in the critical reception of Robert Henryson's *Morall Fabillis*. Although several early studies attempted an overview of Henryson's use of the fable form, the most rewarding serious studies tended to treat each fable as a separate item, and this approach produced some notable essays, which have illuminated our understanding of the local effects Henryson creates in particular cases.[1] An important contribution to a more comprehensive view of the sequence was I. W. A. Jamieson's thesis on Henryson's sources,[2] but even this detailed and scholarly study did not fully engage with the coherence of the *Fabillis*, and the same can be said of John MacQueen's pioneering *Robert Henryson: A Study of the Major Narrative Poems*, which is heavily indebted to Jamieson's work.[3] Yet it is now recognized that the collection is a carefully-structured whole, and that Henryson draws on a wide range of narrative and hermeneutic materials to elevate the essentially simple fable genre to new rhetorical and didactic heights.

The *Fabillis* can be divided into five major sections, three of which are drawn from a single source, the elegiac Romulus collection that was the best-known version of 'Esope' throughout the Middle Ages.[4] To this basic material, itself

---

[1] Among the most important are: John Block Friedman, 'Henryson, the Friars and the *Confessio Reynardi*', *JEGP* 66 (1967), pp. 550–61; I. W. A. Jamieson, 'Henryson's *Taill of the Wolf and the Wedder*', *SSL* 6 (1968–69), pp. 248–57; J. A. Burrow, 'Henryson: *The Preaching of the Swallow*', *Essays in Criticism* 25 (1975), pp. 23–37; Robert Pope, 'A Sly Toad, Physiognomy and the Problem of Deceit: Henryson's *The Paddok and the Mous*', *Neophilologus* 63 (1979), pp. 461–8; idem., 'Henryson's *The Sheep and the Dog*', *Essays in Criticism* 30 (1980), pp. 205–14; Douglas Gray, *Robert Henryson* (Leiden, 1979); pp. 31–161; Craig McDonald, 'The Perversion of Law in Robert Henryson's Fable of the *Fox, the Wolf and the Husbandman*', *MÆ* 49 (1980), pp. 244–53.
[2] I. W. A. Jamieson, 'The Poetry of Robert Henryson: A Study of the Use of Source Material', unpublished Ph.D. thesis (Edinburgh, 1964).
[3] John MacQueen, *Robert Henryson: A Study of the Major Narrative Poems* (Oxford, 1967), pp. 94–221.
[4] This collection has often been attributed to Gualterus Anglicus (Walter the Englishman), and the name is still widely applied in Henryson studies. It is, however, based on one doubtful manuscript attribution, and has now been abandoned by scholars working on the medieval

elaborated in a variety of ways, Henryson added two groups of fables that build upon and extend the penetration of the Aesopic tradition by the more political and more comic tradition of beast-epic, centred in the *Roman de Renart* and including the *fabulae extravagantes*, fables not in the Romulus collection which had developed since the thirteenth century. This essentially symmetrical pattern can be illustrated in tabular form:

0	Prologue	Elegiac Romulus
1	Cock and the Jasp	Elegiac Romulus 1
2	Two Mice	Elegiac Romulus 12
3	The Cock and the Fox	Chaucer, *Nun's Priest's Tale*
4	Fox and the Wolf	Various (?*Roman de Renart*)
5	The Trial of the Fox	?Pseudo–Odo of Cheriton
6	Sheep and the Dog	Elegiac Romulus 4
7	Lion and the Mouse	Elegiac Romulus 18
8	Preaching of the Swallow	Elegiac Romulus 20
9	Fox, the Wolf and the Cadger	?*Roman de Renart*, Branche XIV
10	Fox, the Wolf and the Husbandman	Steinhöwel, Petrus Alfonsi
11	Wolf and the Wedder	Steinhöwel, *Extravagantes*
12	Wolf and the Lamb	Elegiac Romulus 2
13	Paddock and the Mouse	Elegiac Romulus 3

The care with which this design was put into effect has been increasingly recognized since the completion of H. H. Roerecke's important dissertation on the subject in 1969. His arguments were adopted and developed by Denton Fox in his 1981 edition, and are largely confirmed by George D. Gopen.[5] Although some sixteenth-century witnesses, especially the manuscript anthology compiled in 1565–68 by George Bannatyne, arrange their fables in different orders, the careful symmetries of the Bassandyne print of *The Morall Fabillis* (1571) seem to have been an essential element of the final design, and it is difficult to believe that this was not authorial.[6]

Aesopic tradition; the preferable alternatives are elegiac Romulus or (from the provenance of one important manuscript) the Anonymous Neveleti. On this issue see Edward Wheatley, *Mastering Aesop: Medieval Education, Chaucer and his Followers* (Gainesville, Fla., 2000), especially pp. 3–4.

[5] H. H. Roerecke, 'The Integrity and Symmetry of Robert Henryson's *Moral Fables*', unpublished Ph.D. thesis (Pennsylvania State University, 1969); Henryson, *Poems*, ed. Fox, pp. lxxv–lxxxi; George D. Gopen, 'The Essential Seriousness of Robert Henryson's *Moral Fables*: A Study in Structure', *Studies in Philology* 82 (1985), pp. 42–59.

[6] For the suggestion that Bannatyne's order is closer to Henryson's intentions, see John MacQueen, 'The Text of Henryson's *Morall Fabillis*', *IR* 14 (1963), pp. 3–9. On the Bannatyne MS more generally, see *The Bannatyne Manuscript (NLS Adv. MS. 1.1.6)*, introd. Denton Fox and William A. Ringler (London, 1980).

It does not follow from this, however, that Bannatyne's text of the *Fabillis* has no independent value, or that its usefulness is confined to the many places in which its readings are likely to be better than the somewhat anglicized texts of the early printers. In particular, the absence in the Bannatyne MS of the second group of fables drawn from beyond the elegiac Romulus may hint at a significant feature of the collection's transmission: given the poet's desire to create a balanced structure, it would not be surprising if this group ('The Fox, the Wolf and the Cadger', 'The Fox, the Wolf and the Husbandman' and 'The Wolf and the Wedder') were to have been added last, to mirror the earlier triad which Bannatyne describes as 'The Buke of the Tod'. Two of the three were almost certainly drawn from the Aesopic collection made by Heinrich Steinhöwel (1476/7) and must therefore have been written after 1476; if it were possible to determine which of the many versions of this collection Henryson used we could perhaps further limit the date.[7]

The dating of the *Morall Fabillis* is rendered all the more difficult because we know so little about their author and his career. A reference by William Dunbar to the fact that 'In Dunfermelyne he [Death] has done rovne / With maister Robert Henrisoun'[8] suggests that he had died fairly recently when Dunbar wrote these lines, which by general agreement was in the summer of 1505.[9] It also associates Henryson with the burgh of Dunfermline, and by using the title 'Maister' indicates that he was a university graduate. Since sixteenth-century editions of the *Fabillis* describe the author as 'scolmaister of Dunfermling' – for which there is no independent documentary evidence, but which is likely enough – it seems probable that the poet can also be identified with the notary public Master Robert Henryson who witnessed three documents for the abbot of Dunfermline between March and July 1478.[10] Combining functions such as schoolmaster and notary public was not uncommon in fifteenth-century Scotland and both the fact that the elegiac Romulus was a standard grammar-school text, used in the teaching of elementary Latin, and the precision with which Henryson deploys legal terminology and procedure, lend credence to the admittedly circumstantial acceptance of these identifications. It is also probable, though not quite certain, that the master of that name who, as master of Arts and bachelor in Decreets (canon law), was incorporated in the university of Glasgow on 10 September 1462, was the poet; the significance of this procedure is that it was necessary for graduates of another university, and it therefore indicates that Henryson had acquired his academic qualifications

---

[7] On this relationship, see R. J. Lyall, 'Henryson's *Morall Fabillis* and the Steinhöwel Tradition', *FMLS* 38 (2002), pp. 362–81.
[8] 'I that in heill wes and gladnes' (B 21), 81–2. All references are to Dunbar, *The Poems*, ed. Bawcutt.
[9] Dunbar, *The Poems*, ed. Bawcutt, pp. 333–7.
[10] NLS Advocates MS 34.1.3a, fols 63r–64r.

elsewhere.[11] The problem is that he appears nowhere in the extant records of any fifteenth-century university, neither in St Andrews, nor in the Continental universities where Scots most commonly studied, nor anywhere else. Such records are, it is true, frequently fragmentary, and it is conceivable that Henryson studied law in Orléans, where many Scots went and where there are no detailed matriculation, graduation or other lists giving full information about those students forming the Scottish Nation. All we can say for sure, however, is that if the Glasgow master of 1462 is the poet, then he must have spent much of the 1450s studying, and was born no later than about 1435, making him at least seventy at the time of his death.

Such a biographical outline is consistent with the writing of the *Morall Fabillis* in the 1480s, but does little to confirm it. If the Steinhöwel collection is indeed reflected in two fables then these must have been written after 1476; but any more precise dating hinges upon allegedly topical references in several fables, which have been taken as referring to specific events and personalities in the last years of the reign of James III, between the Lauder Bridge crisis of 1482, when the king was seized by his magnates, and his death in 1488.[12] This is an issue to which we shall return below, but even if some degree of topicality is conceded – a point which is at least highly debatable – it does not follow that Henryson completed his sequence while James III was on the throne; it is equally possible that the political lessons that the *Fabillis* undoubtedly draw were directed at his son James IV, who became king as a result of the rebellion in which his father died. The most we can say, then, is that the sequence probably achieved its final form during the final quarter of the fifteenth century.

As the table above illustrates, the selection which Henryson made from the elegiac Romulus includes the Prologue and the first four fables, together with the twelfth, eighteenth and twentieth in the order in which the Latin collection appears in almost all manuscripts. Since he evidently devoted a good deal of attention to the final design of his sequence, it follows that there must have been good reasons both for the choices which he made and the way in which he rearranged the familiar order. What is clear is that the subjects of the three fables which he took from the middle of the elegiac Romulus (the perils of social ambition; the importance of equitable administration of the law; and the hazards of disregarding moral advice) all recur elsewhere in the *Morall Fabillis*, and that these are themes that are at the heart of the Scots poet's moral vision. They help to give the *Fabillis* their strongly sociopolitical emphasis and integrate this into a larger concern with man's desperate spiritual plight; and it is no accident that two of the three occupy a crucial position in the centre of the sequence. By the same token, two of the initial group of four Romulus fables

---

[11] For the incorporation, see *Munimenta Alme Universitatis Glasguensis*, ed. Cosmo Innes, 3 vols, Maitland Club (Glasgow, 1854), vol. 3, p. 69.

[12] For the topical claims, see, for instance, MacQueen, *Robert Henryson*, pp. 150–3, 170–3; Ranald Nicholson, *Scotland: The Later Middle Ages* (1974; rpt 1997), pp. 500 and 509.

are shifted to the final two places in the *Fabillis*, completing the ever-darkening vision of the sequence by showing the triumph of legal anarchy and the fatal consequences of unbridled appetite. Henryson's skilled deployment of his Aesopic materials ensures a degree of coherence to which earlier fable collections do not aspire.

The *Morall Fabillis* open with a version of the Prologue Henryson found in the elegiac Romulus, a connection he emphasizes by quoting the second line (*Dulcius arrident seria picta jocis*, 'serious subjects are more pleasing if combined with humour'). He takes up the standard metaphorical language of his source – flowers and fruit, shell and kernel – and develops it, extending the twelve lines of the Latin to nine rhyme-royal stanzas. In doing so, he makes fully explicit the goal of the fable form in reproving man's 'misleuing' and linking this to the genre's characteristic use of animal characters:

> Na meruell is, ane man be lyke ane beist,
> Quhilk lufis ay carnall and foull delyte,
> That schame can not him renye nor arreist,
> Bot takis all the lust and appetyte,
> Quhilk throw custum and the daylie ryte
> Syne in the mynd sa fast is radicate
> That he in brutal beist is transformate.   (50–6)

Behind this argument lies the Aristotelian model of human psychology, which Henryson also uses in his *Orpheus and Eurydice*: sensual appetites belong to man's animal nature, and must be governed by the rational faculty of the soul. To give oneself up to the senses, then, is indeed to become 'lyke ane beist', and this makes the fable a most appropriate vehicle for demonstrating the individual and social consequences of such behaviour.

Henryson is also careful in his Prologue to emphasize that his work is 'ane maner of translatioun' (32), and to associate it with the authority of 'Esope'. His Latin quotation is part of this strategy, bedding the vernacular text in the school book that would have been familiar to many of his readers. As Edward Wheatley has noted, the use of the elegiac Romulus in grammar schools had led to the accumulation of a substantial body of scholastic commentary, and while we do not know which precise version or versions Henryson used, it is virtually certain that he drew upon this tradition.[13] The voice his narrator assumes has a schoolmasterly quality, drawing attention to the rhetorical skills of his animal characters, who 'to gude purpois dispute and argow, / Ane sillogisme propone, and eik conclude ...' (45–6). He also stresses that the enterprise owes its origin not to his own 'vane presumptioun' but rather to the 'requeist and precept of ane lord', whose name it is unnecessary to provide (33–5). This seems a typically Henrysonian touch, displacing responsibility for the idea but then

---

[13] Wheatley, *Mastering Aesop*, especially pp. 149–89.

declining to identify its true begetter. Naming one's patron being a fairly common ploy in medieval prologues, this reticence creates a curious rhetorical gap right at the outset; should we doubt the aristocratic patron's existence, or might we suspect that his anonymity is linked in some way to the sequence's political themes?

The Prologue's concern with questions of interpretation is neatly highlighted by the opening fable, 'The Cock and the Jasp', in which the Cock rejects the jewel he finds on the grounds that it is inedible. We might be tempted to see this as a laudable contempt for wealth, but Henryson follows elegiac Romulus in – somewhat arbitrarily – interpreting the jasper as wisdom, 'perfite prudence and cunning' (128), and the Cock as a fool who ignores its gifts. His technique is again one of expansion: ten Latin lines become fourteen stanzas, six of them devoted to the *moralitas* which in the original is summed up in a single elegiac couplet. Within the narrative itself, many little touches add to the richness of the fable: the apparent digression about the possibility that careless maidservants were responsible for the jewel's presence in the midden (71–7) ironically evokes the biblical parable of the pearl of great price, while the greatly expanded speech with which the Cock rejects the jasper ends with a passage which introduces a sociopolitical theme absent from the Latin: 'Quhar suld thow mak thy habitatioun? / Quhar suld thow duell, bot in ane royall tour?' (106–7). This deferential posture could be seen as the kind of modesty so notably lacking from such subsequent characters as the Burgess Mouse in 'The Two Mice' and the Wedder in 'The Wolf and the Wedder', but it is completely invalidated by the allegorical interpretation Henryson imposes, since the 'science' the jewel represents is equally desirable in men of every social station. And by the end of the *moralitas* he has strengthened this point considerably, setting the tone for the rest of the sequence by lamenting that 'now, allace, this iasp is tynt and hid. / We seik it nocht, nor preis it for to find' (155–6). This sense that 'nowadays' the claims of moral wisdom are especially disregarded will come to be a leitmotiv of the *Fabillis*, and we can be in little doubt that the narrator's concluding injunction to 'Ga seik the iasp' relates, in part at least, to the reading process on which we have now embarked.

A static and narratively straightforward tale, 'The Cock and the Jasp' gave Henryson limited opportunities to demonstrate his skills as a story-teller. 'The Two Mice', on the other hand, has a more developed plot, and Henryson takes full advantage of this. Here we see the delicate balance between animal and human characteristics exploited to the full: the Burgess Mouse sets out to visit her sister 'Bairfute allone, with pykestaf in hir hand, / As pure pylgryme' (180–1), but as she struggles over the furrows in the ploughed fields she urges her to 'Cry peip anis!' (187). In the same way, the meal which the Burgess Mouse proudly produces imitates 'Ane lordis fair' (271) in almost every respect, but the sisters conclude by eating a candle 'In steid off spyce, to gust thair mouth withall' (287). These details greatly enrich the comic possibilities of the original, but the humour contributes significantly to the fable's moral argument:

whereas in the elegiac Romulus the Burgess Mouse merely whets her sister's desire to experience the good life and the scene is portrayed from the country mouse's point of view, in Henryson the emphasis is laid upon the contempt with which the Burgess Mouse reacts to her hostess's spartan hospitality:

> 'My fair sister,' quod scho, 'haue me excusit;
> This rude dyat and I can not accord.
> To tender meit my stomok is ay vsit,
> For quhy I fair alsweill as ony lord.
> Thir wydderit peis and nuttis, or thay be bord,
> Wil brek my teith and mak my wame ful sklender,
> Quhilk vsit wes before to meitis tender.' (218–24)

Henryson has prepared for this moment with some care, placing the upwardly-mobile Burgess Mouse socially by informing us that she was 'gild brother and made ane fre burges, / Toll-fre als, but custum mair or les' (172–3), parodying the freedoms of the medieval burgh and the social aspirations of its citizens. The elegiac Romulus disposes of the town mouse's rural adventure in six lines; Henryson expands this to eleven stanzas, in which the arrogance of the Burgess Mouse is contrasted with the Uponlandis Mouse's quiet acceptance of her lot. The latter's answers to her sister's criticisms are to the point: she observes that she is the one who stays faithful to family tradition and (Henryson here transfers aphorisms which in the Latin come from the narrator into the voice of one of his characters) that food willingly shared tastes better than that grudgingly provided.

The fable's final episode is also significantly developed: most versions have only one occasion on which the mice's feast is interrupted, but Henryson doubles the effect by bringing in not only the spenser at line 293 but – after the Burgess Mouse has shown her disregard for this danger – 'Gib Hunter, our iolie cat', who seizes the Uponlandis Mouse:

> Fra fute to fute he kest hir to and fra,
> Quhylis vp, quhylis doun, als tait as ony kid.
> Quhylis wald he lat hir rin vnder the stra;
> Quhylis wald he wink, and play with hir buk heid. (330–3)

This typically Henrysonian passage works on at least three levels: it is an acutely observed piece of animal behaviour; it reinforces in concrete terms the perils of the luxurious life; and through its use of the 'quhylis ... quhylis' formula it alludes to a familiar topos of Fortune literature, emphasizing the vicissitudes of human existence. It thus gives sharper point to the fable's moral lesson, and Henryson returns to it in a *moralitas* which is otherwise a fairly straightforward expansion of the traditional reading in favour of 'joyful poverty', observing menacingly: 'Luke to thy self, I warne the well on deid. / The cat cummis and to the mous hes ee' (383–4). This is as close as this *moralitas* comes to allegory, and it continues the pattern of Henryson's much more pointed concern with the consequences of human sinfulness.

Up to this point in the *Fabillis* we have seen the skill with which Henryson develops his Aesopic materials, but he now introduces a much more diverse range of sources. As Arnold Clayton Henderson has pointed out,[14] Henryson was by no means the only writer of the later Middle Ages to explore the territory between Aesopic fable and the more overtly satirical and comic world of the *Roman de Renart*, but he undoubtedly took the integration further and gave it more structural purpose. 'The Cock and the Fox', which owes a great deal to Chaucer's *Nun's Priest's Tale*,[15] introduces this expansion of the sequence's horizons, and this in itself illustrates the complexity of the traditions Henryson was using. An episode in the *Ysengrimus*, the Latin beast epic that is apparently behind the development of the vernacular *Renart*, the story of the vain cock who is tricked by the fox was quickly absorbed into medieval fable collections such as those of Ademar of Chabannes, John of Capua and Odo of Cheriton, so that it is impossible to say whether it belongs more to one tradition or the other. Chaucer's version, of course, gives the fable another generic context; Henryson restores it to its Aesopic roots, but retains much of the narrative sophistication he found in Chaucer and which is characteristic of his own practice. One key alteration, however, shifts the moral weight of the fable quite radically: in place of the opening debate between Chauntecleir and Pertelote, Henryson introduces *three* hens at the moment at which Chantecleir is disappearing into the undergrowth firmly clasped in the fox's jaws. They are, moreover, clearly drawn from the medieval antifeminist tradition, two of them revealing their sexual rapacity and cynicism, while the third offers a moralistic reading of the cock's punishment and 'death' that might on the face of it seem to echo the voice of the narrator, but which is undermined by the fact that Chantecleir is ultimately able to escape.

This explicitly Providential outcome – the narrative informs us that Chantecleir's sudden reversal of roles is 'with sum gude spirit inspyrit' (558) – repeats the comic pattern of 'The Two Mice', with the additional twist that whereas the Uponlandis Mouse is essentially an innocent who is led into danger by her sister's arrogant materialism, it is Chantecleir's own pride that makes him vulnerable to Lowrence's duplicity. The cock's escape, then, reflects a moral balance in which the sinner can still benefit from divine intervention, a possibility that becomes steadily less evident as the sequence's moral vision darkens. The introduction of elements from the beast-epic tradition contributes to this movement by sharpening the social focus, but also by lending a comic dimension which frequently involves a greater degree of violence than is usual

---

[14] 'Having Fun with the Moralities: Henryson's *Fables* and Late-Medieval Fable Innovation', *SSL* 32 (2001), pp. 67–87.

[15] See Donald MacDonald, 'Henryson and Chaucer: Cock and Fox', *Texas Studies in Literature and Language* 8 (1966–67), pp. 451–61.

in the Aesopic fable. We can observe this pattern even within this first triad of fox-and-wolf fables: the violence of 'The Cock and the Fox' is threatened rather than actualized and is ultimately denied by the comic reversal of the ending: that of 'The Fox and the Wolf' is overshadowed by the extended narrative of the fox's confession; and it is only in 'The Trial of the Fox' that the endemic harshness of the *Roman de Renart* begins to dominate Henryson's moral world.

With this darkening of the moral vision the use of beast epic also brings greater narrative complexity. 'The Fox and the Wolf' comprises three main elements, drawn from different traditions and centring on the confession that Lowrence makes to the itinerant friar Wolf 'Waitskaith', or 'Do-Harm'. There is no precise source or analogue for this episode, although, as Denton Fox remarks, the motif of the fox's confession recurs throughout the *Roman de Renart*, and the wolf as confessor does occur in one fable by Odo of Cheriton.[16] There are structural parallels between Lowrence's gulling of Chantecleir in the preceding fable and his treatment of the Wolf here, but with the crucial difference that, since they are both predators, fox and wolf have a great deal in common. This lends satiric point to the ease with which Lowrence is able to negotiate his penance: to his request that the fasting he is required to undertake be lessened somewhat, the Wolf concedes that 'neid may haif na law', to which Lowrence responds with 'that text weill I knaw' (731–2).[17] Henryson is participating here in the medieval antimendicant tradition, and the Wolf's name points towards his complicity in the sinfulness it is his supposed function to absolve. The opening of the fable, however, raises different issues, as Lowrence reads his horoscope and concludes that imminent death confronts him, 'My misleuing the soner bot I mend' (652). In terms of the medieval debate about astrology, the question of whether one can avoid one's fate through one's own actions is not straightforward, but the point is that Lowrence, as his confession illustrates, has no intention of reforming. He apparently believes that by merely observing the form he can somehow change the spiritual reality, and through his laxity as a confessor the Wolf implicitly encourages him in this view.

Lowrence repeats the moral misunderstanding in the fable's third element, in which after a fitful attempt at fishing he pretends to turn a kid into a salmon in a parody of baptism. A version of a group of fables which became attached to the Romulus tradition at a very early date,[18] this episode acquires new point in the sacramental context provided by Lowrence's confession. As he had earlier abused that ritual, he now perverts the ritual of christening. As I have suggested

---

[16] Henryson, *The Poems*, ed. Fox, p. 222.
[17] On the penitential background to this 'text', see *The Vision of Piers Plowman*, ed. A. V. C. Schmidt (London, 1976), passus XX. 10–22.
[18] Gerd Dicke and Klaus Grubmüller, *Die Fabeln des Mittelalters und der frühen Neuzeit: ein Katalog der deutschen Versionen und ihrer lateinischen Entsprechungen* (Munich, 1987), pp. 683–6.

elsewhere,[19] the pattern of error which Lowrence displays here has deep-lying theological roots: in his apparent conviction that words can in themselves constitute reality he reveals traces of nominalism, while his belief that he can avoid the consequences of his actions without true moral reform would have been seen as evidence of Pelagianism. Henryson adds, moreover, a further twist to the fable, in which the fox, shot by the vengeful goatherd in a reprisal for the death of the kid, suggests with his dying breath that the cause of his death is a pleasantry he has just uttered. Even in death he persists in folly; whereas the vain Chantecleir is saved by divine inspiration, Lowrence is so committed to sin that for him there can be no assistance. This contrast is not coincidental, and it is with this fable that death – both that of the innocent kid and that of the recalcitrant fox – enters the sequence for the first time.

The final element of this group, 'The Trial of the Fox', reveals as elaborate a narrative as 'The Fox and the Wolf'. Its core is formed by a version of a fairly obscure fable which attached itself to the collection of Odo of Cheriton, itself a more political adaptation of a story which occurs in the earliest collections of *fabulae extravagantes*.[20] But upon this simple tale of an ass who refuses to attend the Lion's parliament and shows her 'privilege' by kicking the Fox in the head Henryson has lavished all his narrative skill, providing a catalogue of those attending the parliament and adding a Renardian episode in which the fox is accused of murdering a lamb and hanged. He also provides, for the first time in the sequence, an extended allegorical reading of the fable, interpreting the Lion as this world and his parliament as a token of the hold materialism has over sinful man. If we have been inclined to see the punishment of the fox as evidence of royal justice in action, therefore, the *moralitas* forces us to reconsider this reading, and it is significant that the crime for which Lowrence is punished is technically that of murder within a mile of parliament rather than the killing itself. In terms of the *moralitas*, then, it is the Lion's power that Lowrence's death reinforces, and not any more abstract concept of justice.[21] The social world of this fable, even more than those which immediately precede it, owes much to the comic violent, satirical context of the *Roman de Renart*, and Henryson here shows how these materials can be employed to deepen the moral complexity of his initial Aesopic model.

Reverting to the elegiac Romulus for the middle triad of his sequence, Henryson now begins to ring the changes in earnest. The three fables are thematically linked, in that 'The Sheep and the Dog' and 'The Lion and the

---

[19] R. J. Lyall, 'Henryson, the Hens and the Pelagian Fox: a Poet and the Intellectual Currents of his Age', *Older Scots Literature*, ed. Sally Mapstone (2005), pp. 83–94.

[20] Dicke and Grubmüller, *Die Fabeln*, pp. 494–6. For an English version of the sub-Odonian fable, see *Babrius and Phaedrus*, ed. Ben Edwin Perry (Cambridge, Mass. and London, 1965), pp. 557–8.

[21] It is important not to push this point too far: since the fox is interpreted as 'temptationis' in the *moralitas*, any systematic reading back from this interpretation to the detail of the narrative ultimately becomes nonsensical.

Mouse' both confront issues of justice and the administration of the law, while the latter fable and 'The Preaching of the Swallow' deal with the offering of moral instruction and the fate of those who ignore it. In each of the three, moreover, we see the poet playing with the fable form: in 'The Sheep and the Dog' the traditional boundary between the narrative and the *moralitas* is violated when the fiction of talking animals is suddenly allowed to intrude into the latter's rhetorical space; 'The Lion and the Mouse' is provided with a framing dream-vision so that the fable is narrated by Aesop himself; and 'The Preaching of the Swallow' has a thirteen-stanza prologue which establishes its wider doctrinal significance and neatly fits into the beginning of the narrative proper. While these fables are unequivocally part of the mainstream Romulus tradition, Henryson is clearly concerned to push the genre to its limits, and in the process to raise the level of theological (and sociopolitical) discourse of which it is capable. By making Aesop the narrator of his central fable, and by allowing him to express his doubts about the value of fictive instruction in a world in which even 'haly preiching' is ineffective, the Scots poet affects a certain anxiety about his own enterprise, but the emphasis here – reinforced by the tragic ending of 'The Preaching of the Swallow' – is more upon the decadence of the age than upon the limitations of art.

In the Latin verse original, 'The Sheep and the Dog' is a simple tale of the abuse of power. Henryson considerably develops the legal framework, which is inherent in the fable, drawing on his legal expertise to give greater weight to the sense of corrupted justice. He also makes it clear that his primary target is the ecclesiastical courts: it is explicitly a 'consistorie' before which the Dog calls his opponent (1148), and all the terms employed in the narrative relate to this context. This gives much greater significance to the conspiracy of predators and carrion creatures who stack the court's procedures against the Sheep, and while Henryson redresses the balance somewhat in the *moralitas* by there relating the narrative to a temporal sheriff court, the main thrust of the fable itself addresses the abuses of the Church's courts. Another important development lies in the management of the dialogue, scarcely present in traditional versions of the fable. This is a key element in Henryson's narrative art, and it is evident in all his expansions of Aesopic material. Here the Sheep's arguments against his judges make the case against institutionalized injustice fully explicit, while the remarkable intrusion of his complaint into the privileged space of the *moralitas* not only lends additional rhetorical weight to the fable's moral point, but offers an explanation of the miserable conditions 'now in this world' (1299): God's apparent neglect is punishment for 'our grit offence', the general pervasiveness of sin in a society unwilling to contemplate reform. The political dimension of the sequence is thus closely linked to Henryson's larger moral theme: social injustice and misery are symptoms of man's fallen condition.

It is a theme Esope takes up in the prologue to the collection's central fable:

'Now in this warld me think richt few or nane
To Goddis word that hes deuotioun;
The eir is deif, the hart is hard as stane;
Now oppin sin without correctioun,
The e inclynand to the eirth ay doun.
Sa roustit is the warld with canker blak
That now my taillis may lytill succour mak.' (1391–7)

The fable he agrees, after a mild protest, to recount, enacts, however, a more positive political narrative: although the Lion is initially culpable in his neglect of his royal duty, sleeping in the 'fair forest' of 'the warld and his prosperitie' as the *moralitas* explains (1580–2), his willingness to heed the Mouse's eloquent arguments and to pardon her crime of *lèse majesté* both illustrates a more benign view of justice than that we have seen in 'The Sheep and the Dog' and is a key to the Lion's own escape from the nets in which he in his turn is captured. If the preceding fable and Esope's complaint suggest that the world is irredeemably corrupt, then, the fable that he tells indicates the opposite, presenting a process of reform which, significantly, begins with the king himself. Whether or not Henryson was alluding to the events of 1482, it is clear that the contemporary conditions in a more general sense are literally central to his concerns, although the *moralitas* concludes by laying the responsibility for change upon the prayers of 'kirkmen' and the need for 'lordis' to 'keip thair fay / Vnto thair souerane lord' (1618–19).

This 'authoritative' narrative, framed by Esope's scepticism about the effectiveness of the genre in present circumstances, provides the last optimistic fable in the sequence. The remaining six all reflect, in varying degrees, a dark world in which sin, violence and injustice are endemic, and the prospect of effective change seems increasingly remote. This movement is introduced by 'The Preaching of the Swallow', where the Swallow's wisdom is neglected by the other birds, intent upon satisfying their material appetites. There is an echo here, not only of the complaint of Esope but also of the folly of the Cock in the opening fable. But now the narrator provides another level of doctrinal analysis: the first thirteen stanzas constitute a kind of prologue, in which the wonders of the physical world, evidence of God's providential design, are contrasted with man's spiritual blindness. Dark as the poet's moral vision may appear to be, it is informed by a powerful sense of divine majesty and benignity, and it is significant that he chooses to introduce this very un-Aesopic passage at the very moment when he is beginning the *Fabillis*' dark second half with one of his most tragic narratives.[22] The skill with which he manages the formal design, moreover, is evident in his handling of the temporal sequence: commencing the prologue's conventional characterization of the seasons in high summer, Henryson proceeds through autumn and winter (significantly allocated two

---

[22] For an exemplary reading of this fable, see Burrow, *'Preaching of the Swallow'*.

stanzas in contrast to the other seasons' one) to a spring that then becomes the first season of the narrative proper. This ensures that the fable ends in a bleak midwinter in which the desperately hungry birds are massacred by the fowler:

> Allace, it wes grit hart sair for to se
> That bludie bowcheour beit thay birdis doun,
> And for till heir, quhen thay wist weill to de,
> Thair cairfull sang and lamentatioun.   (1874–7)

After this powerful and essentially pessimistic conclusion, the symmetries of Henryson's design required him to introduce a second group of fox-and-wolf fables. As indicated above, it is possible that this triad was the final component to be added to the sequence: they bring another remarkable shift in tone, reaching back across the central group of Aesopic fables to the sub-Renardian world of 'The Trial of the Fox'. 'The Fox, the Wolf and the Cadger', indeed, is the only one of the *Morall Fabillis* that had found no place in the fable tradition proper before Henryson adopted it: its origins are in the *Ysengrimus*, and while moralists such as John Bromyard and Stephen of Bourbon had incorporated it in their collections of exempla, it seems never to have been taken up by Odo of Cheriton or other medieval fabulists who raided the beast-epic for new materials.[23] Henryson's version turns on a tantalisingly obscure pun, for the trick by which the Fox uses the Wolf's greed for the carrier's herrings to get him thoroughly beaten hinges on the promise of a 'nekhering', which the Wolf wrongly understands to be a superior form of fish (2114ff). There is evidence that this rare word meaning 'a blow on the neck' was known in English in the later fifteenth century, and it is possible that it was already associated with this story in Henryson's source.[24] Whatever the truth of this, it adds a good deal to the comic point of the narrative, and to the rivalry of Fox and Wolf, a recurring motif of the *Roman de Renart* and in which the stupidity of the latter is systematically contrasted with the former's cunning – this evidently, is central to the four Fox-Wolf tales of the *Morall Fabillis*. And here, where he is free to devise a *moralitas* of his choosing, Henryson again adopts the allegorical hermeneutic technique he had employed in 'The Trial of the Fox', interpreting the Wolf as man, the Fox as the world, the Cadger as death, and the herring as 'the gold sa reid' (2205–16). Not all the details make sense in these terms, but Henryson seems comfortable with a certain dissonance between narrative and *moralitas*, provided that the main thrust of his argument is clear.

The rivalry of stupid, violent wolf and cunning, duplicitous fox is central to 'The Fox, the Wolf and the Husbandman', one of the two fables Henryson seems to have derived from some version of Heinrich Steinhöwel's printed collection (although he almost certainly knew the *Disciplina clericalis* of Petrus

---

[23] Dicke and Grubmüller, *Die Fabeln*, pp. 271–2.
[24] Henryson, *The Poems*, ed. Fox, pp. 294–5.

Alfonsi, in which the fable also occurs).[25] The comic possibilities of this Renardian interaction bring out Henryson's narrative mastery to the full, while his preoccupation with legal procedure – and especially defective legal procedure – is evident in Lowrence's negotiation of his way into the position of 'iuge amycabill' (2310) in the dispute between the Wolf and the Husbandman. As in the *Roman de Renart*, Lowrence's motivation is complex: he uses the situation to extract a bribe of hens from the Husbandman, but he also seems to enjoy his trickery for its own sake, and the scene in which he leads the Wolf around the landscape, trying to work out how he can deliver the cheese he has promised him, invites our admiration for his improvisational skills:

> Lowrence wes euer remembring vpon wrinkis
> And subtelties, the volff for to begyle;
> That he had hecht ane caboik he forthinkis;
> Yit at the last he findis furth ane wyle,
> Than at him selff softlie couth he smyle.   (2378–82)

We see the smile, but the Wolf clearly does not; and the fact that we have become complicit in the fox's scheme has important moral implications, since the *moralitas* will reveal that he represents 'the Feind ... / Arctand ilk man to ryn vnrychteous rinkis' (2431–2). Other aspects of the moralization, which Henryson substitutes for the much simpler lessons he found in his sources, are more problematic, not least the interpretation of the hens with which the Husbandman bribes the fox, as 'warkis that fra ferme faith proceidis' (2437). Again we have that dissonance that recurs throughout the *Morall Fabillis*, especially where allegory is employed: while there may be some degree of 'Protestantizing revision' involved, it seems that Henryson takes pleasure in confronting his readers with such 'difficult' forms of moral interpretation.[26]

The *moralitas* of the third element of this triad is not allegorical, and here Henryson lends his sequence another kind of symmetry, balancing the fable of 'The Two Mice' with that of 'The Wolf and the Wedder'. Both offer a critique of social climbing, but whereas the opening optimistic tone of the *Fabillis* is preserved in the former case by the escape of both protagonists, here the Wedder suffers the same fate as the other sinners in the sequence's latter half. The Renardian tone of the triad is preserved, however, for the Wedder's death is presented in matter-of-fact terms in a terse couplet (2586–7) which contrasts with the sense of tragedy pervading 'The Preaching of the Swallow', and this ending is linked to a scatological joke that is integral to the fable but to which Henryson gives full comic expression:

---

[25] Henryson, *The Poems*, ed. Fox, pp. 299–300.
[26] Cf. Henryson, *The Poems*, ed. Fox, p. 308. On the problems generated by this *moralitas* and an attempt at an explanation, see Lyall, 'Henryson, the Hens and the Pelagian Fox'.

'Thryis, be my saull, ye gart me schute behind:
Vpon my hoichis the senyeis may be sene;
For feiritnes full oft I fylit the wind.
Now is this ye? Na, bot ane hound, I wene!
Me think your teith ouer schort to be sa kene.'   (2567–71)

The Wedder's mistake, as the fable illustrates and the *moralitas* explains, is believing in the canine role he assumes; initially successful in his defence of his flock, it is his determination to catch the Wolf that leads to his downfall, and the implication is that the presumptuous desire to rise above one's station is compounded by the arrogance that comes from the disguise itself. If the Burgess Mouse's sin is gluttony, or more generally, covetousness, that of the Wedder is pride, and it is a sin for which he pays with his life.

Reverting to the elegiac Romulus for the final phase of the sequence, Henryson now brings in two fables which there immediately follow 'The Cock and the Jasp' but here acquire a much darker significance. Both end in tragedy, presented more starkly than the casual violence of 'The Wolf and the Wedder', and they illustrate two of the major focal points of the *Fabillis* as a whole. In 'The Wolf and the Lamb', Henryson takes over his source's moralization against tyranny, but gives it a more jurisprudential spin, making 'fals peruerteris of the lawis' the first of the '[t]hre kynd of wolfis' now prevailing in the world (2714–15); the others are 'mychtie men' and 'men of heritage' who oppress and exploit the common people (2729, 2742). The social world of the collection, strengthened through the incorporation of so many elements drawn from the *fabulae extravagantes* and their Renardian roots, thus reaches its climax in an Aesopic fable, where the violation of order through the abuse of power seems uncontrolled by any legal constraints. The Lamb has all the best arguments, but they are of no avail against the sheer force of the Wolf. Nor is his innocence of any significance: like the Dog before him, he has no effective answer to a system that grants him no rights at all.

If the social consequences of endemic sin are finally illustrated by 'The Wolf and the Lamb', 'The Paddock and the Mouse' completes the encompassing moral argument about the fallen nature of the world. In the elegiac Romulus this fable of a mouse betrayed by a toad who tricks her into being ferried across a stream illustrates the hazards of listening to the fraudulent, but Henryson adds to this simple moral an allegorical reading derived from the tradition of scholastic commentary, according to which Mouse and Paddock signify the soul and body respectively.[27] Only here does he offer a double reading in his *moralitas*, and the effect is to widen out the fable's significance to take in the whole relationship between the contending elements of human nature. The lesson introduced in the prologue to 'The Preaching of the Swallow', that we are blinded by our corporality, is thus reinforced: by heeding the Paddock's

---

[27] See Wheatley, *Mastering Aesop*, pp. 172–6.

blandishments the Mouse exposes herself to inevitable death, as the birds must die when they fail to heed the Swallow's wisdom. By locating this fable at the end of his sequence, Henryson is able to utter a final, awful warning: in the midst of the vicissitudes of this world, a soul which cannot escape the clutches of physical appetite will necessarily perish.

Dark as this conclusion is, Henryson's *Morall Fabillis* are not lacking in positive doctrine. Seen against the backdrop of later medieval theology, the sequence seems to offer a perspective that is essentially Augustinian: however fallen the world may be, and however recidivist sinful man, divine providence is never entirely withdrawn. It may seem that God is asleep, as the Sheep and Lowrence both claim in very different contexts (1295, 2332), but for those who will respond to it the offer of 'speciall grace' (2447) provides a potential escape route. This is not the place to explore the theological implications of this view, but it seems clear that Henryson's *Morall Fabillis* represent a concerned, carefully-wrought effort to persuade the reader that true repentance is never out of the question. Whatever doubt the narrator, and indeed Esope himself, may have about the efficacy of moral instruction, the sequence's very existence is testimony to its creator's belief that it is not too late to bring about the personal and social reform the world so urgently requires.

7

Orpheus and Eurydice *and* The Testament of Cresseid: Robert Henryson's *'fine poeticall way'*

ANNE M. McKIM

No autograph copies of *Orpheus and Eurydice* and *The Testament of Cresseid* have survived, so we do not know exactly when, or in what order, these poems were composed. The earliest known, but the least complete, copy of *Orpheus and Eurydice* is the edition printed around 1508 by Walter Chepman and Androw Myllar. In his edition of the poem, Denton Fox supplements this text with readings from the Asloan MS (c. 1515–c. 1525), which preserves a fuller but still incomplete version, and from the Bannatyne MS (c. 1568), which is the most complete version.[1] The list of contents in the Asloan MS indicates that *The Testament of Cresseid* was once included in this early sixteenth-century anthology, but the earliest extant Scottish print of the poem, and the best text, dates from the end of the sixteenth century when the Edinburgh bookseller Henry Charteris printed, or possibly reprinted, it in 1593.[2] The *Testament* was also anglicized and inserted after *Troilus and Criseyde* in a compilation of Chaucer's works by the English printer William Thynne, in 1532. This edition and its many successors made the *Testament*, but not Henryson, known to English readers.

In 1639 an English scholar, Sir Francis Kinaston, translated *The Testament of Cresseid* into Latin and identified 'Mr Robert Henderson sometimes cheife schoolemaster in Dumfermling' as the author, but he was unaware that the same poet had composed the *Morall Fabillis* and *Orpheus and Eurydice*, let alone a number of minor poems, for he regrets that 'we haue no more of his work*es*'.[3] Even in Scotland *Orpheus and Eurydice* may not have been widely known as

---

[1] All references are to Henryson, *Poems*, ed. Fox.
[2] For details of the witnesses, including three sixteenth-century fragments, and evidence of the poem's circulation, see Henryson, *Poems*, ed. Fox, pp. xciv–c, and Sally Mapstone, 'The *Testament of Cresseid*, lines 561–7: a new manuscript witness', *Notes and Queries* 230 (1985), pp. 307–10.
[3] On Kinaston, see further, Richard Beadle, 'The Virtuoso's *Troilus*', *Chaucer Traditions: Studies in Honour of Derek Brewer*, ed. Ruth Morse and Barry Windeatt (Cambridge, 1990), pp. 213–33.

Henryson's, as neither the early print nor the Asloan MS attributes the poem to him, although the poet Gavin Douglas knew Henryson was the author of this 'New Orpheus', as he called it, and the early anthologist George Bannatyne assigned the poem, and a number of the *Fabillis*, to '*maister* R H', who elsewhere in his MS is identified as '*maister* R Henrysone'.[4]

Henryson's poetry was certainly appreciated by other poets. He was commemorated by William Dunbar, and emulated by Gavin Douglas, Sir David Lyndsay and others.[5] Kinaston's view that Henryson was 'a learned *and* a witty man' who wrote in 'a fine poeticall way' was no doubt shared by other readers. Although he was a serious, moral poet, his humour, playfulness and irony must have found early as well as more recent admirers. His original audience may have included the royal court at Dunfermline.[6] What does seem indisputable is that Henryson had a sophisticated, poetry-educated audience in mind for the full appreciation of his stylistic and generic range, and of the ironies and subtleties of these richly allusive and intertextual poems, one that would recognize his far from straightforward engagement with his 'sources' and the larger traditions in which he self-consciously worked.

Like the *Morall Fabillis*, *The Testament of Cresseid* and *Orpheus and Eurydice* are substantial narrative poems that retell well-known stories, and while they each conclude with explicit moralizations, Henryson seems less interested in delivering a 'didactic message than in involving his readers in a series of complex moral issues'.[7] As a fifteenth-century schoolmaster, Henryson probably taught his pupils by reading aloud (*DOST*, s.v. *rede*, sense 15), but as a poet he enables his readers to take responsibility for their own learning (*DOST*, *rede*, sense 7, 'to learn or discover by reading a book or other writing').[8] Reading books features prominently in both poems. Early in the *Testament* the poet-narrator reads and summarizes the final book of Chaucer's *Troilus and Criseyde* before turning to 'ane vther quair' in which he 'fand the fatal destenie / Of fair Cresseid' (61–3); and at the beginning of the *moralitas* section of *Orpheus and Eurydice* Henryson presents himself as a reader imparting what he has learned from his reading of Boethius and Trivet: 'I sall the tell sum part, as I haue red' (490).

In his *Fabillis* Henryson encourages the 'reader's involvement in a perpetual play of interpretation', and the same is true of the two poems under

---

[4] Henryson, *Poems*, ed. Fox, pp. xiv, cxiii, lxxxii.
[5] See Dunbar, *Poems*, ed. Bawcutt, 'I that in heill wes' (B 21), 81–2; Bawcutt, *Gavin Douglas* pp. 43–4; Lyndsay, *Selected Poems*, ed. Hadley Williams, p. xv, and Anne McKim, ' "Makand hir mone": Masculine Constructions of the Feminine Voice in Middle Scots Complaints', *Scotlands* 2 (1994), pp. 32–40 (38–40).
[6] William Ramson, 'A Reading of Henryson's *Testament*, or "Quha falsit Cresseid?" ', *Parergon* 17 (1977), pp. 25–35 (27).
[7] C. David Benson, 'Critic and Poet: What Lydgate and Henryson did to Chaucer's *Troilus and Criseyde*', *Writing After Chaucer*, ed. Daniel J. Pinti (New York, 1998), pp. 227–42 (238).
[8] *DOST*'s citation is Henryson's 'Trial of the Fox', 471 (Bannatyne MS).

consideration here.[9] Critics have responded enthusiastically to the poet's encouragement and expectation, producing a wealth of interpretations and counter-interpretations, often consciously presented as 'readings' and 're-readings'.[10] Almost all recent studies of the *Orpheus* and the *Testament* begin by acknowledging the diversity of critical opinions, so much so that in her splendid 1984 review of modern Henryson scholarship Louise O. Fradenburg concluded that 'the genre of the rival reading' had come to dominate critical responses.[11]

Fradenburg's timely assessment highlights major developments in appreciations of Henryson's poetry, especially from the 1960s on. That decade saw the publication of significant new studies of *Orpheus* and the *Testament*, and two important books, John MacQueen's seminal study of Henryson's major narrative poems and Fox's scholarly edition of the *Testament*.[12] Among the main trends in the scholarship that followed, Fradenburg finds an over-emphasis on Henryson's originality and autonomy, itself largely a reaction to studies that had stressed the poet's debt to Chaucer, encapsulated in the 'Scottish Chaucerian' label long attached to Henryson (and Dunbar).[13] Increased attention to Henryson's artistry and rhetorical skills, and to his evident concern with the role of poet, followed.[14] Comparative approaches, in their infancy when Fradenburg wrote her overview, have considered Henryson alongside Chaucer and Lydgate, as well as Middle Scots 'makars', and this has not only heightened appreciation of his achievement, but has also led to a

---

[9] Gregory Kratzmann, 'The Poetics of the "Fenyeit Fabill": Chaucer and the Middle Scots Poets', *Of Lion and Of Unicorn: Essays on Anglo-Scottish Literary Relations in Honour of Professor John MacQueen*, ed. R. D. S. Jack and Kevin McGinley (1993), pp. 16–38 (37).

[10] For example, Susan Aronstein, 'Cresseid Reading Cresseid: Redemption and Translation in Henryson's *Testament*', *SLJ* 21.2 (1994), pp. 5–22; Mairi Ann Cullen, 'Cresseid Excused: A Re-Reading of Henryson's *Testament of Cresseid*', *SSL* 21 (1985), pp. 137–59; Kevin J. Harty, 'Cresseid and Her Narrator: A Reading of Robert Henryson's *Testament of Cresseid*', *Studii Medievali* 23 (1983), pp. 753–65; Jane Roberts, 'On Rereading Henryson's *Orpheus and Eurydice*', *Chaucer and Fifteenth-Century Poetry*, ed. Julia Boffey and Janet Cowen (London, 1999), pp. 103–21.

[11] 'Henryson Scholarship: the Recent Decades', *Fifteenth-Century Studies*, ed. R. F. Yeager (Hamden, Conn., 1984), pp. 65–92 (82).

[12] These include A. C. Spearing, '*The Testament of Cresseid* and the "High Concise Style" ', *Speculum* 37 (1962), pp. 208–25, later published as 'Conciseness and *The Testament of Cresseid*', in his *Criticism and Medieval Poetry* (London, 1964), pp. 118–44; Douglas Duncan, 'Henryson's *Testament of Cresseid*', *Essays in Criticism* 11 (1961), pp. 128–35; Sidney J. Harth, 'Henryson Reinterpreted', *ibid.*, pp. 471–80; Kenneth R. R. Gros Louis, 'Robert Henryson's *Orpheus and Eurydice* and the Orpheus Traditions of the Middle Ages', *Speculum* 41 (1966), pp. 643–55; E. D. Aswell, 'The role of Fortune in *The Testament of Cresseid*', *PQ* 46 (1967), pp. 471–87; John MacQueen, *Robert Henryson* (Oxford, 1967) and *The Testament of Cresseid*, ed. Denton Fox (London, 1968).

[13] 'Henryson Scholarship', *Fifteenth-Century Studies*, ed. Yeager, p. 71.

[14] The pioneers are Spearing, MacQueen, Fox, and Douglas Gray, *Robert Henryson* (Leiden, 1979). Particularly influential is the work of Ian Jamieson: 'Henryson's "Fabillis": an Essay towards a Revaluation', *Words. Wai-te-ata Studies in English* 2 (1966), pp. 20–31, and 'Some Attitudes To Poetry in Late Fifteenth-Century Scotland', *SSL* 15 (1980), pp. 28–42.

revaluation of his poetics, casting important new light on the characteristic tension in his work between moral purpose and the pleasures of poetry.[15] The remainder of this essay will focus on some of the chief interpretative issues that have exercised readers of *Orpheus and Eurydice* and *The Testament of Criseyde*, particularly in the last twenty years.

Orpheus and Eurydice

The story of how Orpheus, through the power of his music, won back his beloved Eurydice from the underworld, only to lose her again forever through a forbidden backward glance, came down to the Middle Ages through Ovid, Virgil and Boethius, and became the subject of various moral commentaries. In medieval romance tradition, the story acquired a happy ending with the reunion of the lovers, exemplified in the Middle English *Sir Orfeo* (c. 1330). A number of readers have seen Henryson's poem as the culmination of these twin medieval Orpheus traditions.[16] Henryson cites only two sources: Boethius's 'gay buke of consolacion' (417), and the moral commentary of the thirteenth-century English Dominican and 'noble theolog', Nicholas Trivet (422). While he may have known the accounts of Virgil and Ovid, there is no reason to doubt that, in the main, his version derives from Boethius's *De Consolatione Philosophiae* III, *met.* 12, with some characteristically amplified narrative details – notably Aristeus's attempted rape of Eurydice and Orpheus's futile search for his vanished spouse in the celestial spheres – taken, like the *moralitas*, from Trivet's well-known commentary on the myth.[17] The poet's debt to Macrobius and Eberhard of Bethune has been widely accepted, but the influence of Boccaccio, Ficino and Poliziano has not.[18]

There has been a steady trickle of critical appreciations of *Orpheus and Eurydice* since the 1960s, which almost dried up in the 1980s and 1990s, only

---

[15] Gregory Kratzmann, *Anglo-Scottish Literary Relations 1430–1550* (Cambridge, 1980), pp. 63–103; Julia Boffey, 'Lydgate, Henryson, and the Literary Testament', *MLQ* 53 (1992), pp. 41–56; Nicholas Watson, 'Outdoing Chaucer: Lydgate's *Troybook* and Henryson's *Testament of Cresseid* as Competitive Imitations of *Troilus and Criseyde*', *Shifts and Transpositions in Medieval Narrative*, ed. Karen Pratt (Cambridge, 1994), pp. 89–108; Ian Jamieson, ' "To preue thare preching be a poesye" ', *Parergon* 8 (1974), pp. 24–36; Denton Fox, 'The Coherence of Henryson's Work', *Fifteenth-Century Studies*, ed. Yeager, pp. 275–81 (278–9); Kratzmann, 'Poetics of the "Fenyeit Fabill" ', *Of Lion and Of Unicorn*, ed. Jack and McGinley, pp. 16–38.

[16] Gros Louis, 'Robert Henryson's *Orpheus*', p. 643, and John Block Friedman, *Orpheus in the Middle Ages* (Cambridge, Mass., 1970), p. 195.

[17] Henryson, *Poems*, ed. Fox, pp. cv–cvii and 384–92 for Trivet's commentary.

[18] See Fox's commentary *passim*; Dorena Allen Wright, 'Henryson's *Orpheus and Eurydice* and the Tradition of the Muses', *MÆ* 40 (1971), pp. 41–7; R. J. Lyall, 'Henryson and Boccaccio: A Problem in the Study of Sources', *Anglia* 99 (1981), pp. 38–59; John MacQueen 'Neoplatonism and Orphism in Fifteenth-Century Scotland: the Evidence of Henryson's "New Orpheus" ', *Scottish Studies* 20 (1976), pp. 69–89 (84), and Matthew P. McDiarmid, *Robert Henryson* (1981), p. 50; R. D. S. Jack, *The Italian Influence on Scottish Literature* (1972), pp. 7–14, and R. J. Lyall, 'Did Poliziano influence Henryson's *Orpheus and Eurydice*?', *FMLS* 15 (1979), pp. 209–21.

to flow again with some vigour in the last few years: six new articles have appeared since 2000, three of them in a 2002 special early Scottish Literature issue of *Forum for Modern Language Studies*. The first major studies of the poem were those by Gros Louis and MacQueen; subsequent readings have largely responded to their arguments. Gros Louis sees Henryson's poem as a 'fully mediaevalized classical myth' that combines allegorical and popular traditions and presents sympathetic characters in a novel and engaging way, whereas for MacQueen Henryson's allegorical purpose is paramount and explicit in the *moralitas*, a view he elaborated in a subsequent article where he argues that the poem is constructed on 'Neoplatonic principles to illustrate Neoplatonic doctrine'. Orpheus and Eurydice lack 'immediacy' because they are exemplary representatives of the intellectual and the appetitive parts of the soul respectively.[19]

The importance of the allegorical tradition is generally recognized, but the emotional power of the story has led a number of critics to agree with Gros Louis about Henryson's sympathetic treatment of convincing characters. Douglas Gray points out that a 'humane interpretation' allowing 'full scope to the emotional tensions of the story' was already part of the allegorical tradition Henryson inherited.[20] For Jamieson, however, the emotional moments in the poem, notably Orpheus's laments (154–83; 401–12) are not 'the dominant poetic mood'.[21] Attempts to define this mood have led critics to describe Henryson's retelling of the myth as variously an 'interior allegorical drama', 'a philosophical tale', a 'spiritual tragedy' and a romance that incorporates the ethical strain of the allegorical tradition.[22]

Henryson's use of romance conventions – the noble lineage of the hero, love by reputation, the identification of Proserpine as the Queen of Fairy, Orpheus's Complaint, the quest structure of the narrative, magic elements, and Orpheus's final bewildered apostrophe to love – has been noted, but Carol Mills has argued that these, and other motifs for which parallels can be found in *Sir Orfeo*, are merely decorative features of Henryson's classical tale.[23] More recently, Alessandra Petrina, developing the view of the poem as a culmination of two medieval literary traditions, has suggested that mixing or 'contamination' of genres causes the troubling disjunction between tale and *moralitas* and explains what for many modern readers is a problem, the

---

[19] Gros Louis, 'Robert Henryson's *Orpheus*', p. 643; MacQueen, 'Neoplatonism and Orphism in Fifteenth-Century Scotland', p. 74.
[20] Gray, *Henryson*, p. 216.
[21] Jamieson, ' "To preue thare preching" ', p. 36.
[22] MacQueen, *Henryson*, p. 38; Gray, *Henryson*, p. 236; Steven R. McKenna, *Robert Henryson's Tragic Vision* (New York, 1994), p. 195; and Friedman, *Orpheus*, p. 146.
[23] Friedman, *Orpheus*, pp. 196–204; Carol Mills, 'Romance Convention and Robert Henryson's *Orpheus and Eurydice*', *Bards and Makars*, ed. A. J. Aitken et al. (Glasgow, 1977), pp. 52–60. See also Enrico Giaccherini, 'From *Sir Orfeo* to "Schir Orpheus": Exile, and the Waning of the Middle Ages', *Displaced Persons*, ed. Sharon Ouditt, Studies in European Cultural Transition 14 (Burlington, 2002), pp. 1–10.

disturbing 'double nature' of Aristeus, portrayed as a sexual predator in the tale but as 'noucht bot gude vertewe' in the *moralitas* (436).[24]

The *moralitas* has certainly given rise to the greatest critical disagreement about the poem. While some have pronounced it 'pretentious, cloudy, prolix' and so 'uninspired' that it must be either an optional extra or someone else's appendix, for others it is 'artfully problematic', cleverly designed to balance the tale with which it is subtly interconnected.[25] Some disappointed readers rate the poem as an early and immature work.[26] Resemblances to Henryson's more acclaimed poems are quite apparent. Readers of the *Fabillis* will not be surprised by the disjunction between narrative and *moralitas*, and may be struck by the consistency in the modes of allegorical representation and characterization. Recent reassessments suggest that the 'jarring' effect readers feel as they move from tale to *moralitas* is engineered by Henryson to retain our attention at the end of his moving tale. The lengthy and ponderous moral application is in a different 'voice' – John Marlin detects a separate speaker or bookish narrator figure – the voice of reason or intellect and, as so often in the *Fabillis*, 'the reader is invited to negotiate apparently valid claims to truth from different sources – from affect and intellect'. The whole poem, in the sum of its parts, thus becomes an embodiment of its theme, which is 'the inherent tension between the soul's faculties'.[27]

Henryson's inventiveness is most marked in the 'agility' with which he interprets his primary sources, according to Johnson, who finds an intertextual and metatextual spirit at play in the poem.[28] The poet stresses the value of these sources at the beginning of the *moralitas*:

> Lo, worthy folk, Boece, that senature,
> To wryte this feynit fable tuke in cure,
> In his gay buke of consolacion,
> For oure doctryne and gude instruction;
> Quhilk in the self, suppose it fenyeit be,

---

[24] Alessandra Petrina, ' "Aristeus Pastor Adamans": The Human Setting in Henryson's *Orpheus and Eurydice* and its kinship with Poliziano's *Fabula di Orpheo*', *FMLS* 38 (2002), pp. 382–95 (385).
[25] Negative views are from H. Harvey Wood, *Two Scots Chaucerians* (London, 1967), p. 20; Wright, 'Henryson's *Orpheus*', p. 47; Giaccherini, 'From *Sir Orfeo* to "Schir Orpheus" ', p. 9; and Dietrich Strauss, 'Some Comments on the *Moralitas* of Robert Henryson's *Orpheus and Eurydice*', *SSL* 32 (2001), pp. 1–12 (9–10); positive views from John Marlin, ' "Arestyus is Nocht but Gude Vertewe": The Perplexing *Moralitas* in Henryson's *Orpheus and Eurydices*', *Fifteenth-Century Studies* 25 (1999), pp. 137–53; Roberts, 'On Rereading', p. 118; and Ian Johnson, 'Hellish Complexity in Henryson's *Orpheus*', *FMLS* 38 (2002), pp. 412–19 (413).
[26] Friedman, *Orpheus*, p. 208; Gray, *Henryson*, p. 209, and MacQueen, *Henryson*, p. 45.
[27] Marlin, ' "Arestyus is Nocht but Gude Vertew" ', pp. 145, 149. On the tradition as gendered, see Kevin McGinley, 'The "Fenyeit" and the Feminine: Robert Henryson's *Orpheus and Eurydice* and the Gendering of Poetry', *Women and the Feminine in Medieval and Early Modern Scottish Writing*, ed. Sarah Dunnigan et al. (Basingstoke, 2004), pp. 74–85.
[28] Johnson, 'Hellish Complexity', pp. 416–17.

> And hid vnder the cloke of poesie,
> Yit maister Trewit, doctour Nicholas,
> Quhilk in his tyme a noble theolog was,
> Applyis it to gude moralitee,
> Rycht full of frute and seriositee.   (415–24)

This defence of poetic fictions is consistent with the more extended apology developed in the prologue to the *Fabillis*, but the view of moral instruction and learning demands brief, special consideration. The 'feynit fable' of Orpheus and Eurydice opens with a similar statement of conviction about learning from noble 'eldirs', specifically how to be virtuous by 'herand reherse' stories of their 'nobilnes' or 'gentilnes'. We can learn, it seems, from both hearing and reading attentively how to 'enclyne' the heart 'to vertu and to worthynes' (4–5) and, with the help of a guide like 'noble theolog', Nicholas Trivet, how to apply what we have heard and read 'to gude moralitee' (422–3). The poet includes himself in this learning process by the repeated use of the first person plural pronouns 'our', 'we', and 'us', as in '*oure* doctryne and gude instruction' (418), and (in the *moralitas*) '*our* mynde', '*our* ressoun', '*our* soule', '*our* hert', '*our* understanding', '*oure* affection', '*oure* fleschly appetyte', '*our* synfull deidis', 'quhen *we* flee', '[s]chawand til *vs*'. While there is certainly a Trivet-inspired focus on our spiritual natures, on the intellectual and passional parts of the soul, the 'human reference' is as present in the *moralitas* as in the tale, and words for the emotional and volitional faculty – 'affectioun' in particular – actually predominate.[29]

The Testament of Cresseid

Readers of *The Testament of Cresseid* encounter a less reliable guide. In this poem Henryson created a narrator who is a poet, reader and critic who comments on Chaucer's *Troilus and Criseyde*, questions received views of Cresseid's reputation, and gets so emotionally involved in her story that he contradicts himself. In effect, the issues of readers' responses and critical interpretation are foregrounded in the poem itself. The aspects of the poem that have fomented most debate are its relationship to Chaucer's poem; its genre; the narrator's role and attitude to his subject; Cresseid's crime and punishment; the status of the gods and the associated question about whether the poem offers a Christian perspective; and the author's perceived anti-feminism.

Various views of the *Testament*'s relationship to Chaucer's *Troilus and Criseyde* have been offered over the years, and the opinion of an early critic, Kinaston, has found modern supporters:

> [W]ittily obseruing, that Chaucer in his 5th booke had related the death of Troilus, but made no mention what became of Creseid, he learnedly takes

---

[29] Henryson, *Poems*, ed. Fox, p. 414.

vppon him in a fine poeticall way to expres the punishment *and* end due to a false vnconstant whore, which commonly terminates in extreme misery.[30]

The *Testament* has been seen as a continuation of Chaucer's poem; an alternative conclusion to it; a penetrating, sometimes ironical, commentary on it; and as bearing a relationship to it not unlike a *moralitas* to a fable.[31] Walter Scheps shows that such views need not be mutually exclusive; he considers the *Testament* is 'a Scottish extension of and reply to an English poem'. The poem's 'Scottishness' has been reconsidered by David Parkinson who outlines prominent features – notably the treatment of exile and disfigurement – it shares with other Middle Scots texts.[32] In contrast, Melvin Storm intentionally excludes extra-textual information and, in a close, nuanced exploration of the inter-textual relationship between the *Troilus* and the *Testament*, shows how the two poems inform each other.[33]

Henryson's independence from his source of inspiration is conveyed in the *Testament* too. He draws attention to the role of *inventioun*, to individual poetic creativeness, in the much-analysed, enigmatic stanza beginning: 'Quha wait gif all that Chauceir wrait was trew?' (64).[34] Questioning the truth value of the *Troilus*, and the second book about Cresseid that the narrator has to hand, has been taken as Henryson's tongue-in-cheek way of authorizing his own new 'narratioun' (65), while simultaneously drawing attention to the fictional nature of stories, a strategy deployed in the *Fabillis* too. Reference to the other book that tells *another* story also promotes the idea that more than one account is in circulation, which is quite credible, as by the fifteenth century a number of poets had contributed to the Criseyde tradition.[35] On the whole, the 'vther quair' (61) has itself been supposed a fiction, like Chaucer's 'Lollius', although there have been several nominations.[36]

The poem's genre, like its relationship to Chaucer's poem, is explicit in the *Testament*:

---

[30] Henryson, *Poems*, ed. Fox, p. xiv. Tatyana Moran, '*The Testament of Cresseid* and *The Book of Troylus*', *Litera* 6 (1959), pp. 18–24, and Nikki Stiller, 'Robert Henryson's Cresseid and Sexual Backlash', *Literature and Psychology* 31.2 (1981), pp. 88–95.
[31] *Testament*, ed. Fox, p. 21.
[32] 'A Climatological Reading of Henryson's *Testament of Cresseid*', *SSL* 25 (1980), pp. 80–7; 'Henryson's Scottish Tragedy', *Chaucer Review* 25 (1991), pp. 355–62.
[33] 'The Intertextual Cresseida: Chaucer's Henryson or Henryson's Chaucer?' *SSL* 28 (1993), pp. 105–22.
[34] *DOST*, like the *OED*, asssigns the first usage of *inventioun* in this sense to Henryson.
[35] See the survey by Gretchen Mieszkowski, 'The Reputation of Criseyde: 1155–1500', *Transactions of the Connecticut Academy of Arts and Sciences* 43 (1971), pp. 73–153.
[36] Eleanor R. Long, 'Robert Henryson's "Uther Quair"', *Comitatus* 3 (1972), pp. 97–101; Robert L. Kindrick, 'Henryson's "Uther Quair" Again: a Possible Candidate and the Nature of the Tradition', *Chaucer Review* 33 (1998), pp. 190–220.

> Ane doolie sessoun to ane cairfull dyte
> Suld correspond and be equiualent:
> Richt sa it wes quhen I began to wryte
> This tragedie. (1–4)

The rhetorical correspondence between a doleful season and sorrowful writing prepares us for a medieval tragedy, that is, a 'literary work of a serious or sorrowful character, with a fatal or disastrous conclusion' (*OED*). Chaucer's first stanza stresses that his poem relates 'the double sorwe of Troilus' in 'woful vers', and he too called his work a 'tragedye' (*Troilus*, V, 1786). Henryson's use of the term seems deliberately to echo Chaucer's and his tragedy to *correspond* to Chaucer's.[37] Although Henryson's understanding of tragedy may derive from Boethius's *De Consolatione Philosophiae* and Trivet's commentary on it, probably Chaucer's extensive use of these sources in *Troilus and Criseyde* exerted a strong influence. Trivet's concept of tragedy as 'a poem about great iniquities beginning in prosperity and ending in adversity' seems especially appropriate to Cresseid's story as told by Chaucer and concluded by Henryson.[38]

The chilly spring opening of the *Testament* evokes courtly associations that predispose the reader to expect 'a tragedy of love', and indeed the story the narrator tells focuses on the consequences of betrayal in love. Read as an allegory, the lovers' courtly relationship becomes a type of those relationships 'seen and judged in terms of Christian morality'.[39] Ramson sees Henryson as a critical 'outsider', satirically mimicking the figure of the poet as courtly lover as he reads his poem aloud to the ladies of the Scottish court.[40] Whoever the 'worthie wemen' addressed in the final stanza of the poem may be, and how, or by whom, the final lines are delivered, they contain a warning against deception in love:

> Now, worthie wemen, in this ballet schort,
> Maid for your worschip and instructioun,
> Of cheritie, I monische and exhort,
> Ming not your lufe with fals deceptioun. (610–13)

Critics have puzzled over Henryson's description of his poem as 'this ballet schort'. If it is a 'deprecatory term', as Fox supposed, then it is quite likely that

---

[37] *DOST* defines 'Traged(i)e' much like the *OED*, citing the *Testament*, 4, as the first instance in Scots.
[38] Boethian readings of the *Testament* include Aswell, 'The Role of Fortune', pp. 471–87; Craig McDonald, 'Venus and the Goddess Fortune in *The Testament of Cresseid*', *SLJ* 4.2 (1977), pp. 14–24; Anne McKim, 'Henryson's "Memoriall of Fair Cresseid" ', *Of Lion and Of Unicorn*, ed. Jack and McGinley, pp. 1–15; Sabine Volk-Birke, 'Sickness unto Death: Crime and Punishment in Henryson's *Testament of Cresseid*', *Anglia* 113 (1995), pp. 163–83.
[39] MacQueen, *Henryson*, pp. 52, 93.
[40] Ramson, 'A Reading', p. 29.

Henryson is consciously imitating Chaucer, who refers to his poem as 'litel bok', 'litel myn tragedye' at the end of *Troilus* (V, 1786).[41] Whereas in Middle Scots poetry *ballatis* were often short, written in a range of metres about diverse subjects, including love, in Middle English, as Fox notes, a 'ballet' was usually a short poem in rhyme royal. It may have amused Henryson to compare his relatively short, tragic poem in rhyme royal (excepting Cresseid's Complaint) to Chaucer's long one in the same metre. Interestingly, Dunbar also links 'ballat making and trigide'.[42]

While there is general agreement that the narrator is a persona, there is a range of views on his role in the poem. For some he is a character, for some a point of view, and for others he is primarily an ironic device. Robert L. Kindrick considers the narrator is 'a fully developed character ... capable of just the kind of patience she [Cresseid] lacks and has the kind of understanding of life she does not gain until the poem's conclusion'.[43] For Carol A. Cole, on the other hand, Cresseid's fall is a vehicle for the narrator's 'coming-to-knowledge'. Others believe he learns little or nothing, seeing him variously as 'sentimental and illogical', 'a figure of ridicule', 'the impotent senex of medieval literary tradition' who attains 'only partial understanding of what he is reading'.[44] For Lesley Johnson, the old, frail narrator is a character through whom the vicarious experience of reading is explored, and who, in resembling the later Cresseid, 'makes her end merely a reflection of his experience'.[45]

Gray, in contrast, regards the narrator as a ' "fictive" projection', not an 'autonomous character', and proposes an analogy with the *Morall Fabillis* in which there is 'a shifting and complex relationship between "poet" and "narrator", but the connection seems to be a fundamental one'.[46] Malcolm Pittock goes even further, detecting the presence of three narrators or 'fictive personae', by which 'elaborate means' Henryson draws attention 'to the fictionality of his own narrative', and undermines *fin amour*.[47] Several critics

---

[41] Henryson, *Poems*, ed. Fox, p. 383, n. 610; Henry Ansgar Kelly, 'Henryson's tragedy of Cresseid', in his *Chaucerian Tragedy* (Cambridge, 1997), pp. 216–59 (218).

[42] Dunbar, *Poems*, ed. Bawcutt, 'I that in heill wes' (B 21), 59. On the range of senses of 'ballat' in Scots, see Bawcutt, *Dunbar the Makar*, pp. 29–31.

[43] R. L. Kindrick, *Robert Henryson* (Boston, 1979), p. 123.

[44] 'Looking for Love in all the Wrong Places', *Michigan Academician* 29 (1997), pp. 511–20 (511); Henryson, *Poems*, ed. Fox, p. xciii; Mieszkowski, 'The Reputation of Criseyde', p. 137; Derek Pearsall, ' "Quha wait gif all that Chauceir wrait was trew?": Henryson's *Testament of Cresseid*', *New Perspectives on Middle English Texts. A Festschrift for R. A. Waldron*, ed. Susan Powell and Jeremy Smith with a personal memoir by Derek Pearsall (Cambridge, 2000), pp. 169–82 (174); Alicia K. Nitecki, ' "Fenyeit of the New": Authority in *The Testament of Cresseid*', *Journal of Narrative Technique* 15 (1985), pp. 120–32 (125, 130).

[45] Lesley Johnson, 'Whatever happened to Criseyde? Henryson's *Testament of Cresseid*', *Courtly Literature, Culture and Context*, ed. Keith Busby and Erik Kooper (Amsterdam, 1990), pp. 313–21 (319).

[46] Gray, *Henryson*, pp. 169–70.

[47] 'The Complexity of Henryson's *The Testament of Cresseid*', *Essays in Criticism* 40 (1990), pp. 198–221 (206–7, 212).

have regarded the figure of Mercury as another projection of the poet who ultimately determines Cresseid's fate, but this role is 'obscured by Henryson the narrator, who claims the role of a mere "speaker" of events against which he even at times dramatically protests'.[48]

It is often accepted that the aged male narrator's attitude to his young female subject, and fellow Venus worshipper, is crucial in the vexed question of whether the poem encourages sympathy for, or condemnation of, Cresseid. The lines that seem to hold the key, 78–91, perplexingly express both compassion ('pietie') and admonishment ('fleschelie lust' and 'brukkilnes'), defence and accusation. Further contradictions take the form of blaming fortune and the 'wickit langage' of Cresseid's detractors for her ignominious reputation, while also assigning to Cresseid responsibility for her actions.

Although there has been considerable debate about the actual crime for which Cresseid is punished, and even more about the appropriateness or otherwise of her terrible punishment, critics tend to agree that Henryson portrays her as a guilty creature who finally comes to admit her blameworthiness. Until recently, there was a consensus that she progresses from blindness to enlightenment, from wilful ignorance and error to wisdom and responsibility, but this essentially humanist view has been challenged, particularly in feminist analyses (discussed below). Readers are reminded early in the poem that in betraying Troilus, Cresseid has offended against the code of love (43–56); she then adds blasphemy to her crimes (354) by blaming Venus and Cupid for her 'infelicitie' (281). Whether her leprosy and death are to be interpreted as punishment for one or the other, or both crimes, has been a matter of critical contention. What is incontrovertible is that she undergoes mental and physical suffering that begins with her rejection by Diomeid and only ends when she dies a leprous beggar. During this painful ordeal she moves from anger to self-pity, from blaming her gods to blaming Fortune, and finally to self-reproach and belated remorse when she admits: 'Nane but my self as now I will accuse' (574).

Henryson's greatest innovation is this emphasis on Cresseid's moral growth, through which he makes the 'change in Cresseid's attitude towards herself … the central event of his story'.[49] Whether she is redeemed, especially given the absence of any explicit Christian reference in the poem, is an unresolved crux.[50] Recent criticism has shifted the discussion away from debating the Christian or

---

[48] Jennifer Strauss, 'To Speak Once More of Cresseid: Henryson's *Testament* Re-considered', *SLJ* 4.2 (1977), pp. 5–13 (12); Priscilla Bawcutt, 'Henryson's "Poeit of the Auld Fassoun" ', *Review of English Studies* n.s. 32 (1981), pp. 429–34; Jill Mann, 'The planetary gods in Chaucer and Henryson', *Chaucer Traditions*, ed. Morse and Windeatt, pp. 91–105 (101).
[49] Mieszkowski, 'The Reputation of Criseyde', p. 132. Cf. Strauss, 'To Speak Once More', p. 8; and Benson, 'Critic and Poet', p. 239.
[50] E. M. W. Tillyard famously claimed that Cresseid achieves Christian salvation in 'The Testament of Cresseid', *Five Poems 1470–1870* (London, 1948), reprinted as *Poetry and its Background* (London, 1955), pp. 5–29 (17). Lee W. Patterson sees the poem as centrally concerned with 'the nature of the Christian experience': 'Christian and Pagan in *The Testament of Cresseid*', *PQ* 52 (1973), pp. 696–714.

pagan nature of Cresseid's experience to focus on issues of power and identity, especially in relation to spirituality and gender. Sabine Volk-Birke sees the poem as about 'the spiritual emancipation of a woman', and Cresseid's 'recognition of her guilt brings with it the recognition of her freedom to act, which confirms her individuality'. Catherine A. Cox finds in this 'text obsessed with errancy' that Cresseid's discursive as well as her sexual 'errancy' are perceived as feminine threats to masculine stability and propriety.[51]

Feminist approaches to the poem have challenged arguments that allow Cresseid agency, whether in a legal, moral or spiritual capacity.[52] Felicity Riddy contends that Cresseid should be read as a voice speaking in 'different genres that provide discontinuous subject positions', and that if her debasement is considered in the light of Kristeva's model of the abject we can see that 'Cresseid's abjection borders and maintains Troilus's truth'. She is allowed only to be 'the agent of her own fall', according to Susan Aronstein, to make an example of herself in a misogynist text that seeks to restore the pre-Chaucerian Criseyde, so the *Testament* brings her to a point where she is able to read herself correctly, 'to read her own story like a man'.[53]

Such readings explore and sometimes challenge longstanding views of Henryson's poem, including its place in medieval anti-feminist tradition. Postmodern approaches have found ambiguities, discontinuities and incoherencies in the text of particular interest, a trend that contrasts with earlier emphases on the poem's 'balance', 'logic' and 'pattern of facts'.[54] Derek Pearsall has responded to such readings with a reminder that the *Testament* is a poem, and what makes it a great poem is its 'poeticness', manifested in its 'intensity, the sense one has in reading the poem that everything that is happening is of enormous significance', and its 'connectivity, the way all its parts knit and work together to make of a linear narrative a *composition* full of echoes and anticipations'.[55]

Ongoing critical debate about the tale-*moralitas* relationship in *Orpheus and Eurydice* and, in *The Testament of Cresseid*, the nature of Cresseid's offence, the narrator's function, the status of Cresseid's dream-vision, the role of the

---

[51] Volk-Birke, 'Sickness unto Death', pp. 182, 177; Catherine S. Cox, 'Froward Language and Wanton Play: The "Commoun" Text of Henryson's *Testament of Cresseid*', *SSL* 29 (1996), pp. 58–72 (63–4).

[52] Marion Wynne-Davies, ' "Spottis blak": Disease and the Female Body in *The Testament of Cresseid*', *Poetica* 38 (1993), pp. 32–52 (52, 43); Jana Mathews, 'Land, Lepers, and the Law in *The Testament of Cresseid*', *The Letter of the Law: Literary Production in Medieval England*, ed. Emily Steiner and Candace Barrington (Ithaca, NY, 2002), pp. 40–56 (63).

[53] Felicity Riddy, ' "Abject Odious": Feminine and Masculine in Henryson's *Testament of Cresseid*', *The Long Fifteenth Century: Essays for Douglas Gray*, ed. Helen Cooper and Sally Mapstone (Oxford, 1997), pp. 229–48 (244, 239); Aronstein, 'Cresseid Reading Cresseid', pp. 15, 9.

[54] Pittock, 'The Complexity', p. 204 and Riddy, ' "Abject Odious" ', p. 236; Nitecki, ' "Fenyeit of the New" ', p. 121; Patterson, 'Christian and Pagan', p. 698, Spearing, '*The Testament of Cresseid* and the "High Concise Style" ', p. 144 and Ramson, 'A Reading', p. 25.

[55] Pearsall, ' "Quha wait gif all that Chaucer wrait was trew?" ', pp. 169, 170, 172.

planetary gods, and Cresseid's final affecting encounter with Troilus, ultimately testifies to this awareness of their 'significance' and 'connectivity'. Henryson's artistry, his long-recognized 'fine poeticall way', continues to be appreciated in the most sensitive studies of his poetry. In their uses of familiar characters from well-known stories, both poems have an exemplary aspect. Nevertheless, Henryson's memorably recreated figures – the haunting portrait of Eurydice in hell, 'warsch and wan and walowit as the wede' (350), Orpheus the forlorn and 'wofull wedow' (414) and 'catiue Creisseid' (408) – linger in the mind long after the reading is over.

8

Religious Verse in Medieval Scotland

PRISCILLA BAWCUTT

The tooth of 'devouring time', changes in aesthetic taste, and, above all, the passionate hostility of the Reformers to any manifestation of papistry have obliterated most of the paintings, sculptures and stained glass of medieval Scotland, and also much of its religious literature. Not a single text exists today of the 'Haliblude', or Corpus Christi, plays, for instance, yet we know that they were regularly performed in Aberdeen and other Scottish burghs.[1] No more than the title now survives of a Scottish 'ballat of disputacoun betuix the body and saull' – this may be an accidental loss, caused by wear and tear to the Asloan Manuscript, but is still deeply regrettable.[2] Other poetic works, although not destroyed, are known to have been censored by sixteenth-century Protestants.[3] Nonetheless the picture is not as black as this might suggest. In recent years much patient research has been devoted to the recovery and study of the imagery and artefacts that survive from this vanished world.[4] Medieval Scottish religious verse is valuable because it illuminates the spiritual beliefs and devotional practices of this period, but it also has intrinsic literary interest. More verse is extant than is always realized, since some is printed in scattered, out of the way publications and can be difficult to locate. Some guidance as to what exists may therefore be helpful to readers.

From the fourteenth century there survives only the Scottish *Legends of the Saints*. This is a massive work, containing over thirty-three thousand lines, in octosyllabic couplets, and largely based, as the author himself claims, on *The*

---

[1] See David McRoberts, 'Material Destruction Caused by the Scottish Reformation', *Essays on the Scottish Reformation 1513–1625*, ed. D. McRoberts (Glasgow, 1962), pp. 415–62 and cf. R. J. Lyall, 'The Lost Literature of Medieval Scotland', *Bryght Lanternis: Essays on the Language and Literature of Medieval and Renaissance Scotland*, ed. J. Derrick McClure and Michael R. G. Spiller (Aberdeen, 1989), pp. 33–47 (34).
[2] See Catherine van Buuren, 'John Asloan and his Manuscript: An Edinburgh Notary and Scribe in the Days of James III, IV and V (c. 1470–c. 1530)', *Stewart Style 1513–1542: Essays on the Court of James V*, ed. J. Hadley Williams (East Linton, 1996), pp. 15–51 (34–5).
[3] See A. A. MacDonald, 'Poetry, Politics and Reformation Censorship in Sixteenth-Century Scotland', *English Studies* 64 (1983), pp. 410–21.
[4] Particularly valuable is John Higgitt, *'Imageis Maid with Mennis Hand': Saints, Images, Belief and Identity in Later Medieval Scotland* (Whithorn, 2003). See also the illustrations in *Angels Nobles and Unicorns: Art and Patronage in Medieval Scotland*, [ed. D. H. Caldwell] (1982).

Golden Legend of Jacobus de Voragine, composed in the thirteenth century. It has a number of individualizing features, such as the inclusion of the Scottish saints Machar, to whom Aberdeen's cathedral is dedicated, and Ninian, whose life describes several miracles said to have occurred in the author's lifetime. Little is known about the author, although he tells us he is a churchman, and often complains of age and ill-health. He is thought to have written an earlier work on the life of the Virgin and Christ not now extant.[5] The narrative style is readable, but unsophisticated. One characteristic is the presence of numerous passages on the efficacy of penance; another is the conclusion of each life with this formulaic prayer on the author's own behalf: 'ovte of this lyf that I ma twyne / but schame, or det and dedly syne' (vol. 1, p. 235). Middle English counterparts to this work, such as *The South English Legendary*, have received much attention in recent years, but the Scottish *Legends* are still neglected by scholars, and would repay investigation into their sources, authorship and style.[6]

The bulk of extant religious verse, however, is very different from the *Legends of the Saints*. It consists chiefly, though not entirely, of lyrics and short poems, is largely devotional in character, and was probably composed in the late fifteenth century. The most important repositories of this verse are three large and carefully composed manuscript anthologies, all belonging to the sixteenth century. The earliest is the Asloan Manuscript (c. 1515–c. 1525). Among the varied contents of this manuscript are a truncated text of Dunbar's *Ballat of the Passioun*, an important text of *The Contemplacioun of Synnaris*, and a group of 'diuers ballatis of our ladye' (fol. 300v); the original list of contents shows that it once also contained other religious lyrics, including 'a ballat of the Incarnacioun' and 'a ballat of our lady of pete'. The Bannatyne Manuscript was completed very much later (1568); yet despite this late date and despite Bannatyne's Protestant sympathies (one of the poems he includes is attributed to Robert Norvell, a friend of John Knox), the first section of the manuscript, the 'Ballatis of theoligie', is particularly rich in interest and contains poems by Henryson, Dunbar, Douglas and other medieval poets.[7] The most important collection of Scottish religious verse, however, is undoubtedly British Library, Manuscript Arundel 285; the compiler of this miscellany, which contains both prose and verse, is unfortunately not known, nor has the manuscript been precisely dated, although it is thought to be pre-Reformation (possibly c. 1540). Focussed chiefly on the Passion, it contains many prayers and devotions to the Crown of Thorns, the Seven Words on the Cross, and the Name of Jesus. J. A. W. Bennett, its editor, noted its great value as a 'guide to

---

[5] See *Legends of the Saints in the Scottish Dialect*, ed. W. M. Metcalfe, 3 vols, STS (1896), vol. 1, 2–4; and Lyall, 'Lost Literature', p. 38.

[6] For a sympathetic treatment, see J. A. W. Bennett, *Middle English Literature* (Oxford, 1986), pp. 62–5, and Regina Scheibe, 'Aspects of the Snake in the *Legends of the Saints*', *Bryght Lanternis*, ed. McClure and Spiller, pp. 67–89.

[7] On the Asloan and Bannatyne Manuscripts, see Introduction, pp. 16–17.

the practices of private devotion observed in Scotland on the eve of the Reformation'.[8]

In contrast to the poems carefully inscribed in these large anthologies there also exist other more scattered manifestations of Scottish piety in this period. Religious feeling was expressed with less formality but with equal intensity in many short, scribbled prayers and poems found in a variety of locations: on the flyleaves, margins, or other blank spaces of books of hours, notaries' protocol books, or students' lecture notes. One book of hours in Edinburgh University Library (MS Laing III.17) contains twelve lines (in couplets) on the efficacy of prayer to the Virgin (*IMEV* 4124).[9] The protocol book of an early sixteenth-century notary, John Feyrn, contains several unpublished fragments of verse, including forty aureate lines, praising Mary, the sister of Martha, as a type of the 'lyf theoricall', that is, the contemplative life. This is possibly an extract from a much larger work on the life of Christ.[10] The so-called Makculloch Manuscript (EUL, MS Laing III.149) is particularly interesting: it originated as a set of Latin lecture notes, written by the well-known scribe Magnus Makculloch when he was a student in Louvain in 1477. Vernacular poems were added to it by a later owner, in the early years of the sixteenth century.[11] The copyists were usually churchmen, notaries or devout laymen. Their names are rarely known, yet it is interesting that one of these manuscripts, a book of hours now in Magdalene College, Cambridge (Pepys Library, MS 1576), belonged to the Hays of Yester at the period when four stanzas were copied into it from a religious poem by Lydgate, 'Cristes Passion' (*IMEV* 2081).[12]

Scottish religious poetry amply confirms Douglas Gray's remark that medieval Latin, especially in the field of religious writing, 'was the mother of the vernacular literatures'.[13] The authors and copyists were educated in Latin,

---

[8] See *Devotional Pieces in Verse and Prose from MS Arundel 285 and MS Harleian 6919*, STS (1955), p. xxiv; also Bennett, 'Scottish Pre-Reformation Devotion: Some Notes on British Library MS Arundel 285', *So Meny People Longages and Tonges: Philological Essays presented to Angus McIntosh*, ed. M. Benskin and M. L. Samuels (1981), pp. 299–308; and A. A. MacDonald, 'Passion Devotion in Late-Medieval Scotland', *The Broken Body: Passion Devotion in Late-Medieval Culture*, ed. A. A. MacDonald et al. (Groningen, 1998), pp. 109–31.

[9] These lines are printed, not wholly accurately, in C. Borland, *A Descriptive Catalogue of the Western Medieval Manuscripts in Edinburgh University Library* (1916), no. 42. The incipit is: 'Quhasaever vthrys [= utters] this orisoun'.

[10] See NAS, NP 1/168, fols. 135r–135v. Protocol book dated: 7 Jan 1525/6–1565.

[11] On this manuscript, see Borland, *Descriptive Catalogue*, no. 205; and *Pieces from The Makculloch and the Gray MSS. together with The Chepman and Myllar Prints*, ed. George Stevenson, STS (1918). On Makculloch, see R. J. Lyall, 'Books and Book Owners in Fifteenth-Century Scotland', *Book Production and Publishing in Britain 1375–1475*, ed. Jeremy Griffiths and D. Pearsall (Cambridge, 1989), pp. 239–56 (245–6); and Walter Bower, *Scotichronicon*, ed. D. E. R. Watt et al., 9 vols (Aberdeen and Edinburgh, 1987–98), vol. 9, pp. 190–1.

[12] The text is printed in M. R. James, *Bibliotheca Pepysiana: A Descriptive Catalogue of the Library of Samuel Pepys, Part III: Mediaeval Manuscripts* (London, 1923), pp. 16–17. See also *Catalogue of the Pepys Library at Magdalene College Cambridge, Volume. 5: Manuscripts, Part i: Medieval*, compiled by R. McKitterick and R. Beadle (Cambridge, 1992), No. 1576.

[13] *Themes and Images in the Medieval English Religious Lyric* (London, 1972), p. 3.

and were familiar with the hymns and liturgy of the church, together with the Psalter and the Scriptures. It is noteworthy how many of the scattered vernacular verses are later additions to works otherwise written in Latin. The Latin influence is unmistakeable, in choice of themes, imagery, diction, and even rhyme-schemes. It may be detected in the titles and refrains of poems, and in short allusions, such as Dunbar's account of kneeling in church before an image of the Virgin, 'Hir halsing with ane *gaude flore*' (*Ane Ballat of the Passioun*, B 1, 7). This brief phrase is packed with meaning: it was then common to start Marian lyrics with *gaude* or *ave* or *salve*, but this recalls a specific hymn, which opened *Gaude flore virginali*, one that was particularly popular in the fifteenth century and often included in books of hours in Scottish ownership, such as MS Pepys 1576.[14] Several Scottish religious poems, of course, were direct translations or paraphrases of Latin works. J. A. W. Bennett noted that many items in MS Arundel 285 were 'versions of Latin prayers that occur regularly in Books of Hours of the period 1450–1550'.[15] One interesting example of dependence upon a Latin source, however, was long unknown to scholars, and discovered comparatively recently. Henryson's 'Forcy as deith is likand lufe', traditionally entitled 'The Annunciation', has been shown by A. A. MacDonald to derive from a Latin poem, '*Fortis ut mors dilectio*'. There is evidence that this Latin poem was known to other Scottish readers in the fifteenth century; one text occurs in a Scottish book of hours.[16] Henryson's rendering is fairly close, and contains exactly the same number of lines, divided into twelve-line stanzas. It is perhaps surprising that Henryson's poem is not highly aureate, although it introduces much alliteration.

Such Latin influences are well known, but the impact upon Scotland of English religious writings is less often acknowledged. Yet there is a mass of evidence to show that Scottish readers often turned to England for spiritual nourishment. *Piers Plowman* was known to Gavin Douglas, and another fourteenth-century religious poem, the alliterative *Pistel of Susan*, was mentioned by Andrew of Wyntoun.[17] Scotticized versions of William of Nassington's *Speculum Vitae* were made in the late fifteenth century, as R. J. Lyall has shown.[18] Many other poems which circulated in Scotland at this time are undoubtedly English in origin, despite a superficial Scottish colouring. Some short examples are the pious couplet: 'In my beginning God me speid / In grace and vertew to proceid'; a quatrain upon the paradoxes of the Incarnation;

---

[14] For Middle English versions, see *Religious Lyrics of the XVth Century*, ed. Carleton Brown (Oxford, 1939), nos. 35 and 36.
[15] *Devotional Pieces*, ed. Bennett, p. xxiv.
[16] 'The Latin Original of Robert Henryson's Annunciation Lyric', *The Renaissance in Scotland: Studies in Literature, Religion, History and Culture Offered to John Durkan*, ed. A. A. MacDonald, Michael Lynch and Ian B. Cowan (Leiden, 1994), pp. 45–65.
[17] See *The Palice of Honour*, in Douglas, *Shorter Poems*, ed. Bawcutt, 1714; and Wyntoun, *Original Chronicle*, ed. Amours, vol. 4, p. 22.
[18] See R. J. Lyall, 'The Lost Literature', pp. 35–6.

and the fourteenth-century 'Earth upon earth' poem, which was wrongly attributed to various Scottish poets, including Dunbar.[19] Hoccleve's poem addressed to the Virgin, 'Moder of God and virgin undefould', was clearly admired by Scottish readers; one copy was made by the theologian John Ireland and another by the compiler of MS Arch. Selden. B. 24, yet both misattributed the poem, calling it an 'Oracio galfridi Chaucere'.[20]

Scottish readers seem to have been particularly attracted to the type of English poem known as the Appeal from the Cross, in which Christ speaks of his suffering and pleads with sinful man to love him in return.[21] One such is the extract from Lydgate's 'Cristes Passion' already mentioned. Another, which opens, 'This is Goddis awne complaint', was copied into the Gray Manuscript, and curiously attributed to an otherwise unknown 'Glassinbery' [= Glastonbury?].[22] A third impressive poem of this type was copied at least twice in Scotland in the early sixteenth century. The best and fullest text is found in MS Arundel 285, where it is called 'the Dollorus Complant of Our Lorde apoune the croce crucifyit'. A fragmentary text also appears in the Makculloch MS; in the Scottish Text Society edition, unfortunately, it is laid out as if it were three separate poems (nos. XV–XVII). The two earliest English texts of this work are northern in provenance (one in the Towneley Plays, one in a manuscript miscellany of Carthusian origin).[23] Proximity to Scotland and the similarities between northern English and Scots would have aided transmission across the Border. It should be noted, however, that the cultural traffic was not in one direction only (see below on *The Contemplacioun of Synnaris*, and 'Ros Mary most of vertewe virginale').

There is a wide thematic range in Scottish religious verse, which cannot be fully illustrated in this chapter. At one extreme is 'In my defens God me defend', a simple mixture of prayer and protective charm, which occurs in a variety of shapes in Scottish manuscripts, including the Gray Manuscript (no. II).[24] In one Scottish book of hours it has been translated into Latin: 'In mea tutione deus me tueatur et portet animam meam ad meum finem'.[25] At the other

---

[19] On these verses, see *IMEV*, nos. 430 and 430.5; 704; and 4181; also P. Bawcutt, 'Dunbar and an Epigram', *SLJ* 13.2 (1986), pp. 16–19.
[20] Cf. Ireland, *Meroure*, ed. Macpherson, Quinn and McDonald, vol. 1, pp. 166–70; and MS Arch. Selden. B. 24, fols 130r–131v.
[21] See Gray, *Themes and Images*, pp. 139–45.
[22] See *Pieces from The Makculloch and the Gray MSS*, ed. Stevenson, pp. 46–50; *IMEV*, 3612; and R. Woolf, *The English Religious Lyric in the Middle Ages* (Oxford, 1968), pp. 216–17.
[23] See *Devotional Pieces*, ed. Bennett, pp. 261–5; *IMEV*, 1119; and the discussion by P. Bawcutt, 'English Books and Scottish Readers in the Fifteenth and Sixteenth Centuries', *ROSC* 14 (2001–02), pp. 1–12 (4–6).
[24] For other versions, see P. Bawcutt, 'The Commonplace Book of John Maxwell', *A Day Estivall: Essays on the Music, Poetry and History of Scotland and England*, ed. A. Gardner-Medwin and J. Hadley Williams (Aberdeen, 1990), pp. 59–68 (64–5).
[25] NLS, MS Dep. 221/5. See Rev. William J. Anderson, 'Andrew Lundy's Primer', *IR* 11 (1960), pp. 39–51 (40).

extreme of verbal and theological subtlety is Douglas's discussion of the Trinity in Prologue X of his *Eneados*, a Prologue fittingly included in Bannatyne's 'ballatis of theoligie'. Most of the poems included in Bannatyne's 'ballatis of moralitie' are also highly devout, their advice on conduct framed by the Christian perspective of Death and the Last Things. These 'mortality' lyrics, which are hortatory in tone and stylistically plain, include many anonymous poems, as well as several of the short pieces attributed to Henryson and Dunbar. Among the more ambitious examples are those which adopt the debate form, such as Henryson's 'Ressoning betuix Aige and Yowth' and 'Ressoning betuix Deth and Man', and Dunbar's 'In May as that Aurora did vpspring' (B 24), a dispute between two symbolic birds concerning human and divine love.

Two themes, however, predominate in these poems: contemplation of the Passion, and veneration of the Virgin Mary. The Bannatyne Manuscript contains several poems on the Crucifixion, one of the most distinctive being Henryson's ballad-like *The Bludy Serk*. In MS Arundel 285 the Passion forms the leading theme of prayers, lyrical poems, and several narratives: in addition to poems by Dunbar and Walter Kennedy, there are the Passion-section of *The Contemplacioun of Synnaris*, the prose *Remembrance of the Passion*, and a work entitled 'Ane Devoit Remembrance of the Passioun of Crist', which is a Scotticized version of part five of Lydgate's *Testament*. All these works derive ultimately from the account of the Crucifixion in the gospels, but contain numerous extra details and incidents. All originate within a devotional tradition deeply influenced by the affective piety of the Franciscans, and by a work formerly attributed to St Bonaventura, the *Meditationes Vitae Christae*. In such works great stress is laid on contemplation of the physical sufferings of Jesus, the intention being to provoke readers into compassion, and thence into contrition and penance.

Dunbar's *Ballat of the Passioun* ('Amang thir freiris within ane cloister', B 1) is profoundly indebted to this tradition. But it is a highly original work, characteristic of Dunbar, both in its brevity (at 144 lines it is shorter than many Passion lyrics) and in the novelty of its form. The story of the Crucifixion is embedded in a dream, a visionary experience that takes place in a church on Good Friday; at its end the dreamer is wakened not by bird song (a familiar motif in love visions) but by the earthquake that accompanied the death of Jesus. In the poem's second allegorical section the dreamer is no mere spectator but a participant, and Christ's Passion is re-enacted in his own heart. He exclaims: 'Pane with Passioun me opprest' (109). Another poem of Dunbar's, *The Tabill of Confessioun* ('To the, O marcifull saluiour myn, Iesus', B 83), which was also copied in MS Arundel 285, has a practical purpose as an aid to penitential self-examination. Yet it too is highly emotional in tone, and pervaded by a similar desire to recall the sufferings of the Crucifixion – 'Thou mak me, Iesu, vnto the to remember' (153) – and, imaginatively, to share them.

Walter Kennedy (1455?–1518) is a poet long overshadowed by Dunbar, and today remembered chiefly as his antagonist in *The Flyting*. Yet Dunbar's comic and scurrilous portrait of Kennedy in that work seems to be a travesty of his real position in society: a member of the powerful Kennedy family, and educated at Glasgow University, he possessed estates in Carrick and Galloway. He boasts, with some justification, in *The Flyting*: 'I haue land, store and stakkis' (362), and 'I am the kingis blude' (417). Kennedy held various benefices, including a canonry at Glasgow Cathedral, but there is no evidence that he was ordained; indeed he had a wife and children.[26] Although not a priest, Kennedy was certainly a 'clerk', and may have been in minor orders; most of his verse (apart from *The Flyting*) is highly devout. Three short moral poems are attributed to him, all penitential in tone, which resemble the shorter poems ascribed to Henryson. Probably the best of these is 'At matyne houre in myddis of the nycht', sometimes known as 'The Praise of Age'. The longest and most interesting of his poems, however, is undoubtedly *The Passioun of Crist*.

In a short Prologue to this work Kennedy reveals something of his motivation for writing: an orthodox desire to stir readers to 'remember' the Passion is strengthened by anger that people in his own time prefer to read vain (that is, secular) stories about the siege of Tyre, 'or Hector, or Troylus' (32, 38). Although Kennedy is likely to have been a native speaker of Gaelic, and elsewhere claims that Gaelic should be 'the gud langage of this land' (*Flyting*, 347), here he is happy to write in the 'Inglis toung', and seeks a wide audience by choosing 'plane termes ... / Quhilk may be tane with small deficulte' (59–60). Kennedy refers somewhat vaguely to his sources as 'Lendulphus and vthiris' (196); 'Lendulphus' is usually taken to refer to Ludolphus of Saxony, author of a prose *Vita Christi*, which was very popular in the late fifteenth century. One of the 'vthiris' may be Philip the Chancellor (c. 1160–1236), whose poem, 'Crux, de te volo conqueri', lies behind the striking Dialogue between the Virgin and the Cross (1093–1162).[27] Kennedy often renders the Latin verse freely, but sometimes follows it remarkably closely: thus 'O lady, sueit the birding I beir now' (1128) corresponds to 'dulce pondus sustineo' (44); and 'Thocht he s[t]aw nocht, he restorit be me' (1139) corresponds to the famous paradox: 'solvit quod nunquam rapuit' (50).

Kennedy's *Passioun of Crist* is a substantial work, with a complex structure. The Crucifixion and the events surrounding it are told lucidly, with occasional lively passages of dialogue. But the narrative is placed within a framework that follows the canonical hours of the divine office in Easter week. It is repeatedly punctuated by exhortations to the reader: 'In the first complyn think with compassioun' (323), and 'Valk of thi sleip, O man, at matyn hour' (393), and:

---

[26] For further information, see Bawcutt, 'Walter Kennedy', *Oxford Dictionary of National Biography*.
[27] On this poem, see also J. A. W. Bennett, *Poetry of the Passion* (Oxford, 1982), pp. 128–36.

> O man, at sext luke with thi inwart sycht
> How thai thi lord led to confusioun;
> Mak rowme to reuth, a place for piete dycht,
> Quhill that thi hert haue perfit compassioun. (645–8)

Kennedy has lavished much care on this poem. He uses rhetorical and metrical devices to highlight important sections of the work: anaphora on 'Hail' thus continues for fourteen lines at the very beginning of the Prologue: *concatenatio* links the first five stanzas of the narrative (as distinct from the Prologue); and, in a sustained lament on Christ's death, each stanza concludes 'allace' (974–1064). There are occasional bursts of internal rhyme in emotive passages, such as two stanzas on the Crucifixion which begin: 'O man, on kne before the tre thou kneill' (792ff.). Such passages recall the verbal fireworks at the end of Kennedy's section of *The Flyting*, and his claim in that work to be 'of rethory the rose' (500).

Immediately following Kennedy's *Passioun* in Manuscript Arundel 285 is *The Contemplacioun of Synnaris*. Its author was William of Touris, a slightly older contemporary of Dunbar and Kennedy, and a Franciscan friar, who studied at the University of Paris between 1465 and 1472, and probably died c. 1505–08. Some scholars associate him with the Observantine friary of Stirling, founded by James IV. Late medieval Franciscan piety provides a valuable context for *The Contemplacioun of Synnaris*, a large and carefully structured work. Its 1560 lines form a series of separate yet inter-related sections, or 'contemplations', each allotted to a different day of the week. The author intended each meditation to have a close relationship with an accompanying 'figour', or symbolic image, but, unfortunately, of the three Scottish copies only one (British Library, Harleian manuscript 6919) provides these illustrations. The work is designed for a wide audience – at its very beginning Touris says that it 'Accordis weill for all stait, condicioun, and degre' (3; cf. also 13).[28] He envisages it as a work of spiritual 'directioun' for all who may read it (see 4 and 1554), and in the course of the work variously addresses not only the powerful, such as 'Princis, prelatis, and officiaris of iustry' (777), but 'all cristin creatouris' (249). He adopts the hortatory tone common in homiletic writing: 'O man, remember' (561).

Each section of the work has a different focus for contemplation. The first, accompanying an image of the world as a globe on a storm-tossed sea, is concerned with justice, and is the most overtly secular in its interests; there is much to link it with other Scottish writings on the *speculum principis* theme. Thursday's meditation on the Four Last Things is characteristic of the late

---

[28] References are to the Arundel text in *Devotional Pieces*, ed. Bennett, pp. 64–169. On the poem and its author, see Bennett, Introduction, pp. v–vii, xxv–xxxii; Sally Mapstone, 'The Advice to Princes Tradition in Scottish Literature 1450–1500', unpublished D.Phil. thesis (Oxford, 1986), pp. 274–315; and John Durkan, 'The Observant Franciscan Province in Scotland', *IR* 35 (1984), pp. 51–7.

fifteenth century, both in the repeated exhortations to 'do penance' and in the anxiety displayed about the imminent coming of Antichrist: 'Gret taikin is the antecrist drawis neir' (713).²⁹ Friday is devoted to heartfelt 'remembrance' (1088) of the Passion of Christ and the Compassion of his mother. The style is fluent, occasionally aureate, and often rhetorical. One passage has a macabre eloquence:

> Think how thi flesche, quhilk now is [fingar] fed,
> Salbe the fude of werme and scorpioun.
>   ...
> For perll, paddokis, for silkis eik serpent.
> Richt terrabill is [this] strang translacioun,
> For gold, gangerallis salbe thi gay garmond.   (545–52)

This illustrates a homiletic tradition that underlies both the 'Complaint of Cresseid' in Henryson's *Testament of Cresseid* and his 'The Thre Deid Pollis'.

The Contemplacioun of Synnaris was probably the most popular of the religious poems. It met the taste of contemporary readers, not only in Scotland but in England, and, perhaps even more surprisingly, its appeal lasted well into the second half of the sixteenth century. Copies of the poem survive not only in three Scottish manuscripts (Asloan, Arundel 285, and Harleian 6919), but also in the printed edition published by Wynkyn de Worde in 1499 (*STC* 5643), which pre-dates these manuscripts, but is not their source. Precisely how the work reached England is not known – Richard Fox, bishop of Durham, seems to have been an intermediary – and the text is much anglicized. At a later date two curious reworkings of the poem were made, both adapted for a Protestant readership. In England Wynkyn de Worde's print formed the basis for *A Dyall of Dayly Contemplacion*, printed by Hugh Singleton in 1578 (*STC* 5644); and in Scotland, as A. A. MacDonald has shown, Bannatyne extracted 112 lines from the Friday section to provide a new, self-contained but rather clumsy lyric on the Passion: 'O wondit spreit and saul in till exile' (no 37).³⁰

There exists a small but interesting cluster of Scottish poems on the Resurrection. By far the most famous is Dunbar's 'Done is a battell on the dragon blak' (B 10), which is accompanied in the Bannatyne Manuscript by three others on this theme: 'Thow that hes bene obedient', 'Surrexit dominus de sepulchro', and 'To the hie potent blisful trinitie'.³¹ MS Arundel 285 contains another text of 'Thow that hes bene obedient', with a slightly altered form of the opening line, and 'O mothir of God, inu[i]olat virgin Mary'.³² These poems

---

²⁹ The tone resembles Dunbar's 'Lucina schyning in silence of the nycht' (B 29); see also Richard Kenneth Emmerson, *Antichrist in the Middle Ages* (Manchester, 1981).
³⁰ See *Bannatyne MS*, ed. Ritchie, vol. 2, p. 80; and A. A. MacDonald, 'Catholic Devotion into Protestant Lyric: The Case of *The Contemplacioun of Synnaris*', *IR* 35 (1984), pp. 58–87.
³¹ *Bannatyne MS*, ed. Ritchie, vol. 2, pp. 85, 87 and 95.
³² *Devotional Pieces*, ed. Bennett, pp. 274–6.

have more in common than their subject. All have a similar metrical shape, consisting of forty lines, disposed in eight-line stanzas, rhyming *ababbcbc*. There is possibly some numerical symbolism in the choice of forty lines. Forty was a common number in the Bible, but one scholar, discussing this aspect of Dunbar's poems, suggests it is based on Christ's Appearance to the Apostles, which lasted forty days.[33] All the poems have refrains, usually in Latin, and often derived from the liturgy or the Scriptures – *A summo celo egressio eius est*, or Dunbar's *Surrexit dominus de sepulchro*, which furnishes the opening line of another poem. All employ traditional and symbolic images for Christ, the Lamb, and his foe, the Dragon. Their phrasing – 'the sing triumphale of the croce', and 'our campioun chryst' – is often closely similar to that of Dunbar. Christ is celebrated as a hero, *Christus miles*. Shared also is the tone of jubilation, appropriate to 'this triumphall fest' of Easter Day.

Nonetheless each poem has its distinctive character. In 'Thow that hes bene obedient', as Rosemary Woolf noted, 'the influence of Passion meditation is still strong':[34]

> Behald thi meik sueit saluiour
> The to inbrace how that he bowis.   (19–20)

'Surrexit dominus de sepulchro' has more of a narrative structure than the others. 'O mothir of God, inu[i]olat virgin Mary' also stands slightly apart from the rest. It has the same length and stanza pattern, but a decasyllabic line, and the diction is more aureate. Its opening might seem to herald a 'ballat of Our Lady', but the second line, which begins 'Exult in ioy', reminds us that the Resurrection was traditionally viewed as one of the Five Joys of the Virgin.[35] Another lyric, 'Ros Mary most of vertewe virginale' (see below, pp. 130–1), illustrates this blending of themes. Largely devoted to praise of the Virgin, it contains two stanzas on the Harrowing of Hell and Resurrection – here too Christ is the 'campioun' who defeats the 'Dragon'.

Devotion to the Virgin Mary was pervasive in late medieval Scotland, and this was reflected in its poetry. Striking instances are often found in otherwise secular compositions. In the romance *Lancelot of the Laik* a passage in praise of the Virgin stands out from its context by the heightened style and sustained anaphora:

> This is the flour that haith the froyt etern,
> This is the flour, this fadith for no schour ... (2086ff.)[36]

---

[33] Cf. T. D. Hill, 'Dunbar's Giant: "On the Resurrection of Christ", lines 17–24', *Anglia* 96 (1978), pp. 451–6.
[34] R. Woolf, *English Religious Lyric*, p. 307.
[35] R. Woolf, *English Religious Lyric*, p. 134.
[36] References are to *Lancelot of the Laik*, ed. Margaret M. Gray, STS (1912).

Richard Holland devised an even longer and more richly ornamented hymn in her praise to be sung by the bird minstrels in *The Buke of the Howlat* (716–54). This opens 'Hale, temple of the Trinite, crounit in hevin!', and is characterized by the common anaphora on *hale*, and numerous traditional images and figures – Mary is the 'seker trone of Salamon', 'worthy wand of Aaron' and 'joyous fleis of Gedion' (751–3).[37] Douglas too expresses his reverence for the Virgin in several Prologues to the *Eneados*. In the seafaring context of Book III, he skilfully converts the traditional image of Mary, *stella maris*, into the lodestar, the shipman's guiding star:

> Be my laid star, virgyne moder but maik;
> Thocht storm of temptatioun my schip oft schaik,
> Fra swelth of Sylla and dyrk Caribdis bandis,
> I meyn from hell, salue al go not to wraik.   (III Prol. 42–5)

In a more complex passage in I Prol. 459–70 he addressed a similar invocation to the Virgin: 'Thou, Virgyn Moder and Madyn, be my muse' (463).

Both these fine passages underwent clumsy Protestant censorship at the hands of whoever it was who prepared the text of the 1553 print of Douglas's *Eneados*. (It is not known whether he was Scottish or English.[38]) III Prol. 42 there reads: 'Be my lede stere, Christ goddis sone but maik', and I Prol. 463 reads: 'Thou Salviour of mankind, be mye muse'. Bannatyne too removed signs of Mariolatry from several of the poems that he copied, including the prayer at the end of Henryson's 'Trial of the Fox' (*Fables*, 1139–44).[39] Surprisingly, however, he made no changes to Holland's eulogy of the Virgin: his text of this passage is virtually identical with that in the Asloan Manuscript.

Some of the poems concerning the Virgin are little more than pious prayers, with a liturgical or scriptural source. One simple example is a five-line paraphrase of the angelic salutation, *Ave Maria*, in the Makculloch Manuscript (no. VIII), which begins: 'Hail, mare, goddis moder ful of grace' (*IMEV* 1065). Another is a couplet, hitherto unpublished:

> Blyssit be the bosum Iesu bair
> And paupes he sowkit, for nowe and euermair.

This is based on a well-known passage (Luke 11: 27), which forms the refrain of a Nativity poem in the Bannatyne Manuscript (vol. 2, pp. 68–71): 'Beatus venter qui te portavit et beata ubera quae suxisti'. The couplet was copied by 'Greynlawe', that is the priest and book owner John Greenlaw, of Haddington,

---

[37] References to *The Howlat* are to *Longer Scottish Poems Vol. 1*, ed. Bawcutt and Riddy; on the Scriptural types of the Virgin, see pp. 333–4.
[38] On the text and annotations of the 1553 edition of the *Eneados*, see Bawcutt, *Gavin Douglas*, pp. 196–7.
[39] Cf. MacDonald, 'Poetry, Politics and Reformation Censorship', passim.

in a copy of Quintin Kennedy's *Ane Litil Breif Tracteit*, c. 1560 (NLS, Acc. 9268, fol. 31v). Greenlaw studied at Glasgow university in the early years of the sixteenth century, and may have known Walter Kennedy, a close relative of Quintin.[40] Some of the pieces in MS Arundel 285, which are based on Latin prayers, are equally artless though suffused with pious feeling: 'I Pray yow, lady' (p. 290), which renders *Obsecro te* (*IMEV* 1343), or 'Haill, glaid and glorius' (p. 294), which renders *Ave gloriosa* (*IMEV* 1044).

Long and extremely ornate compositions were far more characteristic of late medieval Marian poetry, not only in Scotland but throughout western Europe. Dunbar's *Ballat of Our Lady* ('Hale, sterne superne, hale, in eterne', B 16) is the most famous but by no means the only Scottish example of this trend.[41] Three accompany Dunbar's poem in the Asloan Manuscript – 'O hie emprys and quene celestiale', 'Ros Mary most of vertewe virginale' and Kennedy's 'Closter of Crist riche recent flour delys'.[42] All are characterized by alliteration, aureate diction, Latin phrases and refrains, and traditional imagery and symbols. Rosemary Woolf considered that the extreme artifice of such Marian lyrics was perhaps a 'symptom of the decline of medieval devotion'.[43] Yet these Scottish poems are remarkably exuberant and joyful. One, which particularly appeals to modern readers and was by nineteenth-century editors attributed to Dunbar, seems also to have been popular in the sixteenth century: 'Ros Mary most of vertewe virginale'. The text in the Asloan manuscript is the best, but three other copies exist. One was added to the Makculloch Manuscript (no. XII), and another was copied on the flyleaf of a fifteenth-century Italian manuscript of Boethius's *De Consolatione Philosophiae* by one of its Scottish owners. It is there accompanied by a forty-line fragment of a second poem, 'O mortall man plungit in distres', which describes the Five 'Dolours' of the Virgin.[44] In the second half of the sixteenth century the poem reached England, where a copy was included in a collection of poems by William Forrest, a Catholic priest (c. 1581), who wrote admiringly of its piety and eloquence.[45]

Most of these poems to the Virgin combine eulogy with prayer, and have a petitionary purpose. They lay stress on the Virgin's place in the scheme of

---

[40] For further information, see Cornelis H. Kuipers, *Quintin Kennedy (1520–1564): Two Eucharistic Tracts: A Critical Edition* (Nijmegen, 1964); Bawcutt, 'Dunbar and an Epigram'; and John Durkan and Anthony Ross, *Early Scottish Libraries* (Glasgow, 1961), pp. 17–18 and 105–7.

[41] Cf. D. Gray, ' "Hale, Sterne Superne" and its Literary Background', *Dunbar: Essays*, ed. Mapstone, pp. 198–210.

[42] *Asloan MS*, ed. Craigie, vol. 2, pp. 245, 271, and 272.

[43] Woolf, *English Religious Lyric*, p. 281.

[44] For texts of both poems, see Ian C. Cunningham, 'Two Poems on the Virgin (National Library of Scotland, Adv. MS. 18.5.14)', *EBST* 5.5 (1988), pp. 32–40.

[45] On Forrest, see Priscilla Bawcutt, 'Crossing the Border: Scottish Poetry and English Readers in the Sixteenth Century', *The Rose and the Thistle: Essays on the Culture of Late Medieval and Renaissance Scotland*, ed. Sally Mapstone and Juliette Wood (East Linton, 1998), pp. 59–76 (69).

redemption, and her role as intercessor with God. Dunbar calls Mary a 'mediatrice' (67), and in 'Ros Mary' she is likewise termed 'madyn meike most mediatrix for man' (33). She is regularly implored to defend 'man', or 'us', or sinners in general, from the powers of evil. It is slightly less common for the poet to speak on his own behalf, praying for assistance or comfort for 'me', as in Kennedy's 'Closter of Crist'. In the final stanza he beseeches the Virgin to intercede for him with her son, and ends:

> And clenge my saull fra lipper syne inwert,
> And grant that of the hevin I may haf part
> Throw thi request, Mary, as wele thow can,
> Sen hale suple to Kennedy thow art.
> O mater dei, memento mei, thi man. (68–72)

Kennedy's naming of himself here should not be regarded as authorial vanity, a desire to perpetuate his name in the reader's mind. The motivation is religious rather than literary. One might compare Kennedy's use of his own name to the small images of donors, which appear beside the figures of Christ or the Virgin in paintings, or, more specifically, to the owner-portraits sometimes placed, in books of hours, before prayers addressed to the Virgin.[46] An even more interesting precedent occurs in a thirteenth-century manuscript (Cambridge, Fitzwilliam Museum, MS 370) that depicts a monk kneeling before an image of the Virgin. The monk's name is mentioned in the rhyming inscription: 'Fili regna Patris Ricardo da prece matris [Oh Son, grant your Father's kingdom to Richard through the prayer of your mother]'.[47]

The religious verse of this period is hardly 'vivid in the modern memory'.[48] Scottish anthologists, critics, and historians tend to select Dunbar as their 'token' medieval religious poet, and rarely mention his contemporaries. One should not make over-extravagant claims for Walter Kennedy, William of Touris, or the other, often nameless poets mentioned in this chapter, yet their poems deserve more critical recognition. They made a small but significant contribution to the remarkable literary flowering in late medieval Scotland.

---

[46] Cf. Sandra Penketh, 'Women and Books of Hours', *Women and the Book: Assessing the Visual Evidence*, ed. L. Smith and J. H. M. Taylor (London, 1996), pp. 266–81 (271ff.).

[47] For further details, see *The Cambridge Illuminations: Ten Centuries of Book Production in the Medieval West*, ed. Paul Binski and S. Panayotova (London, 2005), pp. 183–4.

[48] A. A. MacDonald's phrase, in 'Religious Poetry in Middle Scots', *History*, ed. Jack, pp. 91–104 (91).

9

William Dunbar

JOHN BURROW

In the summer of 1479 a certain 'Magister Wilelmus Dunbar' graduated as Master of Arts at the university of St Andrews. If this was the poet, as seems very likely, Dunbar was born about the year 1460.[1] There is, however, no further evidence about his life until 1500. In this year, at the age of about forty, he was awarded a 'pensioun' by King James IV, presumably for services in the royal household. This annual salary started at a modest £10, was raised to £20 in 1507 and then in 1510 to a munificent £80. Dunbar got his latest payment from that source in May 1513, shortly before the death of King James at Flodden, and nothing is known of any life he may have had thereafter. He must have been long dead when, in 1530, David Lyndsay lamented the lack of living poets to equal such as 'Dunbar, quhilk language had at large, / As maye be sene in tyll his *Goldin Targe*'.[2]

Dunbar became a priest in 1504, but his hopes of receiving a benefice were evidently disappointed, nor, at first anyway, did he find his royal 'pensioun' adequate to his needs. So he complains in several poems about his straitened circumstances. Yet his life, in court and out, was surely varied and interesting, for men of his sort, *clerici* in royal service, performed many different functions for their masters. As well as acting as a priest and chaplain, Dunbar must have been employed in a variety of secretarial capacities. He also travelled abroad, possibly on occasion as an emissary of the king. Sometimes, too, he was called upon as an acknowledged versifier to celebrate a public occasion, as he does in his poem on the marriage of James IV and Margaret Tudor in 1503, 'Quhen Merche wes with variand windis past' (B 52). He also recorded less formal events at court, such as a dance in which he himself participated, 'Sir Ihon Sinclair begowthe to dance' (B 70).

In the same poem, Dunbar identifies himself as 'Dunbar the mackar' (22), that is, the maker or poet; and he asserts this identity more formally in two other places. In 'I that in heill wes and gladnes' (B 21), he includes makers among

---

[1] On Dunbar's life, see J. W. Baxter, *William Dunbar: A Biographical Study* (1952). More critical are Denton Fox, 'The Chronology of William Dunbar', *PQ* 39 (1960), pp. 413–25, and Bawcutt, *Dunbar the Makar*, pp. 1–8. References are to Dunbar, *The Poems*, ed. Bawcutt. The canon is insecure at its edges: see *ibid.*, pp. 15–17.

[2] See Lyndsay, *Selected Poems*, ed. Hadley Williams, p. 58.

the representatives of every profession, and places himself, modestly but firmly, at the end of a list of brother poets that opens with the names of Chaucer and Gower. In another piece, 'Schir, ye haue mony seruitouris' (B 67), Dunbar the poet keeps different company, among the many professions and crafts that serve King James. Again he comes at the bottom of the list; but here any modesty is belied by the claim he makes for his particular craft:

> Als lang in mynd my work sall hald,
> Als haill in everie circumstance,
> In forme, in mater and substance,
> But wering or consumptioun,
> Roust, canker or corruptioun,
> As ony of thair werkis all.   (28–33)

In explaining why it is that his poems will last as long as – surely longer than – the works of other servants of the king, Dunbar harks back to his days as a student at St Andrews, where he would have learned that, according to Aristotle, 'substances' are compounded of 'matter' and 'form'.[3] It is because his works are complete or whole ('haill') in just these particulars, he claims, that they will have the power to 'hold long in mind'. And so it has been. The best Dunbar poems, of which there are many, do contain their matter 'whole', often most compendiously, within metrical forms which are themselves fully and expertly realized. This is the art which won the admiration of a modern maker, W. H. Auden:

> The first gift of such a poet is verse technique ... His poems never fail to do what he intends them to do. He knows exactly the kind of verse which will suit any given subject, exactly what can be got out of a metre or a stanza form.[4]

For all their wholeness of form and matter, Dunbar's work could not escape the wearing effects of time. Some of his poems survive in copies made during his lifetime, notably those issued by Scotland's first printers, Walter Chepman and Andrew Myllar; but for most we depend upon copies from the later sixteenth century, especially in two large manuscript collections, the Bannatyne Manuscript (1568) and the Maitland Folio Manuscript (1570–86). All the texts have suffered 'corruption' in transmission, and they present many problems to the modern editor.[5] Nor can it be supposed that everything Dunbar wrote has survived. Yet the eighty-four poems currently ascribed to his pen still make up a substantial body of work. The few that can be dated at all exactly prove to

---

[3] So in Aristotle's *De Anima*, Book II, chapter 1. The *De Anima* was a set text in the Master's course at St Andrews; see Baxter, *William Dunbar*, p. 20.
[4] *Criterion* 12 (1933), p. 677 (review of W. Mackay Mackenzie's edition, *The Poems of William Dunbar*, London, 1932).
[5] See Dunbar, *The Poems*, ed. Bawcutt, pp. 4–14.

belong to the documented period, 1500–13; but some of the others surely come from the years before 1500, for already in 1501 Gavin Douglas could name Dunbar in his catalogue of ancient and modern poets.[6]

The surviving corpus of mostly quite short poems exhibits such a wide variety of types that it is hard to give a synoptic account of them. The present essay draws for this purpose upon a general idea about the functions of poetry with which Dunbar himself would have been familiar. 'Every poem and all poetic utterance (*oratio poetica*) is either praise (*laudatio*) or blame (*vituperatio*)'.[7] Such an idea is alien to modern thinking about poetry. As a recent poet has observed, *laus* and *vituperatio* are 'the worst remembered, least understood, of the modes'.[8] Yet these two modes played a large part in the work of poets in earlier times, not least those with court connections like Dunbar. So on many occasions Dunbar will represent his subjects – usually people or places – as superlatively excellent in their kind. The *laudatio* may be expressed quite simply, with eulogistic epithets such as 'fair(est)' or 'bright(est)'; or it may draw upon devices of the high style: elevating tropes and figures of speech and grand diction commonly of a Latin, 'aureate' kind. In marked contrast, *vituperatio* employs a low style for subjects regarded, for whatever reason, as themselves low: these will be treated with dyslogistic epithets, unflattering comparisons, and the like, as in the poet's abusive passages of 'flyting'. Not all Dunbar's poems, of course, devote themselves mainly to praise or blame, the high or the low. He has a plain or middle manner, especially in his poems of morality and of petition. Reserving these for the last part of the present essay, however, I consider first some of Dunbar's writings that exhibit his high-style, laudatory mode.

The court of James IV had no poet laureate – Scotland's first laureate was appointed in 2004 – but four of Dunbar's poems may be described as laureate pieces, in that they address public occasions on behalf of the whole community, as if officially commissioned for the purpose. Two of these relate to the visit from France of the nobleman Bernard Stewart, the first, 'Ballade of ane right noble victorius and myghty lord, Barnard Stewart' ('Renownit, ryall, right reuerend and serene', B 56), welcoming him to Scotland, and the second, 'Illuster Lodouick, of France most cristin king' (B 23), lamenting his sudden death there. These poems show a maker matching both style and metre to his subject, in this case, high matters of public celebration and deploration. Both pieces employ the stanza form that a later king of Scots, James VI,

---

[6] 'Of this Natioun I knew also anone / Greit Kennedie and Dunbar yit vndeid', *The Palice of Honour*, 922–3, in Douglas, *Shorter Poems*, ed. Bawcutt.
[7] Cited from the Latin translation of the Arabic commentary on Aristotle's *Poetics*, in the English rendering in A. J. Minnis and A. B. Scott, *Medieval Literary Theory and Criticism c. 1100–c. 1375: the Commentary Tradition* (Oxford, 1988), p. 289. Aristotle said no such thing in the *Poetics*, but the thought was widely received in medieval treatises on poetry: see Minnis and Scott, *ibid.*, ch. 7, especially pp. 282–4 and 289–92.
[8] Geoffrey Hill, *The Triumph of Love: A Poem* (Harmondsworth, 1999), XXIII, 5–7.

recommended for 'any heich and graue subiectis': the 'Ballat Royal', rhyming with a refrain *ababbcbC*.[9] The 'Ballade' of welcome pulls out all the eulogistic stops, with rhetorical repetitions, extravagant comparisons (Achilles, Hector, Arthur...), and flights of lexical fancy ('Welcum, oure indeficient adiutorie', 25). Another poem in the same ballat-royal stanza celebrates the reception of Queen Margaret by the town of Aberdeen: 'Blyth Aberdeane, thow beriall of all tounis' (B 8). This poem, glorifying the town as well as the queen, shows the principles of *laudatio* extending to non-personal subjects. The *encomium urbis* is an ancient genre.[10]

Much the most ambitious of these 'laureate' pieces, however, is 'Quhen Merche wes with variand windis past' (B 52). This dream-vision approaches its public subject, the royal wedding, quite obliquely, with the poet summoned from his bed by a personified month of May as if he were a lover who has failed to do her honour. But this is not to be an allegory of love. The dreamer follows May into a garden where he finds the goddess Nature presiding over a springtime gathering of birds, beasts and plants – Dunbar recalling, but also outdoing, Geoffrey Chaucer's *Parliament of Fowls*, where Nature assembles only birds. In Dunbar's assembly, Margaret is represented by a Tudor rose, and James variously by a heraldic lion, an eagle, and a thistle (at that time very recently taken as a Scottish royal emblem).[11] The action of the poem consists of nothing more than a sequence of coronations performed by Nature, culminating in the crowning of the rose. She is acclaimed first by the flowers, and then by the birds with such a shout that the dreamer wakes up, just like Chaucer's dreamer at the end of the *Parliament*. The poem is not entirely devoted to praise and celebration, however. Nature gives each of James's three surrogates serious advice on the duties of a king, in the manner of a medieval Regiment of Princes; and the dreamer, more surprisingly, responds at first to May's summons with a very unflattering view of 'busteous' Scottish spring weather (29–35). Yet this May is as beautiful as Botticelli's Primavera, clad all in flowers '[b]almit in dew and gilt with Phebus bemys' (20): this is a May morning when the dew, which releases the fragrance or 'balm' of the flowers, has not yet been dried by the sun. Given the loftiness of its royal occasion, the diction of the poem is less extravagant than one might expect, with rather few conspicuous Latinisms – though the garden is described, not as 'sweet-smelling', but as 'dulce and redolent' (47). Its general manner, though, is lofty

---

[9] *Ane Schort Treatise conteining some revlis and cautelis to be obseruit and eschewit in Scottis Poesie, Poems of James VI of Scotland*, ed. James Craigie, 2 vols, STS (1955–58), vol. 1, p. 80.

[10] In the *Ars Versificatoria* of Matthew of Vendôme, model descriptions of places, like those of persons, are directed either to praise (*praeconium*) or dispraise (*vituperium*): *Les Arts Poétiques du XIIe et du XIIIe Siècle*, ed. E. Faral (Paris, 1924), Section I, paragraphs 109–11. On traditions of praise and blame in medieval writing: E. R. Curtius, *European Literature and the Latin Middle Ages*, trans. W. R. Trask (London, 1953), pp. 154–66.

[11] See Priscilla Bawcutt, 'Dunbar's Use of the Symbolic Lion and Thistle', *Cosmos* 2 (1986), pp. 83–95.

and laudatory, as when Nature tells the thistle that he should honour no flower more than the rose:

> So full of vertew, plesans and delyt,
> So full of blisfull angeilik bewty,
> Imperiall birth, honour and dignite.   (145–7)

An even more ambitious piece in a similar mode is *The Goldyn Targe* ('Ryght as the stern of day begouth to schyne', B 59). It has been suggested that the poem may be an early work, dating perhaps from the 1490s;[12] and this seems very likely, for it has all the air of a 'masterwork', in the old sense of that term, the piece of work by which a craftsman gained the recognized rank of 'master'. It has a difficult nine-line stanza, with only two rhymes in each (as against the easier rhyme royal of 'Quhen Merche wes'); and it opens with a description of another springtime garden that seems to challenge the competition from all earlier dream visions. The sun as it rises is referred to as 'the goldyn candill matutyne' (4), and its drying of the dew prompts a mythological conceit: Phoebus drinks up the tears that Aurora, the dawn, has shed on being parted from him (16–18). The whole scene is brightly lit by a sunlight that reflects off the surface of a river onto the branches of overhanging trees: 'The bewis bathit war in secund bemys / Throu the reflex of Phebus visage brycht' (32–3). 'Reflex' and 'secund bemys' are both ambitiously learned terms from optics.[13] It is in this garden that the narrator, falling asleep, sees an approaching boat, sharply evoked as '[a] saill als quhite as blossum vpon spray' (51), from which disembark two companies, of gods and goddesses. Dunbar names but hardly describes these divinities, resorting to an ancient commonplace of apology in laudatory writing: not even Homer or Cicero with their 'aureate tongis' (71) could do justice to the beauty of the spectacle.[14] There follows the main action of the poem, an allegory of love. The dreamer is defended against the personified charms of a lady by Reason with his golden 'targe' or shield. He finally succumbs, only to be rejected after a very short spell of happiness and left in misery. C. S. Lewis, whilst admiring the brilliance of the poem, was surely right to condemn its action as slight, degenerating at times into 'a mere catalogue of personifications'.[15] It suffers by comparison with the central coronation scenes in 'Quhen Merche wes', whose heraldic grandeur holds out no promise of a story. Yet the dream ends very well, as the gods and goddesses embark, with a loud broadside from the departing ship, which wakes up the

---

[12] Dunbar, *The Poems*, ed. Bawcutt, pp. 413–14.
[13] Cf. 44–5, and see Bawcutt, *Dunbar the Makar*, p. 313, on the similar treatment of sound resounding at lines 25, 108, and 240.
[14] This is the substance of the 'inexpressibility topos' in eulogy: see Curtius, *European Literature*, pp. 159–62.
[15] C. S. Lewis, *The Allegory of Love* (Oxford, 1936), p. 252. For a reading of the poem as erotic fantasy, see A. C. Spearing, *The Medieval Poet as Voyeur* (Cambridge, 1993), pp. 240–8.

dreamer. There follow three stanzas which declare the poem's ambition in the act of apologizing for its inadequacy; for they praise Chaucer, Gower and Lydgate in terms which exemplify the same qualities in Dunbar's own diction: 'fresch anamalit termes celicall' (257), 'tongis aureate' (263). And the very fact of ending the poem with a formal epilogue of this kind marks it as an ambitious successor to such great precedents as Chaucer's *Troilus and Criseyde*.

The four remaining poems in this mode concern religious subjects, for which *laudatio* was always in order: God, Christ, and the Virgin Mary. The most modest of these is 'Thow that in hewin for our saluatioun' (B 80), a poem of uncertain attribution, praying to God on behalf of the author's troubled country.[16] Another piece in the same ballat-royal stanza, 'Done is a battell on the dragon blak' (B 10), is certainly Dunbar's and indeed ranks among his finest achievements. With its clangorous Latin refrain, '*Surrexit dominus de sepulchro*', it celebrates Christ's victory over death and the devil at the Harrowing of Hell and the Resurrection. Writing in the present tense as if on Easter Day itself, Dunbar represents Christ as a champion carrying his cross as a sign of triumph. The poem generates great power from its profusion of images, most of them drawn from the liturgy of the Church:

> He for our saik that sufferit to be slane
> And lyk a lamb in sacrifice wes dicht,
> Is lyk a lyone rissin vp agane
> And as a gyane raxit him on hicht.　　　　　(17–20)[17]

This poem displays Dunbar's mastery of syntax ('wholeness of form', again). Most of the short stanzas, especially the first and the last, shoot off salvoes of simple sentences – 'The fo is chasit, the battell is done ceis' (33) – and against that background even the modest construction of the lines just quoted stands out, with the image in the relative clauses of Christ as sacrificial lamb giving way in the main clauses to the images of the rising lion and the stretching giant. Having suffered in the subordinate clauses, Christ triumphs in the main ones. The syntax generates that 'articulate energy' about which Donald Davie wrote.[18]

'*Rorate, celi, desuper!*' (B 58), a poem celebrating the Nativity, calls upon the whole of creation to acclaim the event, from the archangels down to flowers and fishes. Its refrain is simple and familiar, '*Et nobis puer natus est*'; but the poem has its imaginative source in that other verse of Isaiah which occupies its first line. *Rorate, celi, desuper*, 'Send down dew from above, you heavens' (Isa. 45.8): these words, commonly interpreted as prophetic of the Incarnation, serve here to set off a sequence of acclamations working their way downwards

---

[16] Bawcutt accepts the poem as Dunbar's (*The Poems*, p. 481), though others do not.
[17] See Bawcutt, *Dunbar the Makar*, pp. 178–84; on the giant and source, Ps. 19.5: pp. 180–1.
[18] Donald Davie, *Articulate Energy: An Enquiry into the Syntax of English Poetry*, 2nd edn (London, 1976).

(*desuper*) from the heavens above (*celi*). The one remaining word, '*Rorate*', also plays its part, for the reference to dewfall evokes Dunbar's poetry of dawn: Christ rises as the morning star and as the sun in the east (stanza 1), birds sing a dawn chorus (stanza 5), and the flowers 'lay out their leaves' to greet the returning light (stanza 6). For Dunbar, as for William Langland and many other medieval poets, a text from the Bible or the liturgy could be richly suggestive.

Another poem with its source in the Latin Bible is the extraordinary *Ballat of Our Lady* (B 16). This amplifies Gabriel's salutation, '*Ave, Maria, gracia plena*', into seven flamboyant twelve-line stanzas. Each of these rhymes on only two sounds, with double internal rhyming in the longer lines; so every stanza has to find no less than fifteen *a*-rhymes. The result is a technical *tour de force* of the maker's art, following in the tradition of Latin lyrics honouring the Virgin.[19] The poem shows equal ambition in its language, displaying 'fresch anamalit termes' in a profusion unequalled elsewhere in Dunbar's writing. This diction is drawn from the regular stock of Latin, especially the Latin of the Church, and also from the outer reaches of that language, as when the second stanza rhymes on the words 'habitakle', 'tabernakle', 'signakle', 'vmbrakle', 'makle' and 'mirakle'. The Mary of this poem is the queen and empress of heaven, not the modest virgin of the Nativity, and Dunbar's panegyric matches its high aureate style to the height of the subject:

> Empryce of prys, imperatrice,
>   Bricht polist precious stane,
> Victrice of wyce, hie genitrice
>   Of Ihesu, lord souerayne,
> Our wys pavys fro enemys,
>   Agane the feyndis trayne,
> Oratrice, mediatrice, saluatrice,
>   To God gret suffragane.   (61–8)

Dunbar's Latin and his Latinisms call for some comment. The example of the Mary poem shows how words of Latin origin may contribute, as 'anamalit' or 'aureate' diction, to a high rhetorical style. A phrase such as 'Angelicall regyne' (6) there means the same as 'queen of the angels', but means it differently. Stylistically the expression is, as linguists say, 'marked'. Not that there is always a clear distinction to be drawn between such usages and all the normally unmarked borrowings to be looked for in any everyday piece of early sixteenth-century Scots or English. Among the six rhyme-words cited earlier, one can safely suppose that 'vmbrakle' (Latin *umbraculum*, 'shadow') would have struck a contemporary reader as distinctly marked; but what about 'tabernakle' or 'mirakle'? Both words belong to the regular clerical wordstock; yet in this context, rhyming as they do, they acquire a certain heightened

---

[19] On the tradition, see D. Gray, ' "Hale, Sterne Superne" and its Literary Background', *Dunbar: Essays*, ed. Mapstone, pp. 198–210.

Latinity. The stylistic value of Latin loanwords, in fact, will vary according to use and context. It is not, for most of them, a fixed or intrinsic property.[20]

Latin itself also plays a more direct part in Dunbar's poetry, as when he draws refrains such as '*Et nobis puer natus est*' from ecclesiastical sources. Church Latin was a language very familiar to Dunbar's readers, and he could call upon it freely even for unserious purposes. This he does in the brilliant *Dumbaris Dirige to the King* ('We that ar heir in hevynnis glorie', B 84), a poem addressed to James and his court companions. Writing from Edinburgh, Dunbar jokingly expresses sympathy for the purgatorial sufferings of the royal party then in Stirling, composing a mock-liturgical 'dirge' or Office of the Dead, with a prayer for their return to the celestial joys of the capital. He ends with a passage of Latin which boldly adapts words from the Office and from the Paternoster to the present occasion: thus, '*Credo gustare vinum Edinburgi / In villa viuentium*' parodies (but does not mock) the liturgical words '*Credo videre bona Domini in terra viventium*'.[21] A similar spirit of Goliardic comedy marks another, more systematically bilingual, *jeu d'esprit*. 'I maister Andro Kennedy' (B 19) takes the form of a mock Last Will and Testament dictated by Kennedy, evidently a well-known alcoholic. Its Scots is interlarded with testamentary Latin ('*Nunc condo testamentum meum*') and the Latin of the Church ('*Dies illa, dies ire*', 106), as well as the simplest dog-Latin. The effect is wonderfully racy:

> I maister Andro Kennedy
> *Curro quando sum vocatus.*
> Gottin with sum incuby
> Or with sum freir *infatuatus* ...   (1–4)

For a man like Dunbar, Latin was a living language of many registers, from the formalities of liturgy and law to the mundanities of every day ('I come running when I'm called').

With the drunkard Andrew Kennedy, this discussion has moved into the lower worlds of Dunbar's creations, where *laudatio* has no place, except by way of irony and ridicule – worlds peopled by such as drinkers, fools, tailors, cobblers and Highlanders, as well as charlatans, traitors and devils.

In some of these poems the prevailing spirit is one of wild comedy. 'Off Februar the fyiftene nycht' (B 47) presents a burlesque vision of Hell in Dunbar's elrich manner.[22] The Devil organizes a dance of sinners and then a

---

[20] See discussion and references in John Corbett, 'Aureation Revisited: The Latinate Vocabulary of Dunbar's High and Plain Styles', in *Dunbar: Essays*, ed. Mapstone, pp. 183–97.

[21] For a discussion of 'parody' in 'I maister Andro Kennedy' (B 19) and 'We that ar heir in hevynnis glorie' (B 84), see Elizabeth Archibald, 'William Dunbar and the Medieval Tradition of Parody', *Proceedings of the Third International Conference on Scottish Language and Literature (Medieval and Renaissance)*, ed. R. J. Lyall and F. Riddy (Stirling / Glasgow, 1981), pp. 328–44. Also Bawcutt, *Dunbar the Makar*, pp. 191–203.

[22] See Bawcutt, *Dunbar the Makar*, ch. 7, 'Elrich Fantasyis'.

tournament between a cobbler and a tailor – both notoriously unheroic types, so afraid of each other here that they fart, vomit and shit themselves. For this poem Dunbar selects the common English tail-rhyme stanza, as Chaucer did in his burlesque tale of Sir Thopas, another cowardly hero. Dunbar employs the same form in two other comic pieces, *A Ballat of the Abbot of Tungland* ('As yung Awrora with cristall haile', B 4) and 'Now lythis off ane gentill knycht' (B 39). These both purport to describe exploits of persons known at court. The Abbot of Tungland, a rather mysterious foreign dabbler in medicine and alchemy, tries to fly like Daedalus and ends up in the mud; and the 'gentill knycht' Thomas Norny, evidently a court fool, has the most improbable adventures ascribed to him, perhaps on the occasion of some mock investiture. Norny and the abbot were easy targets for ridicule, like the black girl so unsparingly mocked in 'Lang heff I maed of ladyes quhytt' (B 28); but Dunbar does not confine his mockery to such marginal figures. 'Sir Ihon Sinclair begowthe to dance' (B 70), according to a heading in the Maitland Folio Manuscript, concerns a dance in the private chamber of Queen Margaret, and describes how most of the participants, Dunbar included, make fools of themselves: Sir John and Master Robert Shaw stagger and stumble, the royal almoner releases a fart, and the poet himself, inspired by the beauty of one of the Queen's ladies, 'hoppet lyk a pillie wanton' (25) and lost a shoe. This is one of those pieces that challenge more staid modern notions of the courtly and the clerical.

These poems are far from flattering to their subjects; but for *vituperatio* proper one must look elsewhere. There is one deadly serious example in 'In vice most vicius he excellis' (B 27). This poem attacks a Highland rebel, the 'fell strong tratour, Donald Owyr' (19), advocating his immediate execution.[23] Its stanza consists of an octosyllabic couplet followed by four lines of just four syllables each, as in this parting shot:

> The murtherer ay mvrthour mais,
> And evir quhill he be slane he slais.
>   Wyvis thus makis mokkis,
>   Spynnand on rokkis:
>   Ay rynnis the fox
>   Quhill he fute hais.   (43–8)

Here is occasion to notice a technical point about metrical form. When Dunbar or his scribes wrote the very common inflectional endings '–is' (and also '–it' in verbs), they evidently assumed that readers would perform them either syllabically or not, guided by whatever count of syllables the poem in question has established as its norm. Thus in the four-syllable lines just quoted, where 'mokkis' and 'rokkis' are obviously monosyllabic in rhyme with 'fox', the

---

[23] See Bawcutt, *Dunbar the Makar*, pp. 252–6. In the event, the king did not have Donald executed – a clemency against which the poem argues.

metre requires the same of 'wyvis', 'makis' and 'rynnis': 'Wives thus makes mocks', 'Ay runs the fox'. The force of these heavy short-arm jabs is lost if the lines are mismetred. In another poem, 'Schir, I complane off iniuris' (B 64), Dunbar abuses a certain 'refing sonne off rakyng Muris' (2) for stealing and spoiling his verses: 'That fulle dismemberit hes my meter' (8). He would not have wished modern readers (or editors) to do the same.[24]

A much longer, but also much less serious, exercise in *vituperatio* may be seen in *The Flyting of Dumbar and Kennedie* (B 65).[25] This piece is a full-scale competitive exchange of insults. After short opening exchanges, each man directs an extensive tirade against the other. Dunbar represents Walter Kennedy (not to be confused with the drunkard Andrew Kennedy) as a disreputable Highland 'bard' – a Gaelic word, used pejoratively by Lowlanders. His contribution, like Kennedy's, assembles a whole thesaurus of insult. The man is ugly, misshapen, incontinent, impoverished. He and his mistress go begging at the mill for scraps, with nothing to their name but lice and long nails. Dunbar gleefully imagines him being pursued through the streets of Edinburgh by a rabble of boys and dogs:

> Off Edinburch the boyis as beis owt thrawis,
> And cryis owt, 'Hay, heir cumis our awin queir clerk!'
> Than fleis thow lyk ane howlat chest with crawis,
> Quhill all the brachis at thy botingis dois bark.   (217–20)

A reader of Alexander Pope, that other master of vituperation, might wish for more wit; but this is rougher and wilder stuff. Walter Kennedy was in fact a substantial and well-connected landowner, as well as a poet of repute, and Dunbar's version of him, like his version of Dunbar, touches only lightly on realities.[26] Their poems are best understood as a joint *tour de force* of the maker's art, with grand eight-line stanzas, heavy alliteration, and, at the end of each performance, a great fusillade of internal rhymes. When their exchanges are completed, an amused audience is invited to judge for themselves who came out worst: 'quha gat the war'.

There is another poem that engages with its audience in this fashion by inviting their judgement: *The Tretis of the Tua Mariit Wemen and the Wedo* (B 3). The three women of the title are secretly observed by the narrator as they sit together in a garden, drinking their way through a short Midsummer night and

---

[24] His verse, as we have it, does generally observe the syllable-count, though not with complete consistency. Some editors attempt to remedy metrical defects, attributing them to early printers and scribes, but Bawcutt does not (*The Poems*, pp. 14–15).
[25] Discussed by Bawcutt, *Dunbar the Makar*, pp. 221–39. On such 'rough music' more generally, see D. Gray, 'Rough Music: Some Early Invectives and Flytings', *Yearbook of English Studies* 14 (1984), pp. 21–43.
[26] See Priscilla Bawcutt, 'Walter Kennedy', *Oxford Dictionary of National Biography*. In the quite different context of 'I that in heill wes and gladnes', Dunbar laments the imminent death of 'gud maister Walter Kennedy' (89–91). See also n. 6 above.

boasting to each other over their drinks about how they have deceived and exploited their respective husbands. 'Quhilk wald ye waill to your wif, gif ye suld wed one? [Which would you choose as wife, if you were to wed one of them?]', asks the poet at the end. This is one of Dunbar's longest writings, composed in a long-poem metre, unrhymed alliterative verse. He employs this metre only here (very late in its long history), perhaps because, like James VI, he thought it appropriate for 'flyting or Invectives'.[27] The poem does indeed report much invective. In long vituperative speeches, the women abuse their husbands – variously old and impotent, young and impotent, or middle-aged and despicable – in cascades of alliterating contempt:

> 'I haue ane wallidrag, ane worme, ane auld wobat carle,
> A waistit wolroun na worth bot wourdis to clatter,
> Ane bumbart, ane dronbee, ane bag full of flewme.' (89–91)

In the process, they quite outdo Chaucer's Wife of Bath in exposing the secrets of the marriage bed.[28] The first wife's old husband has, she complains, a stiff beard but a penis 'soft and soupill as the silk' (96). The aggressive female sexuality of all three women and their revulsion from the constraints of marriage might be expected, in a medieval poem, if they were low-life gossips, like the 'cummaris' of 'Richt arely one Ask Wedinsday' (B 57). But they are not. On the contrary, the poet's opening description presents them in high eulogistic style, as elegant ladies whose beauty matches that of the idealized garden in which they sit: they are 'seimlie and soft as the sweit lillies, / Now vpspred vpon spray as new spynist rose' (28–9). Two opposed constructions of womanhood confront each other here without any resolution of the conflict; for at the end of the poem, the narrator calmly resumes his description of the beautiful garden and disposes of the three ladies as if they had never said an improper word: 'Than rais thir ryall rosis in ther riche wedis, / And rakit hame to ther rest throw the rise blwmys' (523–4). What are we to make of this? Perhaps the ladies, who have literally let their hair down (22), are simply enjoying the traditional licences of a Midsummer nightwatch, and the poem is to be read in a purely comic and carnivalesque spirit. Or perhaps Dunbar is implying a strongly anti-feminist argument *a fortiori*: if even such gracious ladies can speak and behave so, then surely all other women must be just as bad or worse. Or perhaps, as A. C. Spearing suggests, the poem manifests 'some of the most damaging consequences of the contradictory attitudes towards women and sexuality built into the dominant structures of medieval thought and feeling and presumably internalized by Dunbar himself'.[29] This last opinion may come

---

[27] *Ane Schort Treatise*, *Poems of James VI*, ed. Craigie, vol. 1, p. 81, on 'tumbling verse'.
[28] Spearing notices also the poem's relation to Chaucer's *Merchant's Tale*, with its portrayal of the marriage between old January and young May: *Medieval Poet as Voyeur*, ch. 13.
[29] Spearing, *Medieval Poet as Voyeur*, p. 253.

nearest the mark. Most readers do find it difficult to focus on the three women, as if the poem itself were suffering from double vision.

I turn now to those other poems of Dunbar in which neither *laudatio* nor *vituperatio* plays a major part. Some of these concern moral or didactic themes and others take the form of verse petitions. They are composed generally in an inbetween style that may be called 'plain',[30] most of them in octosyllabic couplets or else, more commonly, in stanzas.

For these purposes, Dunbar especially favours a stanza of just four or five lines, usually with a refrain, as in the best-known of his didactic pieces, 'I that in heill wes' (B 21).

> No stait in erd heir standis sickir.
> As with the wynd wavis the wickir,
> So waueris this warldis vanite:
> *Timor mortis conturbat me.* (13–16)

This is a typically artful and compendious stanza. The alliterating simile of the waving willow is linked to the preceding maxim with a crisp rhyme, and its key word 'vanite' heralds the return of the poem's ominous refrain, '*Timor mortis conturbat me*'. These words are drawn from the liturgy, the Office of the Dead; but in this poem Dunbar speaks, not as the priest that he was, but as a man subject to the vicissitudes of life, just like his fellow poets and everyone else. Rarely, in fact, do even his didactic poems strike distinctively clerical notes.[31] They speak from common experience, expressed by the pronouns 'we' and 'us', in lines such as these from 'Full oft I mvse and hes in thocht' (B 14):

> How euer this warld dois chynge and varie,
> Let ws no moir in hart be sarie,
> Bot ay be reddie and addrest
> To pas out of this fraudfull farie.
> For to be blyth me think it best. (36–40)

'It seems best to be happy': the refrain sounds a quite unpriestly note, though its counsel coexists easily enough with the poem's awareness of change, death and judgement. Earthly life may be a deceit and an illusion (a 'farie'), but it has to be lived through in time, and we might as well make the best of it.

The finest of the poems composed in this spirit is 'In to thir dirk and drublie dayis' (B 26). Here Dunbar represents himself in the depths of a gloomy Scottish winter, assailed by 'heavy thoughts' about his uncertain livelihood at

---

[30] On the 'middle style' in these poems, see Bawcutt, *Dunbar the Makar*, pp. 367–70.
[31] Even in *Ane Ballat of the Passioun* (B 1), Dunbar represents himself as nothing more than an ordinary Good Friday devotee: 1–7, 141–4. In 'To speik of science, craft or sapience' (B 82), as Bawcutt notes (*The Poems*, p. 484), Dunbar speaks of 'clerkis' as if he were not of their number.

court (stanza 4) and advancing age and approaching death (stanzas 7 and 8). These dark reflections, expressed in chilling speeches by Despair, Age and Death respectively, are countered by the words of Patience and Prudence. Each speaker has just one five-line stanza in which to make his or her points. Thus Prudence:

> And Prudence in my eir sayis ay,
> 'Quhy wald thow hald that will away,
> Or craif that thow may haue no space,
> Thow tending to ane vther place,
> A iournay going everie day?'   (26–30)

For all their ease of rhythm and syntax, these lines are packed with meaning – 'haill in everie circumstance'. Prudence is the virtue that takes long views. She first challenges the gloomy poet with a proverb: Why would you want to hold on to what will certainly go away? (as in Chaucer's *Troilus*, 4, 1628). Or why do you crave for what cannot of its nature be yours for any considerable length of time ['no space']? Picking up the repeated 'thows', Prudence goes on to subjoin her two haunting phrases: 'Thow tending ... / A iournay going ...'. It is the old idea of life as a journey, here given a new twist. Luggage is always an encumbrance on a journey, and if one is travelling 'everie day' it must be best to have none at all. Her rather sinister reference to 'ane vther place' looks forward to the direr warnings of Age and Death which are to follow; yet the poem concludes in a quite different key. Although the personifications have all spoken truths, it is the 'dirk and drublie dayis' of winter that have called them to mind. So as the nights grow shorter, the poet can look forward to more comfortable times; and the poem ends, indeed, with an invocation to 'Symmer', that is, Spring: 'Cum, lustie Symmer, with thi flowris, / That I may leif in sum disport' (49–50).

When Despair spoke of the 'grit trouble and mischeif' (19) to be suffered by the poet as he struggles to survive at court, one may detect a passing hint to King James; but 'In to thir dirk and drublie dayis' can hardly be classed as a petitionary poem, oblique though those often are. More than a dozen other poems, though, make more open appeals – petitions for the bestowal of a benefice, payment of money or a grant of clothing.[32] 'Courtmen' like Dunbar depended on the grace and favour of their masters, which they commonly had to secure by asking – either orally, or in formal written *supplicationes*, or else, where the petitioner was a poet, in verse. One of Dunbar's pieces, 'Off every asking followis nocht' (B 44), insists on the need to make requests and sets out the principles governing the activity. These are summarized in the refrain, 'In asking sowld discretioun be': one had better not bore or exasperate the benefactor. Poets had an advantage here, for they might hope to impress and

---

[32] On Dunbar's poetry of petition, see Bawcutt, *Dunbar the Makar*, pp. 103–30.

entertain by their art. Certainly Dunbar's petitionary poems are as artful as anything he wrote, rising at times to displays of virtuosity. Thus the longest of them, 'This waverand warldis wretchidnes' (B 79), finds twenty-four different words to rhyme with the refrain-word, 'pane', hitting upon some happy finds in the process:

> Kirkmen so halie ar and gude
> That on thair conscience, rowme and rude,
> May turne aucht oxin and ane wane,
> Quhilk to considder is ane pane. (41–4)

These churchmen, enjoying the benefices that Dunbar longs for, have consciences so roomy that one could, we might say, turn a heavy lorry on them. Such are, in the words of one modern poet, the 'chances of rhyme'.[33] No doubt James was amused.

Another poem addressed to the king opens with these words: 'Be diuers wyis and operatiounes / Men makis in court thair solistationes' (B 5). Dunbar's 'solicitations' are indeed diverse. Some of them work in a distinctly poetic and figurative way, employing allegories or sustained metaphors. Most unusually for this genre, one takes the form of a dream vision: 'This hinder nycht, halff sleiping as I lay' (B 75). Dunbar makes more of his personifications here than he does in 'Into thir dirk and drublie dayis' (B 26). The two damsels, Distress and Heaviness, who lie like nightmares on the bedridden poet, represent his state of gloom. The rout of other personifications, who burst into his chamber with bright lights and music, suggests how that weight might be lifted – if only Nobleness and Discretion can prevail with the king against the claims of unworthy competitors. So perhaps, after his abrupt awakening, 'yone ballet maker' (90) may yet get his deserts. Other poems play at some length with cleverly developed comparisons: with birds in 'Schir, yit remember as befoir' (B 68), and with horses in 'Schir, lat it neuer in toune be tald' (B 66). The latter is a Yuletime appeal to the king in which Dunbar plays the fool (one way of furthering a request, according to 'Be diuers wyis and operatiounes', B 5), representing himself as a faithful old carthorse obliged to winter out-of-doors while other horses are stabled in comfort. He asks to be given at least a new 'housing' or horse-cover '[a]ganis this Crysthinmes for the cald' (65–6), referring to the allowance of clothing, the 'livery', that courtmen expected at that season. Evidently James entered into the spirit of the thing, for a subjoined verse '*Respontio regis*' authorizes the Treasurer to take in and house 'this gray hors, auld Dumbar' (70).

Dunbar addresses the king more plainly in three other poems, two of them already mentioned, 'Be diuers wyis and operatiounes' (B 5) and 'Schir, ye haue

---

[33] 'The chances of rhyme are like the chances of meeting – / In the finding fortuitous, but once found, binding', Charles Tomlinson, *Collected Poems*, 2nd edn (Oxford, 1987), 'The Chances of Rhyme', p. 194.

mony seruitouris' (B 67), together with 'Complane I wald, wist I quhome till' (B 9). In all three, encouraged by the unchecked flow of their octosyllabic couplets, Dunbar indulges his love of lists and catalogues. The short 'Be diuers wyis' surveys the various methods of solicitation at court, while 'Complane I wald' complains angrily about the ignobility of many of the types who succeed there. The longer 'Schir, ye haue mony seruitouris' opens with a list of royal servants, ending, as already noticed, with the poet's claim for his own work. There follows a vituperative catalogue, like that in 'Complane I wald', of all those who unworthily enjoy the king's favour – hypocrites, loudmouths, 'Monsouris of France, gud clarat cunnaris' (42), and the rest. This brings the poem to its petitionary moment, a point at which some finesse is called for. 'Be diuers wyis' ostensibly made no claim upon the king's grace, while 'Complane I wald' invoked the poet's long service, but 'Schir, ye haue mony seruitouris' advances a more personal and amusing consideration. Dunbar is suffering from melancholy and his mind is 'set to flyt' (79) because of those sccundrels who are 'all rewardit and nocht I' (67). But if James would only consent to reward him along with the rest, the poet would sing a different tune for him, quite overlooking the many faults of his fellow courtmen. So at last it is not the moralist but the courtier who speaks, coolly acknowledging his self-interested motives in the crowded small world that he inhabits.

Unlike the majority of medieval genres, petitionary verse invited poets to speak about themselves, as did those other royal clerks, Eustache Deschamps in France and Thomas Hoccleve in England. In two poems of this kind, Dunbar speaks in some detail about his own daily life. 'Sanct saluatour, send siluer sorrow!' (B 61) describes some consequences of his empty purse. So, one stanza tells how, when other men with money to spare go off to drink or breakfast together, he has to find an excuse for not joining them, gravely regretting that he is bound to keep a fast until midday:

> Quhen men that hes pursis in tone
> Pasis to drynk or to disione,
> Than mon I keip ane grauetie
> And say that I will fast quhill none.   (16–19)

The second notable instance of personal self-reference is 'My heid did yak yester nicht' (B 35). Here the poet complains that he cannot write anything today – or so he writes – because of suffering last night from a migraine:

> And now, schir, laitlie eftir mes
> To dyt thocht I begowthe to dres,
> The sentence lay full evill till find,
> Vnsleipit in my heid behind,
> Dullit in dulnes and distres.   (6–10)

The poem describes, in Dunbar's best plain manner, a very specific time of distress, as if it were a free-standing autobiographical lyric; but even here there is a petitionary point, marked by the address to King James ('schir'). The poet apologizes to his lord for not writing more, surely in the hope of prompting some sympathetic act of generosity in return.

At a royal court, as Chaucer's Arcite observed, it is '[e]ch man for hymself' (*KnT*, I.1181-2). Many of Dunbar's poems reflect that closed world of rumour and gossip so well portrayed also by his English contemporary John Skelton in the *Bowge of Court*.[34] It is a world of known and named individuals: the court fools – John Bute, Curry, Cuddy Rug – or the dancers in the queen's chamber – Sir John Sinclair, Master Robert Shaw, Mistress Musgrave, 'Dunbar the mackar'. Life at court was, by medieval standards, a highly individualistic and competitive affair. To survive or succeed in it, one had to establish a recognizable identity. Skelton and Dunbar were both priests, but Dunbar, like Skelton, relied mainly on his more distinctive occupation as a poet to single him out: 'Dunbar the mackar' could only be him. Like Skelton, too, he refers quite frequently to himself. These references may be no more than the usual petitionary complaints about poverty and unjustified neglect; but others strike a more personal note. At such moments – in the migraine poem, for example – one can see how autobiographical writing developed, as it did in the poetry of the time, within the matrix of petitionary appeal. Dunbar is not an 'autobiographical' poet in any full later sense of the word, nor does he, like Skelton, draw attention to himself by speaking in a highly idiosyncratic voice. Yet Dunbar does have a distinctive presence in his poems, as Robert Henryson, for instance, does not. He is there as the courtman and, above all, as the master maker, the poet whose works would, as he rightly believed, hold long in mind.

---

[34] On Dunbar as court poet, see Denton Fox, 'Middle Scots Poets and Patrons', *English Court Culture in the Later Middle Ages*, ed. V. J. Scattergood and J. W. Sherborne (London, 1983), pp. 109–27. For a comparison with Skelton, see A. S. G. Edwards, 'Dunbar, Skelton and the Nature of Court Culture in the Early Sixteenth Century', *Vernacular Literature and Current Affairs in the Early Sixteenth Century*, ed. Jennifer Britnell and Richard Britnell (Aldershot, 2000), pp. 120–34.

10

Gavin Douglas

DOUGLAS GRAY

It is strange that the modern reputation of this fine poet has never matched that of his predecessors – and this in spite of an enthusiastic endorsement by C. S. Lewis, and some devoted scholarship and criticism since.[1] While both Henryson and Dunbar have successfully escaped from the prisonhouse of the 'Scottish Chaucerians', Douglas, largely because of his elaborate *Palice of Honour*, seems to have remained there. It may also be partly because his greatest work, his version of Virgil's *Aeneid*, is a translation, and there is, perhaps, a lurking suspicion that translations must be somehow inferior to original compositions. A more certain reason is the difficulty of his language, which is extraordinarily copious and demanding.

Douglas, the son of the fifth Earl of Angus, was a member of one of the most powerful families in fifteenth-century Scotland, whose relations with other great aristocratic Scottish families, and indeed with the Scottish kings, were often extremely uneasy, and sometimes hostile. The evidence shows that he had all the ambition characteristic of the family. He seems to have been born in 1476, and as a younger son was early destined for the church. He was educated at the University of St Andrews, from where he graduated in 1494, and probably at Paris, where he could well have come into contact with humanist thought. Ecclesiastical offices came his way: in 1497 he is recorded as Dean of Dunkeld, and by 1503 he had become Provost of St Giles, a rich collegiate

---

[1] This essay owes much to Priscilla Bawcutt's *Gavin Douglas: A Critical Study* (1976). The account of Douglas's life there (pp. 1–46) is supplemented in her 'New Light on Gavin Douglas', *The Renaissance in Scotland: Studies in Literature, Religion, History and Culture Offered to John Durkan*, ed. A. A. MacDonald, Michael Lynch and Ian B. Cowan (Leiden, 1994), pp. 95–106. References to Douglas are from *Shorter Poems*, ed. Bawcutt, and *Virgil's Aeneid*, ed. Coldwell. See C. S. Lewis, *English Literature in the Sixteenth Century* (Oxford, 1954), pp. 76–90; also Charles R. Blyth, *'The Knychtlyke Stile': A Study of Gavin Douglas' Aeneid* (New York, 1987); Alastair Fowler, 'Virgil for "every gentil Scot" ', *TLS* 22 July 1977, pp. 882–3; Kantik Ghosh, ' "The Fift Quheill": Gavin Douglas's Maffeo Vegio', *SLJ* 22.1 (1995), pp. 5–21; Gerald B. Kinneavy, 'The Poet in *The Palice of Honour*', *Chaucer Review* 3 (1969), pp. 280–303; David Parkinson, 'The Farce of Modesty in Gavin Douglas's *The Palis of Honoure*', *PQ* 70 (1991), pp. 13–25; Ian Simpson Ross, ' "Proloug" and "Buke" in the *Eneados* of Gavin Douglas', *Scottish Language and Literature, Medieval and Renaissance: Fourth International Conference 1984 Proceedings*, ed. D. Strauss and H. W. Drescher (Frankfurt am Main, 1986), pp. 393–407.

church in Edinburgh, in the king's patronage. His name appears frequently in the records, and he knew many of the most distinguished intellectual and political men of his time in Scotland and abroad. The defeat of the Scots at Flodden in September 1513 (not long after he had finished his *Eneados*) deprived him of two brothers and of his king, James IV. He now became increasingly involved in the murky politics of the minority of James V (his nephew the sixth Earl of Angus married Margaret Tudor, widow of James IV) and suffered a number of reverses before, in 1515, he was appointed to the bishopric of Dunkeld. He ended his life as a virtual exile in England in 1522. His works lived on after him, and were read in both Scotland and England; the *Eneados* in particular was well known, and influenced the translation by the Earl of Surrey.[2]

As with some other Scottish poets of the period the canon of Douglas's works is not altogether clear.[3] The two mentioned above are certainly his. Two other poems have also been attributed to him. The first is 'Conscience', a brief punning poem on the cupidity of churchmen, with internal rhyme and elaborate word play, which could well be his.[4] The other is an excellent allegorical poem, the story of 'King Hart', in 'his cumlie castell strang' (1) rejoicing in his youth and beauty, while outside around the wall is something more sinister – 'ane water void, / Blak, stinkand, sowr, and salt as is the sey' (75–6).[5] His adventures with Dame Plesance and his final fall make up the bulk of the story. It is austere in style, with good succinct descriptions and moments of action, processions and battles, and (as in many morality plays) conflict between virtues and vices. The pattern of the traditional Ages of Man unfolds with the arrival at the gate of '[a]ne auld, gudlie man' (435) – 'My name is Age' (443) he announces, and he cannot be kept out. Finally the castle is besieged by the 'hiddous ost' (850) of Decrepitus ('A crudge bak that cairfull cative bure, / And cruikit was his lathlie lymmis bayth', 853–4). Decrepitus smites King Hart's back in two, Death is summoned and King Hart makes a bitter testament. It is an extraordinarily bleak poem, which in the end, like one or two other medieval 'mortality' poems (including some versions of the Dance of Death), seems to concentrate on the decay and dissolution of the body and makes no explicit reference to the salvation of the soul. It seems unlikely to have been written by Douglas. The manuscript ascription is not in the hand of the transcriber of the poem, and it has been argued cogently that stylistically and linguistically the poem is uncharacteristic of Douglas.[6] Finally, there is a mysterious reference by Douglas himself to a work of his youth – he 'Of Lundeys Lufe the Remeid dyd

---

[2] See Priscilla Bawcutt, 'Douglas and Surrey: Translators of Virgil', *Essays and Studies* 27 (1974), pp. 52–67.
[3] See Bawcutt, *Gavin Douglas*, pp. 48–9.
[4] See Bawcutt, 'New Light', pp. 100–6.
[5] See Douglas, *Shorter Poems*, ed. Bawcutt, pp. 141–70.
[6] See Priscilla Bawcutt, 'Did Gavin Douglas write *King Hart*?', *MÆ* 28 (1959), pp. 31–47.

translait; / And syne off hie Honour the Palyce wrait' (*Eneados*, vol. 4, p. 139). This has not been identified.[7]

Douglas probably wrote *The Palice of Honour* in 1501.[8] It is dedicated to James IV, and clearly implies a courtly and sophisticated audience. It is the work of a young man, and one eager to impress. It is hard to disagree with C. S. Lewis that the work's quality 'is prodigality; its vice excess'.[9] Modern readers are overwhelmed – and often repelled – by its plethora of allusion and decorative detail, long catalogues, and elaborate rhetorical style. However, a more sympathetic reading would find it learned and in many ways traditional, though not conventional, flamboyant in style, but genuinely eloquent. It is dazzling and ambitious, boldly and sometimes startlingly imaginative in its handling of common genres and motifs.

It belongs to the well-established genre of the dream vision which had continued to flourish throughout the fifteenth century. Later medieval examples cannot match the subtlety of Chaucer or the strange power of Langland, but at the end of the period the works of Douglas, Dunbar and Skelton triumphantly demonstrate the genre's power and possibilities. The dream's setting is often a scene from the natural world that has been strangely transformed, a beautiful grove or garden, and within the dream the dreamer will find himself in similarly transformed scenes – deserts and rocky landscapes, temples or palaces. Often the dreamer is at the beginning in a state of perplexity or spiritual unease – though when Douglas goes out into a 'garding of plesance' (7) to do his 'obseruance' (6) to May, the sight of that 'heuinly place' (55) exhilarates his spirit, so that he does not know if it is a vision or a delusion, and it is not until he is overwhelmed by an 'impressioun' (105) (probably a 'fiery impression' or exhalation, such as a shooting star or *ignis fatuus*[10]) that he is attacked by a 'dredfull terrour' (117). In the traditional dream narrative, the poet will meet guides or figures of authority who will advise or instruct him, and from these dialogues and from the scenes he encounters he will find some kind of illumination before he is suddenly awakened into the ordinary world. The dream narrative may have unexpected transitions, mysterious juxtapositions, or digressions of a labyrinthine kind. Douglas responded to these possibilities and challenges with enthusiasm, producing an elegant dream vision with intercalated lyrics, a work of great rhetorical skill and metrical and verbal intricacy, which is often at the same time very similar to a romance, filled with magic and the supernatural, and, in a heightened way, similar to the sudden

---

[7] See Bawcutt, *Gavin Douglas*, p. 49. Ruddiman's emendation of 'Lundeys' to 'Ovideis', discussed by Bawcutt, would also make the rhythm uncertain. Douglas seems to be thinking of Ovid, but a translation of the *Remedia* would be a substantial juvenile work. A further – and quite unsubstantiated – guess might be that it was a comic and satiric poem concerning an adventure in love of a character named Lundey.
[8] *Shorter Poems*, ed. Bawcutt, pp. xxvii–xxviii. All references are to the c. 1553 London text.
[9] Lewis, *English Literature*, p. 78.
[10] See Douglas, *Shorter Poems*, ed. Bawcutt, notes to line 105.

elations and anxieties of an actual dream experience. Other genres have also influenced the poem: it seems to be related to the 'encyclopaedic' works of instruction that were immensely popular throughout the Middle Ages, such as the earlier English fifteenth-century *Court of Sapience* or the later *Pastime of Pleasure* of Stephen Hawes – though the long tradition reaches back to Gower and to Alan of Lille.

It is a learned and allusive poem. Echoes of Virgil and (especially) Ovid sit beside allusions to earlier Scottish writers. There are intriguing similarities with some of the allegorical poems of Dunbar, especially *The Goldyn Targe* – although the uncertain dating of this makes questions of 'influence' or possible rivalry difficult to decide.[11] Very clear however is Douglas's debt to Chaucer, notably to the Prologue of *The Legend of Good Women* with its 'trial scene', accusation of blasphemy, and imposition of a penitential literary task, and to *The House of Fame* with its combination of the themes of Fame (a concept closely related to Honour) and of poetry and Chaucer's calling as a poet.

Both Douglas's indebtedness and originality are especially seen in the figure of the dreamer. Chaucer sometimes makes his dreamers appear as naïve, bewildered figures, with a tendency to bookishness and an insatiable curiosity. He uses them as a focus for his characteristic blending of seriousness and humour, and for the dream vision's combination of the private and the public, with 'a personal area of reference and a more public and generalized rhetorical aim'.[12] Douglas vigorously extends this technique, sometimes carrying it to extremes, with his flow of learned allusions and digressions (linked with sly asides) and his constantly talkative manner. The dreamer's terrors and ecstasies are always in the forefront of the poem.

Douglas provides an almost violent alternation of high seriousness and farcical grotesque comedy, as in the scene of the discovery of the concealed dreamer (645 ff.). After seeing the goddess Venus and her followers he is moved to sing a sorrowful lover's lay, rashly concluding 'Wo worth Cupyd, and wo worth fals Venus / Wo worth thaym bayth, ay waryit mot thay be, / Wo worth thair court and cursyt destane' (634-6). One might think here of a parallel to that more serious moment in Henryson's *Testament of Cresseid* when Cresseid 'blasphemes' these gods. Here the punishment is much less grim, but comically painful. The dreamer is discovered and fearfully creeps out of his tree stump to face the wrath of the goddess and her court – which turns into a grotesque 'mobbing' scene:

> Than all the court on me thayr hedis schuke
> Sum glowmand grym, sum grinand with vissage sowr
> Sum in the nek gaue me feil dyntis dowr.

---

[11] See R. J. Lyall, 'The Stylistic Relationship between Dunbar and Douglas', *Dunbar: Essays*, ed. Mapstone, pp. 69–84.
[12] John Norton-Smith, *Geoffrey Chaucer* (London, 1974), p. 5.

Pluk at the craw thay cryit, deplome the ruke
Pulland my hare, with blek my face they bruke. (648–52)[13]

This technique has seemed to some to be a vulgarization of Chaucer's practice, but it is rather a deliberate attempt to achieve a frenetic nightmarish 'eldritch' quality similar to that in some of Dunbar's writing. The daring juxtaposition of a high seriousness that is almost mystical with pantomime knockabout sometimes reminds me (for all the obvious differences) of *The Magic Flute*. And there are variations that are both clever and subtle. The dreamer who often suffers extremes of terror can also answer back to the goddess Venus, showing his legal expertise, or quote a proverb against himself. His comic fear of being transformed into 'a bere, a bair, ane oule, ane ape' (741) is a typically extreme response to a real danger in the presence of these ancient goddesses ('a hart transformyt', 316, is one of the signs of Diana's arrival), and is part of a fascination both serious and playful with metamorphosis throughout a poem that with its constant transformations of scene and mood seems to be mirroring the process. The magicians (1721-8) produce a wonderful series of transformations – a monk from a nutmeg, an ape from a mussel, etc. There is a constant alternation or mingling of 'earnest' and 'game'. After the many noble poets the dreamer sees a band of humbler figures mostly from Scottish popular tales[14] – in a stanza that reads like a surrealist fantasy. The moment when Venus, satisfied with the dreamer's contrition, hands him an unnamed book to 'put in ryme' (1752), identified, no doubt accurately, by a note in the London edition as 'Virgil' (1756), is comically echoed by that in which he sees Catiline trying to get into the palace through a window but being driven off by Cicero ('suddandly Tullius come with a buke / And strake hym doun quhill all his chaftis quuke', 1772-3) – a comic moment, but at the same time a homely demonstration of the power of literary invective.[15]

The twin themes of poetry and Honour are constantly intertwined. References to poetry are found from the Prologue (the poet's 'rurell termes rude', 126) and the opening lament to his 'barrant wyt' (127), and the description of the terrible desert in which he finds himself, strongly reminiscent of that in *The House of Fame*, is suggestive perhaps of barrenness of inspiration. He begins to receive some illumination through a series of set scenes – mysterious and magical processions. In the first is a queen, later identified as Minerva 'the quene of Sapience' (241) by the two outcasts who troop along behind the band of the wise and learned, Achitophel and Synon, self-confessed traitors. This is an intriguingly indirect way to introduce the theme of honour, with the first 'illumination' coming from two wretched outcasts to another, the frightened

---

[13] On the 'mobbing', see David Parkinson, 'Mobbing Scenes in Middle Scots Verse: Holland, Douglas, Dunbar', *JEGP* 85 (1986), pp. 494–509.
[14] Only in the Edinburgh edition: presumably it was deliberately omitted in the London edition.
[15] Cicero's orations against Catiline; see *Shorter Poems*, ed. Bawcutt, note to line 1770.

dreamer, the victim of inconstant Fortune. He begins to learn of true honour through conversation with these 'wrechyt catiuis' (269) who dishonourably misused their wit and wisdom. They remind one of some of the less famous and indeed notorious figures in *The House of Fame*. They are 'negative' figures, but while not exactly penitent, seem to know what Honour is and to want to see the Palace 'And stand on rowme [at a distance] quhare bettyr folk bene charrit [turned away]' (294). There follow the processions of two other powerful goddesses, Diana and Venus, into whose court the dreamer is dragged and condemned.

In the second part the theme of poetry is dominant, and there is a notable lightening of the dreamer's spirits: 'Yone is the court of plesand stedfastnes, / Yone is the court of constant merynes' (844–5). He sees 'Ane heuinly rout' (787) of poets 'With lawrere crownyt in robbis syd all new' (790), both old and new, who are later listed – and he discovers that learning is a necessary part of the poet's calling (and learning of an encyclopaedic kind: later, he goes on an aerial journey, and he sees the events of universal history in Venus's mirror, 1495–1731). He sees the Muses, of whom the ninth, Calliope, takes him under her protection, intercedes for him, and entrusts him to a nymph who has a brisk liveliness. Calliope is the muse of heroic poetry, who celebrates the honour of heroes in appropriate style:

> For sche of nobillis fatis hes the stere
> Till wryt thair worschyp, victory and prowes,
> In kyngly style, quhilk dois thair fame encres.   (875–7)

Later, in the Muses' pavilion, the link between literature and honour is made more explicit, when Calliope summons Ovid, whom she has wittily made into a Scottish official, 'my clerk ... of regestere' (1187), to present the knightly deeds of ancient heroes. The company now rides off with 'syngyng, lauchyng, merines and play' (1252) towards the Palace of Honour.

In the third part we are shown the culmination of the dreamer's journey and the most detailed 'illumination' of the concept of honour. We had been promised that it was a 'sycht of heuynly swete plesance' (1282), but the rock of hard marble stone on which the palace is placed proves very difficult of access (his nymph has to seize him by the hair and carry him aloft as Habbakuk was). He sees frightening scenes of the punishment of the idle and faithless, and a terrible shipwreck. All these 'feirfull wondris sere' (1379) are firmly placed by the nymph in a Christian context, the allegorical journey of man through the uncertainties and disasters of 'this warldis brukkyllnes' (1390). Douglas goes on to fuse Christianity, humanism and chivalry in his vision of ideal honour rather as Spenser was to do. Even here we find links with more 'secular' patterns: the nymph says for instance that men are born the sons of ire, but through baptism receive grace and faithfulness. These qualities, here contrasted with sin and wretchedness, are also an important traditional part of 'courtesy'.

She turns him away from this scene below to consider 'wondris' (1398) and to be vigilant to learn from what he will be shown. His poetic task is not forgotten – 'That thow may bettir endytyng eftirwart / Thyngis quhilkis I sall the schaw or we depart, / Thow sall haue fouth of sentence ...' (1399–1401). The great palace of honour is indeed 'lyke to parradyce' (1413) – it is placed in the East, beyond Hebron, and sounds like the Earthly Paradise, or a restored Eden. The wondrous palace stands in a 'plane of peirles pulcritude' (1414) whose plenitude echoes and transforms the vision of the work of nature that we saw in the garden at the very beginning of the dream. Gone are the deserts and monsters of earlier visions. Here the created species live in peace and tranquillity – 'Till noy the small the grete bestis had na will, / Nor rauanus fowlys the littill volatill' (1421–2).

The dreamer's learning process continues with the sight of knights in the service of Venus jousting for their ladies' sakes, and then in the visions afforded by the goddess's wonderful mirror of the 'dedes and fetes of euery erdly wycht' (1496) from Creation to the coming of the Antichrist, an overlong list by any standards, but somewhat enlivened by vivid details, for example, the giant with six fingers on each hand (1529). The allegorical narrative continues with a description of the Prince of Honour's household – Liberality his Treasurer, Constance his secretary, Temperance his cook, Conscience his Chancellor. This statement of the ideal works interestingly on several levels: it is clearly by implication 'advice to a prince', and is also applicable to every individual Christian; furthermore, to anyone familiar with 'court satire' or with real medieval courts, the remark that Conscience the Chancellor 'for na meid, will pronounce a fals sentence' (1811) must have underlined an awareness that there was a large gap between the ideal and the actuality. But in the vision 'euery vertew and plesance' (1826) is subject to the rule of Honour.

The dreamer, marvelling at the richly ornamented gate, is unceremoniously pushed through into the Palace by his nymph. The wonders that he now sees are overwhelming. An intense light shines from the Palace's walls, and its rich gleaming stones are like those of Otherworld palaces or of the heavenly Jerusalem in the *Apocalypse*. Finally, he and his nymph ascend the ten steps of topaz leading to the hall. The door is shut, but through a chink he can see the interior, 'Rial Princis in plate and armouris quent / Of byrnist gold' (1919-20), and enthroned, 'a god armypotent' (1921),[16] the sight of whose 'fyry vissage brycht' overwhelms the dreamer's senses (1948–51) and he lies in a swoon until his nymph rescues him. It is reminiscent in some ways of an intense spiritual experience, of a mystic vision perhaps, or of the way Lancelot is smitten down in the *Queste del Saint Graal*.

The nymph's discourse on the nature of Honour (1963–2015) is the most explicit 'statement' that we are given, and it seems to me to be a satisfactory one in its poetic context. I differ in this from some critics who think it

---

[16] Or 'Omnipotent' (Edinburgh text); see *Shorter Poems*, ed. Bawcutt, note to line 1921.

ambiguous or confused. Douglas was not writing a scholastic tract on the concept, but trying to illuminate the idea (or cluster of ideas) through dramatic scenes and visions. Douglas shares the admiration many of his contemporaries had for those men who seem to embody in their lives the ideals of knighthood, men like the Chevalier Bayard or the Scottish 'flower of chivalry' Lord Bernard Stewart.[17] He also seems to be aware of the more intellectual and 'humanist' view of 'nobility of soul' as against a nobility dependent on birth. It is true that much is traditional (and can sometimes be found in proverbs),[18] but Douglas treats it with intelligence and eloquence. It is also true that in Douglas's time Honour was a popular poetic subject, both in English and even more in French writing,[19] but his poem is very distinctive. The topic had an obvious attraction for courtly writers – of panegyrics, chivalric biographies or 'mirrors for princes' – but it is important to remember that it had a considerable social importance in medieval life. Honour, in the sense of the value placed upon oneself and which is felt to be placed on one by society, seems then to have had what is for us an unusual intensity (as it has still in some 'traditional' societies), accompanied by an intense hatred for treachery or the breaking of tacit bonds of friendship, kin or community.

The dream moves to its close dramatically as the dreamer, following his nymph across a bridge fearfully and uncertainly, falls off into the water – and finds himself awake in the garden where he first went to sleep. In spite of the birds' song and the flowers he is filled with sorrow, cursing the time he awoke and wishing to have remained in that 'lusty yle' (2104). He would have wished, he says, to see how the wretches that betrayed honour were punished. (There seems to be no obvious need to read more into this melancholy mood than extreme disappointment at the ending of a transforming vision.) So he makes an end, sitting under a tree, with a splendidly elaborate poem in praise of honour, and then dedicates his book to the king.

This young man's poem already shows an extraordinary talent. It is particularly interesting to see how his developing poetic 'voice' looks forward to his masterpiece, the *Eneados*. Firstly, the variety of his style is impressive. He uses a very wide range of vocabulary, and delights equally in self-consciously using a clerkly Latinate word like *adiutory* (1288), or *subsequent* (1441), or terms from his 'rural' vernacular like *smy* (705) or *skauppis* (144). In this he closely resembles Dunbar. He moves easily from the highly ornate to the simple ('cald as a key', 674), and is always sensitive to acoustic effects. He handles different stanza forms with virtuosity. Secondly, much of the poem's power comes from his narrative skill. The story moves with a remarkable

---

[17] Bayard's life was written by the 'Loyal Serviteur' (Jacques de Mailles) in 1527. On Bernard Stewart, celebrated by Dunbar, see Douglas Gray, 'A Scottish "Flower of Chivalry" and his Book', *Words: Wai-te-ata Studies in Literature* 4 (1974), pp. 22–33.
[18] B. J. Whiting and H. W. Whiting, *Proverbs, Sentences, and Proverbial Phrases from English Writings Mainly before 1500* (Cambridge, Mass., 1968), H445 ff; cf. D239, M159, N12.
[19] See Bawcutt, *Gavin Douglas*, p. 51.

energy, varied by shifts of mood and rhythm, by dialogues and descriptions. He gives to scenes of terror especially a highly emotional quality – as in the vivid eyewitness account of the shipwreck:

> It wes a pietuus thyng (allake allake)
> Till here the duylfull cry quhen that scho strake
> Maist lamentabill the peryst folk till se,
> Sa famyst, drokyt, mait, forwrocht, and wake.   (1369–72)

Virgil was to offer him many such 'pietuus' scenes.

Douglas fulfilled the task imposed upon him by Venus and finished his translation of Virgil's epic (together with the thirteenth book added by the humanist Maffeo Vegio) on 22 July 1513. He used an edition made by Badius Ascensius (probably that of 1501).[20] It was made, he says, at the request of his kinsman and patron Henry, Lord Sinclair, of whom he speaks with warmth and affection. However, he evidently intended it for a wider audience – it will be pleasant and profitable to many a man, and it will also be useful for those who would expound Virgil to children: 'Thank me tharfor, masteris of grammar sculys, / Quhar ye syt techand on your benkis and stulys' ('Heir the translatar direkkis hys buk', *Eneados*, vol. 4, p. 189, 47-8). In the 'Exclamatioun aganyst detractouris', he triumphantly addresses his 'wlgar Virgill' – 'Now salt thou with euery gentill Scot be kend, / And to onletterit folk be red on hight, / That erst was bot with clerkis comprehend'.[21]

Each book is preceded by a prologue, which often contains an interesting discussion of the circumstance of composition or the style or the matter of the book he is translating. Thus Prologue IV discusses earthly love and its dangers, Prologue XI true knighthood, and Prologue XIII contains a comic encounter between Douglas and Maffeo Vegio. They sometimes establish the mood and the patterns of imagery which are to recur through the following book – in Prologue II, for instance, the scene is set for the tragic fall of Troy ('Dyrk beyn my muse with dolorus armony', 1) and ends with an appropriate proverb, 'All erdly glaidness fynysith with wo' (21). In the Prologues we see Douglas as a scholar and literary critic and as an expositor, explaining and discussing problems that face the Christian reader. The distinctive narrator's voice, familiar from *The Palice of Honour*, is firmly established. Like Chaucer, Douglas is intimate with his audience, now addressing fellow enthusiasts for Virgil, now fellow Christian readers, now critics and detractors of Virgil or of himself. He is a presenter of Virgil's books and a commentator on them, and indeed the Prologues sometimes act rather like the commentaries included in his Virgil. But they also reveal Douglas the creative artist, struggling with his great task. The Prologues themselves, written in a remarkable variety of metres

---

[20] See Bawcutt, *Gavin Douglas*, pp. 95–102; Bawcutt, 'Gavin Douglas and the text of Virgil', *EBST* 4.6 (1973), pp. 213–31.
[21] Douglas, *Virgil's Aeneid*, ed. Coldwell, vol. 4, pp. 192–3.

and styles,[22] sometimes become poems in their own right. Prologue VII brilliantly creates a bleak wintry Northern landscape that more than rivals that in *Sir Gawain and the Green Knight*:

> The grond fadyt, and fawch wolx all the feildis,
> Montane toppis slekit with snaw ourheildis;
> On raggit rolkis of hard harsk quhyn stane
> With frosyn frontis cauld clynty clewis schane.   (37–40)

This and Prologue XII (devoted to spring) were published separately in modernized form in the eighteenth century when the taste for 'seasonal' writing returned.[23]

The Prologue to the first book opens with an ecstatic and highly ornamented praise of Virgil, 'gem of engyne and flude of eloquens' (4). Douglas singles out his combination of 'sentence' and vividness: 'Sa quyk, lusty and maist sentencyus, / Plesand, perfyte and feilabill in all degre, / As quha the mater beheld tofor thar e' (12–14), and his concision, 'Sa wysly wrocht with nevir a word invane' (30). He touches on some of the perennial problems of translation, and launches into a fierce and entertaining attack on Caxton's *Eneydos* of 1490, a prose work that is based on a French retelling of the epic. He speaks with scholarly horror of 'this Caxton' (220) and his errors; he has produced a book without 'sentence or engyne' (147); he has allowed the story of Dido to become half of the volume instead of a twelfth part; the fifth book is 'ourhippit quyte' (175), and the whole thing is 'na mair lyke Virgill, dar I lay, / Than the nycht owle resemblis the papyngay' (261–2). Caxton's book is an example of a long medieval tradition of Virgilian paraphrase, adaptation and rewriting, but it is probably oversimplifying to say that Douglas is attacking this whole tradition. He certainly knew something of the newer Italian humanism of the time – he refers to Landino, 'Lawrens of the Vaill [Lorenzo Valla]' (I Prol. 127), and others – and this lies behind his insistence on the need to translate as accurately as possible the actual text of Virgil as well as to pass on his general 'sentence'. But he can also be placed at the end of the older, wider tradition of 'medieval humanism' in which allusions can be expanded, commentary worked into the text, and the characters of the epic will be made to look, speak and feel as if they were contemporary medieval figures (so that Priam will have a hauberk, and Orpheus a harp, not a lyre). Douglas has links with both strands, having the heightened sense of 'authenticity', 'faithfulness' and close attention to the text emphasized by the newer philological humanism and also the intense feeling characteristic of medieval humanism that the story is not remote but close to contemporary experience. Religion was, of course, a crucial difficulty

---

[22] See Bawcutt, *Gavin Douglas*, pp. 164–91.
[23] See J. A. W. Bennett, 'The Early Fame of Gavin Douglas's *Eneados*', *MLN* 61 (1946), pp. 83–8. Douglas knew the *Eclogues* and the *Georgics* and used *Georgics* II in his Prologue to Book XII; see Bawcutt, *Gavin Douglas*, pp. 87–90.

for the Christian translator and the Christian reader. For Douglas, Virgil is pagan, but he is a great philosopher full of 'sentence', and much of what he says is compatible with Christianity or may foreshadow it. Douglas will sometimes use contemporary terms like 'priest', 'purgatory' or 'hell', sometimes indicate the difference ('as was the gyss that tyde', I. xi. 9) or sometimes leave ancient ceremonies, such as funerals with the embalming of the body, without any comment at all.

Douglas produced an eminently readable version, unmarred by pedantry or stiff 'classicism'. It moves with enormous verve, and does full justice to the excitement of the narrative. Much of Virgil's delicate melody and elegance of style is lost, and much of his concision, for Douglas regularly expands, either because of the exigencies of his couplet form, or because he wishes to work in an explanatory gloss, or simply because he is excited by the subject-matter. But the sheer energy of the translation is impressive (as in the famous example of his version of 'laetitia exsultans' as he 'hoppit vp for ioy, he was so glaid', XII. xii. 6).

Dryden attempted 'to make Virgil speak such English, as he would himself have spoken if he had been born in England and in this present age'.[24] Douglas made him speak in the language of Scotland in a tough energetic diction combined with more learned clerkly elements. As he showed in the *Palice* he was both sensitive and boldly experimental in matters of style and language. In the Prologue to Book IX he speaks of the royal style 'heroycall' as proper for the subject and fitted for the ear of a noble patron, but he is happy to use his examples of low style, 'scroggis, broym, haddir or rammale' (IX Prol. 37) or their equivalents in his epic narrative. Indeed he seems to be fashioning an epic language out of his own vernacular with its 'haymly playn termys famyliar' (*Eneados*, vol. 4, p. 190, 94), even though he speaks modestly of 'our tungis penuryte', using a word that is hardly unlearned! (I Prol. 380). He praises Virgil's variety: '... He altyrris hys style sa mony way, / Now dreid, now stryfe, now lufe, now wa, now play' (V Prol. 33–4) and seems to be imitating it, in the larger scenes and emotions and in the details of diction. Alongside learned words ('pronuba', IV. iv. 78) and echoes of Latin words ('thair labour is besy and fervent for to se', I. vii. 34, for 'fervet opus'), we find a host of homely terms – a shepherd 'amang the scroggy rammell settis the fyre' (X. vii. 112). And he can give such terms a moving simplicity – when in Virgil Evander says 'I ask not for joy in life – that cannot be – but to bear tidings to my son in the shades below' ('Manis ... sub imo'), Douglas turns the phrase 'amang the gostis law in skowgis dern', XI. iv. 102). He can also imitate a lighter movement – a bird 'skummand the fludis law' (IV. v. 149) – or a comic one – the Trojans laugh seeing a man fall 'and, hym behaldand swym, thai keklit all' (V. iv. 40), especially to 'se hym spowt salt watir of hys throte' (V. iv. 42). There are imitations of Virgilian locutions ('the wollyt scheip', III. x. 9) or

---

[24] *The Poems of John Dryden*, ed. J. Kinsley, 4 vols (Oxford, 1968), vol. 3, p. 1055.

syntax ('Ane active bow apon hir schuldir bar', I. vi. 24), but these are much fewer than in Surrey, a more self-consciously neo-classical poet. Douglas prefers his own rhetorical devices, expanding a Virgilian phrase by means of doublets – or triplets – so that 'fit gemitus' becomes 'thai schowting, gowling and clamour abowt him maid' (VI. iii. 123). This is clearly an example of his liking for an emphatic style, but it is also an example of his imaginative participation in a scene (in this case the funeral of Misenus) which has inspired in him a powerful emotional response – and, typically, he prefers to emphasize the involvement of the bystanders rather than the general mood. It is similar to his fondness for his homely terms and dramatically colloquial expressions: 'Howe, say me yonkeris', says Venus (I. vi. 29). But Virgil's style seems to have had a profound and pervasive influence on him. He can find a Virgilian solemnity – 'placis of silence and perpetuall nycht' (VI. iv. 60). Indeed his typical 'strong lines' are very often good literal translations, simple and with a distinctive resonance:

> The lattir day is cummyn of Dardanus end,
> The fatale tyme quham na walyng may mend.
> We war Troianys, vmquhile was Ilion,
> The schynand glory of Phrygianis now is gone.   (II. vi. 55–8)

He achieves a remarkable fusion of learned and popular diction, with a responsiveness to Virgil's 'royal style' and an awareness of the possibilities of the Scottish vernacular. His search for copiousness or 'fouth' of language is similar to Dunbar's.

His little additions often testify to Douglas the educator and commentator (the 'flude Simois', I. iii. 12, 'Latium, quhilk now is Italy', I. i. 57, 'Avernus the well, / Quhilk lowch is situate at the mouth of hell', IV. ix. 81–2) and do not disturb the modern reader, but there are a few that stand out in the narrative flow (like the learned reference to the woodpecker, a bird 'clepit a speicht with ws / Quhilk in Latyn hait Pycus Marcyus', VI. iii. 91–2). A few cases raise the question of narrative voices in the poem. That of Douglas the presenter is clearly heard throughout all the Prologues. It is this voice that summons us at the end of the first Prologue, 'gevis audiens and draw neir' (I Prol. 503); but the first line of Book I, 'The batalis and the man I wil discrive' is that of Virgil, mediated through Douglas, and this voice speaks for long stretches of narrative. But sometimes that of Douglas seems to 'intrude' or blend with that of Virgil (the 'Syrene, that we Marmadynnys clepe', V. xiv. 71, where the 'we' is Douglas and his audience, yet somehow is connected with that of Virgil). Odder at first sight are the rare cases when Douglas's 'we' is placed in the speech of a character in the narrative: Anchises 'explains' Jove's lightning to Aeneas – 'with his fyry levin ... / That we intill our langage clepe fyreflauch' (II. x. 155–6); later Evander tells him that 'we' call nymphs and fauns 'fairfolkis, or than elvys' (VIII. vi. 7). I suspect that these are not cases where

Douglas with his natural loquacity was unable to resist an attack of commentator's twitch,[25] but rather an extreme example of the narrator/translator's total involvement in the narrative and of a 'medieval' humanist's sense that it is all very close to his world – the characters, like the settings, have been more or less Scotticized and speak 'our language': vividness and nearness to experience are prized above all. I also suspect that Douglas was responding to what has been called Virgil's 'subjective style' – he 'not only reads the minds of his characters; he constantly communicates to us his own reactions to them and to their behaviour'.[26] In some cases the practice of amplifying seems to be due to simple enthusiasm. One example occurs in a simile in Book XII which compares the advance of the Trojans to a tempest approaching from the sea that causes terror in the hearts of the countrymen. Here Douglas is so carried away by the dramatic scene evoked that he makes the countrymen burst into direct speech:

> Quhilk, with sair hartis quakand, 'Allake, allaik!'
> Says, 'Lo, yon bub sall stryke dovn growand treys,
> Doun bet our cornys, and by the ruyt vpheis,
> And far onbreid ourturn all doys vpstand:
> Hark! heir the swouch cumis brayand to the land' –
> On siclyke wyss ....   (XII. viii. 28–33)

This imaginative involvement is often seen in his treatment of Virgil's imagery, which brings events and emotions before our very eyes.[27] Throughout the work he is responsive to this – in large scenes (like the death of Laocoon and his sons) and in small images and similes (his forceful translation 'he hoppit vp for ioy, he was so glaid', XII. xii. 6, emphasizes the visual element implicit in Virgil's words). He was well aware of the way in which Virgil again and again uses imagery to represent emotions and mental states (Dido compared to the stricken deer or Aeneas to an oak battered by the storm, for instance). Much of Virgil's skill comes through in Douglas's version, often in a vigorous though less subtle way. I wonder if his vivid and pictorial style was encouraged by a knowledge of illustrated Virgils, like the spectacular edition of Sebastian Brant (1502): there is no direct evidence in Douglas's text, however, that he used it. He responds especially to exciting scenes, battles and storms in particular, but also to strange events, portents and wonders, like the eerie appearance of Lavinia, who seemed 'Tobe involuyt in yallo reky lyght' (VII. i. 114), or the whirlpool that belches all its sand into the underworld river Cocytus:

---

[25] See Bawcutt, *Gavin Douglas*, p. 129; Douglas Gray, 'Virgil in Late Medieval Scotland', *Focus on Literature and Culture*, ed. G. Bystydzienska and L. Kolek (Lublin, 1994), p. 20.
[26] Brooks Otis, *Virgil. A Study in Civilized Poetry* (Oxford, 1963), chapter 3.
[27] See Douglas Gray, ' "As quha the mater beheld tofor thar e": Douglas's Treatment of Virgil's Imagery', *Palace*, ed. Houwen et al., pp. 95–123.

> With holl bysme and hydduus swelch onrude,
> Drumly of mud, and skaldand as it war wod,
> Popland and bulrand furth on athir hand
> Onto Cochitus all his slyke and sand.   (VI. v. 3–6)

Sometimes one of his little additions will use both extra visual details and a homely simile: the deep cave above Avernus is protected by the dark lake and forest gloom – in Douglas it is 'closit ... / With a fowle layk, als blak as ony craw, / And skuggis dym of a ful dern wod schaw' (VI. iv. 6–8).

Douglas is sensitive to scenes of pathos – of which there are many in Virgil's 'epic of grief'. He often intensifies or draws attention to them by exclamations and the use of traditional formulae. 'Allace, quhat reuth was it he not eschapit!' (IX. vii. 164) he exclaims at the death of Nisus, later indicating his involvement by transforming the 'Rutulian victors' into 'The schamful victouris, thir Rutilyanys' (IX. vii. 177). He certainly knew and was influenced by the highly emotional 'pitous' style of late medieval poets such as Chaucer, Lydgate and Henryson.[28] Modern readers sometimes find this over-emotional and over-elaborate, and occasionally Douglas is wordy. Yet at the same time he can imitate Virgil's concision, as in his rendition of Camilla's terse and soldierly dying speech: here, although he slightly expands her final words (iamque uale'), he keeps the sense of brevity – 'Adew for evir! I haue na mar to say' (XI. xv. 136).

He is also aware of Virgil's iterative imagery, those larger patterns of repetitions and subtle echoes of images and motifs that have a cumulative effect.[29] Not surprisingly he cannot reproduce all of these, but there are some clear cases where he is trying to do so, or trying to produce echoic patterns of his own. So the parallel between the two serpents coming from Tenedos to destroy Laocoon and the coming of the Greeks from Tenedos would be evident to Douglas's readers, although they would not find an exact replica of the verbal repetitions that emphasize it. But they would be aware of sinister words associated with snakes – not exactly Virgil's but close to his 'sinuat' and 'insinuat' – in Douglas's own pattern of 'crap' (II. iv. 48, 51) and the great horse that 'slydis' (II. iv. 74) – Virgil's 'inlabitur' – into the city. In Book IV he frequently translates Virgil's adjective 'infelix' by 'fey' (sometimes supported by other emotive adjectives, 'onsylly', 'onhappy', etc.).

Virgilian ideas are often discussed in the Prologues, but in the text Douglas allows them to remain embedded in the narrative's figures and scenes. Here he does not use the allegorical interpretations with which he must have been familiar, and it seems to me that some of the interpretations suggested by modern critics – that Aeneas is the 'model for a prince' and that Douglas

---

[28] See Douglas Gray, ' "Pite for to here – Pite for to see": Some Scenes of Pathos in Late Medieval Literature', *PBA* 87 (1995), pp. 67–99.
[29] See Bawcutt, *Gavin Douglas*, p. 87.

manipulated the poem to demonstrate its political implications, for instance – are exaggerated, and encourage a very narrow reading of the work.[30] He seems in fact more concerned to follow Virgil than to manipulate him. Although for Douglas Aeneas demonstrates 'euery vertu belangand a nobill man' (I Prol. 325), he is also more than simply an idealized princely hero. Douglas allows his moods and emotions to emerge from the sequence of Virgil's scenes, from the time he first appears, as potential victim, in the great storm when 'euery thing mannasit the men to de, / Schawand the ded present tofor thar e' (I. ii. 67–8), 'murnand' and raising his hands to the stars, lamenting 'with petuus voce' (a Douglas addition) how happy were those who died at Troy (I. iii. 2–6). Douglas seems to be very interested in the hero's emotions – sudden fear or hurried excitement, his 'hasty dreid' (VI. iv. 111) when confronted by monsters in the underworld. He emphasizes that Aeneas is 'reuthfull' (his common choice for 'pius', and one that emphasizes a particular aspect of *pietas*). The hero is a man of feeling as well as a man of action, and Douglas seems often to share Virgil's melancholy and pity at the brevity of man's life.

Douglas depicts Aeneas as 'gentill' and 'curtas' and a great warrior. He translates the battle scenes with considerable gusto, using emphatic alliteration ('Our all the planys brays the stampand stedis / Full galyart in thar bardis and weyrly wedis', XI. xii. 5–6), and drawing on the techniques of earlier and contemporary Scottish verse narrative genres, the romance and the heroic chronicle like the *Bruce* and the *Wallace*. His additions (like 'this douchty Eneas' and 'the nobill knycht') emphasize the idea of the heroic warrior, who fights not just 'ardens' but 'as wod lyon'. Just as Douglas was much closer to ancient ideas of honour and kinship than his modern readers are, so the horrors and the glories of (pre-industrial) warfare would have been better known to him, by hearsay if not by experience. In the Prologue to Book XI ('Thow hie renown of Martis chevalry, / Quhilk gladis euery gentill wight to heir') he continues his reflections in *The Palice of Honour*, and presents an ideal of a chivalry both temporal and spiritual, a prowess which is 'moral vertuus hardyment' and magnanimity.

But he carefully presents Aeneas's moments of indecision, doubt and melancholy, and the characteristic mingling of emotions that Virgil had given him. In Book IV, when Mercury brings him the message that he must leave Carthage, Aeneas is horrified: 'heu! Quid agat'. Douglas makes a little addition: 'Allace! quhat suld he do? oneth he wist' (IV. vi. 8) – not, I think, simply for the sake of explicitness, but also to draw the reader further into an imaginative understanding of Aeneas's quandary. There are similar moments in Aeneas's meetings with Dido later in Book IV, and in Book VI. In his general treatment of Dido Douglas seems to keep the Virgilian blend of detachment and involvement. I do not think that he presents Dido in the narrowly moralistic

---

[30] See Bawcutt, *Gavin Douglas*, pp. 124–5; Douglas Gray, 'Gavin Douglas and "the gret prynce Eneas"', *Essays in Criticism* 51 (2001), pp. 18–34 (20–2).

way that some critics have claimed, and I think that interpretations claiming a conflict between Douglas the churchman and Douglas the courtly poet are much exaggerated: in the Prologue to Book IV he criticizes inordinate love, but his 'pite' for Dido leads him to address her directly 'sen I suld *thy* tragedy endyte, / ... / *Thy* lusty pane begouth on this maneir' (264, 270). Douglas's imaginative involvement throughout is very intense: in this it resembles Virgil's, though that is characteristically more understated, and is a technique recommended by the rhetorician Quintilian in his discussion of *enargeia*, a quality which Douglas's writing as well as Virgil's clearly possesses.[31]

In the final battle of Aeneas and Turnus there are darker and uneasy undertones: violence and pathos are intermingled, and Aeneas reacts with both fury and hesitation. Here Douglas clearly means to involve his readers – Aeneas 'begouth inclyne hym to reuth and mercy, / Abydand lang in hovir quhat he suld do' (XII. xiii. 128–9). But when he sees the 'fey gurdill' of Pallas on Turnus's shoulder, a moment emphasized by Douglas with the exclamation 'lo!' (XII. xiii. 131), 'All full of furour kyndlys he inhy / Full brym of ire and terribill' (XII. xiii. 142–3), and the deed of vengeance is done. The final lines of Virgil's epic are grim and austere:

> ... and tharwithall
> The cald of deth dissoluyt hys membris all.
> The spreit of lyfe fled murnand with a grone,
> And with disdeyn vnder dyrk erth is goyn.   (XII. xiv. 151–4)

Douglas took leave of his Virgil with a mixture of pride and humility. His treatment of Maffeo Vegio's additional book is less reverential, especially in the Prologue, and seems to be the beginning of an elaborate leavetaking.[32] We cannot but lament that this most talented and lively poet – and perhaps the most promising of his generation – wrote no more, but his achievement is a great one, and he deserves to be read (as he hopefully predicted) 'Throw owt the ile yclepit Albyon' (Conclusio, vol. 4, p. 187, 11).

---

[31] *Institutio oratoria* 6. 2. 30ff. He remarks on the great power of imagination, and suggests that we must identify with the sufferer and persuade ourselves that their miseries have befallen us. On Dido, see Christopher Baswell's *Virgil in Medieval England* (Cambridge, 1995), p. 279; Marilynn Desmond, *Reading Dido: Gender, Textuality, and the Medieval Aeneid* (Minneapolis, 1994), pp. 163–94 and James Simpson, *Reform and Cultural Revolution: The Oxford English Literary History, Volume 2, 1350–1547* (Oxford, 2002), pp. 91–2.

[32] It is followed by a number of poems bidding farewell – a Conclusio, boldly adapting a conclusion of Ovid to a translation of Virgil, which is triumphant, serious and lighthearted (after my death 'The bettir part of me salbe vpheld / Abufe the starnys perpetually to ryng, / And heir my naym remane, but enparyng; / Throw owt the ile yclepit Albyon / ... / My muse sal now be cleyn contemplatyve, / ... / Adew gallandis, I geif you all gud nycht, / And God salf euery gentill curtas wight!' (8–11, 16, 23–4); a Direction, to Lord Sinclair, warmly written, and claiming that Aeneas's fame is now secure; an Exclamation against detractors and uncourteous readers; and a statement of 'the tyme, space and dait of the translatioun of this buke'.

11

Medieval Romance in Scotland

RHIANNON PURDIE

The medieval romances of Scotland have received considerably less attention than those of many other European literatures. This is partly because there are not many of them: only twelve are known, and three of these were discovered in the 1970s.[1] It is also to do with difficulties in defining the corpus of medieval Scottish romance. Beyond the usual problem of deciding how far to stretch the definition of 'romance', students of the medieval Scottish romance may also encounter problems with the labels 'medieval' and 'Scottish'. Can texts that survive only in copies from the later seventeenth century, such as *Roswall and Lillian* or *Eger and Grime*, really be called 'medieval'? This chapter argues that they can, but it is a point that cannot be taken for granted. The nationality of anonymous medieval texts is usually determined by their language, but Older Scots is notoriously difficult to distinguish from Northern Middle English: where earlier scholars had enthusiastically claimed romances such as *Sir Tristrem* and the *Awntyrs off Arthure at the Terne Wathelyn* for Scotland, more recent analysts of their dialect have politely returned them to England.[2] This serves as an uncomfortable reminder that the 'Scottishness' of many of our texts remains open to challenge. However, these inconveniences for modern scholars should not be allowed to obscure the fact that romances were both composed and enthusiastically read in medieval and early modern Scotland, and

---

[1] See Marion Stewart, 'A Recently-Discovered Manuscript: "ane taill of Sir colling ye kny^t" ', *Scottish Studies* 16 (1972), pp. 23–39, and '*King Orphius*', *Scottish Studies* 17 (1973), pp. 1–16.

[2] See Angus McIntosh, 'Is *Sir Tristrem* an English or a Scottish Poem?', *In Other Words: Transcultural Studies in Philology, Translation and Lexicology presented to Hans Heinrich Meier*, ed. J. L. MacKenzie and R. Todd (Dordrecht and Providence, RI, 1989), pp. 85–95. F. J. Amours claims the *Awntyrs* for Scotland via the unidentifiable poet 'Huchowne of the Awle Ryale' in his edition, *Scottish Alliterative Poems in Riming Stanzas*, STS (1897), pp. li–lxxxii. Priscilla Bawcutt recently unmasked a 'Scottish' fragment of *Sir Lamwell* as a copy of an English print: '*Sir Lamwell* in Scotland', *The Scots and Medieval Arthurian Legend*, ed. Rhiannon Purdie and Nicola Royan (Cambridge, 2005), pp. 83–93. In the same volume's 'The Search for Scottishness in *Golagros and Gawane*', pp. 95–107, Purdie reasserts the Scottishness of *Golagros*. See also Deanna Delmar Evans, 'Re-evaluating the case for a Scottish *Eger and Grime*', *The European Sun: Proceedings of the Seventh International Conference on Medieval and Renaissance Scottish Language and Literature*, ed. Graham Caie, Roderick J. Lyall, Sally Mapstone and Kenneth Simpson (East Linton, 2001), pp. 276–87.

that medieval Scottish romance, like that of other cultures, developed some distinguishing features of its own.[3]

The Medieval Scottish Romances

The Buik of Alexander	(1438)[4]
The Buik of King Alexander the Conquerour	(c. 1460); by Sir Gilbert Hay[5]
Clariodus	(c. 1503–49)[6]
Eger and Grime or 'Graysteel'	(probably before 1497)[7]
Florimond of Albany (fragment)	(before c. 1550)[8]
Golagros and Gawane	(15th century; before 1508)[9]
King Orphius (fragments)	(before c. 1550)[10]
Lancelot of the Laik (incomplete)	(before c. 1490)[11]
Rauf Coilyear	(15th century; before c. 1501)[12]
Roswall and Lillian	(before 1603; 16th century?)[13]
Scottish Troy Book (fragments)	(15th century)[14]
Sir Colling the Kny^t	(before c. 1582)[15]

---

[3] In contrast, A. S. G. Edwards stresses their dependence upon English and French models, and concludes that one cannot really speak of 'Scottish romance': 'Contextualising Middle Scots Romance', *Palace*, ed. Houwen et al., pp. 61–73 (69).

[4] *The Buik of Alexander*, ed. R. L. Graeme Ritchie, 4 vols, STS (1921–29).

[5] Hay, *Buik*, ed. Cartwright. For discussion of Hay's text see above, Chapter 5.

[6] *Clariodus: A Metrical Romance*, ed. D. Irving (1830).

[7] For both versions of the text: *Eger and Grime*, ed. J. R. Caldwell, Harvard Studies in Comparative Literature, vol. 9 (Cambridge, Mass., 1933). For the Percy Folio text: *Middle English Metrical Romances*, ed. W. H. French and C. B. Hale, 2 vols (New York, 1964), vol. 2, pp. 671–7. For the Huntington-Laing text (on which term see note 24 below): *Early Popular Poetry of Scotland and the Northern Border*, ed. D. Laing, rev. W. C. Hazlitt, 2 vols (London, 1895), vol. 2, pp. 119–210. Finally, see Purdie, *Shorter Scottish Medieval Romances*, STS, forthcoming. This edition also includes *Roswall and Lillian*, *Sir Colling ye kny*^t, *Florimond* and *King Orphius*.

[8] Unannotated transcription by J. D. McClure, 'The *Florimond* Fragment', *SLJ*, Supplement 10 (1979), pp. 1–10.

[9] In *Scottish Alliterative Poems*, ed. Amours (the edition used here), and more recently with normalized spelling in *Sir Gawain: Eleven Romances and Tales*, ed. Thomas Hahn, TEAMS Middle English Texts (Kalamazoo, 1995): both editors provide excellent critical discussion.

[10] Stewart, '*King Orphius*'.

[11] '*Lancelot of the Laik*' and '*Sir Tristrem*', ed. Alan Lupack, TEAMS Middle English Texts (Kalamazoo, 1994), or *Lancelot of the Laik*, ed. Margaret M. Gray, STS (1912).

[12] In *Scottish Alliterative Poems*, ed. Amours; also *Medieval English Romances*, ed. Diane Speed, 2 vols, 3rd edn (Durham, 1993) and *Longer Scottish Poems: Vol. 1*, ed. Bawcutt and Riddy.

[13] See O. Lengert's parallel-text edition of the Long and Short Versions, 'Die Schottische Romanze "Roswall and Lillian" ', *Englische Studien* 16 (1892), pp. 321–56 and 17 (1892), pp. 341–77. The Short Version is too late a redaction to concern us here.

[14] *Barbour's des Schottischen Nationaldichters Legendensammlung nebst den Fragmenten seines Trojanerkrieges*, ed. C. Horstmann, 2 vols (Heilbronn, 1881–82), vol. 2, pp. 215–307.

[15] Stewart, 'A Recently-Discovered Manuscript'.

The initial difficulty of deciding what kinds of texts to include is immediately apparent from this list. Many readers, for example, will have looked for Sir David Lyndsay's *Squyer Meldrum*, or perhaps Barbour's *Bruce* and Hary's *Wallace*. Generic boundaries are notoriously permeable, and these three texts – particularly *Meldrum* – certainly borrow romance conventions. *Meldrum*, however, is a biography of Lyndsay's friend, 'Gude Williame Meldrum' (71),[16] and its humour depends on the *incongruity* of describing a real friend's life in the language of romance, a genre that normally deals with the idealized heroes of a fictionalized (if not necessarily fictional) past. Something of this generic tension is also visible in Barbour's *Bruce*, written a half-century after Bruce's death. Barbour calls his text a 'romanys' when he begins his moving account of Bruce's personal suffering (I:446), but this is only after a lengthy introduction in which he meticulously distinguishes between 'storys' that are 'nocht bot fabill' (I:1-2) and those that are 'suthfast' (I:3).[17] He assures his readers that he will 'put in wryt a suthfast story' (I:13), thus aligning himself with a historiographical tradition that, at least in theory, 'schawys ye thing rycht as it wes' (I:8) rather than indulging in the fantasies of romance. This is also the case with Hary's *Wallace*.

The list above is presented alphabetically because a chronological list is impractical: relatively accurate dates can be determined for some of the texts, but for others even the century is uncertain. By the standards of medieval romance this corpus is rather late, although we can still describe most – perhaps all – of these texts as the products of a 'medieval' literary culture thanks to the extension of that period traditionally granted to Scottish literature.[18] The earliest datable Scots romance is from 1438, if the scribal colophon of the *Buik of Alexander* is trustworthy. The latest (probably *Roswall and Lillian*) may only just scrape in before 1600. The language of the earliest extant version of *Roswall*, a 1663 Edinburgh print, is lightly scotticized seventeenth-century English with only occasional archaic rhymes to betray its age. This is not a problem for readers interested in the literary tastes of late seventeenth-century Scotland, but it is a deeply unsatisfactory situation for those attempting to learn more about Older Scots poetry. *Eger and Grime*, or 'Graysteel' as it is also known, would seem to be on surer footing with its host of sixteenth-century citations as well as the payment recorded in 1497 to 'tua fithelaris that sang Graysteil to the King [James IV]'.[19] There are several sixteenth- and early seventeenth-century references to either 'syr egeir and syr gryme',[20] or 'Gray-Steill' (three hundred copies of which were listed as part of the stationer

---

[16] Lyndsay, *Selected Poems*, ed. Hadley Williams.
[17] Barbour, *Bruce*, ed. McDiarmid and Stevenson.
[18] Cf. the temporal range of R. James Goldstein's 'Writing in Scotland, 1058–1560', *The Cambridge History of Medieval English Literature*, ed. David Wallace (Cambridge, 1999), pp. 229–54, and *History*, ed. Jack.
[19] *TA*, vol. 1, 330: 19 April 1497.
[20] *The Complaynt of Scotland (c. 1550)*, ed. A. M. Stewart, STS (1979), fol. 50v.

Thomas Bassandyne's stock for 1577).[21] A tune called 'Gray Steel' was recorded in the Robert Gordon of Straloch lute book of 1627–29, reminding us irresistibly of that performance for James IV.[22] The problems come in attempting to match these citations with the surviving copies. The first copy, of 1474 lines, appears in the famous Percy Folio manuscript of c. 1650: there is nothing of Scotland left in its language (its occasional Northern rhymes could equally well be English); it has some nonsensical gaps in sense and it bears suspiciously strong evidence of memorial transmission.[23] The second version, generally known as Huntington-Laing [hereafter HL],[24] of 2860 lines, is represented by three almost identical Scottish prints dating from 1669–1711. HL is, like *Roswall*, presented in lightly scotticized seventeenth-century English; the text is riddled with gaps and errors and refers to Grime as 'Grahame' all the way through, although rhyme always demands 'Grime'. The two versions have different endings and cannot even agree on the heroine's name.[25] Critics disagree over whether HL represents a 'corrupt and expanded version of the source of the [Percy Folio]',[26] or something closer to the 'original' text.[27] One recent critic allows that Percy and HL may descend from separate written texts, but argues that these predecessors are themselves 'fruits of a common oral tradition, one with roots deeply grounded in Celtic folklore'.[28] This is probably true of many romances, including *Eger and Grime*, but it brings us no closer to identifying what might have been performed for James IV, or sold by Bassandyne, or referred to by John Davidson in 1574 when he wrote: 'Euen of Gray-Steill, wha list to luke, / Their is set foorth a

---

[21] These and other references are collected in Caldwell, pp. 6–13 and Laing, rev. Hazlitt, vol. 2, pp. 119–23.

[22] See John Purser, 'Greysteil', *Stewart Style 1513–1542: Essays on the Court of James V*, ed. J. Hadley Williams (East Linton, 1996), pp. 142–52. He observes that the Huntington-Laing text (on which see note 24 below), united with this musical score, would take a perfectly feasible two and half hours to perform (p. 146).

[23] Noted by David C. Fowler in *A Literary History of the Popular Ballad* (Durham, NC, 1968), pp. 142–6 and examined in detail by Demelza Jayne Curnow, 'Five case studies of the transmission of popular Middle English verse romances', unpublished Ph.D. dissertation, University of Bristol, 2002, pp. 132–77. Curnow finds instances of the exact repetition of widely separated passages, a feature characteristic of memorially-transmitted texts but not of written transmission.

[24] *The History of Sir Eger, Sir Grahame, and Sir Gray-Steele*: one of its prints is held by the Huntington Library, San Marino, California, and it was first edited by David Laing.

[25] The Percy Folio version ends with happy marriages all round. The HL version continues with Grime's death, Eger's confession that it was Grime who defeated Graysteel, and Eger's eventual marriage to Grime's widow. This lady is called Lillias throughout HL, but 'Loosep(a)ine' in Percy.

[26] French and Hale, *Middle English Metrical Romances*, p. 671.

[27] Caldwell votes decisively for HL (p. 20), citing Georg Reichel's study, 'Studien zu der schottischen Romanze: The History of Sir Eger, Sir Grime, and Sir Gray-Steel', *Englische Studien* 19 (1894), pp. 1–66.

[28] Evans, 'Re-evaluating', p. 286.

meikle buke'.²⁹ For this latter description the longer HL version would seem to be a better candidate than Percy. The fact that some other ballad-romances in the Percy Folio are late abridgements of medieval romances may also weigh in HL's favour.³⁰ However, HL remains a problematical text, riddled with gaps, errors, and clumsy modernizations. Unless a new, earlier text of *Eger and Grime* is uncovered, the chasm between *Eger and Grime*'s late-medieval citations and its faulty early modern copies will remain unbridgeable.

Such problems of dating aside, there are some useful general observations we can make about the small corpus of Scottish medieval romance. Firstly, it manages despite its size to address all three traditional 'matters' of romance. Antiquity is represented by the *Troy Book* fragments, the *Alexander* books and *Florimond* (a fictional grandfather of Alexander, whose title 'of Albany' refers to Albania rather than Scotland); Britain by *Lancelot* and *Golagros*; and France (somewhat tenuously) by *Rauf*, which includes Charlemagne among its characters. One might also argue that medieval Scottish literature adds a 'matter' of its own with the heavily romanticized historical narratives of the *Wallace* and the *Bruce*.³¹ These two monumental texts seem to take the place, for a Scottish audience, of the so-called 'ancestral romances' of England, which featured heroic forbears such as Guy of Warwick and Bevis of Hampton.³²

Secondly, Scottish romancers seem to have had clear preferences when it came to form. Conveniently for a chapter in a *Companion to Medieval Scottish Poetry*, no prose romances are known to exist. This is rather a striking divergence from English tradition, which by this period is leaning heavily towards prose as its favoured medium for new romances. Both English and French prose romances circulated in Scotland,³³ but Scottish authors did not seem inclined to imitate them. Indeed, both *Clariodus* and *Lancelot of the Laik* are re-versifications of prose sources, which rather suggests the lengths to

---

²⁹ *A Memorial of the Life and Death of Robert Campbel of Kinyeancleugh and his Wife Elizabeth Campbel*, 15–16. It was composed, according to the author's dedication, in 1574, but printed in Edinburgh, twenty-one years later, in 1595. Quoted from Laing, rev Hazlitt, vol. 2, pp. 120–2.

³⁰ For discussion of the relationship between the Percy ballad-romances and their medieval romance antecedents, see: Fowler, *Literary History*, pp. 132–82; Richard Firth Green, 'The Ballad and the Middle Ages', *The Long Fifteenth Century: Essays for Douglas Gray*, ed. H. Cooper and S. Mapstone (Oxford, 1997), pp. 163–84 (pp. 166–70); Thomas J. Garbáty, 'Rhyme, Romance, Ballad, Burlesque, and the Confluence of Form', *Fifteenth-Century Studies: Recent Essays*, ed. R. F. Yeager (Hamden, Conn., 1984), pp. 283–301 (291–7). See also Gillian Rogers, 'The Percy Folio Manuscript Revisited', *Romance in Medieval England*, ed. M. Mills, J. Fellows and C. M. Meale (Cambridge, 1991), pp. 39–64.

³¹ However, see the reservations expressed above on their generic classification. On the idea of a 'matter of Scotland', see R. James Goldstein, *The Matter of Scotland: Historical Narrative in Medieval Scotland* (Lincoln, Nebr. and London, 1993).

³² On both Anglo-Norman and Middle English versions of such romances, see Susan Crane, *Insular Romance: Politics, Faith and Culture in Anglo-Norman and Middle English Literature* (Berkeley and Los Angeles, 1986).

³³ Priscilla Bawcutt, 'English Books and Scottish Readers in the Fifteenth and Sixteenth Centuries', *ROSC* 14 (2001–02), pp. 1–12 (8–9).

which Scottish romancers would go to avoid prose.[34] Rhyming couplets are the dominant form in what survives, whether four-stress / octosyllabic (*Buik of Alexander, Eger and Grime, Florimond, King Orphius, Roswall*, the *Scottish Troy Book*) or the more stately five stress / decasyllabic variety popularized by Chaucer (*Clariodus, Buik of King Alexander the Conquerour*, and *Lancelot*). *Golagros* and *Rauf* use a complex rhymed-alliterative stanza of thirteen lines. *Sir Colling* swings along in an idiosyncratic version of ballad metre. While all of these forms would have been familiar to Scottish writers from English literature, further proof that the Scottish romancers did not simply replicate the English tradition can be found in the complete absence of tail-rhyme romance in the Scottish corpus, although it makes up a full third of the corpus of Middle English metrical romance and was especially popular in the North.[35] As in the case of prose, its absence from the Scottish corpus is not due to lack of example: the circulation of several tail-rhyme romances is attested and Chepman and Myllar printed the tail-rhyme *Eglamour of Artois* in Edinburgh in 1508.[36] Most tellingly of all, William Dunbar uses the measure for his satiric *Schir Thomas Norny* ('Now lythis off ane gentill knycht', B 39). *Norny* owes much to Chaucer's equally satiric tail-rhyme *Tale of Sir Thopas*, but it also betrays independent knowledge of the tail-rhyme romances.[37] The fact that Dunbar uses tail-rhyme for satire here (and elsewhere)[38] may indicate why Scottish romancers avoided it. Even at the mechanical level of style, then, the Scottish romance tradition is distinguishable from the Middle English tradition which is often assumed to overwhelm it.

Old French romance has, as one might expect, provided the inspiration for several of the Scottish romances. The most straightforward handling of French source material is demonstrated by *Florimond*, whose extant 504 lines present a careful, often line-by-line translation of the late twelfth-century romance

---

[34] The 1578 Edinburgh print of John Rolland's *The Seuin Seages* (itself completed 1560) seems to expect a preference for verse in vernacular Scots literature when it advertises itself repeatedly as being 'translatit out of prois in Scottis meter' on its title page, at the beginning of the tale, and in the author's prologue and epilogue, where Rolland relates how 'this quair was clene compleit / Out of plane prois' for one of his aunts ('Ane schort schawing quhair and quhen, and at quhais requeist this buik was translatit out of prois in Scottis Meter', 10–11); cf. 'The Prologue', 122–6: *The Seuin Seages*, ed. G. F. Black, STS (1932).
[35] See the forthcoming study of the tail-rhyme romances by Purdie: *Anglicizing Romance: Tail-Rhyme and Genre in Medieval English Literature*. The rarer form of unrhymed alliterative romance also fails to find a footing in Scotland.
[36] Bawcutt, 'English Books', p. 8.
[37] See Elizabeth Roth Eddy, 'Sir Thopas and Sir Thomas Norny: Romance Parody in Chaucer and Dunbar', *Review of English Studies* n.s. 22 (1971), pp. 401–9; Dunbar, *The Poems*, ed. Bawcutt, vol. 2, pp. 369–72.
[38] *A Ballat of the Abbot of Tungland* ('As yung Awrora with cristall haile', B 4); 'Off Februar the fyiftene nycht' (B 47, printed by some editors as two poems, 'The Dance of the Sevin Deidly Synnis' and 'The Soutar and Tailyouris War', beginning 'Nixt that a turnament wes tryid'); and 'Quha will behald of luve the chance' (B 50).

Florimont by Aimon de Varennes;[39] the translator shows considerable technical skill in reproducing the smooth octosyllabic couplets (rather than a rough four-stress equivalent) of his source. It breaks off abruptly at the equivalent of line 647 of the Old French text, long before the introduction of the eponymous hero. However, the *Complaynt of Scotland*'s citation of 'floremond of albanye that sleu the dragon be the see' refers to a youthful exploit of Florimond's that occurs nearly 2,000 lines later in the French text,[40] suggesting that our fragment was copied from a much longer Scots text, perhaps even a complete translation of similar length to its 13,680-line source.

Golagros draws its plot from two separate sections of the First Continuation of *Perceval*, although they have been so altered as to be barely recognizable.[41] *Lancelot* is based on a part of the Old French non-cyclic prose *Lancelot* which tells of Arthur's wars with Galiot.[42] Both of these Arthurian texts deal with the topical issue of sovereignty (demands for tribute are the cause of contention in both), and each shows Arthur being offered extensive political advice. The adviser in *Lancelot*, Amytans, is present in the French source although his advice has been significantly expanded,[43] but Spynagros, the advisory figure in *Golagros*, is an entirely new invention.[44] Along with the extensive direct borrowing from the *Secreta Secretorum* seen in Hay's *Buik of King Alexander*, these texts demonstrate the confidence with which some Scottish romancers adapted the narrative genre of romance to accommodate a well-documented local appetite for advisory material.[45] A very different handling of French source material, meanwhile, can be seen in *Clariodus*, whose plot is lifted without alteration from its Burgundian source, *Cleriadus et Meliadice*,[46] but whose aureate diction incongruously mimics that of William Dunbar.[47]

---

[39] *Florimont: ein Altfranzösischer Abenteuerroman*, ed. Alfons Hilka (Göttingen, 1932).
[40] Fol. 50v. *The Complaynt* is very unlikely to be referring to a French text: see '*The Complaynt* as Defence and Illustration of the Vernacular' in Stewart's Introduction, pp. xxix–xxxiii.
[41] See Purdie, 'Search for Scottishness', and W. R. J. Barron, '*Gologros and Gawain*: A Creative Redaction', *Bibliographical Bulletin of the International Arthurian Society* 26 (1974), pp. 173–85.
[42] See the introduction to *'Lancelot of the Laik'*, ed. Lupack.
[43] See Karl Heinz Göller, *König Arthur in der Englischen Literatur des Späten Mittelalters* (Göttingen, 1963), pp. 137–42; Flora Alexander, 'Late Medieval Scottish Attitudes to the Figure of King Arthur: A Reassessment', *Anglia* 93 (1975), pp. 17–34 (23–8); Douglas Wurtele, 'A Reappraisal of the Scottish *Lancelot of the Laik*', *Revue de l'Université d'Ottawa* 46 (1976), pp. 68–82; Elizabeth Archibald, '*Lancelot of the Laik*: Sources, Genre, Reception', *The Scots and Medieval Arthurian Legend*, ed. Purdie and Royan, pp. 71–82.
[44] Discussed in detail in Purdie, 'Search for Scottishness', pp. 101–3.
[45] See S. L. Mapstone, 'The Advice to Princes Tradition in Scottish Literature, 1450–1500', unpublished D.Phil. thesis (Oxford, 1986).
[46] *Cleriadus et Meliadice: roman en prose du XVe siècle*, ed. G. Zink, Textes Littéraires Français 328 (Paris and Geneva, 1984).
[47] See Purdie, '*Clariodus* and the Ambitions of Courtly Romance in Later Medieval Scotland', *FMLS* 38 (2002), pp. 449–61.

Surprisingly, the one medieval Scottish romance that actually belongs to the 'matter of France', *Rauf Coilyear*, has no known French source.[48] *Rauf* is part of a group of 'king in disguise' tales popular in England and on the continent, although it is unlike any other known member of this group. Its closest relation is the Middle English comic tale of *John the Reeve*, known to us from a tail-rhyme recension in the Percy Folio.[49] It is mentioned in the same breath as *Rauf* by both Douglas and Dunbar,[50] and is a probable source for *Rauf*.[51] Both stories tell of a king travelling incognito (Charlemagne in *Rauf*, Edward I in *John*) who spends a night as the guest of an unsuspecting churl. The churl is later invited (or summoned) to court, where he learns his guest's real identity. They are related to other 'imperious host' tales such as the Middle English *Sir Gawain and the Carle of Carlisle* and *Sir Gawain and the Green Knight*.[52] Significantly, *Golagros* is another member of this group. With varying degrees of sophistication, these texts explore the value of courtesy and stress the dignity of the individual irrespective of his social class. This is expressed in recognizably similar terms in *Rauf* and *Golagros*: Rauf sternly reminds his guest 'to mak me lord of my awin' (128), while Gawain, with his intuitive courtesy, calms an anxious host with: 'To mak you lord of your avne, me think it grete skill' (147). A cornerstone of courtesy and social harmony in *Rauf* and *Golagros* is the ability to trust and be trusted. Again, this is dramatized in notably similar ways, which set them apart from their analogues. In *John the Reeve*, the hero is merely summoned to court. Rauf, however, makes the journey because he and his guest have exchanged promises: he to come to court, and the guest to help him get a good price for his coals. Rauf's wife fears that he will be betrayed, but he is determined to uphold his promise (367–81). On his way he meets Roland, who has been instructed by Charlemagne to bring back the first person he finds on the road. They argue until Roland (rather surprisingly given his usual literary reputation) determines to find a diplomatic solution: 'Lat se how we may disseuer with sobernes aneuch, / And catche crabitnes away' (525–6). He agrees to trust Rauf to come to court on his own, while Rauf promises to meet him the next day. Such laying-aside of personal pride in order to find a diplomatic (and peaceful) solution is precisely what Gawain does at the end of

---

[48] Amours notes, however, the inclusion of a French proverb, 'charbonnier est maître chez soi', *Alliterative Poems*, p. xxxviii. On the analogues, *Medieval English Romances*, ed. Speed, vol. 1, pp. 196–202.
[49] Edited in Laing, rev. Hazlitt, vol. 1, pp. 250–83.
[50] Douglas, *Palice of Honour*, 1711–12; Dunbar, 'Schir, yit remember as befoir' (B 68), 33.
[51] It was probably composed before the 1461 accession of Edward IV: 'Of that name [Edward] were Kings 3' (16). On the English 'king in disguise texts' generally, see Rachel Snell, 'The Undercover King', *Medieval Insular Romance: Translation and Innovation*, ed. J. Weiss, J. Fellows and M. Dickson (Cambridge, 2000), pp. 133–54.
[52] See Glenn Wright, 'Churl's Courtesy: *Rauf Coilyear* and its English analogues', *Neophilologus* 85 (2001), pp. 647–62. Auvo Kurvinen surveys Middle English and continental 'imperious host' tales but finds no evidence for the influence of the English *Carle* romances on *Rauf*: *Sir Gawain and the Carl of Carlisle in two versions* (Helsinki, 1951), pp. 81–5 (81).

Golagros when he allows himself to be led back to Golagros's castle in apparent defeat in order to preserve Golagros's honour and his life. Gawain must swallow some serious doubts: 'To leif in thi laute, and thow war vnlele, / Than had I cassin in cair mony kene knight' (1107–8). The empty-handed Roland likewise spends an uncomfortable stanza wondering 'gif the Coilyearis lawtie was leill' (602). With their depiction of the unglamorous art of compromise, these romances are much closer to such texts as the advice-filled *Buik of King Alexander the Conquerour* than they might first appear. In this context, the much more downbeat ending of the HL version of *Eger and Grime*, with its deaths and shamefaced confessions, does not look nearly so out of place.

The *Scottish Troy Book* is in some ways the most shadowy work in our corpus of medieval Scottish romances: it is represented only by fragments patched into a much larger chunk of Lydgate's *Troy Book*, the whole patchwork exercise being preserved in two manuscripts in which the relevant sections were copied in the early sixteenth century.[53] (Both poets are translating Guido delle Colonne's Latin prose *Historia Destructionis Troiae*.) It has occasionally been assumed that the Scottish fragments were composed specifically to fill lacunae in a Lydgate manuscript,[54] but this would hardly explain why they are in four-stress couplets while Lydgate's couplets are decasyllabic: they seem rather to have been imported from a complete, independent Scottish *Troy Book*. Despite the fact that over 3,700 lines of this text survive, it remains something of a 'lost text' of Older Scots literature, doomed forever to be 'the bits in the Lydgate manuscripts' that are neither by Lydgate nor, despite one scribe's optimistic claim, by Barbour.[55]

At the opposite end of the scale, at least in terms of size, lie *Sir Colling the Kny^t* and the fragments of *King Orphius*. Both of these romances are closely associated with later ballad tradition. *King Orphius* is obviously related to, but not derived from, the Middle English *Sir Orfeo*: it may represent an independent translation from the same (presumably French) source.[56] In it, Orphius's queen is called Issabell and they are king and queen of 'Portingale' (Portugal), as opposed to the Thrace of classical legend or the Winchester of the Middle English *Sir Orfeo*. This detail identifies *King Orphius* as the referent of

---

[53] Cambridge, University Library Kk.5.30, and Oxford, Bodleian Library, Douce 148. See Angus McIntosh, 'Some Notes on the Language and Textual Transmission of the *Scottish Troy Book*, *Archivum Linguisticum* n.s. 10 (1979), pp. 1–19; *Lydgate's Troy Book*, ed. Henry Bergen, 4 vols, EETS ES 97, 103, 106, 126 (1906–35), vol. 4, 46–50, 88–91. On Kk.5.30, see also Bawcutt, 'Sir Lamwell', pp. 84–5.

[54] See, for example, M. P. McDiarmid, 'The Metrical Chronicles and Non-alliterative Romances', *History*, ed. Jack, pp. 27–38 (32).

[55] In Kk.5.30 Fragment I concludes: 'Heir endis barbour and begynnis the monk' (fol. 9r). Fragment II opens with: 'Her endis the monk ande begynnis Barbour' (fol. 304v); ed. Horstmann, vol. 2, pp. 227, 229.

[56] Stewart, '*King Orphius*', p. 14.

the *Complaynt*'s 'Opheus kyng of portingal',[57] while 'Queen Issabell' is a detail that links our text directly to the nineteenth-century Scots versions of a ballad of 'King Orfeo'.[58] Scholars had previously suspected the 'Orfeo' ballads of being nineteenth-century creations based on published editions of the Middle English *Sir Orfeo*, but such shared details, absent from *Sir Orfeo*, attest to a separate and continuous Scots textual tradition from at least the early sixteenth century to modern times.

The *King Orphius* fragments were part of a much longer text. *Sir Colling*, on the other hand, seems more or less complete at 246 lines.[59] It is an earlier version of the Percy Folio's *Sir Cawline*, a text written in standard *abcb* ballad quatrains and included by Child in his great ballad collection.[60] *Sir Colling* has the alternation between four-stress and three-stress lines characteristic of ballad, but it shows no regular stanza division despite several long chains of rhyming lines.[61] It also has a Scottish setting (the only Scots romance that does)[62] in Argyll and a suggestion of historicity: Sir Colling fought with 'Edvaird ye bruce ... / In Irland biyond ye sie' (9–10) as did a real Sir Colin Campbell of Argyll.[63] However, we are soon back in familiar romance territory as he slices off the hand of an 'alreche' knight and defeats a three-headed challenger. Where *King Orphius* has clear links back to medieval romance tradition and forwards to later ballad tradition, the brief *Sir Colling* represents a real hybrid of ballad and romance. Ballad tradition is generally (though not universally) thought to have developed over the later fifteenth and sixteenth centuries.[64] In

[57] Priscilla Bawcutt, '*King Orphius* and "Opheus Kyng of Portingal" ', *Notes and Queries* 48.2 (2001), pp. 112–14.

[58] See Francis J. Child, *The English and Scottish Popular Ballads*, 5 vols (Boston and New York, 1882–98), no. 19; Patrick Shuldham-Shaw, 'The Ballad "King Orfeo"', *Scottish Studies* 20 (1976), pp. 124–6; Dorena A. Wright, 'From *Sir Orfeo* to *King Orphius*', *Parergon* 27 (1980), pp. 9–11.

[59] However the scribe concludes rather mysteriously: 'This is ye end of ye maist pairt of Sir Collyne ye kny^t'.

[60] Child, *Ballads*, no. 61. Child's version of 201 lines omits the first two stanzas of Percy 'as belonging to another ballad', but they are paralleled in *Sir Colling* (quoted in Stewart, 'A Recently-Discovered Manuscript', p. 32).

[61] Stewart, 'A Recently-Discovered Manuscript', pp. 30–2.

[62] *Eger and Grime* is sometimes described as having a Scottish setting. However, the texts only tell us that both heroes are from Bea(l)m (possibly Bohemia – certainly nowhere recognizably Scottish). Graysteel lives in 'the land that was forbidden' (HL 128, P 108), 'a forbidden countrye' (P 410), 'the land of doubt' (HL 1447, 1864), 'this ffar countrye' (P 343). Lillias / Loosepine lives nearby in the land of her father, Earl Gares / Goris ('Earle Gares Land', P 1398, 1428). The wild landscape described in parts of the poem sounds very Scottish, but this is also the case with *Rauf Coilyear* and *Golagros and Gawane*, which are explicitly set in France. One critic has recently tried to place *Eger and Grime* in the Border region by interpreting Graysteel's 'land of doubt' as a historical area known as 'the Debateable Land': see Evans, 'Re-evaluating', pp. 280–3.

[63] This 'Schyre Colyne Cambell' appears briefly in *Barbour's Bruce*, ed. McDiarmid and Stevenson, 16:119–32.

[64] Thus for example Fowler, *Literary History*, pp. 3–19. Green, 'Ballad and the Middle Ages', argues for origins earlier in the Middle Ages. On the difficulties of identifying the beginning of

England this follows the great period of metrical romance composition, but in Scotland it overlaps significantly with it, and this is reflected in the histories of *King Orphius* and *Sir Colling*.

A final feature of medieval Scottish romance that deserves mention here is one that extends to medieval Scottish literature generally: a strong sense that texts are circulating in a relatively small, self-consciously interconnected literary culture. Studies of manuscript and book circulation in this period see the same names recurring, while the Older Scots poets themselves often make a point of praising fellow makars within their poems.[65] Many of the Scottish romances likewise cite each other, and are in turn mentioned in other Scottish works.[66] Before any of our texts were composed, the romance tastes of later generations of Scottish readers were foreshadowed in Barbour's *Bruce*: it describes Bruce reading 'Ferambrace' (a Charlemagne-cycle romance) to his men, and also cites Tydeus of Thebes, Gaudifer, Alexander and King Arthur.[67] 'Gaudifer' is the hero of the Old French Alexander-cycle *Fuerre de Gadres* ('Foraging of Gaza'), a text that would later be translated in both Scottish *Alexander* books. It is probably one of these Scots versions that Lyndsay has in mind when he mentions 'Gaudefer' at the foray of Gaza in *Squyer Meldrum* (1281-2). He continues:

> This worthie squyer courageous
> Micht be compairit to Tydeus,
> Quhilk faucht for to defend his richtis
> And slew of Thebes fiftie knichtis.
> Rolland with Brandwell, his bricht brand,
> Faucht never better, hand for hand;
> Nor Gawin aganis Golibras,
> Nor Olyver with Pharambras.
> I wait he faucht that day als weill

a recognizable ballad tradition, see Holger Olof Nygard, 'Popular Ballad and Medieval Romance', *Ballad Studies*, ed. E. B. Lyle (Cambridge, 1976), pp. 1–19.

[65] The most famous round-up of the early stars of Scotland's literary firmament is probably Dunbar's 'I that in heill wes and gladnes' (B 21), also known as the 'Lament for the Makars'. The extremely learned Douglas offers three poets 'of this natioun ... / Gret Kennedy and Dunbar, yit undede, / And Quyntyne ...' to balance his citation of the three English poets Chaucer, Gower and Lydgate in his *Palice of Honour*, 922–4. Lyndsay, in his *Testament of the Papyngo*, allows his own citation of Chaucer, Gower and Lydgate (all in line 12) to be completely overwhelmed by the ensuing praise for sixteen Scottish writers (16–54). For more general discussion of the citation of authors and texts in Older Scots literature, see R. J. Lyall, 'The Lost Literature of Medieval Scotland', *Bryght Lanternis: Essays on the Language and Literature of Medieval and Renaissance Scotland*, ed. J. D. McClure and M. J. Spiller (Aberdeen, 1989), pp. 33–47.

[66] See the long list of stories in the *Complaynt of Scotland* (cited in the discussion of *Florimond*, *Orphius* and *Eger and Grime* above); see also note 50 and the discussion of Lyndsay's *Meldrum*, below.

[67] Barbour, *Bruce*, ed. McDiarmid and Stevenson: 'Ferambrace', 3:437; summary of Gaudifer and the *Fuerre de Gadres*, 3:73–87; the ambush of Tydeus, 6:181–270.

> As did Sir Gryme aganis Graysteill,
> And I dar say he was als abill
> As onie knicht of the Round Tabill.   (1309–20)

Tydeus is a hero of the Old French *Roman de Thèbes* (perhaps what Barbour had in mind) but also, by the fifteenth century, of Lydgate's *Siege of Thebes*. A copy of this was owned at the end of the sixteenth century by Duncan Campbell of Glenorchy,[68] whose other books included the fragment of *Florimond* and both known manuscripts of Hay's *Buik of King Alexander the Conquerour*. Campbell married Elizabeth Sinclair, a member of the same Sinclair family that had in previous generations provided patrons for Gavin Douglas and Sir Gilbert Hay, as well as apparently commissioning a large manuscript compilation of Scottish and English verse now known as Oxford, Bodleian Library, Arch. Selden. B. 24.[69]

Legends of Charlemagne's douzepers ('Rolland' and 'Oliver'), including the *Fierabras* branch ('Pharambras'), are evidently still popular in Lyndsay's day, as is Arthurian romance, but we now also see Scots texts appearing in this summary of contemporary romance reading: *Golagros* ('Golibras') and *Eger and Grime*. The long version of *Roswall and Lillian* adds a few more to the list, slipping in *Florimond* and *Clariodus* alongside several characters from the history of Troy:[70]

> Princes to him could not compare,
> Ulisses nor Gandifere [i.e. 'Gaudifer']
> Achilles nor Troyalus,
> Nor yet his father Priamus,
> Nor the gentle Clariadus [i.e. 'Clariodus],
> Nor the fair Philmox, nor Achilles,
> Nor Florentine of Almanie [i.e. 'Florimond']
> Was never half so fair as he;
> Nor knight Sir Lancelot du Lake.   (15–23)

---

[68] Priscilla Bawcutt, 'The Boston Public Library Manuscript of Lydgate's *Siege of Thebes*: Its Scottish Owners and Inscriptions', *MÆ* 70 (2001), pp. 80–94.

[69] See Julia Boffey, 'Bodleian Library, MS Arch. Selden B. 24 and Definitions of the "Household Book" ', *The English Medieval Book: Studies in Memory of Jeremy Griffiths*, ed. A. S. G. Edwards, V. Gillespie and R. Hanna (London, 2000), pp. 125–34; Julia Boffey and A. S. G. Edwards, 'Bodleian Library Arch. Selden B. 24 and the "Scotticization" of Middle English Verse', *Rewriting Chaucer: Culture, Authority and the Idea of the Authentic Text 1400–1602*, ed. T. A. Prendergast and B. Kline (Columbus, OH, 1999), pp. 166–85. The collection contains several pieces by Chaucer as well as the unique copy of the *Kingis Quair*. See above, chapter 4.

[70] It might also be noted that *Roswall*'s setting in 'Bealm' recalls *Eger and Grime*, while the name 'Lillian' recalls the HL *Eger*'s 'Lillias'.

The *Roswall*-poet's familiarity with the actual text of *Clariodus* is suggested by another list of names, garbled in the extant prints, which is directly paralleled in a passage from *Clariodus*:

> Of fairer forsooth I read of nane.
> Not the noble French queen,
> Nor yet the lady Pelicane [var. Pellan] *sheen*,
> Nor yet Helen, that fair ladie,
> Nor yet the true Philippie [var. Philledy]   (*Roswall*, 340–4)

> And with thy bright hairis thou Palexine,
> And thou faire Heline, with thy hairis quhyte,
> And Candas with thy culloure of delyte,
> And with thy trewth thou [chaist] Penelope. (*Clariodus* IV, 1196–9)

These are Polyxena, Helen and Penelope from the story of Troy, known to earlier Scottish readers from Lydgate's *Troy Book* and, presumably, the lost *Scottish Troy Book*. The names seem to be meaningless to the seventeenth-century printers of *Roswall* in its Long Version, and all such citations are absent from the eighteenth-century prints of the Short Version. This suggests that the Long Version of *Roswall* is a sixteenth-century text, composed after *Clariodus* had joined the list of local favourites, but long before it reached the hands of the baffled seventeenth-century printers.

Scotland enjoyed an era of intense poetic creativity in the fifteenth and sixteenth centuries, and the Scottish medieval romances were a part of it. This is not to claim that every romance-poet rivalled the brilliance of Henryson, Dunbar or Douglas, but simply to recognize that many poets made conscious use of a local poetic tradition alongside the dominant traditions of England and France. Some borrowed style and technique from other Scottish poets; some catered for the strong interests of their Scottish audiences in the arts of diplomacy and the proper conduct of rulers, remoulding their source materials to address such concerns. Still others simply borrowed from other romances (Scottish or otherwise) in the best self-referential tradition of romance composition. Despite the difficulties faced by the modern reader in trying to reassemble the corpus of Scottish romance, it is evident that Scotland did move beyond a mere appreciation of English and French medieval romance to develop a confident romance tradition of its own.

12

Sir David Lyndsay

JANET HADLEY WILLIAMS

Best known today as author of the ambitious play first performed in the 1550s, *Ane Satyre of the Thrie Estaitis*, Sir David Lyndsay has been associated principally with the reign of Mary Queen of Scots (1542–67) and with the major political issue of that day, the authorization of religious reform. Yet Lyndsay, the oldest son of an established family of middle-ranking landholders in Fife, was born in about 1486, near the end of James III's reign (1460–88). Much of his poetry was written over twenty years before the Marian era.[1]

Lyndsay's name appears in the court records of Mary's grandfather, James IV (1488–1513). He is possibly the 'Lyndesay' briefly attached to the stable of the first Prince James, who had died by February 1508;[2] and probably the 'David Lindesay' who by 1511 was among those servitors paid regularly and well. In that year, too, he was supplied with a 'play coit [coat] ... for the play playt in the King and Quenis presence in the Abbay', a plausible beginning to what was to be his long-term involvement in the entertainment of king and court. By 1512, Lyndsay was usher (doorkeeper) to the surviving Prince James.

These dates mark the fact that the beginning of Lyndsay's career in the royal household coincided with the presence there of some older servitors who were part-time poets of great skill – William Dunbar, Walter Kennedy, and James Inglis among others – and thus with a period of poetic self-assurance. There is no evidence of any concurrent literary activities of Lyndsay's own; yet, when in the following reign he began to write, the influence of these writers is often evident, as is his awareness of the changed conditions to which he had now to adapt and respond.

With James IV's unexpected death at Flodden late in 1513, and the coronation of the seventeen-month-old prince, Lyndsay became 'kepar of the Kingis grace' or 'maister uschar'. In this unstable environment of minority rule, he shared the

---

[1] Lyndsay was probably twenty-one by 19 October 1507, when his feudal superior, Patrick Lord Lindsay of the Byres, made him the customary grant of the lands of Garmylton-Alexander, near Haddington, East Lothian: *The Poetical Works of Sir David Lyndsay*, ed. David Laing, 3 vols (1879), vol. 1, p. ix; and Carol Edington, *Court and Culture in Renaissance Scotland: Sir David Lindsay of the Mount* (Amherst, Mass., 1994), p. 14.

[2] Accurate quotations from government sources for this and subsequent biographical details are gathered in *The Works of Sir David Lindsay of the Mount 1490–1555*, ed. Douglas Hamer, 4 vols, STS (1931–36), vol. 4, pp. 245–77.

responsibility of James's safekeeping, sleeping in the king's bedchamber with the schoolmaster and chamber attendants.[3] The multi-tasking in which David Lyndsay was involved – as cupbearer, server, carver, privy purse master – he later recalled in verse.[4] He also described in more detail his particular concern, the after-school recreation. Lyndsay sang to the king, accompanying himself on the lute; danced energetically to James's favourite tunes;[5] told stories (chivalric romances, ancient prophecies, folk tales) and acted out 'fairsis' (short dramas):

> And sumtyme lyke ane feind transfegurate
> And sumtyme lyke the greislie gaist of Gye,
> In divers formis, oft tymes disfigurate,
> And sumtyme dissagyist full plesandlye.
> So, sen thy birth, I have continewalye
> Bene occupyit, and aye to thy plesoure.   (*Dreme*, 15–20)

In 1524, when the governor, John, Duke of Albany, returned to France, the newly-powerful dowager queen Margaret and her supporters raised James to his position as king.[6] Then, by taking custody of James, Margaret's estranged second husband, Archibald Douglas, Earl of Angus, seized power. Lyndsay was replaced at court, but at first continued to receive his pension, his full dismissal probably impeded by his marriage to a Douglas or, perhaps, as he claimed, by the influence of the fourteen-year-old king.[7] James knew his bargaining power; he had escaped from his stepfather by 1528. Lyndsay was reinstated and by 1530 had written (and probably published) two considerable poems, *The Dreme*, an advisory work marking the king's assumption of personal rule, and *The Complaynt of Schir David Lindesay*, a more overt petition for promotion.[8] He was appointed herald, an office in which he represented both crown and kingdom. Its duties included diplomatic travel, the devising of state ceremonies, and execution of royal proclamations.[9] His concern for Scotland's social order in later poems reflects this deepening involvement in the country's public affairs.

---

[3] 'Ordinance for the Keeping of James V', Historical Manuscripts Commission, *Report on the Manuscripts of the Earl of Mar and Kellie* (London, 1904), pp. 11–12.
[4] *The Dreme*, 21–4. All references are to Lyndsay, *Selected Poems*, ed. Hadley Williams unless noted otherwise.
[5] See further, Janet Hadley Williams, 'Music and Sir David Lyndsay', *Notis Musycall: Essays on Music and Scottish Culture in Honour of Kenneth Elliott*, ed. Gordon Munro et al. (Glasgow, 2005), pp. 133–41.
[6] *Acts of the Parliaments of Scotland*, ed. T. Thomson and C. Innes, 12 vols (1814–75), vol. 2, 286–7, 290.
[7] Lyndsay married Janet Douglas, a court 'semestair', c. 1522: *TA* V, 196, 301, 314. For Lyndsay's claim: *Complaynt*, 272.
[8] See *Works of Lindsay*, ed. Hamer, vol. 4, pp. 15–20; Douglas Hamer, 'The Bibliography of Sir David Lindsay', *The Library* 10 (1929), pp. 1–42.
[9] See Thomas Innes of Learney, *Scots Heraldry*, rev. M. R. Innes (London, 1978), pp. 4–11.

Before the late 1530s, when Lyndsay received a knighthood and became senior herald (Lyon King of Arms),[10] he had travelled widely in the cause of his heraldic duties. At the Habsburg court he negotiated on trading matters and held confidential discussions on the king's marriage prospects. His preliminary report of this trip survives, a rare example of his prose, its details of current political rumours and imperial tournaments suggesting that Lyndsay was a keen observer of all aspects of government.[11] His four visits to the artistically lively French court during the negotiation and celebration of the marriage of James V and Princess Madeleine could only have strengthened his interest in literature and the allied arts.[12] On a number of occasions Lyndsay also travelled through England or to its court: for James's installation by proxy with the Order of the Garter, for instance, and to return the same collar, garter and statutes after the king's death. His last much later journey to protestant Denmark, to request assistance against English attack and negotiate a trade treaty, gave Lyndsay opportunities to observe literary as well as political matters in a country where the preparation of a vernacular translation of the bible was being given royal encouragement.[13]

At home, in these same years, Lyndsay helped to reinvigorate the public image of the Scottish monarch and his court: the self-confident *Testament and Complaynt of our Soverane Lordis Papyngo* (published in England as well as Scotland), and the changes to the design of the royal arms are aspects of his contribution.[14] Lyndsay also devised welcoming tableaux for James's two queens, and the funeral of the first, Princess Madeleine, who died before her formal entry into Edinburgh could take place.[15] His *Deploratioun of the Deith of Quene Magdalene*, a stylized expression of national mourning, was part of this latter task; his *Justing betwix James Watsoun and Jhone Barbour* was a more intimate court entertainment linked to the arrival of Marie de Guise, James's second wife. In addition, Lyndsay accompanied diplomatic visitors, such as Burgundy herald (in Scotland to invest the king with Charles V's Order

---

[10] See George Seton, *Law and Practice of Heraldry* (1863), p. 480.
[11] See *The Letters of James V*, ed. Denys Hay (1954), pp. 191, 193–4, 302–4, and Janet Hadley Williams, ' "Of officiaris serving thy senyeorie": David Lyndsay's diplomatic letter of 1531', *Palace*, ed. Houwen et al., pp. 125–40.
[12] See Janet Hadley Williams, 'Writing and Publishing in Sixteenth-Century Scotland: Some French Connections', *Renaissance Reflections: Essays in memory of C. A. Mayer*, ed. Pauline M. Smith and Trevor Peach (Paris, 2002), pp. 129–44 (130–1, 135–41).
[13] T. L. Christensen, 'The Earl of Rothes in Denmark', *The Renaissance and Reformation in Scotland: Essays in honour of Gordon Donaldson*, ed. Ian B. Cowan and Duncan Shaw (1983), pp. 60–74 (67–9); Janet Hadley Williams, 'Shady Publishing in Sixteenth-Century Scotland: the Case of Sir David Lyndsay's Poems', *Bulletin of the Bibliographical Society of Australia and New Zealand* 16 (1992), pp. 97–105 (101–3).
[14] See further, Janet Hadley Williams, 'James V of Scots as Literary Patron', *Princes and Princely Culture 1450–1650*, vol. 1, ed. Martin Gosman, Alasdair MacDonald and Arjo Vanderjagt (Leiden, 2003), pp. 172–98 (191–2).
[15] See further, Robert Lindesay of Pitscottie, *The Historie and Cronicles of Scotland*, ed Æ. J. G. Mackay, 3 vols, STS (1899–1922), vol. 1, pp. 378–9.

of the Golden Fleece), and Henry VIII's envoy, Ralph Sadler.[16] Funeral arrangements for James V in 1542 were another melancholy responsibility. Afterwards Lyndsay acted for the Earl of Arran's initially-reformist interim government, in 1546 negotiating with the reformers (all Fife men he probably knew), who after assassinating Cardinal David Beaton had seized St Andrews Castle.[17] In his *Tragedie of the Cardinall* (1547) Lyndsay did not maintain the professional neutrality required for the negotiations, but his use of the wraith of a repentant Beaton as the poem's speaker, evoking the literary antecedents of Boccaccio, Chaucer and Lydgate, also recognized the political undesirability of associating the reformist cause with aggressive polemic.[18]

By then in his sixties, Lyndsay spent more time on his estate near Cupar, to the benefit of his writing.[19] An affectionate tribute, in the form of a heroic romance, *The Historie of Ane Nobil and Vailyeand Squyer, William Meldrum*, with an appended *Testament*, was circulated locally, c. 1550, and published only after the poet's death. Lyndsay's masterpiece, *Ane Satyre*, was completed and performed in Cupar in 1552,[20] then in Edinburgh for the queen regent and city populace in 1554.[21] His most widely-read work, *Ane Dialog betwix Experience and ane Courteour*, a mix of scriptural translation, religious history and direct counsel, begun perhaps in 1548, was published in 1554, a year before his death. These later works, in theme, metrics, genre and style, have many links with earlier writing, as will be noted. As poetic responses to the rapidly changing political and religious circumstances of mid-century Scotland they are also of great interest, but an in-depth study is beyond the scope of this chapter.

David Lyndsay does not present himself as a poet, a term he explicitly associated with the classical writers and with those he regarded as the best of his own day.[22] Even speaking tongue-in-cheek, Lyndsay rejects that role, in the *Answer to the Kingis Flyting* conceding defeat before his mock-quarrel with James is well begun, on the grounds that he is not a poet, and must '... do as dog dois in his den, / Fald baith my feit, or fle fast frome your flyting. / ... / Proclamand yow, the prince of poetry' (17–18, 21). His writing can recall

---

[16] *Letters*, ed. Hay, pp. 221–2.

[17] M. H. B. Sanderson, *Cardinal of Scotland: David Beaton 1494–1546* (1986), pp. 222–8.

[18] See further, Janet Hadley Williams, 'The Earliest Surviving Text of Lyndsay's *Tragedie of the Cardinall*: An English Edition of a Scottish Poem', *Literature, Letters and the Canonical in Early Modern Scotland*, ed. Theo van Heijnsbergen and Nicola Royan (East Linton, 2002), pp. 22–34.

[19] One heraldic duty is recorded, the trial of a messenger in January 1554, at which Lyndsay presided: *Works of Lindsay*, ed. Hamer, vol. 4, p. 274.

[20] For the play's history: R. J. Lyall, 'The Linlithgow Interlude of 1540', *Actes du 2e Colloque de Langue et de Littérature Ecossaises (Moyen Age et Renaissance)*, ed. Jean-Jacques Blanchot and Claude Graf (Strasbourg, 1978), pp. 409–21; *Works of Lindsay*, ed. Hamer, vol. 2, pp. 1–6.

[21] *Extracts from the Records of the Burgh of Edinburgh AD 1528–1557*, ed. James D. Marwick, Scottish Burgh Records Society (1871), pp. 197, 198–9, 282, 284.

[22] See *Papyngo*, stanzas one and two.

Dunbar's in its theatrical and recreative qualities, as in his jesting claim that the court parrot could:

> Bark lyk ane dog, and kekell lyke ane ka,
> Blait lyke ane hog and buller lyke ane bull,
> Gaill lyke ane goik and greit quhen scho wes wa,
> Clym on ane corde, syne lauch and play the fule:
> Scho mycht have bene ane menstrall agane Yule. (*Papyngo*, 94–8)

Lyndsay does not place himself with the latter entertainers; when in *The Complaynt* he asks the king for reward, he explicitly dissociates himself from the 'baird', or Gaelic-speaking travelling minstrel-entertainer (49–50). He alludes, in part, to Dunbar's similar distinction in his *Flyting* with Kennedy (B 65, 17–21), but Lyndsay's point is slightly different. Whereas Dunbar comments upon his value as a poet in the 'Inglis' tradition and consequent contempt for the Gaelic, Lyndsay is less concerned with his own portrayal as writer than with the fact that these 'bairds' were frequently associated with extortioners and beggars. As a faithful servitor, he hopes his own request will be distinguished from theirs. Indeed after this one petition (in which Lyndsay writes more about the king's needs than his own), he does not follow Dunbar's often wittily satiric emphasis on self-depiction. Advice in the diverse forms Lyndsay knew were congenial to the king, not personal ambition, is uppermost, especially in the poems of the 1530s and early '40s.

Similarly Lyndsay does not mention the word 'makar', Dunbar's frequent preference. This could be traditional poetic 'modesty', which he understood well: in his *Papyngo*, in a rhyme royal stanza distinguished by internal rhyme and sustained alliteration, Lyndsay disowned his work as 'but [without] rhetoric so rude' (1179). Yet his omission (not only of 'makar' but of the related 'mak' and 'makyng') could also imply an uneasiness with the idea that the crafting of a poem is higher than, or of equal importance to, its content. It is revealing that Lyndsay uses indefinite or general terms ('dyting', 'mater', 'indyte', 'complaynt', 'tragedie') of his own writing, and none for himself as their author. Arguably this is because, unlike the majority of the Scottish writers mentioned earlier, David Lyndsay was not a churchman, nor, possibly, a university graduate.[23] He knew French and Latin, had read widely, and admired those with more learning,[24] but he did so as a well-placed layman. His writing is not deeply informed, as these poets' work so often is (especially in its highly-patterned rhetoric) by the Christian Latin tradition of liturgy and Scripture. None of his poems is devotional, although several are seriously concerned with the state's responsibilities towards the church.

---

[23] See further, Edington, *Court and Culture*, pp. 12–13.
[24] See *Ane Dialog*, 594–600.

His debts are to secular writing. They include those to the French tradition of the *sottie* or fools' play in *Ane Satyre*;[25] the *épitre* or verse epistle in *The Complaynt* and *The Answer to the Kingis Flyting*,[26] and to the long-lasting modes of *déploration* and *complainte* in his *Deploratioun*.[27] The play's discriminating use of the thirteen-line stanza, however, recalls its employment in medieval English moralities[28] and the Scottish *Buke of the Howlat*, while the *Deploratioun*'s heightened rhetoric owes much to the English lament tradition.[29] Generally, Lyndsay drew most deeply on the poetic traditions, the vernacular emphasis, and the metrical innovations associated with earlier English writers, especially Chaucer and Lydgate, and with Scottish writers, particularly Henryson, Douglas and Dunbar, all of whom he praised in the *Papyngo*'s opening catalogue of great poets. The few following illustrations represent many more.

For his *Dreme* and *Ane Dialog* Lyndsay adopted the mode of dream vision allegory derived from French sources such as the *Roman de la Rose*, yet made popular by Chaucer's distinctive works (*Parliament of Fowls, Book of the Duchess*), and used inventively by James I, Henryson (*Testament of Cresseid*) and Douglas (*Palice of Honour*) among others. He did so with some care: in *Ane Dialog* the early signals of a vision are deliberately unfulfilled, and imply disquiet at the use of such forms. Chaucer's translation of Boethius's *Consolation of Philosophy* perhaps had particular resonance, suggesting to Lyndsay the value of a female figure of authority in *The Dreme*; but her name, 'Dame Remembrance', was possibly prompted by Hay's depiction of 'Memor ... kepare of all things that cummys before', as member of a wise king's 'grete Counsale' in *The Buik of King Alexander the Conquerour*.[30] Lyndsay explicitly linked Chaucer's *Troilus and Criseyde* to *Squyer Meldrum*, not only by verbal echoes and a common authorial stance, but by carefully pointed comparisons and contrasts between the pairs of lovers.[31] His *Papyngo*, telling of the fall of a talented but plump and vain court parrot, is in the *de casibus* tradition of writing exemplified by Chaucer's *Monk's Tale* and Lydgate's *Fall of Princes*. The

---

[25] See A. J. Mill, 'The Influence of Continental Drama on Lyndsay's *Ane Satyre of the Thrie Estaitis*', *MLR* 25 (1930), pp. 425–42; Jean-Claude Aubailly, *Le Monologue, le Dialogue et la Sottie* (Paris, 1976); and Heather Arden, *Fools' Plays: A study of satire in the 'sottie'* (Cambridge, 1980).

[26] On this form see Yvonne LeBlanc, *Va Lettre Va: The French Verse Epistle (1400–1550)* (Birmingham, Ala., 1995).

[27] See Hadley Williams, 'Writing and Publishing in Sixteenth-Century Scotland', *Renaissance Reflections*, ed. Smith and Peach, pp. 134–41.

[28] On English affinities see Gregory Kratzmann, *Anglo-Scottish Literary Relations 1430–1550* (Cambridge, 1980), pp. 195–226.

[29] Cf. for example John Skelton's 'Upon the dolorus dethe and muche lamentable chaunce of the mooste honorable Erle of Northumberlande', *John Skelton: The Complete English Poems*, ed. John Scattergood (Harmondsworth, 1983), pp. 29–35.

[30] Hay, *Buik*, ed. Cartwright, vol. 3, 9743–4 and 9732–4. References are to this edition.

[31] For examples: Lyndsay, *Selected Poems*, ed. Hadley Williams, notes to *Squyer Meldrum*, 898–916, 1002–4, and 1473.

parrot's embedded high style complaint, however, is reminiscent of several others, especially Cresseid's against Fortune in Henryson's *Testament*. In the latter poem's light, the bird's brief references to her physical changes ('feddrem fair' to 'catyue carion') add tragi-comic touches.

The tradition of historical verse in Scots, including the works of John Barbour, Blind Hary, and the anonymous poet of *The Buik of Alexander*, was also well known to Lyndsay. *Squyer Meldrum*'s four-stress couplets are those of (among others) Barbour's *Bruce*, and words, phrases and episodes in the poem echo Hary's *Wallace*.[32] Lyndsay further builds a heroic context by citing also the Scottish alliterative romance *Golagros and Gawain* and *Eger and Gryme*, and the English *Sir Ferumbras*.[33] Several of the heroes mentioned, including Gowmakmorne and Finn Mac Coul, belong to Gaelic legend, but their presence does not necessarily imply Lyndsay's in-depth knowledge of these sources; other Scottish poets list them in a similar manner.[34] Andrew Wyntoun's popular work was another likely source of inspiration: both *Ane Dialog* and *The Original Chronicle* are deeply concerned with Scotland's place in Christian world history.

The many works of 'advice to princes' were of most importance to Lyndsay: he offers princely counsel in semi-dramatic guises in six of his poems, and his panoramic play greatly adds to that pre-occupation and the dramatic devices used to convey it.[35] The name of Sir Gilbert Hay, author-translator of *The Buke of the Gouernaunce of Princes* and other prose works of advice, appears in the *Papyngo*'s catalogue of poets, presumably for the advisory *Buik of King Alexander the Conquerour*, or for poems now lost.[36] In particular the *Buik*'s 'Regiment' (9355–10107), Aristotle's counsel to the young King Alexander,[37] has parallels of situation and content to Lyndsay's advice to the youthful King James in *The Dreme* and *Papyngo*. Both writers express the traditional commonplaces,[38] yet both emphasize that an earthly king's success requires an acknowledgement of God's central place, a just and generous treatment of the people, and rule in consultation.[39] This last is also argued by the poet of the

---

[32] Cf. *Meldrum*, 45, *Wallace*, 12:1434; *Meldrum*, 691–6, *Wallace*, 12:312–19.
[33] See Purdie, 'Medieval Romance in Scotland', pp. 175–6, above.
[34] *Ane Satyre*, 2087; *Meldrum*, 317. Cf. *Bruce*, 3:67–75; Douglas, *Palice*, 1715–16.
[35] See Claude Graf, 'Audience Involvement in Lindsay's *Satyre of the Thrie Estaitis*', *Scottish Language and Literature, Medieval and Renaissance: Fourth International Conference 1984 Proceedings*, ed. Dietrich Strauss and H. W. Drescher (Frankfurt am Main, 1986), pp. 423–35.
[36] For one now lost, see *Asloan Manuscript*, ed. Craigie, vol. 1, p. xiv.
[37] Lyndsay possibly refers directly to this, or another similar work: *Papyngo*, 307.
[38] See R. J. Lyall, 'Politics and Poetry in Fifteenth and Sixteenth Century Scotland', *SLJ* 3.2 (1976), pp. 5–29; and Sally Mapstone, 'The Advice to Princes Tradition in Scottish Literature, 1450–1500', unpublished D.Phil. thesis (Oxford, 1986).
[39] Cf. *Buik*, 9395–8 and *Dreme*, 1037–41, 364–8; *Buik*, 7319–25, 7336 and *Papyngo*, 336–8; and *Buik*, 9789–92, 10006–11 and *Papyngo*, 298–303. Note also the reference to the impact of 'bakwart' policy, *Buik*, 9659–72 and its dramatization in *Ane Satyre*, initiated by a stage direction (after 2315) that the Three Estates now enter, 'gangand bakwart led be thair vyces'.

Thre Prestis of Peblis, foreshadowing Lynday's stance on the interrelationship of the king and the three estates in part two of *Ane Satyre*.

Robert Henryson's moral seriousness and comprehensive concern for society were highly congenial to Lyndsay, but his appreciation is also apparent in many small but distinct allusions to the earlier poet. One example is *The Dreme*'s description of Hell, which contains many echoes of Henryson's *Orpheus* (310–44).[40] Yet this is no mere imitation; Lyndsay gives greater prominence to the churchmen among Hell's inhabitants by his strategic departures from Henryson's text. The same poem's portraits of the planets recall Henryson's in *The Testament of Cresseid*, but they, too, are deftly selective echoes, by which Lyndsay presents the planets as monarchs rather than gods, as befits his kingship theme. In *The Complaint and Publict Confessioun of the Kingis Auld Hound, callit Bagsche*, Lyndsay highlights the limited extent to which the dog is prepared to suffer for his sins during Lent by echoing the imperfect confession of Henryson's wily fox (*Fabillis*, 698–732).[41]

Lyndsay spoke perceptively of William Dunbar's 'language ... at large' (*Papyngo*, 17). He learned much from him, most obviously in the skilled use of courtly diction, as seasonal descriptions in the *Papyngo* and *Ane Dialog* reveal.[42] He appreciated Dunbar's keen sense of comedy, redeploying his petitionary expressions (*Bagsche*); adopting his righteous, mock-puzzled stance (*Complaynt*), or the intimate, near-impertinent, or dryly witty tones in which Dunbar addressed his king (*Answer*). Lyndsay's lightly satiric treatment of the matter of trailing gowns, with its compliments to the queen and flattering criticism of the king (for not suppressing this fashion as he has other civil disorders), might be called 'Dunbarian' (*Ane Suplication in Contemptioun of Syde Taillis*).[43]

Gavin Douglas, however, was for Lyndsay 'Abufe vulgare poetis prerogatyve' – superior among other writers in Scots (*Papyngo*, 29). The *Papyngo* contains both brief and more extended echoes of *The Palice of Honour*; here, too, is a tribute to Douglas's energetic and inventive Scots translation of Virgil's Latin (*Papyngo*, 33–4). In *Ane Dialog*, Lyndsay, like Douglas, stresses the need for access to works presently in Latin, though of a different kind – the country's laws and the basic statements of faith (636–54). Seeking a wider audience than Douglas hoped for, *Ane Dialog* is stylistically less demanding than, if metrically as varied as, the *Eneados*. His debts to Douglas reveal that, at the end of the medieval period, accepted notions about poetry and its uses are being questioned. *Ane Dialog*'s prologue, rejecting the Muses for the Christian God – 'I mon go seik ane muse more confortabyl [than

---

[40] All references are to Henryson, *The Poems*, ed. Fox.
[41] For *Bagsche* and *Syde Taillis*: *Works of Lindsay*, ed. Hamer, vol. 1, pp. 92–9 and 118–22. See also the discussion in Lyall, 'Henryson's *Morall Fabllis*', p. 97, above.
[42] See Janet Hadley Williams, 'Dunbar and His Immediate Heirs', *Dunbar: Essays*, ed. Mapstone, pp. 85–107 (101–4).
[43] *Ibid.*, pp. 104–6.

the pagan gods of antiquity] ... Beseikand the gret God to be my muse' (241, 243) – echoes yet modifies Douglas's re-application of Virgil's homage to Jupiter (X Prol. 150–2).

The date of Lyndsay's earliest known work marks the beginning of James V's personal rule (c. 1526–28). At least seven more poems followed before the king's death (1542),[44] and another three during the early Marian period. This might seem unimpressive beside the over eighty poems Dunbar wrote during or near James IV's reign. Yet he is atypical, not only in the quantity, but in the brevity of his poems. Several major works, including *The Goldyn Targe*, are less than 300 lines; others are much shorter. By contrast, Lyndsay's most polished poems, *The Dreme* and *The Papyngo*, are over 1000 lines; others vary from 500 (*Complaynt*) to around 200 (*Bagsche, Deploratioun, Syde Taillis*), with two of the later works much longer (*Squyer Meldrum* and its *Testament* over 1800 lines; *Ane Dialog* over 6000). Douglas's known output is comparable (although Lyndsay speaks of the latter's works 'in nowmer more than fyve', *Papyngo*, 32). Extant are *The Palice*, just over 2000 lines; the *Eneados*, of many thousands of lines (its Prologues alone from c. 100 to 500 lines each); and *Conscience*, of only four seven-line stanzas. Henryson's *Fabillis* are almost 3000 lines, *The Testament of Cresseid* just over 600; his twelve shorter poems closer to Dunbar's in length. In both diversity of length and expansive tendency Lyndsay's verse is typical of late medieval Scottish writing.

This can also be said of his choice and imaginative use of a variety of genres (kinds of verse). Among them are the dream vision, petitionary complaint, bird fable, beast fable, mock flyting, elegy, testament, heroic romance, and joust burlesque.[45] In *The Dreme* Lyndsay combines two literary kinds, epistle and dream vision, for a structurally tight, thematically coherent and richly varied tone and content. The opening epistle, lightly petitionary, is affectionate panegyric; the concluding epistle is austerely formal counsel. The multi-sectioned vision at the centre is an entertaining story (enlivened by tours through Hell, the planets, and heaven itself), and a repository of directly expressed advice, supported by many facts and figures (some, taking advantage of the dream medium's distancing effect, highly critical of Scotland's present state), systematically presented for the use of a newly-powerful king. In *Bagsche*, by contrast, Lyndsay's opening line, 'Allace, quhome to suld I

---

[44] *Kitteis Confessioun*, published by Charteris in 1568 with the title: '... compylit (as is beleuit) be Schir Dauid Lindesay of the Mount', is otherwise unconnected to him. For the text: *Works of Lindsay*, ed. Hamer, vol. 1, pp. 124–7.

[45] On Scottish poets' generic diversity: Denton Fox, 'Middle Scots Poets and Patrons', *English Court Culture in the Later Middle Ages*, ed. V. J. Scattergood and J. W. Sherborne (London, 1983), pp. 109–27 (120–2); Dunbar, *Selected Poems*, ed. Bawcutt, p. 8; A. A. MacDonald, 'William Stewart and the Court Poetry of the Reign of James V', *Stewart Style 1513–1542: Essays on the Court of James V*, ed. Janet Hadley Williams (East Linton, 1996), pp. 179–200; Hadley Williams, 'Dunbar and His Immediate Heirs', *Dunbar: Essays*, ed. Mapstone, p. 94.

complayne', strongly suggests a petition akin to Dunbar's 'Quhom to sall I compleine my wo' (B 54), or 'Complane I wald, wist I quhome till' (B 9). The bathetic lament a few lines later: 'In Court na Dog wyll do for me' (4), humorously qualifies this impression, and turns the poem into a mixture of beast fable and exemplum on court life: the speaker is a deerhound out of royal favour for 'prydfull presumptioun' (142). Animal and human spheres interact as James V's courtiers are named and their parts recorded. The poem thus modulates further, to be entertaining yet pointed advice on the nature of authority – how its misuse by the favourite (dog or courtier) will eventually attract just punishment by the king and, ultimately, God:

> Put na pure tyke frome his steiding,
> Nor yit na sillie Ratchis raif:
> He sittis abone that seis all thing,
> And of ane knicht can mak ane knaif.   (165–8)

It is in *The Testament of the Papyngo*, however, that Lyndsay's use of several genres and modes, for both comic and serious purposes, is most striking. His opening is a high-style eulogy to vernacular poets past and present, among whom, Lyndsay admits modestly, he has no place. In keeping, seemingly, his own narrative begins with the sober plainness of a sermon with a text: 'Quho clymmit to hycht, perforce his feit mon faill', but fleeting allusions to the courtly *chanson d'aventure* are interposed. The juxtaposition gives the poet-narrator a useful ambivalence, placing him within his poem (as he tells how he, with the parrot on his hand, walked out into an idealized garden 'to repose ... / Amang the flowris', 102, 104), yet apart from it, as, in the manner of Henryson ('Lion and the Mouse', 'Preaching of the Swallow') or Dunbar (*The Tretis*), he recalls how he knelt under a hawthorn, to 'heir and se and be unsene' (189), as the bird makes her complaint. She addresses advisory epistles to James V and her 'brether of Courte'; and receives three birds of prey, a magpie, raven and kite, purporting to be her 'holye executouris', who join her in a 'Commonyng' or dialogue (the apt linking of clerical garb and avian colourings recalling Holland's *Howlat* and its theme). Similarly, the poet-narrator then overhears the papyngo's confession and testament, in which she bequeathes her goods (her physical attributes) to other needy birds (her heart excepted, given to the king), but leaves nothing to the greedy Church that has offered her no succour. At the last, with Henrysonian disengagement, the narrator tells how he saw the argumentative raptor-clerics fly away with the dead parrot's bodily parts, 'all out of my sycht' (1171). The poem's witty combination of literary kinds, assuming a well-read audience, asserts the self-confidence of James V and his court, but it mingles with both some astute social commentary and princely counsel.

Like other late medieval poets Lyndsay observes a traditional decorum,[46] in which choice of metre is governed by the kind of poem being written. The *Complaynt* and *Syde Taillis* are composed in the popular four-stress couplets that give these poems, both addressed to the king, the informal intimacy of one-to-one conversation. The narratives *Squyer Meldrum* and *Ane Dialog* also make use of this flexible measure, but in consort with others, as will be discussed below. The burlesque *Justing*'s five-stress couplets were common in narrative verse, comic or serious, as in Hay's *Buik*.

Lyndsay's more courtly works of the reign, *The Deploratioun* and *Papyngo* (except for the opening), are appositely in the formal but adaptable rhyme royal, a five-stress, seven-line stanza (*ababbcc*). His use of the same stanza for *The Answer to the Kingis Flyting* indentifies Lyndsay's real intention there: in other literary flytings metrical virtuosity plays an important part in the display of skills (as in Dunbar's five-stress eight-line stanza, with a different rhyme scheme for each part, for his flyting with Kennedy). In Lyndsay's 'flyting', however, despite notable wordplay and promising bursts of dense alliteration, the rhyme-royal stanza – considered suitable for writing of some formality rather than for the display of poetic ingenuity demanded of a literary flyting – confirms that this poem has been composed as a piece of advice to the king. *Bagsche*'s four-stress eight-line stanza (*ababbcbc*), frequently chosen for sober didactic works,[47] also suggests that the poem has a serious message. Lyndsay employs the more elaborate five-stress nine-line stanza (*aabaabbab*) for *The Dreme*'s 'Exhortatioun', the *Papyngo*'s opening and *Ane Dialog*'s 'Epistill'. He thus highlights the importance of the content, but also demonstrates his expertise, inspired by Chaucer's original use of the stanza for the courtly 'compleynt' in *Anelida and Arcite*, and by those of earlier Scottish poets, Hary (*Wallace*, II:171–359), Douglas (*Palice*), Dunbar (*Goldyn Targe*) and John Bellenden ('Proheme')[48] among them.

Lyndsay's attitude to decorum is further revealed in his use of metrical change within a single work. In the *Papyngo* he thus modestly separates the opening praise for the work of others from his own following piece; in his romance biography, *Squyer Meldrum*, he sobers the tone by appending a testament in rhyme royal stanzas, its final stanza, in turn, adding a more elaborate if still genial eight-line prayer in alternating Scots and Latin. At the end of *The Dreme* Lyndsay uses a single two-stress eight-line prayer stanza (*aaabaaab*) to universalize what has been so sharply directed in the preceding 'Exhortatioun'. Later, in his long *Ane Dialog*, Lyndsay makes far greater use of metrical change to organize his material into easily-distinguished sections of

---

[46] See further, A. J. Aitken, 'The Language of Older Scots Poetry', *Scotland and the Lowland Tongue*, ed. J. Derrick McClure (Aberdeen, 1983), pp. 18–49.

[47] Cf. the anonymous 'Man, hef in mynd and mend thi myss', *Pieces from The Makculloch and the Gray MSS. together with The Chepman and Myllar Prints*, ed. George Stevenson, STS (1918), pp. 13–14.

[48] *Bannatyne MS*, ed. Ritchie, vol. 2, pp. 9–20 (fols 4r–8v).

narrative, thematic argument, or commentary.[49] In *Ane Satyre* he excels in his use of a variety of forms (including the alliterative thirteen-line stanza, rhyme royal, and four- and five stress couplets), using the changes from one to the next to draw attention to his most important themes, and advance the dramatic action.[50]

Like his metrics, Lyndsay's style and diction are varied yet always apt. In his prologues to *The Dreme, Papyngo,* and *Ane Dialog,* for example, he writes competently in the 'high' style of which Douglas and Dunbar were masters, his diction like theirs including Latinate terms such as 'angelicall', 'imperiall', 'ornat', or 'cristalline', and coined words such as 'impurpurit'. Yet his examples of this rarely have the density of, for instance, Douglas's description of the 'Court Rethoricall' in his *Palice* (835–924). Lyndsay more often uses a plainer, or 'middle' style in which rich rhetorical ornament is absent. He had precedents in Henryson's *Fabillis,* and in many of Dunbar's moral or more personal pieces – 'Schir, at this feist of benefice' (B 62), or 'My heid did yak yester nicht' (B 35). Lyndsay recognized the subtle skill of this less adorned verse, especially its usefulness in engaging the reader in what seems to be direct and conversational, as in the aside to the king: '... I sall mak the payment / Efter the daye of Jugement– / Within ane moneth, at the leist!' (*Complaynt,* 475–7). He used this middle style for narrative as well as instruction, enriching or undercutting it at need. The papyngo's farewell to her haunts is one example: with courtly formality she addresses Stirling, with its 'touris hie' and 'Chapell Royall'; Linlithgow with its 'palyce of plesance'; and Falkland with its 'polyte park', 'fallow deir' – and bad ale! (633–46). *Ane Satyre* amply demonstrates Lyndsay's accomplished use of varieties of the 'low' style, but a vernacular diction of insults, oaths and flyting is also a notable feature of *The Complaynt,* where the frequent switching between colloquial and more formal levels of language creates a series of mini-dramas that bring court innuendo to vivid life yet also provide soberly oblique comment on the reprehensible and responsible behaviour thus exposed.[51]

Perhaps influenced by the use of Lyndsay's poetry as a source of historical information about pre-Reformation Scotland, modern critical commentary is frequently pre-occupied by Lyndsay's anti-clerical stance. As a result it sometimes fails to appreciate or examine his strengths as a poet. In much of Lyndsay's writing, it is true, there is an implicit belief that poetry serves particular moral purposes, but in this it is akin to Henryson's. If Lyndsay owed much to the English and Scottish poetic traditions of the late fourteenth and

---

[49] See further, Lyndsay, *Selected Poems,* ed. Hadley Williams, p. 314.
[50] See, for a perceptive analysis, John J. McGavin, 'The Dramatic Prosody of Sir David Lindsay', *Of Lion and Of Unicorn: Essays on Anglo-Scottish Literary Relations in Honour of Professor John MacQueen,* ed. R. D. S. Jack and Kevin McGinley (1993), pp. 39–66.
[51] See further, Graf, 'Audience Involvement', *Scottish Language and Literature,* ed. Strauss and Drescher, pp. 423–35.

fifteenth centuries, he did not draw on them unthinkingly. Like those before him he selected, invented, or changed the emphases; his satire is not 'general' but directed to the Scottish king's responsibility (and, later, to that of the acting minority leaders) to govern self and realm. The moral seriousness of such topics overlies the playfulness, agile changes of diction, and the metrical care with which they are often presented, but the latter should not be forgotten in assessing Lyndsay. The wider audience that Dunbar and others had begun to attract through the printing press, moreover, played a larger role with Lyndsay's poems. Almost all were published soon after composition, *The Papyngo*, *Tragedie* and *Ane Dialog* also in England, the first two in Lyndsay's lifetime.[52] Because these earliest editions are lost, their role in reaching a literate audience beyond the court is under-appreciated. That they did so is confirmed by their use as models by Robert Sempill and others for their own even more sharply defined satire in the middle and later sixteenth century,[53] and in the popularity of Lyndsay's works, printed many times, into the eighteenth century.[54]

---

[52] See Hamer, 'The Bibliography', pp. 2–28; and A. J. Mann, *The Scottish Book Trade 1500–1720* (East Linton, 2000), pp. 110, 212.
[53] For the poems of Sempill and others, see *Satirical Poems of the Time of the Reformation*, ed. James Cranstoun, 2 vols, STS (1891–93). For a note on Lyndsay's influence: Roderick Lyall, 'Complaint, Satire and Invective in Middle Scots Literature', *Church, Politics and Society 1408–1929*, ed. Norman Macdougall (1983), pp. 44–64 (58–9).
[54] See further, William Geddie, *A Bibliography of Middle Scots Poets*, STS (1912), pp. 268–317; *Works of Lindsay*, ed. Hamer, vol. 4, pp. xlvi–liv.

13

Guide to Further Reading

PRISCILLA BAWCUTT
JANET HADLEY WILLIAMS

This Guide provides a brief, selective introduction to medieval Scottish poetry, not a complete bibliography on the subject. Key books and articles from the past are listed, but the main emphasis lies on works published in the last twenty years. Further information will also be found in the relevant chapters.

Note that between 1975 and 1997 *SLJ* published a useful Supplement containing 'The Year's Work in Scottish Literary and Linguistic Studies'.

For shortened references, see List of Abbreviations, pp. viii–x.

Introduction

PRINCIPAL MANUSCRIPT AND PRINTED COLLECTIONS

Asloan MS. Ed. Craigie.
Bannatyne MS. Ed. Ritchie.
The Bannatyne Manuscript. National Library of Scotland Advocates' MS. 1.1.6. Introd. Denton Fox and William A. Ringler. [Facsimile.] London, 1980.
The Chepman and Myllar Prints. A Facsimile. Introd. William Beattie. 1950.
See also at: http://www.nls.uk/digitallibrary/chepman/page.htm.
Devotional Pieces in Verse and Prose From MS. Arundel 285 and MS. Harleian 6919. Ed. J. A. W. Bennett. STS, 1955.
Maitland Folio MS. Ed. Craigie.
Ratis Raving and Other Early Scots Poems on Morals. With an appendix of the other pieces from Cambridge University Library MS. Kk.1.5, No. 6. Ed. R. Girvan. STS, 1939.
The Works of Geoffrey Chaucer and 'The Kingis Quair': A Facsimile of Bodleian Library, Oxford, MS Arch. Selden. B. 24. Introd. Julia Boffey and A. S. G. Edwards, appendix B. C. Barker-Benfield. Cambridge, 1997.

BIBLIOGRAPHIES

Geddie, William. *A Bibliography of Middle Scots Poets*. STS, 1912. This continues to be a valuable reference work.

Ridley, Florence H. 'Middle Scots Writers'. *A Manual of the Writings in Middle English 1050–1500*, ed. Albert E. Hartung. Vol. 4. New Haven, Conn., 1973. Pp. 961–1060, 1123–284.

Scheps, Walter and J. A. Looney. *Middle Scots Poets: A Reference Guide to James I of Scotland, Robert Henryson, William Dunbar and Gavin Douglas*. Boston, Mass., 1986.

LITERARY AND CULTURAL STUDIES

Bawcutt, Priscilla. ' "My bright buke": Women and their Books in Medieval and Renaissance Scotland'. *Medieval Women: Texts and Contexts in Late Medieval Britain: Essays for Felicity Riddy*. Ed. Jocelyn Wogan-Browne et al. Turnhout, 2000. Pp. 17–34.

Bawcutt, Priscilla. 'Scottish Manuscript Miscellanies from the Fifteenth to the Seventeenth Century'. *English Manuscript Studies 1100–1700* 12 (2005). Pp. 46–73.

Boffey, Julia. 'The Maitland Folio Manuscript as a Verse Anthology'. *Dunbar: Essays*. Ed. Mapstone. Pp. 40–50.

Boffey, Julia and A. S. G. Edwards. 'Bodleian MS Arch. Selden. B. 24: The Genesis and Evolution of a Scottish Poetical Anthology'. *Poetica* 60 (2003). Pp. 31–46.

Cunningham, I. C. 'The Asloan Manuscript'. *The Renaissance in Scotland: Studies in Literature, Religion, History and Culture Offered to John Durkan*. Ed. A. A. MacDonald, Michael Lynch and Ian B. Cowan. Leiden, 1994. Pp. 107–35.

Durkan, John and Anthony Ross. *Early Scottish Libraries*. Glasgow, 1961.

Fox, Denton. 'The Scottish Chaucerians'. *Chaucer and Chaucerians*. Ed. D. S. Brewer. London, 1966. Pp. 164–200.

Fradenburg, Louise Olga. *City, Marriage, Tournament: The Arts of Rule in Late Medieval Scotland*. Madison, Wis., 1991.

Goldstein, R. James. 'Writing in Scotland 1058–1560'. *The Cambridge History of Medieval English Literature*. Ed. David Wallace. Cambridge, 1999. Pp. 229–54.

History. Ed. Jack.

Kratzmann, Gregory. *Anglo-Scottish Literary Relations 1430–1550*. Cambridge, 1980.

Lyall, R. J. 'Books and Book Owners in Fifteenth-Century Scotland'. *Book Production and Publishing in Britain 1375–1475*. Ed. Jeremy Griffiths and Derek Pearsall. Cambridge, 1989. Pp. 239–56.

Mapstone, Sally. *Scots and their Books in the Middle Ages and the Renaissance: An exhibition in the Bodleian Library, Oxford*. Oxford, 1996.

Older Scots Literature. Ed. Sally Mapstone. 2005.

Van Buuren, Catherine, 'John Asloan and his Manuscript: An Edinburgh notary and scribe in the days of James III, IV and V (c. 1470–c. 1530)'. *Stewart Style 1513–1542: Essays on the Court of James V*. Ed. Janet Hadley Williams. East Linton, 1996. Pp. 15–51.

LANGUAGE

DOST. See also at: http://www.dsl.ac.uk/dsl/

The Concise Scots Dictionary. Ed. Mairi Robinson. Aberdeen, 1985.

Aitken, A. J. 'The Language of Older Scots Poetry'. *Scotland and the Lowland Tongue: Studies in the language and literature of Lowland Scotland in honour of David Murison*. Ed. J. Derrick McClure. Aberdeen, 1983. Pp. 18–49.

Aitken, A. J. *The Older Scots Vowels: A History of the Stressed Vowels of Older Scots from the Beginnings to the Eighteenth Century*. Ed. Caroline Macafee. STS, 2002.

Bawcutt, Priscilla. '*DOST* and the Literary Scholar'. *Perspectives on the Older Scottish Tongue: A Celebration of DOST*. Ed. Christian J. Kay and Margaret A. Mackay. 2005. Pp. 5–17.

John Barbour, Andrew of Wyntoun, Blind Hary

EDITIONS

Barbour's Bruce. Ed. McDiarmid and Stevenson.

Barbour, John. *The Bruce*. Ed. with trans. A. A. M. Duncan. Canongate Classics 78. 1997. (The 1999 reprinted edition is defective.)

Bower, Walter. *Scotichronicon*. Gen. ed. D. E. R. Watt. 9 vols. Aberdeen and Edinburgh, 1987–98.

Hary's Wallace. Ed. McDiarmid.

Blind Harry. *The Wallace*. Ed. Anne McKim. Canongate Classics 112. 2003.

Wyntoun, *Original Chronicle*. Ed. Amours.

BIBLIOGRAPHY

Edward D. Kennedy. 'Chronicles and Other Historical Writing'. *A Manual of the Writings in Middle English 1050–1500*. Vol. 8. New Haven, Conn., 1989. Pp. 2679–700, 2891–926.

SECONDARY STUDIES

Crawford, Barbara E. (ed). *Church, Chronicle and Learning in Medieval and Early Renaissance Scotland: Essays Presented to Donald Watt on the Occasion of the Completion of the Publication of Bower's 'Scotichronicon'*. 1999.

Ebin, Lois. 'John Barbour's *Bruce*: Poetry, History, and Propaganda'. *SSL* 9 (1972). Pp. 218–47.
Goldstein, R. James. ' "For he wald vsurpe na fame": Andrew of Wyntoun's Use of the Modesty *Topos* and Literary Culture in Early Fifteenth-Century Scotland'. *SLJ* 14.1 (1987). Pp. 5–18.
Goldstein, R. James. *The Matter of Scotland: Historical Narrative in Medieval Scotland*. Lincoln, Nebr. and London, 1993.
Kliman, Bernice W. 'Speech as a Mirror of *Sapientia* and *Fortitudo* in Barbour's *Bruce*'. *MÆ* 44 (1975). Pp. 151–61.
Kliman, Bernice W. 'John Barbour and Rhetorical Tradition: A Summary'. *Actes du 2e Colloque de Langue et de Littérature Ecossaises (Moyen Age et Renaissance)*. Ed. Jean-Jacques Blanchot and Claude Graf. Strasbourg, 1978. Pp. 162–84.
McClure, J. Derrick. 'Blind Hary's Metrics'. *Older Scots Literature*. Ed. Sally Mapstone. 2005. Pp. 147–64.
McKim, Anne. 'James Douglas and Barbour's Ideal of Knighthood'. *FMLS* 17 (1981). Pp. 167–80.
McKim, Anne. ' "Gret Price off Chewalry": Barbour's Debt to Fordun', *SSL* 24 (1989). Pp. 7–29.
Moll, Richard J. ' "Off quhat nacioun art thow?" National Identity in Blind Hary's *Wallace*'. *History, Literature, and Music in Scotland, 700–1560*. Ed. R. Andrew McDonald. Toronto, 2002. Pp. 120–43.
Scheps, Walter. 'William Wallace and his "Buke" '. *SSL* 6 (1968–9). Pp. 220–37.
Scheps, Walter. 'Middle English Poetic Usage and Blind Hary's *Wallace*'. *Chaucer Review* 4 (1970). Pp. 291–302.
Wilson, Grace. 'Andrew of Wyntoun: More than just "That Dreich Clerk" '. *Scotia* 10 (1986). Pp. 1–13.

Richard Holland: The Buke of the Howlat

EDITIONS

Longer Scottish Poems, Vol. 1. Ed. Bawcutt and Riddy. Pp. 43–84.
Scottish Alliterative Poems in Riming Stanzas. Ed. F. J. Amours. STS, 1897. Pp. 47–81.

SECONDARY STUDIES

Alexander, Flora. 'Richard Holland's "Buke of the Howlat" '. *Literature of the North*. Ed. David Hewitt and Michael Spiller. Aberdeen, 1983. Pp. 14–25.
Beattie, William. 'An Early Printed Fragment of the "Buke of the Howlat" '. *EBST* 2 (1938–45). Pp. 393–7.

Brown, Michael. ' "Rejoice to hear of Douglas": The House of Douglas and the Presentation of Magnate Power in Late Medieval Scotland'. *SHR* 76 (1997). Pp. 161–84.

Brown, Michael. *The Black Douglases: War and Lordship in Late Medieval Scotland 1300–1455*. East Linton, 1998.

Donaldson, Robert. 'An Early Printed Fragment of the "Buke of the Howlat" – Addendum'. *EBST* 5.3 (1980–3). Pp. 25–8.

McDiarmid, Matthew P. 'Richard Holland's *Buke of the Howlat*: An Interpretation'. *MÆ* 38 (1969). Pp. 277–90.

Mackay, Margaret. 'Structure and Style in Richard Holland's *Buke of the Howlat*'. *Proceedings of the Third International Conference on Scottish Language and Literature (Medieval and Renaissance)*. Ed. R. J. Lyall and Felicity Riddy. Stirling / Glasgow, 1981. Pp. 191–206.

Mapstone, Sally. 'The Wisdom of Princes: Advice Literature in Late Medieval Scotland' (forthcoming).

Parkinson, David. 'Mobbing Scenes in Middle Scots Verse: Holland, Douglas, Dunbar'. *JEGP* 85 (1986). Pp. 494–509.

Riddy, Felicity. 'Dating *The Buke of the Howlat*'. *Review of English Studies* n.s. 37 (1986). Pp. 1–10.

Riddy, Felicity. 'The Alliterative Revival'. *History*. Ed. Jack. Pp. 39–54.

Scheibe, Regina. 'The Major Professional Skills of the Dove in *The Buke of the Howlat*'. *Animals and the Symbolic in Medieval Art and Literature*. Ed. L. A. J. R. Houwen. Groningen, 1997. Pp. 107–37.

Stewart, Marion. 'Holland of the Howlat'. *IR* 23 (1972). Pp. 3–15.

Stewart, Marion. 'Holland's "Howlat" and the Fall of the Livingstones'. *IR* 26 (1975). Pp. 67–79.

Turville-Petre, Thorlac. *The Alliterative Revival*. Cambridge, 1977.

Bodleian Library MS Arch. Selden. B. 24

THE MANUSCRIPT

The Works of Geoffrey Chaucer and 'The Kingis Quair': A Facsimile of Bodleian Library, Oxford, MS Arch. Selden. B. 24. Introd. Julia Boffey and A. S. G. Edwards, appendix B. C. Barker-Benfield. Cambridge, 1997.

EDITIONS

James I of Scotland, *The Kingis Quair*. Ed. John Norton-Smith. 2nd edn, Medieval and Renaissance Texts. Leiden, 1981.

The Kingis Quair of James Stewart. Ed. Matthew P. McDiarmid. London, 1973.

Fifteenth-Century Dream Visions: An Anthology. Ed. Julia Boffey. Oxford, 2003. Pp. 90–157.

The Quare of Jelusy. Ed. John Norton-Smith and I. Pravda. Middle English Texts 3. Heidelberg, 1976.

Wilson, Kenneth G. '*The Lay of Sorrow* and *The Lufaris Complaynt*: An Edition'. *Speculum* 29 (1954). Pp. 708–26.

SECONDARY STUDIES

Boffey, Julia. 'Chaucerian Prisoners: The Context of *The Kingis Quair*'. *Chaucer and Fifteenth-Century Poetry*. Ed. Julia Boffey and Janet Cowen. London, 1991. Pp. 84–102.

Boffey, Julia and A. S. G. Edwards. 'Bodleian MS Arch. Selden. B. 24 and the "Scotticization" of Middle English Verse'. *Rewriting Chaucer: Culture, Authority, and the Idea of the Authentic Text, 1400–1602*. Ed. T. A. Prendergast and B. Kline. Columbus, OH, 1999. Pp. 166–85.

Boffey, Julia. 'Bodleian Library MS Arch. Selden. B. 24 and Definitions of the "Household Book" '. *The English Medieval Book: Studies in Memory of Jeremy Griffiths*. Ed. A. S. G. Edwards, Vincent Gillespie, and Ralph Hanna. London, 2000. Pp. 125–34.

Boffey, Julia and A. S. G. Edwards. 'Bodleian MS Arch. Selden. B. 24: The Genesis and Evolution of a Scottish Poetical Anthology'. *Poetica* 60 (2003). Pp. 31–46.

Burrow, J. A. 'The Poet and the Book'. *Genres, Themes and Images in English Literature from the Fourteenth to the Fifteenth Century: The J. A. W. Bennett Memorial Lectures, Perugia, 1986*. Ed. Piero Boitani and Anna Torti. Tübingen, 1988. Pp. 230–45.

Carretta, Vincent. '*The Kingis Quair* and *The Consolation of Philosophy*'. *SSL* 16 (1981). Pp. 14–28.

Ebin, Lois A. 'Boethius, Chaucer, and *The Kingis Quair*'. *PQ* 53 (1974). Pp. 321–41.

Edwards, A. S. G. 'Bodleian Library MS Arch. Selden B.24: A "Transitional" Collection'. *The Whole Book: Cultural Perspectives on the Medieval Miscellany*. Ed. Stephen G. Nichols and Siegfried Wenzel. Ann Arbor, Mich., 1996. Pp. 53–67.

Epstein, Robert. 'Prisoners of Reflection: The Fifteenth-Century Poetry of Exile and Imprisonment'. *Exemplaria* 15.1 (2003). Pp. 159–98.

Frankis, P. J. 'Notes on Two Fifteenth Century Scots Poems'. *Neuphilologische Mitteilungen* 61 (1960). Pp. 203–13. [*The Lay of Sorrow, The Lufaris Complaynt.*]

James, Clair F. '*The Kingis Quair*: The Plight of the Courtly Lover'. *New Readings of Late Medieval Love Poems*. Ed David Chamberlain. Lanham, Md, 1993. Pp. 95–118.

Jeffery, C. D. 'Anglo-Scots Poetry and *The Kingis Quair*'. *Actes du 2e Colloque et de Langue et Littérature Ecossaises (Moyen Age et Renaissance)*. Ed. Jean-Jacques Blanchot and Claude Graf. Strasbourg, 1978. Pp. 207–21.

Jeffery, C. D., '*The Quare of Jelusy*, lines 141–6'. *Notes and Queries* n.s. 27 (1980). Pp. 500–1.

Mapstone, Sally. 'Kingship and the *Kingis Quair*'. *The Long Fifteenth Century: Essays for Douglas Gray*. Ed. Helen Cooper and Sally Mapstone. Oxford, 1997. Pp. 51–69.
Petrina, Alessandra. *'The Kingis Quair' of James I of Scotland*. Padova, 1997.

Sir Gilbert Hay and The Buik of King Alexander the Conquerour

EDITIONS

Hay, *Buik*. Ed. Cartwright.
The Prose Works of Sir Gilbert Hay. Ed. Jonathan A. Glenn. 2 vols. STS, 1993 and 2005.

SECONDARY STUDIES

Bawcutt, Priscilla. 'The Boston Public Library Manuscript of Lydgate's *Siege of Thebes*: Its Scottish Owners and Inscriptions'. *MÆ* 70 (2001) Pp. 80–94.
Bunt, Gerrit H. V. 'A Wife There was for Alexander the Great'. *A Wyf Ther Was: Essays in Honour of Paule Mertens-Fonck*. Ed. Juliette Dor. Liège, 1992. Pp. 41–8.
Bunt, Gerrit H. V. *Alexander the Great in the Literature of Medieval Britain*. Mediaevalia Groningana 14. Groningen, 1994.
Cary, George. *The Medieval Alexander*. Cambridge, 1956.
Cartwright, John. 'Sir Gilbert Hay and the Alexander Tradition'. *Scottish Language and Literature, Medieval and Renaissance: Fourth International Conference 1984 Proceedings*. Ed. Dietrich Strauss and Horst W. Drescher. Frankfurt am Main, 1986. Pp. 229–38.
Cartwright, John. 'Sir Gilbert Hay's Alexander: A Study in Transformations'. *MÆ* 60 (1991). Pp. 61–72.
Cartwright, John. 'Basilisks, Brahmins and Other Aliens: Encountering the Other in Sir Gilbert Hay's Alexander'. *SSL* 26 (1991). Pp. 334–42.
The Medieval French Alexander. Ed. Donald Maddox and Sara Sturm Maddox. Albany, NY, 2002.
McDiarmid, Matthew P. 'Concerning Sir Gilbert Hay, the Authorship of *Alexander the Conquerour* and *The Buik of Alexander*'. *SSL* 28 (1993). Pp. 28–54.
Mapstone, Sally. 'The Advice to Princes Tradition in Scottish Literature, 1450–1500'. Unpublished D.Phil. thesis. Oxford, 1986.
Mapstone, Sally. 'The Scots *Buke of Phisnomy* and Sir Gilbert Hay'. *The Renaissance in Scotland: Studies in Literature, Religion, History and Culture Offered to John Durkan*. Ed. A. A. MacDonald, M. Lynch and I. B. Cowan. Leiden, 1994. Pp. 1–44.
Ross, D. A. J. *Studies in the Alexander Romances*. London, 1985.

Saldanha, Kathryn. '*The Thewis of Gudwomen*: Middle Scots Advice with European Connections?' *The European Sun: Proceedings of the Seventh International Conference on Medieval and Renaissance Scottish Language and Literature*. Ed. G. Caie, R. J. Lyall, S. Mapstone and K. Simpson. East Linton, 2001. Pp. 288–99.

Van Duin, Deborah. ' "Na Man micht Noumber the Riches": The City of Segar in Sir Gilbert Hay's *Buik of King Alexander*'. *English Studies* 77 (1996). Pp. 517–29.

Robert Henryson

EDITIONS

Henryson, *The Poems*. Ed. Fox.
The Poems of Robert Henryson. Ed. G. Gregory Smith. 3 vols. STS, 1906–14.
Selected Poems of Robert Henryson and William Dunbar. Ed. Douglas Gray. Harmondsworth, 1998.
Longer Scottish Poems, Vol. 1. Ed. Bawcutt and Riddy. Pp. 134–70 ('The Two Mice', 'The Lion and the Mouse' and 'The Fox, the Wolf and the Cadger'). Pp. 170–93 (*Testament*).

BIBLIOGRAPHY

Gray, Douglas. *Robert Henryson*. Authors of the Middle Ages, Vol. 3, No. 9. Ed. M. C. Seymour. Aldershot, 1996.

SECONDARY STUDIES

Archibald, Elizabeth. 'The Incestuous Kings in Henryson's Hades'. *Scottish Language and Literature, Medieval and Renaissance, Fourth International Conference 1984 Proceedings*. Ed. Dietrich Strauss and Horst W. Drescher. Frankfurt am Main, 1986. Pp. 281–9.

Aronstein, Susan. 'Cresseid Reading Cresseid: Redemption and Translation in Henryson's *Testament*'. *SLJ* 21.2 (1994). Pp. 5–22.

Benson, C. David. 'Troilus and Cresseid in Henryson's *Testament*'. *Chaucer Review* 13 (1979). Pp. 263–71.

Bitterling, Klaus. 'Insular and Continental Traditions behind Robert Henryson's *Fables*'. *Older Scots Literature*. Ed. Sally Mapstone. 2005. Pp. 70–82.

Boffey, Julia. 'Lydgate, Henryson, and the Literary Testament'. *MLQ* 53 (1992). Pp. 41–56.

Burrow, John. 'Henryson: *The Preaching of the Swallow*'. *Essays in Criticism* 25 (1975). Pp. 25–37.

Clark, George. 'Henryson and Aesop: The Fable Transformed'. *English Literary History* 43 (1976). Pp. 1–18.

Dunnigan, Sarah. 'Feminizing the Text, Feminizing the Reader? The Mirror of "Feminitie" in the *Testament of Cresseid*'. *SSL* 33–4 (2004). Pp. 107–23.

Fox, Denton. 'The Coherence of Henryson's Work'. *Fifteenth-Century Studies: Recent Essays*. Ed. Robert F. Yeager. Hamden, Conn., 1984. Pp. 275–81.
Fradenburg, Louise O. 'Henryson Scholarship: the Recent Decades'. *Fifteenth-Century Studies: Recent Essays*. Ed. Robert F. Yeager. Hamden, Conn., 1984. Pp. 65–92.
Friedman, John Block. 'Henryson, the Friars, and the *Confessio Reynardi*'. *JEGP* 66 (1967). Pp. 550–61.
Gray, Douglas. *Robert Henryson*. Leiden, 1979.
Greentree, Rosemary. *Reader, Teller and Teacher: The Narrator of Robert Henryson's 'Moral Fables'*. Frankfurt am Main, 1993.
Gros Louis, Kenneth R. R. 'Robert Henryson's *Orpheus and Eurydice* and the Orpheus Traditions of the Middle Ages'. *Speculum* 41 (1966). Pp. 643–55.
Henderson, Arnold Clayton. 'Having Fun with the Moralities: Henryson's *Fables* and Late-Medieval Fable Innovation'. *SSL* 32 (2001). Pp. 67–87.
Jamieson, Ian. 'The Beast Tale in Middle Scots: Some Thoughts on the History of a Genre'. *Parergon* 2 (1972). Pp. 26–36.
Jamieson, Ian. ' "To preue thare preching be a poesye": some thoughts on Henryson's poetics'. *Parergon* 8 (1974). Pp. 24–36.
Johnson, Ian. 'Hellish Complexity in Henryson's *Orpheus*'. *FMLS* 38 (2002). Pp. 412–19.
Khinoy, Stephan, 'Tale-Moral Relationships in Henryson's *Moral Fables*'. *SSL* 17 (1982). Pp. 99–115.
Lyall, R. J. 'Did Poliziano Influence Henryson's *Orpheus and Eurudices?*' *FMLS* 15 (1979). Pp. 209–21.
Lyall, R. J. 'The Bannatyne "Additions" to Henryson's *Orpheus and Eurydice*'. *Neuphilologische Mitteilungen* 81 (1980). Pp. 416–23.
Lyall, R. J. 'Henryson and Boccaccio: A Problem in the Study of Sources'. *Anglia* 99 (1981). Pp. 38–59.
Lyall, R. J. 'Henryson's *Morall Fabillis* and the Steinhöwel Tradition'. *FMLS* 38 (2002). Pp. 362–81.
Lyall, R. J. 'Henryson, the Hens and the Pelagian Fox: a Poet and the Intellectual Currents of his Age'. *Older Scots Literature*. Ed. Sally Mapstone. 2005. Pp. 83–94.
McDiarmid, Matthew P. *Robert Henryson*. 1981.
McDonald, Craig. 'The Perversion of Law in Robert Henryson's Fable of the *Fox, the Wolf, and the Husbandman*'. *MÆ* 49 (1980). Pp. 244–53.
McDonald, D. 'Narrative Art in Henryson's *Fables*'. *SSL* 3 (1965). Pp. 101–13.
McDonald, D. 'Henryson and Chaucer: Cock and Fox'. *Texas Studies in Literature and Language* 3 (1966–67). Pp. 451–61.
McGinley, Kevin J. 'The Fenyeit and the Feminine: Robert Henryson's *Orpheus and Eurydice* and the Gendering of Poetry'. *Woman and the Feminine in Medieval and Early Modern Scottish Writing*. Ed. Sarah M.

Dunnigan, C. Marie Harker and Evelyn S. Newlyn. Basingstoke, 2004. Pp. 74–85.

Machan, Tim William. 'Robert Henryson and Father Aesop: Authority in the *Moral Fables*'. *Studies in the Age of Chaucer* 12 (1990). Pp. 193–214.

McKim, Anne, 'Henryson's "Memoriall of Fair Cresseid" '. *Of Lion and Of Unicorn: Essays on Anglo-Scottish Literary Relations in Honour of Professor John MacQueen*. Ed. R. D. S. Jack and Kevin McGinley. 1993. Pp. 1–15.

McKim, Anne, ' "Makand hir mone": Masculine Constructions of the Feminine Voice in Middle Scots Complaints'. *Scotlands* 2 (1994). Pp. 32–40.

MacQueen, John. *Robert Henryson: A Study of the Major Narrative Poems*. Oxford, 1967.

Mann, Jill. 'The planetary gods in Chaucer and Henryson'. *Chaucer Traditions*. Ed. R. Morse and B. Windeatt. Cambridge, 1990. Pp. 91–106.

Mapstone, Sally. 'The Origins of Criseyde'. *Medieval Women: Texts and Contexts in Late Medieval Britain. Essays for Felicity Riddy*. Ed. Jocelyn Wogan-Browne et al. Turnhout, 2000. Pp. 131–47.

Marlin, John. ' "Arestyus is Nocht but Gude Vertewe": The Perplexing *Moralitas* in Henryson's *Orpheus and Eurudices*'. *Fifteenth-Century Studies* 25 (1999). Pp. 137–53.

Parkinson, David. 'Henryson's Scottish Tragedy'. *Chaucer Review* 25 (1991). Pp. 355–62.

Patterson, Lee W. 'Christian and Pagan in *The Testament of Cresseid*'. *PQ* 52 (1973). Pp. 696–714.

Powell, Marianne. *Fabula Docet: Studies in the Background and Interpretation of Henryson's Morall Fabillis*. Odense, 1983.

Riddy, Felicity. ' "Abject odious": Feminine and Masculine in Henryson's *Testament of Cresseid*'. *The Long Fifteenth Century: Essays for Douglas Gray*. Ed. Helen Cooper and Sally Mapstone. Oxford, 1997. Pp. 229–48.

Roberts, Jane. 'On Rereading Henryson's *Orpheus and Eurydice*'. *Chaucer and Fifteenth-Century Poetry*. Ed. Julia Boffey and Janet Cowen. London, 1991. Pp. 103–21.

Scheps, Walter. 'A Climatological Reading of Henryson's *Testament of Cresseid*'. *SSL* 25 (1980). Pp. 80–7.

Storm, Melvin. 'Intertextual Cresseida: Chaucer's Henryson or Henryson's Chaucer?' *SSL* 28 (1993). Pp. 105–22.

Twycross-Martin, Henrietta. 'Moral Pattern in *The Testament of Cresseid*'. *Chaucer and Fifteenth-Century Poetry*. Ed. Julia Boffey and Janet Cowen. London, 1991. Pp. 30–50.

Watson, Nicolas. 'Outdoing Chaucer: Lydgate's Troy Book and Henryson's *Testament of Cresseid* as Competitive Imitations of *Troilus and Criseyde*'. *Shifts and Transpositions in Medieval Narrative: A Festschrift for Elspeth Kennedy*. Ed. Karen Pratt. Woodbridge, 1994. Pp. 89–108.

Wheatley, Edward. 'Scholastic Commentary and Robert Henryson's *Morall Fabillis*: The Aesopic Fables'. *SP* 91 (1994). Pp. 70–99.
Wheatley, Edward. *Mastering Aesop: Medieval Education, Chaucer and his Followers*. Gainesville, Fla., 2000.

Religious Verse in Medieval Scotland

EDITIONS

Legends of the Saints in the Scottish Dialect. Ed. W. M. Metcalfe. 3 vols. STS, 1896.
Devotional Pieces in Verse and Prose from MS. Arundel 285 and MS. Harleian 6919. Ed. J. A. W. Bennett. STS, 1955.
Pieces from The Makculloch and the Gray MSS. together with The Chepman and Myllar Prints. Ed. George Stevenson. STS, 1918.
An edition of Kennedy's poems is forthcoming, edited by Nicole Meier for the Scottish Text Society.

SECONDARY STUDIES

Bennett, J. A. W. 'Scottish Pre-Reformation Devotion: Some Notes on British Library MS. Arundel 285'. *So Meny People Longages and Tongues: Philological Essays in Scots and Mediaeval English presented to Angus McIntosh*. Ed. M. Benskin and M. L. Samuels. 1981. Pp. 299–308.
Bennett, J. A. W. *Poetry of the Passion*. Oxford, 1982.
Diehl, Patrick. *The Medieval European Religious Lyric*. Berkeley and London, 1985.
Ditchburn, David. 'The Religious Bonds'. *Scotland and Europe: The Medieval Kingdom and its Contacts with Christendom, c.1215–1545*. East Linton, 2001. Pp. 32–92.
Galbraith, James. 'The Middle Ages'. *Studies in the History of Worship in Scotland*. Ed. Duncan Forrester and D. Murray. 2nd edn, 1996. Pp. 19–35.
Gray, Douglas. *Themes and Images in the Medieval English Lyric*. London, 1972.
Gray, Douglas. ' "Hale, Sterne Superne" and its Literary Background'. *Dunbar: Essays*. Ed. Mapstone. Pp. 198–210.
Higgitt, John. *'Imageis Maid with Mennis Hand': Saints, Images, Belief and Identity in Later Medieval Scotland*. Whithorn, 2003.
MacDonald, A. A. 'Poetry, Politics and Reformation Censorship in Sixteenth-Century Scotland'. *English Studies* 64 (1983). Pp. 410–21.
MacDonald, A. A. 'Catholic Devotion into Protestant Lyric: the Case of the *Contemplacioun of Synnaris*'. *IR* 35 (1984). Pp. 58–87.
MacDonald, A. A. 'Religious Poetry in Middle Scots'. *History*. Ed. Jack. Pp. 91–104.

MacDonald A. A. 'The Latin Original of Robert Henryson's Annunciation Lyric'. *The Renaissance in Scotland: Studies in Literature, Religion, History and Culture Offered to John Durkan*. Ed. A. A. MacDonald, M. Lynch and I. B. Cowan. Leiden, 1994. Pp. 45–65.

MacDonald, A. A. 'Passion Devotion in Late-Medieval Scotland'. *The Broken Body: Passion Devotion in Late-Medieval Culture*. Ed. A. A. MacDonald, H. N. B. Ridderbos and R. M. Schlusemann. Groningen, 1998. Pp. 109–31.

Woolf, Rosemary. *The English Religious Lyric in the Middle Ages*. Oxford, 1968.

William Dunbar

EDITIONS

Dunbar, *The Poems*. Ed. Bawcutt.
The Poems of William Dunbar. Ed. James Kinsley. Oxford, 1979.
William Dunbar: Selected Poems. Ed. Priscilla Bawcutt. Harlow, 1996.

BIBLIOGRAPHY

Gray, Douglas. *William Dunbar*, Authors of the Middle Ages, Vol. 3, No. 10. Ed. M. C. Seymour. Aldershot, 1996.

SECONDARY STUDIES

Archibald, Elizabeth. 'Tradition and Innovation in the Macaronic Poetry of Dunbar and Skelton'. *MLQ* 53 (1992). Pp. 126–49.

Bawcutt, Priscilla. 'The Earliest Texts of Dunbar'. *Regionalism in Late Medieval Manuscripts and Texts: Essays celebrating the publication of 'A Linguistic Atlas of Late Mediaeval English'*. Ed. Felicity Riddy. Cambridge, 1991. Pp. 183–98.

Bawcutt, Priscilla. 'Images of Women in the Poems of Dunbar'. *Etudes Ecossaises* 1 (1992). Pp. 49–58.

Bawcutt, Priscilla. *Dunbar the Makar*. Oxford, 1992.

Bawcutt, Priscilla. ' "Nature Red in Tooth and Claw": Bird and Beast Imagery in William Dunbar'. *Animals and the Symbolic in Mediaeval Art and Literature*. Ed. L. A. J. R. Houwen. Groningen, 1997. Pp. 93–105.

Bawcutt, Priscilla. 'New Texts of William Dunbar, Alexander Scott and Other Scottish Poets'. *Scottish Studies Review* 1 (2000). Pp. 9–25.

Bawcutt, Priscilla. 'William Dunbar'. *Edinburgh History of Scottish Literature*. Volume I. Ed. Ian Brown et al. 2006. Pp. 649–69.

Bawcutt, Priscilla. 'Dunbar and his Readers: From Allan Ramsay to Richard Burton'. *SSL* 35 (forthcoming, 2006). Pp. 1–20.

Baxter, J. W. *William Dunbar: A Biographical Study*. 1952.

Corbett, John. 'Aureation Revisited: The Latinate Vocabulary of Dunbar's High and Plain Styles'. *Dunbar: Essays*. Ed. Mapstone. Pp. 183–97.
Edwards, A. S. G. 'Editing Dunbar: The Tradition'. *Dunbar: Essays*. Ed. Mapstone. Pp. 51–68.
Fox, Denton. 'Dunbar's *The Golden Targe*'. *ELH* 26 (1959). Pp. 311–34.
Fox, Denton. 'The Chronology of William Dunbar'. *PQ* 39 (1960). Pp. 413–25.
Glenn, Jonathan. 'Classifying Dunbar: Modes, Manners, and Styles'. *Dunbar: Essays*. Ed. Mapstone. Pp. 167–82.
Gray, Douglas. ' "Hale, Sterne Superne" and its Literary Background'. *Dunbar: Essays*. Ed. Mapstone. Pp. 198–210.
Hadley Williams, Janet. 'Dunbar and His Immediate Heirs'. *Dunbar: Essays*. Ed. Mapstone. Pp. 85–107.
Higgins, Iain Macleod. 'Tit for Tat: The Canterbury Tales and "The Flyting of Dunbar and Kennedy" '. *Exemplaria* 16 (2004). Pp. 165–202.
Lyall, R. J. 'Moral Allegory in Dunbar's "Golden Targe" '. *SSL* 11 (1974). Pp. 47–65.
Lyall, R. J. 'The Stylistic Relationship between Dunbar and Douglas'. *Dunbar: Essays*. Ed. Mapstone. Pp. 69–84.
McClure, J. Derrick. 'Dunbar's Metrical Technique'. *Dunbar: Essays*. Ed. Mapstone. Pp. 150–66.
McDiarmid, Matthew P. 'The Early William Dunbar and his Poems'. *SHR* 59 (1980). Pp. 126–39.
Mapstone, Sally. 'William Dunbar and the Book Culture of Sixteenth-Century Scotland'. *Dunbar: Essays*. Ed. Mapstone. Pp. 1–23.
Reiss, Edmund. *William Dunbar*. Boston, 1979.
Ross, Ian Simpson. *William Dunbar*. Leiden, 1981.
Roth, Elizabeth. 'Criticism and Taste: Readings of Dunbar's *Tretis*'. *SLJ*, Supplement 15 (1981). Pp. 57–90.
Singh, C. 'The Alliterative Ancestry of Dunbar's "The Tretis of the Tua Mariit Wemen and the Wedo" '. *Leeds Studies in English* n.s. 7 (1974). Pp. 22–54.

Gavin Douglas

EDITIONS

Douglas, *Virgil's Aeneid*. Ed. Coldwell.
Douglas, *Shorter Poems*. Ed. Bawcutt.
Gavin Douglas. The Palis of Honoure. Ed. David Parkinson. TEAMS, Kalamazoo, Mich., 1992.

SECONDARY STUDIES

Baswell, Christopher. *Virgil in Medieval England: Figuring the 'Aeneid' from the Twelfth Century to Chaucer*. Cambridge, 1995.

Bawcutt, Priscilla. 'Gavin Douglas and the Text of Virgil'. *EBST* 4, pt 6 (1973). Pp. 213–31.
Bawcutt, Priscilla. *Gavin Douglas: A Critical Study*. 1976.
Bawcutt, Priscilla. 'The "Library" of Gavin Douglas'. *Bards and Makars*. Ed. Adam J. Aitken, Matthew P. McDiarmid and Derick S. Thomson. Glasgow, 1977. Pp. 107–26.
Bawcutt, Priscilla. 'William Dunbar and Gavin Douglas'. *History*. Ed. Jack. Pp. 73–89.
Bawcutt, Priscilla. 'New Light on Gavin Douglas'. *The Renaissance in Scotland: Studies in Literature, Religion, History and Culture Offered to John Durkan*. Ed. A. A. MacDonald, M. Lynch and I. B. Cowan. Leiden, 1994. Pp. 95–106.
Blyth, Charles R. 'Gavin Douglas' Prologues of Natural Description'. *PQ* 49 (1970). Pp. 164–77.
Blyth, Charles R. *'The Knychtlyke Stile': A Study of Gavin Douglas' Aeneid*. New York, 1987.
Cairns, Sandra. '*The Palice of Honour* of Gavin Douglas, Ovid and Raffaello Regio's Commentary on Ovid's *Metamorphoses*'. *Studi Umanistici Piceni* 4 (1984). Pp. 17–38.
Canitz, A. E. Christa. ' "In our awyn langage": The Nationalist Agenda of Gavin Douglas's *Eneados*'. *Vergilius* 42 (1996). Pp. 25–37.
Ghosh, Kantik. ' "The Fift Quheill": Gavin Douglas's Maffeo Vegio'. *SLJ* 22 (1995). Pp. 5–21.
Gray, Douglas. ' "As quha the mater beheld tofor thar e": Douglas's Treatment of Vergil's Imagery'. *Palace*. Ed. Houwen et al. Pp. 95–123.
Gray, Douglas. 'Gavin Douglas and "the gret prynce Eneas" '. *Essays in Criticism* 51 (2001). Pp. 18–34.
Kinneavy, Gerald B. 'The Poet in *The Palice of Honour*'. *Chaucer Review* 3 (1969). Pp. 280–303.
Lyall, R. J. 'The Stylistic Relationship between Dunbar and Douglas'. *Dunbar: Essays*. Ed. Mapstone. Pp. 69–84.
Morse, Ruth. 'Gavin Douglas: "Off Eloquence the flowand balmy strand" '. *Chaucer Traditions: Studies in Honour of Derek Brewer*. Ed. R. Morse and B. Windeatt. Cambridge, 1990. Pp. 107–21.
Norton-Smith, John. 'Ekphrasis as a Stylistic Element in Douglas's *Palis of Honoure*'. *MÆ* 48 (1982). Pp. 240–53.
Parkinson, David. 'The Farce of Modesty in Gavin Douglas's *The Palis of Honoure*'. *PQ* 70 (1991). Pp. 13–25.
Pinti, Daniel. '*Alter Maro, alter Mapheus*: Gavin Douglas's Negotiation of Authority in *Eneados* 13'. *Journal of Medieval and Renaissance Studies* 23 (1993). Pp. 323–44.
Pinti, Daniel. 'The vernacular Gloss(ed) in Gavin Douglas's *Eneados*'. *Exemplaria* 7 (1995). Pp. 443–64.

Spearing, A. C. *The Medieval Poet as Voyeur: Looking and Listening in Medieval Love-Narratives*. Cambridge, 1993. Pp. 231–40.

Starkey, Penelope Schott. 'Gavin Douglas's *Eneados*: Dilemmas in the Nature Prologues'. *SSL* 11 (1974). Pp. 82–98.

Medieval Romance in Scotland

EDITIONS

The Buik of Alexander. Ed. R. L. Graeme Ritchie. 4 vols. STS, 1921–29.

Hay, *Buik*. Ed. Cartwright. (See above, pp. 199–200.)

Clariodus: A Metrical Romance. Ed. D. Irving. Maitland Club, 1830.

Eger and Grime. Ed. James Ralston Caldwell. Harvard Studies in Comparative Literature 9. Cambridge, Mass., 1933.

[*Florimond of Albany*.] McClure, J. Derrick, 'The *Florimond* Fragment'. *SLJ*, Supplement 10 (1979). Pp. 1–10. Unannotated transcript of the fragment.

[*Golagros and Gawane*.] *Scottish Alliterative Poems in Riming Stanzas*. Ed. F. J. Amours. STS, 1897. Pp. 1–46.

[*King Orphius*.] Stewart, Marion. '*King Orphius*'. *Scottish Studies* 17 (1973). Pp. 1–16. A transcript from Edinburgh, NAS RH 13/35, with appended discussion.

Lancelot of the Laik. Ed. Margaret M. Gray. STS, 1912.

[*Rauf Coilyear*.] *Longer Scottish Poems Vol. I*. Ed. Bawcutt and Riddy. Pp. 94–133.

[*Rauf Coilyear*.] *Medieval English Romances*. Ed. Diane Speed. 2 vols. 3rd edn, Durham, 1993. Pp. 196–235 and 306–20.

The Taill of Rauf Coilyear printed by Robert Lekpreuik at St Andrews in 1572. [Facsimile.] Introd. William Beattie. 1966.

[*Roswall and Lillian*.] 'Die Schottische Romanze "Roswall and Lillian" '. Ed. O. Lengert. *Englische Studien* 16 (1892). Pp. 321–56. 17 (1892). Pp. 341–77. A parallel-text edition of the Long and Short Versions.

[*Scottish Troy Book* fragments.] *Barbour's des Schottischen Nationaldichters Legendensammlung nebst den Fragmenten seines Trojanerkrieges*. Ed. C. Horstmann. 2 vols. Heilbronn, 1881–82.

[*Sir Colling*.] Stewart, Marion. 'A Recently-Discovered Manuscript: "ane taill of Sir colling ye kny'" '. *Scottish Studies* 16 (1972). Pp. 23–39. A transcript from Edinburgh, NAS RH 13/35, with appended discussion.

SECONDARY STUDIES

Archibald, Elizabeth. '*Lancelot of the Laik*: Sources, Genre, Reception'. *The Scots and Medieval Arthurian Legend*. Ed. Rhiannon Purdie and Nicola Royan. Cambridge, 2005. Pp. 71–82.

Barron, W. R. J. '*Gologros and Gawain*: A Creative Redaction'. *Bibliographical Bulletin of the International Arthurian Society* 26 (1974). Pp. 173–85.

Bawcutt, Priscilla. '*King Orphius* and "Opheus Kyng of Portingal" '. *Notes and Queries* 48.2 (2001). Pp. 112–14.

Bawcutt, Priscilla. 'English Books and Scottish Readers in the Fifteenth and Sixteenth Centuries'. *ROSC* 14 (2001–02). Pp. 1–12.

Edwards, A. S. G. 'Contextualising Middle Scots Romance'. *Palace*. Ed. Houwen et al. Pp. 61–73.

Evans, Deanna D. 'Re-evaluating the Case for a Scottish *Eger and Grime*'. *The European Sun: Proceedings of the Seventh International Conference on Medieval and Renaissance Scottish Language and Literature*. Ed. G. Caie, R. J. Lyall, S. Mapstone and K. Simpson. East Linton, 2001. Pp. 276–87.

Hasler, Antony J. 'Romance and Its Discontents in *Eger and Grime*'. *The Spirit of Medieval English Popular Romance*. Ed. Ad Putter and Jane Gilbert. Harlow, 2000. Pp. 200–18.

Jack, R. D. S. 'Arthur's Pilgrimage: A Study of *Golagros and Gawane*'. *SSL* 12 (1974–75). Pp. 3–20.

McIntosh, Angus. 'Some Notes on the Language and Textual Transmission of the *Scottish Troy Book*'. *Archivum Linguisticum* n.s. 10 (1979). Pp. 1–19.

Mapstone, Sally. 'The Scots, the French, and the English: an Arthurian Episode'. *The European Sun: Proceedings of the Seventh International Conference on Medieval and Renaissance Scottish Language and Literature*. Ed. G. Caie, R. J. Lyall, S. Mapstone and K. Simpson. East Linton, 2001. Pp. 129–44.

Pinti, Daniel J. 'Court, King and Community in *The Taill of Rauf Coilyear*'. *Chaucer Yearbook* 3 (1966). Pp. 73–85.

Purdie, Rhiannon. '*Clariodus* and the Ambitions of Courtly Romance in Later Medieval Scotland'. *FMLS* 38 (2002). Pp. 449–61.

Purdie, Rhiannon. 'The Search for Scottishness in *Golagros and Gawane*'. *The Scots and Medieval Arthurian Legend*. Ed. Rhiannon Purdie and Nicola Royan. Cambridge, 2005. Pp. 95–107.

Smith, Janet M. 'The Romances'. *The French Background to Middle Scots Literature*. 1934. Pp. 1–31.

Wright, Dorena. 'From "Sir Orfeo" to "King Orphius" '. *Parergon* 27 (1980). Pp. 9–11.

Wright, Glenn. 'Churl's Courtesy: *Rauf Coilyear* and its English Analogues'. *Neophilologus* 85 (2001). Pp. 647–62.

Sir David Lyndsay

EDITIONS

The Works of Sir David Lindsay of the Mount 1490–1555. Ed. Douglas Hamer. 4 vols. STS, 1931–36. For detailed description of earlier Lyndsay editions, see vol. 4, pp. 5–122.

Sir David Lyndsay: Selected Poems. Ed. Janet Hadley Williams. Glasgow, 2000.

Sir David Lindsay of the Mount: 'Ane Satyre of the Thrie Estaitis'. Ed. Roderick Lyall. Canongate Classics 18. 1989.

Four Morality Plays. Ed. Peter Happé. Harmondsworth, 1979. Pp. 431–615.

Longer Scottish Poems Vol. I. Ed. Bawcutt and Riddy. Pp. 247–68 and 394–402 (*Squyer Meldrum*, lines 849–1516).

SECONDARY STUDIES

Axton, Marie. '*Ane Satyre of the Thrie Estaitis*: The First Edition and its Reception'. *A Day Estivall: Essays on the Music, Poetry and History of Scotland and England in Honour of Helena Mennie Shire*. Ed. Alisoun Gardner-Medwin and Janet Hadley Williams. Aberdeen, 1990. Pp. 21–34.

Burger, Glenn D. 'Poetical Invention and Ethical Wisdom in Lindsay's *Testament of the Papyngo*'. *SSL* 24 (1998). Pp. 164–80.

Cairns, Sandra. 'Sir David Lindsay's *Dreme*: Poetry, Propaganda, and Encomium in the Scottish Court'. *The Spirit of the Court*. Ed. Glynn S. Burgess and R. A. Taylor. Cambridge, 1985. Pp. 110–19.

Edington, Carol. *Court and Culture in Renaissance Scotland: Sir David Lindsay of the Mount*. Amherst, Mass., 1994.

Graf, Claude. 'Audience Involvement in Lindsay's *Ane Satyre of the Thrie Estaitis*', *Scottish Language and Literature, Medieval and Renaissance: Fourth International Conference 1984 Proceedings*. Ed. Dietrich Strauss and Horst W. Drescher. Frankfurt am Main, 1986. Pp. 423–35.

Hadley Williams, Janet. 'The Lyon and the Hound: Sir David Lyndsay's *Complaint and Confessioun of Bagsche*', *Parergon* 31 (1981). Pp. 3–11.

Hadley Williams, Janet. 'David Lyndsay and the Making of King James V'. *Stewart Style 1513–1542*. Ed. Janet Hadley Williams. East Linton, 1996. Pp. 201–26.

Hadley Williams, J. 'Lyndsay and Europe: Politics, Patronage, Printing'. *The European Sun: Proceedings of the Seventh International Conference on Medieval and Renaissance Scottish Language and Literature*. Ed. G. Caie, R. J. Lyall, S. Mapstone and K. Simpson. East Linton, 2001. Pp. 333–46.

Kantrowicz, Joanne Spencer. *Dramatic Allegory in Lindsay's 'Ane Satyre of the Thrie Estaitis'*. Lincoln, Nebr., 1975.

Lyall, R. J. 'The Linlithgow Interlude of 1540'. *Actes du 2e Colloque de Langue et de Littérature Ecossaises (Moyen Age et Renaissance)*. Ed. Jean-Jacques Blanchot and Claude Graf. Strasbourg, 1978. Pp. 409–21.

McGavin, John J. 'The Dramatic Prosody of Sir David Lindsay'. *Of Lion and Of Unicorn: Essays on Anglo-Scottish Literary Relations in Honour of Professor John MacQueen*. Ed. R. D. S. Jack and Kevin McGinley. 1993. Pp. 39–66.

McGinley, Kevin J. ' "That Every Man May Knaw": Reformation and Rhetoric in the Works of Sir David Lyndsay'. *Literature Compass* 2 (2005), RE 144. Pp. 1–15. See at: http://www.literature-compass.com (doi:10.1111/j.1741-4113.2005.00144.x).

Mill, Anna J. 'The Influence of Continental Drama on Lyndsay's *Ane Satyre of the Thrie Estatis*'. *MLR* 25 (1930). Pp. 425–42.

Reid, David. 'Rule and Misrule in Lindsay's *Thrie Estaitis* and Pitcairne's *Assembly*'. *SLJ* 11.2 (1984). Pp. 5–24.

Riddy, Felicity. '*Squyer Meldrum* and the Romance of Chivalry'. *Yearbook of English Studies* 14 (1974). Pp. 26–36.

Walker, Greg. 'Sir David Lindsay's *Ane Satire of the Thrie Estaitis* and the Politics of Reformation'. *SLJ* 16.2 (1989). Pp. 5–17.

Index of Manuscripts

Cambridge
  Fitzwilliam Museum, 370 131
  Magdalene College, Pepys Library, 1576 121, 122
  Magdalene College, Pepys Library, 2553 (Maitland Folio) 17, 66, 134, 141
  St John's College, G.19 (187) (John Mirk's *Festial* and *Quattuor Sermones*) 8, 64 n.4
  Trinity College Library, 0.3.12 (*Eneados*) 16
    scribe of (Geddes) 16
  University Library, Kk.1.5 No. 6 16, 63 n.2, 83 n.28
  University Library, Kk.5.30 (*Scottish Troy Book* fragments) 77 n.10, 173 n.53
  University Library, Ll.5.10 (Reidpeth) 66

Edinburgh
  NAS, GD 45/31/I–II (Dalhousie) 7, 64 n.4
  NAS, GD 112/71/9 (*Alexander the Conquerour*) 76, 176
  NAS, GD 112/22/2 (*Florimond of Albany* fragment) 11, 166, 169, 170–1, 176
  NAS, NP 1/168 121 n.10
  NAS, RH13/35 (*Sir Colling* and other verse and prose fragments) 166, 170, 173–5
  NLS, Acc. 9253 (Gilbert Hay's prose translations) 64 n.4, 76 n.5
  NLS, Acc. 9268 130
  NLS, 16500 (Asloan) 3 n.10, 16, 50, 66, 76, 105, 106, 119, 120, 127, 129, 130
  NLS, 21000 (Murthly Hours) 9
  NLS, Adv. 1.1.6 (Bannatyne) 14, 15, 17, 18, 50, 65, 66, 90–1, 105, 106, 120, 121, 129, 134
    part I, 'ballattis of theoligie' 17, 120, 124, 127
    part II, 'ballatis full of wisdome and moralitie' 14, 17, 124
    part III, 'ballettis mirry' 17
    part IV, 'ballatis of luve' 17
    part V, 'fabillis wyiss and sapient' 17, 50, 91, 129
    and *Morall Fabillis* 90–1
  NLS, Adv. 18.5.14 130
  NLS, Adv. 19.2.2 35 36 n.3
  NLS, Adv. 34.1.3a 91 n.10
  NLS, Adv. 34.7.3 (Gray) 123
  NLS, Adv. 35.1.7 (Coupar Angus MS of *Scotichronicon*) 46
  NLS, Adv. 72.1.37 (Book of the Dean of Lismore) 5
  NLS, Dep. 221/5 (Andrew Lundy's Primer) 123 n.25
  University Library, Laing III.17 121
  University Library, Laing III.149 (Makculloch) 121, 123, 129, 130, 189 n.49
    scribe of 121

London
  British Library, Additional 16165 67 n.15, 69 n.21
  British Library, Additional 27879 (Percy Folio) 168–9, 172, 174
  British Library, Additional 40732 (*Alexander the Conquerour*) 76, 176
  British Library, Arundel 285 16–17, 120–1, 122, 123, 124, 126, 127, 130
  British Library, Cotton Caligula B. I. (Lyndsay's letter, fol. 313) 181
  British Library, Cotton Nero D. XI (Wyntoun) 39 nn.13 and 14
  British Library, Cotton Vitellius E. XI (Fordun, *Chronica gentis Scotorum*) 65
  British Library, Harley 6919 (*Contemplacioun of Synnaris*) 126, 127

Oxford
  Bodleian Library, Arch. Selden. B. 24 7, 8, 16, 63–74

and Chaucer 63–4, 65–6, 67–8, 70, 71–3
complaints in 71–3
and Hoccleve 71–3, 123
illumination of 64
Kingis Quair in 67–71
  lyrics in 68–9
  textual integrity of 70–1
make-up of 64, 66
Parliament of Fowls in 71 n.30
provenance of 64, 176; *see also* Sinclair, family of
scribes of 8, 63, 64 n.4, 65, 66, 67, 70–2, 72 n.33

short verse texts in 65–6
Bodleian Library, Douce 148 (Scottish *Troy Book* fragments) 77 n.10, 173 n.53
Bodleian Library, Fairfax 16 74 n.41

Warminster
  Longleat House Library, Longleat 252a 3 n.10

Wemyss
  Wemyss Castle, Wemyss MS (Wyntoun) 39 nn.13 and 14

General Index

Aberdeen 3, 11, 31, 35, 119, 136
  St Machar, Cathedral of 32, 120
  University of 30
Aberdeen Breviary 17
Achitophel and Synon 153
Ademar of Chabannes 96
Adornes, Anselm (*Itinerarium*) 6
advice to princes, *see* speculum principis tradition
Aeneas 160, 162–4
Aesop, fable tradition of 89–90, 90 n.4, 92–3, 96, 97, 98, 99–101, 103, 104
Aimon de Varennes (*Florimont*) 171
Aitken, A. J. 13, 189 n.48
Alan of Lille (*Planctu Naturae, De*) 54, 152
Albany, Duke of, *see* Stewart
Alexander III, king of Scots (1249–86) 41
Alexander, the Great 166, 167, 169, 170, 171, 175
Alexander, Flora 171 n.43
Alexander, tradition of 75, 77–9, 80, 81, 82, 83–4, 86, 87, 88, 169, 171, 175
Alexandri Magni Iter ad Paradisum 78
Alexandre de Paris (*Roman d'Alexandre*) 77, 78, 81, 82, 84, 85
  Fuerre de Gadres, Li, in 77, 87, 175
  Voeux de Paon, Les, in 77, 83, 87
Alexis, Guillaume (*Débat de l'Omme et de la Femme*) 11
Alfonsi, Petrus, Spanish theologian 90, *Disciplina clericalis* 101–2
allegory, in Older Scots poetry 12, 53, 70, 81–2, 83, 94, 96, 98, 101, 102, 103, 109, 110, 113, 124, 136–7, 145, 146, 150, 152, 154, 155, 162, 164
alliteration, in Older Scots poetry 10, 13, 49, 50–1, 122, 130, 142, 143, 144, 163, 170, 183. 185, 189, 190
Anderson, William J. 123 n.25
anglicization, in Older Scots poetry 91, 106, 127
Anglicus, Gualterus (Walter the Englishman) 89–90 n.4
animals, in Older Scots poetry 15, 69, 94–104, 136, 146, 186, 188
anthologies, *see* miscellanies

anti-feminism, in Older Scots poetry 65, 66, 96, 116, 143
anti-mendicant tradition, medieval 97
Arbuthnet, Alexander 87
Archibald, Elizabeth 140 n.21, 171 n.46
Arden, Heather 184 n.25
Aristotle 77 n.11, 81, 82, 93, 134
Arn, Mary-Jo 68 n.16
Aronstein, Susan 107 n.10, 116
Arran, Earl of, *see* Hamilton
Arthur, legendary king of Britain 51, 165, 171, 175
Asloan, John 16
Asloan MS, *see* Index of MSS
Assembly of Ladies, The 73
astrology, medieval debate about 97
Aswell, E. D. 107 n.12
Aubailly, Jean-Claude 184 n.25
Auchinleck Chronicler 79
Auden, W. H. 134
audience, *see* readers
Awntyrs off Arthure at the Terne Wathelyn 51, 165

Babel 56, 57
Babylon 39, 56
Badius, Jodocus (Badius Ascensius) 157
Balfour-Melville, E. 67 n.13
'balat', 'ballatis' 2, 5, 14, 17, 113–4, 119, 120, 122, 124, 128, 130
ballad tradition, in Older Scots poetry 13, 124, 174–5
'ballat of disputacoun betuix the body and saull' (Asloan MS) 119
Bannatyne, George 17, 106
Bannatyne Manuscript, *see* Index of MSS
Bannerman, J. W. M. 29 n.43
Bannockburn, battle of (1314) 36, 41, 43
Barbour, John 2–3, 4, 6, 14–15, 41, 43, 58, 87, 167, 173
  Bruce, The 2, 4, 9, 10, 14–15, 16, 18, 35, 37, 40, 41–4, 49, 58–9, 163, 167, 169, 175, 185
Barker-Benfield, B. C. 63 n.2
Barns of Ayr 46
Barratt, Alexandra 73 n.38
Barron, W. R. J. 171 n.41

Barry, Henry 87
Basle, Council of 56
Bassandyne, Thomas 90, 167–8
Baswell, Christopher 164 n.31
Bawcutt, Priscilla 1–18, 4 n.11, 6 n.29, 8 n.41, 9 n.46, 10 n.52, 11 nn.57 and 58, 12 n.61, 14 n.70, 15 nn.76 and 78, 16 n.81, 20–1 n.5, 27 n.34, 70 n.28, 81 n.27, 115 n.48, 119–31, 123 nn.19 and 24, 125 n.26, 130 n. 45, 136 n.11, 150 nn.2 and 6, 157 n.20, 165 n.2, 174 n.57
Baxter, J. W. 133 n.1
Bayard, Chevalier de (Pierre Terrail) 156
Beadle, Richard 105 n.3
Beaton, David, cardinal 182
beast epic, tradition of 90, 96, 97, 101–2
Beattie, W. 4 n.15, 17 n.86, 50 n.3, 66 n.8
Beaufort, Joan, wife of James I 70
Bellenden, John 5, 6
   'Proheme' 5, 189
   Chronicles 6; *see also* historiographical tradition
Bennett, J. A. W. 120–1, 122, 125 n.27, 158 n.23
Benson, David C. 106 n.7
Berwick 21
Bevis of Hampton 169
Bible 8, 38, 39, 56, 122, 128, 129, 139
   Isaiah 138–9
   Luke 129
   Matthew (pearl of great price parable) 94
   Psalms 42, 47, 122
Biggar, fictitious battle of 44
Binski, Paul 131 n.47
birds, in Older Scots poetry 49–56, 67, 68, 71, 94, 100, 103–4, 124, 129, 136, 139, 146, 183, 187, 188
bird parliament, in Older Scots poetry 50, 51, 53, 54–6, 59
'Blak be thy bandis and thy wede also' (Selden MS) 65
Blind Hary, *see* Hary
Blyth, Charles R. 149 n.1
Boardman, Stephen 19 n.1, 20 n.3, 36 n.6, 37 n.10, 60 n.26
Boccaccio, Giovanni 14, 108, 182; *see also* 'Greneacres A Lenvoye'
Boece, Hector 10, 18, 30
   Scotorum Historiae 6
Boethius, Anicius Manlius Severinus 38, 65, 66, 10
   Consolation of Philosophy, The 67, 68, 69, 70, 71, 106, 108, 113, 130, 184; *see also* Walton
   De musica 68

Boffey, Julia 17 n.85, 63–74, 63–4 n.3, 64 n.4, 65 n.7, 68 n.16, 108 n.15
Bohun, Henry de (nephew of the Earl) 43
Bonet, Honoré, *L'Arbre des Batailles* 76
book collectors, early Scottish 7–8, 86–7
Book of Cupid, see Clanvowe
Book of the Dean of Lismore 5
books of hours 9, 121, 122, 123, 131
Booton, Harold 11 n.54
Borders 31–2
Borland, C. 121 n.9
Bower, Walter 6, 7, 19, 32, 36, 37–8
   Scotichronicon 6, 19, 35, 36, 39, 40, 41, 42, 44, 46
Bowge of Court (Skelton) 148
Boyd, Thomas, Earl of Arran 8
Brant, Sebastian 161
Breviaire des Nobles, Le (Chartier) 11
Bromyard, John 101
Broun, Dauvit 32 n.62, 37 n.9
Brown, Keith M. 22 n.8
Brown, Michael 20 n.2, 22 n.11, 57 n.21, 67 n.13
Brown, Peter 69 n.24
Bruce, Robert the, *see* Robert I
Bruce, The, see Barbour
Buik of Alexander 9, 11, 87, 166, 167, 169, 170, 185
Buik of King Alexander the Conquerour, The 7, 10, 75–88, 166, 170, 171, 173, 176, 184, 185, 189
   Aristotle, role of, in 77 n.11, 81, 82, 185
   attribution to Gilbert Hay 75–7
   Candace, role of, in 83–4
   Caractor, oriental prince in 79, 84
   date of 77
   death of Alexander in 85
   Diogenes exemplum in 84
   Earthly Paradise and 79
   kingship, young, in 79–81
   Nectanabus, dying speech of, in 83
   pirate exemplum in 84–5
   Poisoned Maiden exemplum in 82
   'Regiment of kingis with the buke of phisnomy' and 76, 81, 82, 87, 185
   Roxanne, role of, in 85
   sources of 77–86
   travels, exotic, noted in 78–9, 81, 82
'buk of Gud Maneris, a' 8
'buke contenand four bukis of the sentence, ane' 8
'buke of curtasy and nortur' (Asloan MS) 76
Buke of the Chess, The 14
Bunt, Gerrit V. 76 n.9, 85 nn.32 and 33

Burgundy 171
  and Scotland 14, 20, 171, 181
burlesque, in Older Scots poetry 52, 140–1, 187, 189
Burns, J. H. 5 n.17
Burrow, J. A. 89 n.1, 133–48

Cadiou, Andrew 3, 11
  Porteous of Nobelnes 4, 11, 18
Caldwell, D. H. 119 n.4
Calin, William 70 n.24
Calliope, muse of heroic poetry 154
Cameron, Jamie 20 n.2
Campbell, clan and family of 79 n.19, 86
  as book collectors 86–7
Campbell, Sir Colin, of Argyll 174
Campbell, Duncan, 7th laird of Glenorchy 86, 176
Carretta, Vincent 68 n.17
Cartwright, John 77 n.13, 79 n.16
Cary, George 84 n.31
Catiline (Lucius Sergius Catilina) 153
Caxton, William 8, 13–14, 158
  Book of Good Manners 14
  Cordial 14
  Dicts or Sayings of the Philosophers 8
  Eneydos 14, 158
  Paris and Vienne 14
  Recuyell of the Historyes of Troye 14
censorship, *see* Protestantism
chanson d'aventure, in Older Scots poetry 52, 188
Charlemagne, Emperor 169, 172, 175
  and douzepers (Roland, Oliver) 175–6
Charles V, Emperor (1519–55) 32–3, 181
Charles VII, king of France (1422–61) 57
Charteris, Henry 87, 105, 187 n.46
Chartier, Alain (*Breviaire des Nobles*) 11
Chaucer, Geoffrey 2, 11–13, 17, 69, 73, 107, 134, 151, 152, 157, 162, 170, 182, 184
  and attributions to 65, 66, 71, 72, 123
  and 'Lollius' 112
  Anelida and Arcite 12, 73, 148, 189
  Boece (English trans. of Boethius) 184
  Book of the Duchess, The 184
  Canterbury Tales, The 12
    'Knight's Tale' 67, 68, 148
    'Monk's Tale' 184
    'Nun's Priest's Tale' 90, 96
    'Sir Thopas, Tale of' 141, 170
    'Squire's Tale' 73
    'Wife of Bath's Tale' 143
  'Complaint of Mars' 63, 72, 73
  'Complaint of Venus' 63, 66, 71, 72
  House of Fame, The 73, 152, 153, 154
  Legend of Good Women, The 63, 71, 72, 73, 152
  Parliament of Fowls, The 49, 54–5, 63, 65, 67, 71, 71 n.30, 136, 184
  Troilus and Criseyde 12, 63, 64, 65, 66, 68, 71, 73, 105, 106, 111–12, 113, 114, 138, 145, 184
  'Truth' 63, 65, 71
'Chaucerian' and 'Non-Chaucerian' poetry 13, 65–6, 68, 70, 71, 72, 73, 107, 151–3, 184
Chepman, Walter 17
Chepman and Myllar prints 4, 14, 17, 50, 66, 105, 134, 170
Cherry, A. F. 8 n.37
Chesnutt, Michael 7 n.36
Child, Francis J. 174
chivalric biographies, *see* exemplary lives
chivalry, as theme, in Older Scots poetry 51, 78, 154–6, 163
Christianity, Christian beliefs 26, 38, 39, 42, 111, 113, 115, 124, 154, 157, 158, 159, 183, 185, 187
Christine de Pizan 71, 73
Christensen, T. L. 181 n.13
'Christis Kirk' tradition 15
Chronica Gentis Scotorum, *see* Fordun
Chronicles of England, The 13–14
Church, pre-Reformation, in Scotland
  administration of 26
  Catholicism, state of 26, 27, 121; *see also* Protestantism
  clergy 26–7
  benefactions to 28–9
  devotions
    Marian 122, 124, 128–31
    Passion 120–1, 123, 124, 125–7, 128
  and donor patrons 131
  and education 29–30, 91–2, 93
  and endowments 29
  foundations, religious 28, 38
  and heresy 27–8
  and hospitals 28
  hymns of 122
  liturgy of 122, 124, 125, 128, 129, 138, 139–40, 144, 183
  and miracles 120
  and pilgrimage 10, 28, 94
  relics, veneration of 28
  religious orders
    Carthusian 28
    Dominican 28
    Observant Franciscan 28, 124, 126
  Rome, relations with 26–7, 49, 52–3
  royal involvement in 27

sacraments
  baptism 97–8
  confession 97
  penance 16, 97, 120, 124, 127
  saints, cults of 28, 29
  song schools of 30
Cicero, Marcus Tullius 153
Clanvowe, Thomas
  Book of Cupid (*Cuckoo and the Nightingale*) 63, 66, 67, 71 n.32
Clariodus 11, 166, 169–70, 171, 176, 177
Cleriadus et Meliadice 171
'Closter of Crist riche recent flour delys' (Kennedy) 130, 131
Cocytus, river of Hades 161–2
Cole, Carol A. 114
Colkelbie Sow 15
comic poetry, medieval English and Scottish 15, 16, 17, 52, 55, 67–8, 90, 94–5, 96, 97, 98, 101–3, 124–5, 141, 143, 152–3, 157, 159, 172, 185, 188, 189; see also eldritch
complaint, in Older Scots poetry 2, 12, 15, 50, 54, 66, 67, 69, 71–3, 85, 100, 109, 123, 152, 184, 185, 187, 188
Complaynt of Scotland 171
Comyn, Sir John (d. c.1306) 43
concatenation, use of, in Older Scots poetry 50–1, 126
Consolation of Philosophy, see Boethius
Contemplacioun of Synnaris, see Touris
Copland, William 18
Corbett, John 140 n.20
Corpus Christi, feast of
  plays of 119
  processions of 31
Court of Sapience 152
courtesy, theme of, in Older Scots poetry 154, 172
Coutts, Winifred 23 n.15
Cowan, I. B. 28 n.40
Cox, Catherine S. 116
Crane, Susan 169 n.32
Crawford, Barbara E. 7 n.35
Cuckoo and the Nightingale, see Clanvowe
Cullen, Mairi Ann 107 n.10
culture, fifteenth-century Scottish
  and the common man or woman 30–1
  English mediation in 14, 167
  female literacy and 9
  Highlands and 28–9, 31, 49, 183
  laicization of 4, 8, 17, 19, 29, 183
  non-centralized form of 7, 20
  regional diversity of 20, 87
Cunningham, I. C. 16 n.82, 130 n.44
Cupar 182

Curnow, Demelza Jayne 168 n.23
Curtius, E. R. 136 n.10

Darius of Persia 78, 79
Davenport, W. A. 73 n.37
David II (1329–71) 37, 43
Davidoff, Judith M. 52 n.8
Davidson, John 168–9
Davie, Donald (*Articulate Energy*) 138
Débat de l'Omme et de la Femme, Le (Guillaume Alexis) 11
debate, in Older Scots poetry 11, 83, 124
Declaration of Arbroath (1320) 59, 61
Deguileville, Guillaume de 67
Deidis of Armorie 11
Denmark 21, 28, 181
Deschamps, Eustace 147
Desmond, Marilynn 164 n.31
'Deuise prowes and eke humylitee' (Selden MS) 65, 66, 71
'Devoit Remembrance of the Passioun of Crist, Ane' (MS Arundel 285) 124
devotion, private 14, 17, 47, 119, 120–1, 124; see also Church
Diana, goddess 153, 154
Dicke, Gerd and Klaus Grubmüller (*Die Fabeln des Mittelalters*) 97 n.18
didactic and moral verse 9, 10, 11, 14, 16, 17, 50, 61, 66, 89, 106, 126, 135, 144, 189
Dido, queen of Carthage 158, 161, 163–4
Ditchburn, David 6 n.26, 22 n.7, 28 n.37
'Dollorus Complant of Our Lorde apoune the croce crucifyit, the' (MS Arundel 285) 123
Donaldson, Robert 50 n.3
Douglas, earls of 22, 57
Douglas, family of 20, 41, 49, 50, 51, 56, 57–8, 59–60, 61–2, 149, 180
  Archibald, 5th Earl of Angus 149
Douglas, Archibald, 6th Earl of Angus 150, 180
Douglas, Archibald, Master 57
Douglas, Archibald, 4th Earl of Douglas (c. 1372–1424) 57
Douglas, Archibald, 1st Earl of Moray 7, 49, 57, 60 n.23
Douglas, Gavin, Bp of Dunkeld (1515–22) 1, 3, 4, 5, 7, 8, 10, 12, 13, 15, 18, 27, 106, 120, 122, 149–64, 172, 176, 177, 184, 186, 187, 188, 189, 190
  and Chaucer 12, 149, 152, 157, 189
  and Dunbar 135, 152, 156
  and James IV 150, 151
  and *King Hart* 150
  and translation 158–61

'Conscience' 150, 187
Eneados 1, 3 n.10, 4, 7, 8, 9, 13, 14, 16, 18, 129, 149, 150, 151, 153, 156, 157–64, 186, 187
  Book XIII (Maffeo Vegio) 157, 164
  narrative voices in 160–1
'Of Lundeys Lufe the Remeid' 150–1
Palice of Honour 2, 5, 18, 50, 73, 149, 151–7, 159, 163, 172 n.50, 175 n.65, 184, 186, 187, 189, 190
  Edinburgh edition of 153 n.14
  London edition of 153
  themes in 153–5
  Prologues to *Eneados* 15, 124, 129, 157–9, 160, 162–3, 164, 186–7
Douglas, Hugh, Earl of Ormond 57, 60 n.23
Douglas, James 'The Gross', of Balvenie, 7th Earl of Douglas 57, 60 n.23
Douglas, Sir James , 'The Good' ('The Black Douglas') 36, 41, 43, 57–8, 59, 60
Douglas, William, 8th Earl of Douglas (d. 1452) 60 n.23, 79
Douglas, James, Master, *later* 9th Earl of Douglas 60 n.23
Douglases, Black 61
Downie, Fiona 20 n.5
drama, religious 123, 150
  'Haliblude' (Corpus Christi) 119
drama, secular
  and Abbot of Unreason 31
  'fairsis' 180
  Queen of May 31
  Robin Hood and Little John 31
  Satyre of the Thrie Estaitis, Ane 179, 182, 184, 190
dramatic elements, in Older Scots poetry 55, 109, 115, 156, 160, 161, 172, 185, 190
dream visions, allegorical 12, 16, 46, 63, 69, 71, 99, 117, 124, 136, 137–8, 146, 151–3, 154, 155, 156, 184, 187
  guides in 151, 184
Dunbar, Elizabeth, Countess of Moray 7, 9, 49, 59
Dunbar, William 1, 2, 3, 5, 10, 15–16, 17, 18, 66, 106, 107, 114, 120, 123, 124, 126, 130, 131, 133–48, 149, 151, 152, 153, 156, 160, 170–1, 172, 177, 179, 183, 184, 186, 187, 190
  as 'mackar' 133, 135, 148, 183
  and Chaucer 12–13, 107, 134, 138, 189
  and Gower 134, 138
  and *Grands Rhétoriqueurs* 10

and Henryson 91, 106, 148
and Holland 50
and Villon 10
Ballade of Barnard Stewart, The ('Renownit, ryall', B 56) 9, 135–6
Ballat of Our Lady, Ane ('Hale, sterne superne', B 16) 66 n.9, 130, 131, 139–40
Ballat of the Abbot of Tungland, A ('As yung Awrora with cristall haile', B 4) 141, 170 n.38
Ballat of the Passioun, Ane ('Amang thir freiris', B 1) 120, 122, 124, 144 n.31
'Be diuers wyis and operatiounes' (B 5) 146–7
'Be mery, man, and tak nocht fer in mynd' (B 6) 66 n.9
'Blyth Aberdeane, thow beriall of all tounis' (B 8) 136
'Complane I wald, wist I quhome till' (B 9) 147, 188
'Done is a battell on the dragon blak' (B 10) 66 n.9, 127, 128, 138
Dumbaris Dirige to the King ('We that ar heir in hevynnis glorie', B 84) 140
Flyting of Dumbar and Kennedie, The ('Schir Iohine the Ros', B 65) 3, 5, 15, 124–5, 142, 183, 189
'Full oft I mvse and hes in thocht' (B 14) 144
Goldyn Targe, The ('Ryght as the stern of day' B 59) 2, 8–9, 73, 133, 137–8, 152, 187
'I maister Andro Kennedy' (B 19) 140
'I that in heill wes' (B 21) 2, 3, 50 n.4, 76, 91, 106 n.5, 114 n.42, 133–4, 142 n.26, 144, 175 n.65
'Illuster Lodouick, of France most cristin king' (B 23) 9, 135
'In May as that Aurora did vpspring' (B 24) 124
'In to thir dirk and drublie dayis' (B 26) 144–5
'In vice most vicius he excellis' (B 27) 141–2
'Lang heff I maed of ladyes quhytt' (B 28) 141
'Lucina schyning in silence of the nycht' (B 29) 127 n.29
'My heid did yak yester nicht' (B 35) 147–8, 190
'Now lythis off ane gentill knycht' (*Schir Thomas Norny*, B 39) 13, 141, 170

'Off Februar the fyiftene nycht' (B 47) 140–1, 170 n.38
'Off every asking followis nocht' (B 44) 145–6
'Quha will behald of luve the chance' (B 50) 170 n.38
'Quhat is this lyfe bot ane straucht way to deid' (B 51) 66 n.9
'Quhen Merche wes with variand windis past' (B 52) 56, 133, 136, 137
'Quhom to sall I compleine my wo' (B 54) 188
'Richt arely one Ask Wedinsday' (B 57) 143
'*Rorate, celi, desuper!*' (B 58) 138–9
'Sanct saluatour, send siluer sorrow!' (B 61) 147
'Schir, at this feist of benefice' (B 62) 190
'Schir, I complane off iniuris' (B 64) 142
'Schir, lat it neuer in toune be tald' (B 66) 15, 146
'Schir, ye haue mony seruitouris' (B 67) 134, 146–7
'Schir, yit remember as befoir' (B 66) 146, 172 n.50
'Sen that I am a presoneir' (B 69) 66 n.11
'Sir Ihon Sinclair begowthe to dance' (B 70) 133, 141
Tabill of Confessioun, The ('To the, O marcifull saluiour myn, Iesus', B 83) 124
'This hinder nycht, halff sleiping as I lay' (B 75) 146
'This hindir nycht in Dumfermeling' (B 76) 3
'This waverand warldis wretchidnes' (B 79) 146
'Thow that in hewin for our saluatioun' (B 80) 138
'To speik of science, craft or sapience' (B 82) 144 n.31
Tretis of the Tua Mariit Wemen and the Wedo, The ('Apon the Midsummer Ewin', B 3) 142–3, 188
Duncan, Douglas 107 n.12
Dundee 25, 29
Dunfermline 3, 91, 106
Dunkeld 3, 149, 150
Dunlop, David 21 n.6
Durkan, John 1 n.2, 3 n.10, 9 n.45, 27 n.35, 28 nn.40 and 41, 30 n.50, 126 n.28

Dyall of Dayly Contemplacion, A 127

'Earth upon earth' 121
Easson, D. E. 28 n.40
Eberhard of Bethune 108
Ebin, Lois 68 n.17
economy, of Scotland 23–5
  and beggars 26
  and building work 24
  burghs (royal, ecclesiastical, baronial), roles of 25
  and devaluation of coinage 24
  and domestic trade 24
  guilds, craft, roles of 25–6
  inflation 24
  merchants, roles of 25
  and overseas trade (wool, salmon, coarse cloth, hides) 24, 25
  and sumptuary laws 24
  and work, male and female 26
Edinburgh 3, 16, 18, 25, 26, 28, 29, 30, 65, 66, 87, 105, 121, 140, 142, 150, 167, 170, 181, 182
Eddy, Elizabeth Roth 170 n.37
Edington, Carol 4 n.12, 32 n.62
education
  chaplains, as teachers of the nobility 30
  Education Act (1496) 30
  in Highlands 30
  Latin, role in; *see* Latin
  learned professions 3, 30
  schools, for girls 30
  schools, grammar 30, 91, 93
  schools, song, *see* Church
  study abroad 10, 30, 75, 92, 121, 126, 149
  universities 3, 30, 91–2, 125, 133, 149, 183
Edward I, king of England (1272–1307) 42, 46, 172
Edwards, A. S. G. 63 n.2, 64 nn.3 and 4, 70 n.28, 148 n.34, 166 n.3, 176 n.69
Effesoun, Siege of 83
Eger and Grime ('Graysteel') 165, 166, 167–9, 170, 173, 176, 185
Eglamour of Artois 18, 170
Elderton, William 17
eldritch (elrich) poetry, in Older Scots 15, 140–1, 153; *see also* comic poetry
elegy, in Older Scots poetry 187
Elegy, French, on dauphine Margaret 6, 11
Elphinstone, William, Bp of Aberdeen 8
Emmerson, Richard Kenneth 127 n.29
Eneados, see Douglas
England 147, 156, 159

and Scotland 1, 2, 4, 10, 11–12, 13–14, 18, 19, 20, 21, 22, 32, 36, 40, 42, 45–6, 47, 49, 51, 59, 61, 63, 67, 72–3, 105, 114, 122, 123, 127, 130, 150, 165, 169, 172, 174–5, 177, 181, 182, 184, 191
English Chaucerians 13, 63
English (language)
  Middle English 4, 139, 168, 172
  Old English 4
epistle, in Older Scots poetry 82, 184, 187, 188
Epistola Alexandri ad Aristotelem 78
Epstein, Robert 70 n.25
Erkinholme, battle of (1455) 49
'Erse', *see* Gaelic
Erskine, family of 86–7
Erskine, Thomas, 2nd Lord 7, 86
eulogy, in Older Scots poetry 41, 129, 130, 188
Europe
  and Scotland 1, 4, 14, 19, 20, 21, 27, 29, 31, 32, 73, 74, 92, 130, 165, 181
Evander 159, 160
Evans, Deanna Delmar 165 n.2
Ever Green, The (Ramsay) 18
Ewan, Elizabeth 19–33, 21 n.5, 26 n.28, 31 n.54
Ewyne, Thomas 77 n.10
excerptions, poetic 65, 87, 121, 123
exemplary lives, in Older Scots poetry 117
  of saints, *see* Legends of the Saints
  of secular figures 35–47, 57, 75, 78, 79–80, 82, 84, 88, 109, 117, 156, 167, 182, 188, 189

fable 3, 14, 15, 17, 49, 50, 52, 53, 59, 61, 89–104, 112, 167, 187, 188
fabulae extravagantes 90, 98, 103
fabliau 15
Falkirk, battle of (1298) 44
Falkland 190
Fawcett, R. 28 n.42
Felix V, anti-pope (1439–49) 56–7, 60 n.23
feminism, and Older Scots poetry 116
Fergus Gaist 15
Ferguson, F. S. 8 n.44
Feyrn, John, notary 121
Ficino, Marsilio 108
Fierabras, 'Ferambrace', 'Pharambras' 175, 176, 185
Fife 7, 9, 179, 182
Finn Mac Coul, hero, Ossianic cycle 185
Fisher, Keely 15 n.78, 31 n.57
Five 'Dolours' of the Virgin 130
Five Joys of the Virgin 128
Flodden, battle of (1513) 19, 21, 133, 150, 179
Florimond of Albany 11, 166, 169, 170–1, 176
flyting 3, 13, 15, 31, 135, 143, 147, 182, 187, 189, 190
Foray of Gadres 87
Fordun, John of 37
  Chronica Gentis Scotorum 35, 39, 40, 65
Forrest, William 130
fortune, theme of, in Older Scots poetry 59, 61, 67, 69, 95, 113, 115, 154, 185
Fowler, Alastair 149 n.1
Fowler, David C. 168 n.23
Fox, Denton 5 n.19, 13, 18 n.87, 90, 97, 105, 107, 108 n.15, 113, 133 n.1, 148 n.34, 187 n.47
Fox, Richard, Bp of Durham 127
Fradenburg, L. O. 32 n.63, 65 n.5, 107
France 1, 10, 156
  and Scotland 1, 10–11, 14, 18, 19, 20–1, 33, 57, 68 n.16, 69–70, 77–8, 82–3, 87, 135, 147, 169–71, 172, 177, 180, 181, 184
Franciscan order, *see* Church
Frankis, P. J. 66 n.11, 72 n.34
Fraser, James E. 44 n.28
Fraser, William 8 n.39
Frederick III, Emperor (1452–93) 56–7
freedom, cause of, in Older Scots poetry 32, 42, 49
Freiris of Berwick, The 15
Friedman, John Block 89 n.1, 108 n.16
Fuerre de Gadres, *see* Alexandre de Paris
Fuog, Karin E. C. 69 n.24
Furrow, Melissa 15 n.73

Gaelic ('Erse'), use of, in Scotland 5, 30, 31, 49, 52, 86–7, 125, 142, 183, 185
Galbraith, James 26 n.30
Galloway, provincial lordship of 5, 26, 29, 59, 125
Garbáty, Thomas 169 n.30
Gaudifer, romance hero 175, 176
Gaullier-Bougassas, Catherine 81 n.24
Geddes, Matthew 16
Geddie, William (*A Bibliography of Middle Scots Poets*) 2
Gemmill, Elizabeth 23 n.16
Gerson, Jean 11
Gesta Annalia 44
Gesta Romanorum 82
Ghosh, Kantik 149 n.1
Giaccherini, Enrico 109 n.23

Gillies, William 5 n.18
Gillies, William A. 86 n.38
Glasgow
  archbishopric of 26
  Cathedral 3, 28, 125
  University of 30, 91–2, 125, 130
'Glassinbery', poet 123
  'This is Goddis awne complaint' (Gray MS) 123
'Go go fro my window' (Selden MS) 66
Golagros and Gawane 11, 16, 51, 166, 169, 170, 171, 172–3, 175–6, 185
Goldstein, R. James 2 n.7, 3 n.8, 15 n.73, 35–47, 70 n.25
Golibras, *see* Golagros
Göller, Karl Heinz 171 n.43
Goodare, Julian 86 n.38
Gopen, George D. 90
Gourlaw, Robert 87
Government, of Scotland 20
  chief officers of 21
  College of Justice and 22
  council, role of 22
  king, role of 21
  local authorities, role of 22, 25–6
  nobility, role of 20, 22
  Parliament, role of 22, 25, 31, 38, 80, 98
Gower, John 2, 13, 67, 134, 138, 152
  Confessio Amantis 13
'Goweir, ane Inglis buke of' 8
Gowmakmorne, hero in Gaelic legend 185
Graf, Claude 185 n.35
Grands Rhétoriqueurs 10
Grant, Alexander 20 n.2, 22 n.12
Gray, Douglas 15 n.76, 89 n.1, 109, 114, 121, 130 n.41, 149–64, 156 n.17, 161 nn.25 and 27, 162 n.28, 163 n.30
Graye, James 63 n.2
'Graysteel', *see Eger and Grime*
Great Michael 21
Greece 39, 40
Green, Richard Firth 169 n.30
Greenlaw, John, of Haddington 129–30
Greer Fein, Susanna 51 n.5
'Greneacres A Lenvoye vpon John Bochas' (Selden MS) 65
Gros Louis, Kenneth R. R. 107 n.12, 109
Guido delle Colonne (*Historia Destructionis Troiae*) 173
Guy of Warwick 169
'Gye, gaist of' (Guido de Corvo) 180
Gyre Carling, The 15, 52

Haddington 31, 130, 179 n.1

Hadley Williams, Janet 1–18, 52 n.7, 179–91, 180 n.5, 181 nn.11, 12, 13 and 14, 182 n.18, 186 n.44
'Haill, glaid and glorius' (MS Arundel 285) 130
'Hail, mare, goddis moder ful of grace' (Makculloch MS) 129
Hamer, Douglas 180 n.8
Hamilton, James, 2nd Earl of Arran 182
Harth, Sidney J. 107 n.12
Harty, Kevin J. 107 n.10
Harward, Vernon 12 n.61, 45 n.30
Hary 2, 7, 18, 36, 44, 46, 62, 87
  and Chaucer 12
  Wallace, The 2, 3, 4, 5, 7, 10, 12, 18, 35, 40, 42, 44–7, 62, 163, 167, 169, 185, 189
Havely, Nick 54 n.13
Hawes, Stephen (*Pastime of Pleasure*) 152
Hay, family of Yester 121
Hay, Sir Gilbert 3, 11, 75–7, 79, 82, 86, 176
  Buke of the Gouernaunce of Princis 7, 76, 185
  Buke of the Law of Armys 7, 76
  Buke of the Ordre of Knychthede 7, 76
  'document of Sir gilbert hay' 76; *see also Buik of King Alexander the Conquerour*
Hay, William, laird of Ardendracht 8
Helen, of Troy 177
Henderson, Arnold Clayton 96
Henry IV, king of England (1399–1413) 20
Henry VI, king of England (1422–61, 1470–71) 21
Henryson, Robert 1, 3, 4, 10, 18, 53, 91–2, 105–6, 120, 148, 149, 177, 184, 190
  and Chaucer 12, 106–7, 111–14
  Bludy Serk, The 124
  'Forcy as deith is likand lufe' (*The Annunciation*) 122
  'Garmont of Gud Ladeis' 17
  Morall Fabillis 4, 7, 9, 12, 14, 15, 18, 53, 89–104, 105–7, 110, 112, 114, 187, 190
    and Aesopic tradition 89–91, 93, 96–7, 98, 99–100, 103, 104
    and courts, corrupt 99
    and government, corrupt 98–9, 102–3
    comedy in 94–5, 96–7, 101–3
    date of composition 91
    dialogue in 94–5, 97, 99
    moralitates 94, 95–6, 98, 98 n.21, 99, 100, 101, 102, 102–3

GENERAL INDEX

'Cock and the Fox, The' 15, 90, 96, 97
'Cock and the Jasp, The' 90, 94, 103
'Fox and the Wolf, The' 90, 97, 98, 186
'Fox, the Wolf and the Cadger, The' 90, 91, 101
'Fox, the Wolf and the Husbandman, The' 90, 91, 101–2, 104
'Lion and the Mouse, The' 90, 98–100, 188
'Paddock and the Mouse, The' 90, 103–4
'Preaching of the Swallow, The' 53, 90, 99, 100, 102, 103–4, 188
'Prologue, The' 90, 92, 93, 94, 111
'Sheep and the Dog, The' 90, 98–9, 104
'Trial of the Fox, The' 90, 97, 98, 101, 129
'Two Mice, The' 90, 94–5, 96, 102
'Wolf and the Lamb, The' 90, 103
'Wolf and the Wedder, The' 90, 91, 94, 102–3
Orpheus and Eurydice 11, 73, 93, 105–11, 186
   Aristeus, role in 108, 110
   moralitas 106, 108, 109–11, 116–17
'Ressoning betuix Aige and Yowth, The' 124
'Ressoning betuix Deth and Man, The' 124
Sum Practysis of Medecyne 52
Testament of Cresseid, The 9, 12, 53, 73, 105–8, 111–17, 152, 185, 186, 187
   'Complaint of Cresseid' in 127
'Thre Deid Pollis, The' 127
heraldry, in Older Scots literature 4, 11, 49, 50, 56–9, 60 n.23, 64–5, 136, 137
Heroides (Ovid) 73
Hesylryg, Sir William 45
Higgitt, John 9 n.46, 28 n.38
Highlands 5, 20, 25, 30, 31, 141, 142
Hill, Geoffrey 135 n.8
Hill, T. D. 128 n.33
Historia Alexandri 87
Historia de Preliis 77–8, 81, 82, 83–5
historiographical tradition, in Older Scots literature 2–3, 6, 10, 35–47, 125, 163, 167, 169, 185
Hoccleve, Thomas 17, 71, 147
   Letter of Cupid 63, 71, 72, 73

'Mother of God' 63, 71, 123
Holland, Richard 3, 4, 18, 49–50, 52
   Buke of the Howlat, The 5, 7, 9, 49–62, 188
   date of 59–61
   Gaelic in 52
   and heraldry 56–9
   Marian hymn in 129
   and Odo of Cheriton 52
Holy Blood, cult of 29, 119
Holy Land 6, 28, 58
Homer 2, 137
Homildon Hill, battle of (1402) 20
homiletic tradition, in Older Scots poetry 127
honour, as a theme in Older Scots poetry 42, 45, 83, 84, 136, 137, 153–4, 155–6, 163, 173
Howard, Henry, Earl of Surrey 150, 160
'Huchowne of the Awle Ryale' 165 n.2
humanism 1, 30, 115, 149, 154, 156, 157, 158, 161
Hundred Years War 20
'Hye quene of lufe' (*Kingis Quair*) 68 n.20

'I Pray yow, lady' (MS Arundel 285) 130
imagery, in Older Scots poetry 13, 119, 130, 157, 161
   animal 15, 188
   corporeal 81–2
   of dawn 139
   of emotions 161
   estates 94–6
   heraldic 58, 136–7
   iterative 162
   Latin derivation of 122, 138
   legal 99–100, 103
   of love 82–3
   Marian 122, 128–31
   mythological 137
   political 5, 55–7, 81–2, 98, 100, 136–7, 181
   religious 97, 124, 128–31, 138
   seasonal 53–4, 68, 100–1, 137, 142–3, 151, 156, 188
   scatological 102–3
   symbolic 56, 58, 59, 126–7
   theological 124
imperium, idea of 32
'In my beginning God me speid' 122
'In my defens God me defend' (Gray and other MSS) 123
Inchcolm, monastery 38
Inglis, James 179
Innes, Thomas, of Learney 180 n.9

'inventioun', in Older Scots poetry 112
Ireland, John, theologian 4, 6, 10, 11
  and Chaucer 12
  and Hoccleve 123
  Meroure of Wyssdome, The 4, 6, 11
  treatise on the doctrine of special grace 6
  treatise on the Immaculate Conception of the Virgin 6
Ireland 40, 42
Isles, *see* Lordship of the Isles
Itinerarium (Adornes) 6

Jack, R. D. S. 108 n.18
Jacobs, Nicholas 70 n.28
James I, king of Scots (1406–37) 1, 6, 10, 12, 19–20, 28, 41, 42, 61, 64, 67, 68 n.18, 184
  and Chaucer 12, 184; *see also Kingis Quair*
James II, king of Scots (1437–60) 6, 19, 20, 21, 57, 60, 61, 62
  and sister Margaret 6
  and Douglas family 20, 79
James III, king of Scots (1460–88) 6, 19–20, 21, 22, 28, 32, 36, 79, 92, 179
James IV, king of Scots (1488–1513) 1, 10, 19–20, 21, 22, 26, 27, 65, 79, 86, 92, 126, 133, 135, 140, 148, 150, 151, 156
  court of 5, 6, 133, 134, 140, 141, 145, 146–7, 179
  and music 5, 167–8
  and printing 17
  pilgrimages of 28, 29
James V, king of Scots (1513–42) 5, 19, 20, 21, 27, 32–3, 79, 150, 179–80, 181–2, 187
  court of 6, 188
  and heraldic orders 181–2
  regalia and 33, 181
James VI, king of Scots (1567–1625) 12, 16, 79, 86, 135–6
  Ane Schort Treatise 12, 135–6, 143
James, Clair F. 68 n.17
James, M. R. 121 n.12
Jamieson, I. W. A. 89, 107 n.14, 108 n.15, 109
Jeffery, C. D. 63 n.3
John of Capua 96
John the Reeve 172
Johnson, Ian 110 n.25
Johnson, Lesley 114 n.45
Johnston, Patrick 3

Kelly, Henry Ansgar 114 n.41

Kennedy, Andrew 140, 142
Kennedy, Quintin (*Litil Breif Tracteit*) 130
Kennedy, Walter 2, 3, 4, 5, 10, 18, 66, 124, 125, 126, 120, 130, 131, 142, 179
  'At matyne houre in myddis of the nycht' (*Praise of Age*) 125
  'Closter of Crist riche recent flour delys' 130, 131
  Flyting of Dumbar and Kennedie, The (B 65) 3, 5, 15, 124–5, 126, 142, 183, 189
  Passioun of Crist, The 125–6
  Dialogue between the Virgin and the Cross in 125
Kerrigan, John 73 n.37
Kinaston, Sir Francis 105, 106, 111–12
Kindrick, R. L. 112 n.36, 114
'king in disguise' tales 172
King Berdok 15
King Hart 80, 150
'King Orfeo', ballad 174
King Orphius 166, 170, 173–5
Kingis Quair, The (James I) 10, 12, 16, 63, 64, 67–71, 72, 73, 184
kingship, *see speculum principis* tradition
Kinneavy, Gerald B. 149 n.1
Knox, John 120
Kratzmann, Gregory 11 n.58, 107 n.9, 184 n.28
Kristeva, Julia 116
Kurvinen, Auvo 172 n.52
Kynd Kittok 15

Laing, David 18
lairds, position of 7, 8, 22–3, 29, 36, 86
lament, *see* complaint
Landino, Cristoforo 158
Lanark 45
Lancelot 155
Lancelot of the Laik 10, 11, 14, 73, 80, 81 n.26, 128, 166, 169–70, 171, 176
Langland, William (*Piers Plowman*) 122, 139, 151
Latin, use of, in Scotland 2, 4–5, 6, 8, 18, 30, 35, 37, 39, 40, 41 n.21, 45 n.29, 49, 65, 77–8, 80, 91, 93–4, 121–2, 123, 125, 128, 130, 135, 136, 138–9, 140, 156, 159–60, 173, 183, 186, 189, 190
Lauder Bridge 92
Lavinia, wife of Aeneas 161
Lay of Sorrow, The 63, 71–3
LeBlanc, Yvonne 184 n.26
Legends of the Saints 4, 9, 16, 119–20
Letter of Cupid, see Hoccleve
Lewis, C. S. 70, 137, 149, 151
libraries, early Scottish 7–8

GENERAL INDEX

Lichtoun's Dreme 15
Liddale, Sir James, of Halkerstone 7, 36 n.5
Linlithgow Palace 190
Litil Breif Tracteit, Ane (Kennedy) 130
'Lokert, Schir Mungo, of the Le' 3
Lollardy 27–8
Long, Eleanor R. 112 n.36
lordships, development of 22
Lordship of the Isles, MacDonald 20, 22, 29, 32
Loudon Hill, battle of (1307) 44
Louis XI, king of France (1461–83) 6
Louvain 121
love poetry, courtly 2, 10, 12, 16, 17, 45, 63, 66, 67, 68, 69, 70, 71, 73, 82–4, 113, 114, 115, 124, 136–7, 152, 184
Low Countries 25, 29
Lowlands 20, 31, 86, 142
Ludolphus of Saxony (*Vita Christi*) 125
Lufaris Complaynt, The 63, 71–3
Lull, Raymond, *Libre de Caballeria* 76
Lyall, R. J. 3 n.10, 5 n.19, 89–104, 91 n.7, 98 n.19, 108 n.18, 119 n.1, 122, 152 n.11, 182 n.20, 185 n.38, 191 n.55
Lydgate, John 2, 13, 17, 67, 69 n.22, 107, 138, 162, 184
   Complaint of the Black Knight, The 13, 18, 63, 65, 67, 69, 71, 72
   'Cristes Passion' (Pepys MS 1576) 121, 123
   Fall of Princes, The 65, 182, 184
   Siege of Thebes 176
   Temple of Glass 69, 73
   Testament 124
   Troy Book 77 n.10, 173, 177
Lyle, Robert, Lord Lyle 8
Lynch, M. 25 n.26, 26 n.27
Lyndsay, Sir David 2, 3, 4, 5, 18, 106, 179–91
   and Chaucer 12, 182, 184, 189
   and Douglas 184, 186–7, 189, 190
   and Dunbar 133, 179, 183, 186, 187, 188, 189, 190, 191
   and Henryson 184, 185, 186, 187, 188, 190
   as herald 180–1
   and Holland 50
   and *Kitteis Confessioun* 187 n.46
   letter, diplomatic, of 180
   and Reformation 190–1
   Answer to the Kingis Flyting, The 182, 184, 186, 189
   Complaint of Bagsche, The 15, 186, 187, 188
   Complaynt of Schir David Lindesay 180, 183, 184, 186, 187, 189, 190
   Deploratioun of the Deith of Quene Magdalene 181, 184, 187, 189
   Dialog betwix Experience and ane Courteour, Ane 182, 184, 185, 186, 187, 189–90, 191
   Dreme, The 12, 180, 184, 185, 186–7, 189, 190
   Justing betwix James Watsoun and Jhone Barbour 181, 189
   Satyre of the Thrie Estaitis, Ane 179, 182, 184, 186, 190
   Squyer Meldrum 167, 175–6, 182, 184, 185, 187, 189
   Suplication in Contemptioun of Syde Taillis, Ane 186, 187, 189
   Testament of the Papyngo, The 2, 12, 50 n.4, 76, 175 n.65, 181, 183, 184–5, 186, 187, 188, 189, 190, 191
   Testament of Meldrum, The 182, 187
   Tragedie of the Cardinell, The 182, 191
lyric genre, in Older Scots poetry 63, 73
   appeals from the Cross 123
   complaints of Christ 123
   love 16, 17, 66, 68–9, 73
   Marian 66, 120, 121, 122, 123, 128–31, 138–9
   'mortality' 124
   religious 120, 121, 124, 127–8, 138–40

McClure, J. Derrick 4 n.14, 166 n.8
MacColl, Alan 71 n.29
McDiarmid, Matthew P. 52 n.9, 76 n.9, 108 n.18, 173 n.54
MacDonald, A. A. 17 n.83, 29 n.47, 119 n.3, 122, 127, 131 n.48, 187 n.47
McDonald, Craig 89 n.1, 113 n.38
MacDonald, Donald 96 n.15
Macdougall, Norman 20 nn.2 and 5
Macfarlane, Leslie J. 8 n.38, 29 n.46
McGavin, John 30 n.53, 190 n.52
McGinley, Kevin 110 n.27
McGladdery, Christine 20 n.2
MacGregor, Martin 29 n.43
Machaut, Guillaume de
   Dit de la fonteinne amoreuse 69
   Remède de Fortune 73
McIntosh, Angus 165 n.2, 173 n.53
McKenna, Steven R. 109 n.22
McKim, Anne 105–17, 106 n.5, 113 n.38
MacQueen, John 1, 68 n.18, 89, 90 n.6, 107, 108 n.18, 109
McRoberts, David 29 n.45
Macrobius, Ambrosius Theodosius 108

Madeleine de Valois, first wife of James V 181
Magic Flute, The (Mozart) 153
Mair, John 6, 10, 13, 18, 30
   Historia Maioris Britanniae 6, 13–14
Maitland, Sir Richard 17
Major, John, *see* Mair
makar, maker 2, 76, 107, 133–4, 135, 139, 146, 148, 175, 183
Makculloch, Magnus 121
Makculloch MS, *see* Index of MSS
'Man be als mery as tho' (Selden MS) 66
'Man, hef in mynd and mend thy myss' (Makculloch MS) 189 n.49
'Mandvile' (*Mandeville's Travels*) 6
Mann, A. J. 191 n.54
Mann, Jill 115 n.48
manrent, bonds of 22
Mapstone, Sally 5 n.19, 6 n.23, 14 n.72, 38 n.11, 49 n.1, 70, 76, 105 n.2
Margaret of Denmark, wife of James III 21, 28
Margaret Tudor, wife of James IV 21, 133, 141, 150, 179–180
Marie de Guise, second wife of James V and queen regent 181, 182
Marjory, daughter of Robert I 36
Marlin, John 110
Marot, Clément 10 n.52
Martin, Florentine 8–9
Martin, Joanna 75–88, 81 n.27
Mary, *see* Virgin Mary
Mary of Gueldres, wife of James II 20, 21, 28, 60 n.23
Mary, queen of Scots (1542–67) 79, 179
Mason, Roger 1 n.1, 6 n.24, 30 n.48
Mathews, Jana 116 n.52
Matthew de Vendôme (*Ars Versificatoria*) 136 n.10
Maxwell, Robert, Bp of Orkney 8
'maying and disport of Chaucere, The' (Selden MS) 71
Meditationes Vitae Christae (formerly attrib. St Bonaventura) 124
men, voices of, in Older Scots poetry 71, 72–3, 115
Menteith, Earl of, in *The Wallace* 46
Meroure of Wyssdome, *see* Ireland
Mersar 3
metre, in Older Scots poetry 12, 51, 114, 128, 134, 135, 141–2, 143, 157, 170, 189
Middle English (language) 4, 49, 51, 75, 108, 114, 120, 122, 165, 170, 172, 173, 174

Middle Scots poets 1, 2, 107, 152, 187, 188
   education 3, 10–11, 121–2
   laicization 4, 121
   language of 4–5, 13
Mieszkowski, Gretchen 112 n.35
Mill, Anna J. 31 n.57, 184 n.25
Mills, Carol 109
Minerva, goddess 153
Minnis, Alastair J. 37 n.8, 135n.7
Mirk, John (*Festial*) 8, 64 n.4
miscellanies, manuscript 5, 16, 17, 50, 63–74, 120–1, 123
Miskimin, Alice 68 n.18
mock-conjurations 15
morality plays, English 123, 150, 184
Moran, Tatyana 112 n.30
Moray Cathedral 3, 49
Murthly Hours, The, *see* Index of MSS
music, and Older Scots poetry 5, 49, 68, 167–8, 180
Musgrave, Mistress 148
Muslims, in Spain 41, 58–9
'My frende gif thou will be a seruitur' (Selden MS) 66
Myllar, Androw 17, 105; *see also* Chepman and Myllar prints

narrator, role of, in Older Scots poetry 46, 50, 52–4, 69, 71, 72, 77–9, 83, 85–7, 93–96, 99, 100, 102, 104, 106, 110–12, 113, 114–15, 116
Nassington, William of (*Speculum Vitae*) 122
national identity, of Scotland 31–2
Nativity, the, in Older Scots poetry 129, 138–9
Nature, in Older Scots poetry 51–6, 136–7
Neoplatonism 109
Neveleti, Anonymous 90 n.4
Nicholas V, pope (1447–55) 56
Nitecki, Alicia K. 114 n.44
nobility, the 19–20, 22, 28, 29, 32, 58, 156
nominalism 98
Northern Renaissance 1
Norvell, Robert 120
Norton-Smith, J. 74 n.41, 152 n.12
notaries public 3, 11, 16, 49, 91, 121; *see also* protocol books
Nygard, Holger Olof 175 n.64

'O hie emperice and quene celestiall' (Selden and Asloan MSS) 66, 71 n.32, 130
'O lady I shall me dress with besy cure' (Selden MS) 66

'O mortall man plungit in distres' (NLS Adv. 18.5.14) 130
'O mothir of God inu[i]olat virgin Mary' (MS Arundel 285) 127–8
'O Venus clere, of goddis stellifyit' (Selden MS) 68 n.20
'O wondit spreit and saul in till exile' (Bannatyne MS) 127
Odo of Cheriton (*Fabulae*) 52, 90, 96, 97, 98, 101
origin myth, of Scotland 39–40
  'Gadeill-Glaiss' (Gaythelos) 40
  'Sir Newill' 40
  Scota 40; *see also* historiographical tradition
Original Chronicle; *see* Wyntoun
Orkney, Earl of, *see* Sinclair, William
Orkney 21, 26, 31, 32
Orléans, Charles d' 67–8, 68 n.16, 69
Orléans 92
Orosius, Paulus 39
Orpheus 108, 109, 158, 166, 173–5; *see also* Henryson
Otis, Brooks 161 n.26
Otterburn, battle of (1388) 20
Ovid (Publius Ovidius Naso) 73, 108, 151 n.7 152, 154, 164 n.32
  Heroides 73
'Owyr, Donald' 141
Oxford, Bodleian Library, Arch. Selden. B. 24, *see* Index of MSS

Paisley Abbey 41
Palice of Honour, *see* Douglas
Paradise, Earthly 79, 155
Paris, University of 10, 11, 126, 149
Parkinson, David 112, 149 n.1, 153 n.13
parliament, *see* Government
Passion, devotion 120–6, 127, 128
Pastime of Pleasure (Hawes) 152
Paston, Anne 8
Patterson, Lee 115 n.50
Pearsall, Derek 114 n.44, 116
Pelagianism 98
Penance, sacrament of 16, 97, 120, 124, 127
Penelope, wife of Ulysses 177
Penketh, Sandra 131 n.46
Perceval, First Continuation of 171
Percy Folio manuscript, *see* Index of MSS
personae, poetic 15, 52, 54, 114–15, 136, 151, 188
Perth 25, 28
Perthshire 5, 86
Peterson, C. 65 n.6

petitions, in Older Scots poetry 7, 69, 130, 135, 144, 145–8, 180, 183, 186, 187, 188
Petrina, Alessandra 67 n.14, 109, 110 n.24
Philip the Chancellor ('Crux, de te volo conqueri') 125
Phillips, Helen 69 n.24
Piers Plowman (Langland) 122, 139, 151
pilgrimage, *see* Church
Pistel of Susan 122
Pittock, Malcolm 114
Planctu Naturae, De (Alan of Lille) 54, 152
Poliziano, Angelo 108
Polyxena, daughter of Priam and Hecuba of Troy 177
Pope, Alexander 142
Pope, Robert 89 n.1
population, of Scotland 22–6
  in burghs 25
  family, as basic social unit of 23
  on farms 23, 25
  and literacy 30
  and occupations 23, 24–5
  and poor 26
  and women 23
Porteous of Noblenes, *see* Cadiou
postmodernism, and Older Scots poetry 116
prayer, in Older Scots poetry 41, 52, 53, 71, 100, 120, 121–3, 124, 129, 130–1, 140, 189
prayer books, *see* books of hours
Priam, king of Troy 158
printing, in Scotland 17–18, 29, 191; *see also* Chepman and Myllar prints
prophecy 44, 46
Proserpine, queen of Fairy 109
Protestantism 16, 18, 119, 120–1, 182
  and censorship 102, 119, 120, 127, 129, 179
protocol books 50 n.3, 121; *see also* notaries
proverbs, in Older Scots poetry 55, 145, 153, 156, 157, 172 n.48
Prudence, as virtue 145
Purdie, Rhiannon 165–77, 165 n.2, 170 n.35, 171 n.47
Purser, John 168 n.22
Pynson, Richard 65

Quare of Jelusy, The 12, 63, 71–3
querelle des femmes 73
Queste del Saint Graal 155
'Quhen sall your merci rew upon your man' (Selden MS) 68 n.20

Quinn, William 69 n.23
Quintilian (*Institutio oratoria*) 164
  and *enargeia* 164
'Quintine' 2

Ramsay, Allan (*Ever Green*) 18
Ramsay, John, Lord Bothwell 8
Ramsay, John 35
Ramson, William 106 n.6, 113
Ratis Raving 3, 9, 13, 14, 16
Rauf Coilyear 10, 16, 51, 166, 169, 170, 172
readers, early Scottish and English 8–9, 11, 13–14, 30, 35–6, 38, 44, 47, 50, 53–4, 64–5, 72, 76, 86–7, 105, 106, 111–12, 123, 126–7, 151, 157, 162, 164, 165, 175, 177, 188, 191; *see also* book collectors
Reformers, Reformation, *see* Protestantism
refrains, Latin, in Older Scots poetry 122, 128, 129, 130–1, 140, 144
Regimen Sanitatis 8
'Regiment of kingis with the buke of phisnomy, the' (Asloan MS) 76, 81, 185
Regimine Principum, De 10, 14
Reichel, Georg 168 n.27
relics, *see* Church
religious verse 16, 17, 29, 119–31
Remembrance of the Passion (MS Arundel 285) 124
Renaissance 1
Restalrig, Chapel of 28
Resurrection, in Older Scots poetry 127–8, 138
Riddy, Felicity 41 n.17, 51 n.5, 56 n.17, 116
Robert I, king of Scots (1306–29) 35–6, 41, 43–4, 60
  Edward Bruce, brother of 42
Robert II, king of Scots (1371–90) 6, 19, 36, 37, 43, 61
Robert III, king of Scots (1390–1406) 19
Roberts, Jane 107 n.10
Roerecke, H. H. 90
Rogers, Gillian 169 n.30
Roland 172–3, 175–6; *see also* Charlemagne
Rolland, John
  Court of Venus, The 87
  Seuin Seages, The 170 n.34
Roman d'Alexandre, *see* Alexandre de Paris
Roman de la Rose 184
Roman de Renart 90, 96, 97, 98, 101, 102, 103

Roman de Thèbes, Old French romance 176
Roman de Toute Chevalerie 84
romance, 'ancestral' 169
romance, Arthurian 2, 51, 165, 171, 175–6
romance, 'matter' of 169
romances, Middle English 51, 75, 108, 165, 169–70, 172–5
romances, Old French 170–1, 175–6
romances, Older Scots 2, 10, 11, 13, 14, 15, 16, 18, 45, 51, 77, 78–9, 80, 81–4, 108, 109, 128, 151, 163, 165–77, 174, 180, 182, 189, 187, 189
  Buik of Alexander, The 9, 11, 87, 166, 167, 169, 170, 185
  Buik of King Alexander the Conquerour, The (Hay) 7, 10, 75–88, 166, 169, 170, 171, 173, 176, 184, 185, 189
  Clariodus 11, 166, 169–70, 171, 176, 177
  Eger and Grime ('Graysteel') 165, 166, 167–9, 170, 173, 176, 185
    Percy Folio MS 168–9, 172
    Huntington-Laing 168–9
  Florimond of Albany 11, 166, 169, 170–1, 176
  Golagros and Gawane 11, 16, 51, 166, 169, 170, 171, 172–3, 175–6, 185
  King Orphius 166, 170, 173–5
  Lancelot of the Laik 10, 11, 14, 73, 80, 81 n.26, 128, 166, 169–70, 171, 176
  Rauf Coilyear 10, 16, 51, 166, 169, 170, 172
  Roswall and Lilian 165, 166, 167, 168, 170, 176–7
  Scottish Troy Book 77 n.10, 166, 169, 170, 173, 177
  Sir Colling 166, 170, 173–5
Rome 26, 39
Romulus, elegiac, fable collection of 89–90 n.4, 90, 91, 92–5, 97, 98, 99, 103
'Ros Mary most of vertewe virginale' (Asloan, Makculloch and other MSS) 123, 128, 130, 131
Roslin 7, 28, 76
Ross, D. A. J. 87 n.41
Ross, Ian Simpson 149 n.1
Ross, earldom of 8, 29, 32
Roswall and Lilian 165, 166, 167, 168, 170, 176–7
Roull (Rowle), John 3, 15
  Cursing Vpoun the steilaris of his fowlis 15
Roxburgh, siege of (1460) 21
Royan, Nicola 6 n.25, 49–62

Ruddiman, Thomas 18, 151 n.7
Rymour, Thomas 44

St Andrew 46
St Andrews
  archbishopric of 26, 27
  Castle 182
  University of 30, 92, 133, 134, 149
St Augustine 38, 104
  Confessions 38
St Catherine, of Siena 28
St Duthac 28
St Edmund 47
St Edward 47
St Giles, collegiate church of 3, 5, 28, 29, 149–50
St Kentigern 28
St Machar 120
St Machar, Cathedral of, *see* Aberdeen
St Margaret, wife of Malcolm III 28
St Mary, church of, Dundee 29
St Ninian 28, 120
St Oswald 47
St Thomas 28
St Thomas (Becket) 47
Sadler, Ralph, Henry VIII's envoy 182
Saldanha, K. 14 n.71, 77 n.11, 83
Sanderson, M. H. B. 8 n.43, 9 n. 46, 25 n.23, 182 n.17
Saracens 58–9
Sark River, battle of (1448) 60 n.23
satire and invective, in Older Scots poetry 5, 15, 52, 56, 96, 97, 98, 113, 153, 155, 170, 183, 186, 191
Scheibe, Regina 56 n.14, 120 n.6
Scheps, Walter 2 n.3, 112
Scheves, William, Abp of St Andrews 8
Scota, *see* origin myth
Scotland
  and Burgundy 14, 20, 171, 181
  and England 1, 2, 4, 10, 11–12, 13–14, 18, 19, 20, 21, 22, 32, 36, 40, 42, 45–6, 47, 49, 51, 59, 61, 63, 67, 72–3, 105, 114, 122, 123, 127, 130, 150, 165, 169, 172, 174–5, 177, 181, 182, 184, 191
  and Europe 1, 4, 14, 19, 20, 21, 27, 29, 31, 32, 73, 74, 92, 130, 165, 181
  and France 1, 10–11, 14, 18, 19, 20–1, 33, 57, 68 n.16, 69–70, 77–8, 82–3, 87, 135, 147, 169–71, 172, 177, 180, 181, 184
Scotorum Historiae, *see* Boece
Scots (language) 6, 7, 13, 31, 39, 67, 121, 122, 123, 139, 149, 159–60, 167, 171, 174, 175–6, 185, 186, 189

'Inglis' 4–5, 8, 125, 183
Early Scots 4, 37
Middle Scots 4, 107, 112, 114
Older Scots 4, 61, 88, 89, 173
  and Northern Middle English 165
'Scottis' 4, 17
Scott, A. B. 135 n.7
Scottish Chaucerians 13, 107, 149
Scottish Lydgatians 13
Scottish Nation, at University of Orléans 92
Scotticization, Scottification, Scottishness 11, 63, 64 n.3, 71 n.30, 72, 112, 122, 161, 165
scribes 8, 16, 35, 37, 63, 64 n 4, 65, 66, 67, 69 n.21, 70–1, 72, 86, 121, 141, 150, 165, 167, 173
seasonal description, in Older Scots poetry 12, 100–1, 136, 137, 144–5, 158, 186
Secretum Secretorum 76, 78, 81, 82, 171
Sempill, Robert 191
Seton, George 181 n.10
Shaw, Frances J. 24 n.22
Shaw, Quintin 3, 5
'Suppois the courte' 5 n.21
Shaw, Master Robert 141, 148
Shetland 21, 31, 32
Shire, Helena M. 33 n.65
Shirley, John 67 n.15
Shuldham-Shaw, Patrick 174 n.58
Siege of Thebes (Lydgate) 8, 176
Siege of Tyre 87
Simpson, James 164 n.31
Sinclair, family of 7, 16, 64, 176
  as book collectors 7–8, 16, 76 n.4
  as literary patrons 7, 157, 164 n.32, 176
Sinclair, Sir David, of Sumburgh 8
Sinclair, Elizabeth, wife of Duncan Campbell of Glenorchy 176
Sinclair, Henry, 3rd Lord (d. 1513) 7, 8, 64, 65, 157, 164 n.32
Sinclair, Henry, Bp of Ross (d. 1565) 8
Sinclair, Sir John 141, 148
Sinclair, Sir Oliver, laird of Roslin 7–8, 76
Sinclair, William, Earl of Orkney and Caithness (d. 1480) 7, 28, 76
Singleton, Hugh 127
Sir Cawline (Percy Folio MS) 174
Sir Colling 166, 170, 173–5
Sir Gawain and the Carle of Carlisle 172
Sir Gawain and the Green Knight 158, 172
Sir Orfeo 108, 109, 173–4
Sir Tristrem 165
Skelton, John 148, 151, 184 n.29

Bowge of Court 148
Smith, G. Gregory 13 n.66
Smith, Janet M. 10 n.51
Snell, Rachel 172 n.51
sources, prose, versified in Scots 11, 119–20, 169–71
South English Legendary, The 120
Spain 40–1, 58
Spearing, A. C. 70 n.25, 107 n.12, 137 n.15, 143
Spectacle of Luf, The 77 n.11
speculum principis tradition 14, 32, 36–7, 49, 55, 61, 70, 75, 78–82, 126, 136, 155, 162–3, 171, 173, 177, 180, 183, 185–6, 188, 189, 191
Speculum Vitae (Nassington) 122
Spenser, Edmund 154
Spiller, Michael R. G. 70 n.25
Stanley, Eric 68 n.18
stanza forms, in Older Scots poetry 10, 11, 72–3, 94, 121, 128, 129, 141, 143, 185
  and Chaucer 12
  and concatenation 50–1
  alliterative thirteen-line 10, 49–2, 54, 170, 184, 190
  ballade 11
  'ballat royal' (eight-line) 135–6, 138
  decasyllabic couplets 10, 75, 170, 189, 190
  eight-line 45, 66, 128, 142, 189
  nine-line (*Anelida*) 12, 73 n.39, 137, 189
  octosyllabic couplets 37, 87, 119, 141, 144, 170–1, 189, 190
  quatrains 122, 174
  rhyme royal (seven-line) 10, 12, 65, 66, 68, 93, 114, 183, 189, 190
  tail-rhyme 141, 170
  ten-line 11, 73 n.39
  'Troilus verse' 12
  twelve-line 122, 139
Steer, K. A. 29 n.43
Steinhöwel, Heinrich 90, 91, 92, 101
Stell, Geoffrey 24 n.21
Stephen of Bourbon 101
Stewart, Alexander, Duke of Albany 36 n.5
Stewart, Bernard, 3rd seigneur d'Aubigny 9, 135, 156
Stewart, Sir David, of Rosyth 7
Stewart, John, Duke of Albany (c. 1482–1536) 180
Stewart, Marion 49 n.1, 60 n.23, 165 n.1
Stewart, Murdoch, Duke of Albany (c. 1362–1425) 19

Stewart, Robert, Duke of Albany (c. 1340–1420) 19
Stewart, Walter 36, 41
'Stewart of Bute' 62
'Stewartis Orygenale' 36 n.6
Stiller, Nikki 112 n.30
Stirling 28, 140
  Castle 79, 190
  Chapel Royal 190
  Observantine friary of 126
Storm, Melvin 112
Straloch lute book, of Robert Gordon 168
Strauss, Dietrich 110 n.25
Strauss, Jennifer 115 n.48
style, in Older Scots poetry 1
  high, courtly, aureate, Latinate 2, 10, 12–13, 50–2, 62, 121, 122, 126, 127, 128, 130, 135–7, 139–40, 143, 150, 151, 154, 156, 160, 185, 186, 188, 190
  'pitous', of Chaucer, Lydgate and Henryson 162
  'royal style "heroycall"' 159–60
  middle, plain 13, 125, 135, 144, 150, 156, 160, 162, 188, 189, 190
  low 15, 52, 100, 135, 142, 159, 188, 190; *see also* flyting
Summers, Joanna 70 n.25
'Surrexit dominus de sepulchro' (Bannatyne MS) 127–8, 138
Surrey, *see* Howard
symbolism, number 128

Tain 28, 29
tales, popular 13, 153, 172, 180
Talis of the Fyve Bestes, The 15
  'Boar's Tale' 87 n.44
  'Unicornis Tale' 15
Taylor, Jane H. M. 85 n.32, 131 n.46
Testament of Cresseid, see Henryson
testaments, in Older Scots poetry 43, 53, 140, 150, 187, 188, 189
Thewis of Gudwomen, The 14 n.71, 83
'This is Goddis awne complaint' ('Glassinbery') 123
'This warldly Ioy is onuly fantasy' (Selden MS) 66
'Thow that hes bene obedient' (Bannatyne MS; MS Arundel 285) 127–8
Thre Prestis of Peblis, The 10, 14, 80, 186
'Thy bagynyng Is barane brutulnesse' (Selden MS) 66
Thynne, William 105
Tillyard, E. M. W. 115 n.50
'To the hie potent blisfull trinitie' (Bannatyne MS) 127

Tomlinson, Charles 146 n.33
Torrie, E. P. D. 25 n.25
Touris, William of 3, 10, 14, 126, 131
   Contemplacioun of Synnaris 10, 14,
     120, 123, 124, 126, 127
tournaments 32, 141, 181
Towneley plays 123
towns, Scottish
   crafts in 25, 31
   festivals in 30, 31
   government of 25–6, 30
   hospitals in 28
   inhabitants of 26
   location of 25
   parish and 31
   poems celebrating 136, 190
   religious foundations in 28
   saints, patron, of 31
   schools in 30
   worship in 29, 31
tragedy, in Older Scots poetry 2, 102, 103,
   109, 113–14, 164
translation 149, 158
   of French works into English 14, 67–8,
     71, 158
   of French works into Scots 11, 18, 77–
     8, 87, 170–1, 173
   of Latin works into Scots 4, 6, 9, 77–8,
     82, 89–90, 92, 98, 99, 101, 108, 120,
     122, 129–30, 149, 150, 157–9, 160–1,
     171, 173, 182, 186
Treaty of Perpetual Peace (1503) 21
Trivet, Nicholas 106, 108, 111, 113
'Troilus verse', *see* stanza forms
Troy, story of, in Older Scots poetry 53,
   157, 163, 169, 173, 176–7
Troy Book, Scottish 166, 169, 170, 173,
   176
truth-telling, and Older Scots poetry 14,
   36, 37, 38, 41
Tucker, Marie-Claude 10 n.50
Turnus, king of the Rutili 164
Turville-Petre, Thorlac 51 n.5
Tydeus of Thebes, romance hero 175, 176

'V de F', scribe 63 n.2
Valla, Lorenzo 158
van Buuren, Catherine 16 n.82
van Duin, Deborah 78 n.14
van Heijnsbergen, Theo 17 n.83
Vegio, Maffeo 157, 164
Venus 55. 63, 66, 69, 71, 72, 87, 115,
   152–5, 157, 160
Verneuil, battle of (1424) 57
versification, in Scots, of prose sources 11,
   119–20, 169–71

Virgil (Publius Virgilius Maro) 1, 2, 14,
   108, 158, 159–61, 164
   Aeneid 149, 152, 153, 157, 161–3,
     186–7
Virgin Mary 29, 46, 52, 124, 127–31, 138,
   139
Vita Christi (Ludolphus of Saxony) 125
Voeux de Paon, *see* Alexandre de Paris
Volk-Birke, Sabine 113 n.38, 116
Voragine, Jacobus de (*Golden Legend*)
   120
*Voyage d'Alexandre au Paradis Terrestre,
   Le* 78

Wallace, Sir William 35, 44, 47; *see also*
   Hary
Wallace, Sir William, of Craigie 7
Wallace, The, *see* Hary
Walton, John (metrical translation of
   Boethius) 65, 66
Warbeck, Perkin 21
Wars of Independence (1296–1342) 3, 32,
   40, 49
Wars of the Roses 21
Watry, P. B. 18 n.88
Watson, Nicholas 108 n.15
Wemyss, Sir John, of Leuchars and
   Kincaldrum 7
Wemyss version (*Original Chronicle*) 39
Wheatley, Edward 90 n.4, 93
Whithorn 28, 29
Whyte, Ian D. 22 n.7
William of Touris, *see* Touris
Wilson, Kenneth G. 72 n.34
women, voices of, in English and Scots
   poetry 71, 72, 82, 83–4, 115, 142–4
Wood, H. Harvey 110 n.25
Woolf, Rosemary 123 n.22, 128, 130
Worde, Wynkyn de 127
Wormald, Jenny 20 n.2, 22 n.13
'Worschippe, ye that loveris bene, this
   May' (Selden MS) 68
Wright, Dorena Allen 108 n.18, 174 n.58
Wright, Glenn 172 n.52
Wurtele, Douglas 171 n.43
Wynne-Davies, Marion 116 n.52
Wyntoun, Andrew of 2, 3, 7, 32, 37, 40,
   87, 122
   Original Chronicle 2, 9, 10, 16, 35, 37,
     38–40, 44–5, 185

Yeoman, Peter 28 n.38
Ysengrimus, Latin beast epic 96, 101

www.ingramcontent.com/pod-product-compliance
Ingram Content Group UK Ltd.
Pitfield, Milton Keynes, MK11 3LW, UK
UKHW021319180426
11947UKWH00015B/1314